Lecture Notes in Computer S

Commenced Publication in 1973
Founding and Former Series Editors:
Gerhard Goos, Juris Hartmanis, and Jan van Le

Stéphane Grumbach Liying Sui
Victor Vianu (Eds.)

Advances in Computer Science – ASIAN 2005

Data Management on the Web

10th Asian Computing Science Conference
Kunming, China, December 7-9, 2005
Proceedings

 Springer

Volume Editors

Stéphane Grumbach
LIAMA, CNRS, Institute of Automation
P.O. Box 2728, Beijing 100080, P.R. China
E-mail: stephane.grumbach@inria.fr

Liying Sui
Victor Vianu
University of California at San Diego
Computer Science and Engineering Department
San Diego, La Jolla, CA 92093-0404, USA
E-mail: {lsui,vianu}@cs.ucsd.edu

Library of Congress Control Number: 2005937050

CR Subject Classification (1998): H.2, H.3, H.4, C.2, H.5, I.2, J.1

ISSN   0302-9743
ISBN-10   3-540-30767-2 Springer Berlin Heidelberg New York
ISBN-13   978-3-540-30767-9 Springer Berlin Heidelberg New York

Springer is a part of Springer Science+Business Media

springeronline.com

© Springer-Verlag Berlin Heidelberg 2005
Printed in Germany

Typesetting: Camera-ready by author, data conversion by Scientific Publishing Services, Chennai, India
Printed on acid-free paper   SPIN: 11596370   06/3142   5 4 3 2 1 0

Preface

The series of annual Asian Computing Science Conferences (ASIAN) was initiated in 1995 by AIT, INRIA and UNU/IIST to provide a forum for researchers in computer science from the Asian region and to promote interaction with researchers from other regions. The first nine conferences were held respectively in Bangkok, Singapore, Katmandu, Manila, Phuket, Penang, Hanoi, Mumbai and Chiang Mai. The 10th ASIAN conference was held in Kunming, China, December 7-9, 2005.

Each year, the conference focuses on a different theme at the cutting edge of computer science research. The theme of ASIAN 2005 was data management on the Web. Four distinguished speakers were invited to the conference: Mariano Consens (University of Toronto), Richard Hull (Bell Laboratories, Lucent Technologies), Tova Milo (Tel Aviv University) and Prabhakar Raghavan (Yahoo Research and Stanford University).

This year, 91 papers were submitted from 11 countries. The Program Committee selected 17 regular papers and 21 short papers. This volume contains the papers based on the invited talks, the regular papers, and the short papers. We wish to thank the Program Committee and the external referees for their work in selecting the contributed papers.

The conference was organized by Yunnan University in Kunming, the capital of the southern province of Yunnan, which has strong historical ties with South-East Asia. Yunnan University is part of the Greater Mekong Subregion Academic and Research Network (GMSARN), which aims to strengthen the cooperation between academic institutions in the region. We warmly thank the Local Organization Committee, and particularly Prof. Shaowen Yao, for their sustained efforts in the organization of the conference.

We thank the Steering Committee for inviting us to organize the 10th ASIAN conference in China. We also thank the Database Society of the China Computer Federation, CCFDBS, for the promotion of the conference in China. The conference received financial support from the French Embassy in China, INRIA, and Yunnan University, for which we are grateful.

Finally, many thanks to Liying Sui, Proceedings Chair, for the preparation of this volume.

October 2005 Stéphane Grumbach
Victor Vianu

Organization

Steering Committee

Stéphane Grumbach (INRIA, France)
Joxan Jaffar (NUS, Singapore)
Gilles Kahn (INRIA, France)
Kanchana Kanchanasut (AIT, Thailand)
R.K. Shyamasundar (TIFR, India)
Kazunori Ueda (Waseda University, Japan)

Conference Chair:	Stéphane Grumbach (INRIA, France)
Program Chair:	Victor Vianu (UC San Diego, USA)
Local Organizing Chair:	Yongxue Fan (Yunnan University, China)
Proceedings Chair:	Liying Sui (UC San Diego, USA)

Program Committee

Alin Deutsch (UC San Diego)
AnHai Doan (University of Illinois at Urbana-Champaign)
Wenfei Fan (University of Edinburgh/Bell Labs)
Mong-Li Lee (National University of Singapore)
Maurizio Lenzerini (University of Rome "La Sapienza")
Xiaofeng Meng (Renmin University)
Tova Milo (Tel Aviv University)
Riichiro Mizoguchi (Osaka University)
Frank Neven (Limburg University)
Krithi Ramamritham (IIT Bombay)
Luc Segoufin (INRIA-Futurs)
Jérôme Simeon (IBM T.J. Watson Research Center)
Jayavel Shanmugasundaram (Cornell University)
Kyuseok Shim (Seoul National University)
Jianwen Su (UC Santa Barbara)
Dan Suciu (University of Washington)
Victor Vianu (PC Chair, UC San Diego)
Shaowen Yao (Yunnan University)
Masatoshi Yoshikawa (Nagoya University)
Zheng Zhang (Microsoft China)

Local Organization Committee

Colin Campbell (Yunnan University)
Yongxue Fan (Yunnan University)
Zhongmin Wang (Yunnan University)
Chao Yi (Yunnan University)
Zhijie Zheng (Yunnan University)
Liping Zhou (Yunnan University)

External Referees

Serge Abiteboul
Geert Jan Bex
Rajendra Bose
Chavdar Botev
Bogdan Cautis
Adina Crainiceanu
Pedro DeRose
Floris Geerts
David Gross-Amblard
Wynne Hsu
Ushio Inoue
Ying Jiang
Hideyuki Kawashima
Anastasios Kementsietsidis
Naotake Kitagawa
Yoonkyong Lee
Prakash Linga

Joan Lu
Akira Maeda
Akiyoshi Matono
Robert McCann
Takashi Menjo
Jun Miyazaki
Manabu Ohta
Neoklis Polyzotis
Nicoleta Preda
Mayssam Sayyadian
Feng Shao
Warren Shen
Manpreet Singh
Stijn Vansummeren
Stratis Viglas
Bogdan Warinschi
Wensheng Wu

Sponsoring Institutions

AIT
INRIA, France
UNU/IIST

Table of Contents

Peer-to-Peer Data Management

Web Services and Electronic Commerce

Data Mining and Search

XML

Data Streams and Publish/Subscribe Systems

III Short Papers

Security and Privacy

Semantic Web and Data Integration

Peer-to-Peer Data Management

Web Services and Electronic Commerce

Data Mining and Search

XML

Data Streams and Publish/Subscribe Systems

Web-Based Applications

Towards a Unified Model for Web Services Composition (Extended Abstract)

Richard Hull

Bell Labs Research, Lucent Technologies,
600 Mountain Avenue, Murray Hill, NJ 07974, USA
hull@lucent.com
http://db.bell-labs.com

1   Introduction

The web services paradigm, which finds roots in Service-Oriented Computing [ACKM04, PG03], promises to enable rich, flexible, and dynamic interoperation of highly distributed and heterogeneous web-hosted services. Substantial progress has already been made towards this goal (e.g., emerging standards such as SOAP, WSDL, BPEL) and industrial technology (e.g., IBM's WebSphere Toolkit, Sun's Open Net Environment and JiniTM Network technology, Microsoft's .Net and Novell's One Net initiatives, HP's e-speak). Several research efforts are already underway that build on or take advantage of the paradigm, including the DAML-S/OWL-S program [OWL-S, MSZ01, Grü03, SPAS03], the Semantic Web Services Initiative (SWSI) [SWSI] and Web Service Modeling Ontology (WSMO) [WSMO] groups, and automata-based and other models for web services [BFHS03, HBCS03, BCG+03, BCH05].

A key research challenge in web services concerns (semi-)automatic discovery and composition of web services, in order to construct new web services with desired properties or capabilities. This extended abstract provides a short review of selected works in this young and ambitious area. A more comprehensive overview of this area may be found in [HS05]. However, the reader is urged to consult the primary sources for a much more complete discussion of both the results obtained so far, and the questions that are motivating further investigation.

The fundamental work in web services composition has centered on three models, each coming with a different approach to the composition problem. The OWL-S model for web services focuses on how web services interact with the "real world", represented abstractly using (time-varying) first-order logic predicates and terms. A representative composition result [NM02] here uses a translation into Petri nets. The "Roman" model for services [BCG+03, BCDG+04a] focuses on an abstract notion of "activities" (without modeling how they impact the world), and in essence model web services as finite state automata with transitions labeled by these activities. A powerful composition result is obtained using a reduction to Propositional Dynamic Logic (PDL). The Conversation

S. Grumbach, L. Siu, and V. Vianu (Eds.): ASIAN 2005, LNCS 3818, pp. 1–10, 2005.
© Springer-Verlag Berlin Heidelberg 2005

model [BFHS03, FBS03] (see also [HNK02]) focuses on messages passed between web services, and again uses finite state automata to model the internal processing of a service, with transitions labeled by message sends and message reads. A key result here concerns determination of the "local" behavior of individual services, if they are required to conform to a given "global" behavior (as might be specified using choreography constraints, reminiscent of WS-Choreography [WSCDL04]).

The bulk of the current survey focuses on two recent efforts, that hold the promise of providing a unifying framework for the growing body of research on automated web services composition. The first effort is the work on FLOWS [BGHM04, GHM05, SWSO], which provides a first-order logic ontology for web services, described in Section 2. The second effort is focused on Colombo, a new model for web services and their composition, described in Section 3. Brief remarks concerning selected related works are provided in Section 4.

2   FLOWS

FLOWS forms part of a recent W3C Member Submission [SWSF]. The FLOWS ontology is an extension of the Process Specification Language (PSL) [GM03, PSL], an ISO standard that was originally developed to specify and share specifications of manufacturing processes. PSL draws inspiration from the family of situation calculii [Rei01], and allows a formal, logic-based specification of the possible execution paths taken by a process or a family of processes. PSL itself has a core theory and several extensions; FLOWS is an extension of PSL Outercore. Speaking intuitively, the models of PSL Outercore correspond to trees, whose nodes correspond to occurrences of atomic processes, with an edge connecting node n_1 to node n_2 if the process occurrence associated with n_2 could occur immediately after the process occurrence associated with n_1. With this as a starting point, it is now intuitively natural to describe properties of web services (and their compositions) by specifying constraints on those execution trees.

The FLOWS ontology is very general, and can be used in connection with a broad array of web services models. Nevertheless, FLOWS does provide some key building blocks for specifying typical web services applications. Speaking loosely, these building blocks can be viewed as a synthesis of key elements from the OWL-S model and from the message-based perspective of the Services Oriented Architecture and the WSDL standard. A typical (although not required) approach to specifying a web services application in FLOWS is illustrated in Figure 1. The figure shows three web services, corresponding to processes that might be performed by a Store, a Warehouse, and a Bank. Occurrences of these web services have the ability to interact with an abstraction of the "real world"; in FLOWS the world is modeled as first-order constants and predicates, whose contents can vary over time. These are called *domain-specific fluents*. (For a given FLOWS theory, there is a natural representation of these fluents in terms of (possibly infinite) relations in the sense of database theory.) Importantly, some

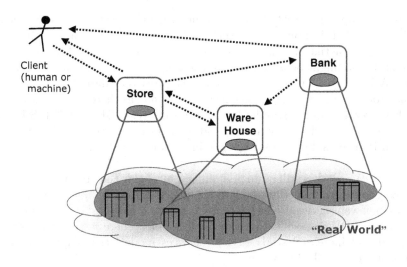

Fig. 1. Schematic view of unified web services model

of the predicates used to model the "real world" might be accessible exclusively by (the occurrences of) exactly one web service, while other predicates might be accessible by (the occurrences of) more than one web service. As suggested by Figure 1, constructs are provided in FLOWS to describe the communication between web services through the passing of messages. Optionally, an application domain specification using FLOWS can use a channel construct, to provide some structure for how messages are passed.

FLOWS includes objects of type *service*. These can be related to several types of object, including non-functional properties (e.g., name, author, URL), and also to its *activity*. This is a PSL activity, and as such may be specified using first-order formulae that act essentially as constraints on the possible executions of the service. In general, the activity of a service will have specialized kinds of subactivities. This includes (*FLOWS*) *atomic processes*, which are based on OWL-S atomic processes with inputs, outputs, pre-conditions and conditional effects. Some of these atomic processes, as in OWL-S, are *domain-specific*, in that they interact with the "real world" as represented in the application domain, and others are *service-specific*, in that they focus on the standardized mechanics of services, e.g., message-passing and channel management.

The flow of information *between services* can occur in essentially two ways: (a) via message passing and (b) via shared access to the same "real world" fluent (e.g., an inventory database, a reservations database). With regards to message passing, FLOWS models *messages* as (conceptual) objects that are created, read, and (possibly) destroyed by web services. A message life-span has a non-zero duration. Messages have types, which indicate the kind of information that they can transmit. FLOWS also includes a flexible *channel* construct.

To represent the acquisition and dissemination of information *inside a Web service*, FLOWS follows the spirit of the ontology for "knowledge-producing actions" developed in [SL03]; this also formed the basis for the situation calculus semantics of OWL-S inputs and effects [NM02]. This provides a mechanism for abstracting the actual information transfer from the lower-level details of how the information might be encoded into messages (e.g., as XML documents).

FLOWS is very open-ended concerning the process or data flow between the atomic processes inside a services. This is intentional, as there are several process models for services in the standards and literature (e.g., BPEL, OWL-S Process Model, Roman model, Mealy model) and many other alternatives besides (e.g., rooted in Petri nets, in process algebras, in workflow models, in telecommunications).

The FLOWS work is still quite preliminary, but holds the promise of providing a unifying foundation for the study and comparison of these many variations on the notion of web service. Being based in first-order logic, most decision problems concerning FLOWS specifications are undecidable. There is thus the need for continued and increased study of web services models that capture different subsets of the overall FLOWS model.

3   Colombo

We now turn to a second work that helps to provide a unifying model for web services composition. This is very recent work, described in [BCD+05b] (and also [BCD+05a]). This work follows the high-level perspective of Figure 1, and studies what is essentially a subset of FLOWS, in which decision procedures for specific composition synthesis problems can be developed. The work introduces Colombo, a formal model for web services that combines

(a) A world state, representing the "real world", viewed as a database instance over a relational database schema
(b) Atomic processes in the spirit of OWL-S,
(c) Message passing, including a simple notion of ports and links, as found in web services standards (e.g., WSDL, BPEL)
(d) The use of "guarded automata", that represent the (observable or advertised) internal behavior of web services, where the individual transitions correspond to atomic processes, message writes, and message reads.

The first three elements parallel in several aspects the core elements of FLOWS. The fourth element is reminiscent of the guarded automata of [FBS04a, FBS04b], although in Colombo (i) the notion of OWL-S atomic processes is incorporated as a new kind of transition, and (ii) only scalar values can be manipulated, rather than XML documents.

Colombo also includes

(e) a "local store" for each web service, used manage the data read/written with messages and input/output by atomic processes; and
(f) a simple form of integrity constraints on the world state

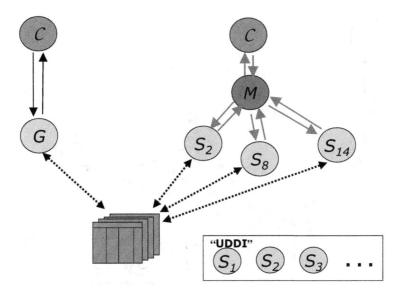

Fig. 2. Illustration of Mediator Synthesis

Using the Colombo model, [BCD+05b] develops a framework for posing composition problems, that closely parallels the way composition might be done using standards-based web services. One composition problem is called the *mediator synthesis* problem. This focuses on how to build a mediator service that simulates the behavior of a target web service, where the mediator can only use message passing to get the pre-existing web services to invoke atomic processes (which in turn impact the "real world"). The mediator synthesis problem is illustrated in Figure 2. As suggested on the left side of that figure we assume that a (virtual) "goal service" $\mathcal{G}$ is given as a Colombo guarded automata. As such, $\mathcal{G}$ includes atomic processes that can manipulate "real world" relations, and also messaging ports that can be used by a hypothetical client $\mathcal{C}$. Also provided as input is a set of Colombo web services $\mathcal{S}_1$, ..., $\mathcal{S}_n$. (These can be viewed as existing in a generalized form of "UDDI" directory). The challenge, as suggested on the right side of Figure 2 is to (i) select a subset of services from the UDDI directory, (ii) synthesize a new service M (a "mediator"), and (iii) construct "linkages" between M, the chosen services, and the client $\mathcal{C}$, so that the set of possible behaviors of the system involving M and the selected services, at least as can be observed by $\mathcal{C}$, by the invocations of atomic processes, and by the impact on the "real world", is identical to the set of possible behaviors of $\mathcal{G}$.

A second problem studied in [BCD+05b], called *choreography synthesis*, is illustrated in Figure 3. The inputs for this problem are identical to those of the mediator synthesis problem. However, in choreography synthesis the challenge is to select elements of the "UDDI" directory and then to construct a linkage for message passing that goes between those services and the client, so that the overall system simulates the goal service (i.e., there is no "new" service involved).

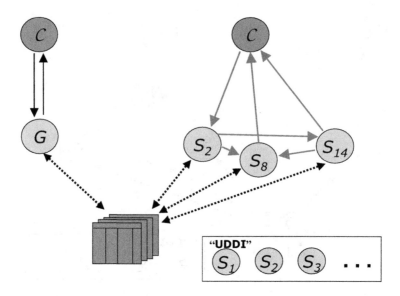

Fig. 3. Illustration of Choreography Synthesis

Under certain restrictions, [BCD⁺05b] demonstrates the decidability of the existence of a solution to the mediator synthesis problem, and similarly for the choreography synthesis problem. Further, a method for building a solution for a given synthesis problem is provided if a solution exists. These results are based on (a) a technique for reducing potentially infinite domains of data values (in the "real world") into a finite set of symbolic data values, and (b) in a generalization of [BCDG⁺04a], a mapping of the composition problem into PDL. The results reported in [BCD⁺05b] rely on a number of restrictions; a broad open problem concerns how these restrictions can be relaxed while still retaining decidability. Also, the worst-case complexity as reported in [BCD⁺05b] is doubly exponential time; it is hoped to reduce that at least to exponential time.

4   Selected Related Work

We close this brief survey by mentioning briefly some selected related works. The Web Services Modeling Ontology (WSMO) [WSMO] effort is developing an ontology for web services and their composition, with a foundation different than that of FLOWS. WSMO allows the specification of a web service at four levels: (a) "Capabilities", which are reminiscent of the OWL-S input, output, pre-condition, and conditional effect; (b) "Choreography", which concerns the possible sequencings of messages and effects on the world that a service can have, from the perspective of a client calling the service; (c) "Orchestration", which concerns the possible sequencings of messages that a service can make when invoking other services; and (d) "Implementation", which focuses on the internal processing of the web service. The Choreography and Orchestration components are described using Abstract State Machines [Bör03], which provide a very basic formalism that can be used to simulate many process models (e.g., flowcharts, finite state machines, Petri nets). This approach is fundamentally procedural, in contrast with the more declarative approach of FLOWS. We note also that FLOWS specifications may be better suited than WSMO Choreography or Orchestration specifications for expressing historical properties and constraints concerning transaction compensations.

In [DSV04], a rule based language was developed for specifying interactive (i.e., human-machine) Web services. The rules may access associated (relational) databases. Web service properties are defined using a linear temporal first-order logic. Based on the Abstract State Machine techniques [Spi03], it was shown that some properties are verifiable for a subclass of Web services; see also [DMS+05]. It remains open if the results just mentioned can be applied in connection with the emerging WSMO effort.

The papers [PMBT05, PTBM05, TP04] study synthesis problems similar to the mediator synthesis problem described for Colombo. For example, [TP04] develops an approach to build a mediator that combines OWL-S services to behave according to a behavior specification given in the EaGle language (a variant of CTL, that incorporates preferences and handling of subgoal failures); and [PTBM05] does something analogous but starting with BPEL services. The work just mentioned does not attempt to represent the impact of services on the "real world"; reference [PMBT05] builds on the previous work by incorporating limited knowledge about the values being passed and manipulated by the web services, thus capturing some aspects of impact on the world. We note that the EaGle specifications used can be incomplete in ways that a Colombo goal service cannot be. All of this work is based on using a planning tool to synthesize a mediator, rather than the use of a logical framework as in Colombo.

Finally, we mention Meteor-S [POSV04], which can be viewed as an extension of WSDL to position input/output data types into domain ontologies. In [AVMM04], web service "operations" are modeled essentially as OWL-S atomic processes (with input, output, pre-condition, and conditional effect), and composition is acheived using a "Semantic Process Template" (SPT). The SPT is essentially a workflow whose actions are semantically-described operations. The style of composition developed there is reminiscent of the "customized" approach to composition presented in [MS02].

Acknowledgements. The author wishes to thank his collaborators for many fruitful discussions and inspirations, including Michael Benedikt, Daniela Berardi, Tevfik Bultan, Diego Calvanese, Vassilis Christophides, Guiseppe De Giacomo, Xiang Fu, Cagdas Gerede, Michael Grüninger, Oscar Ibarra, Grigorios Karvounarakis, Maurizio Lenzerini, Massimo Mecella, Sheila McIlraith, and Jianwen Su.

References

[ACKM04]   G. Alonso, F. Casati, H. Kuno, and V. Machiraju. *Web Services. Concepts, Architectures and Applications.* Springer-Verlag, 2004.

[AVMM04]   R. Aggarwal, K. Verma, J. Miller, and W. Milnor. Constraint Driven Web Service Composition in METEOR-S. In *Proc. IEEE Intl. Conf. on Services Computing* (IEEE-SCC), 2004.

[BCD$^+$05a]   D. Berardi, D. Calvanese, G. De Giacomo, R. Hull, and M. Mecella. Automatic composition of web services in Colombo. In *Proc. of 13th Itallian Symp. on Advanced Database Systems*, June 2005.

[BCD$^+$05b]   D. Berardi, D. Calvanese, G. De Giacomo, R. Hull, and M. Mecella. Automatic Composition of Transition-based Semantic Web Services with Messaging. Proc. Intl. Conf. on Very Large Databases (VLDB), Trondheim, Norway, September, 2005

[BCDG$^+$04a]   D. Berardi, D. Calvanese, G. De Giacomo, M. Lenzerini, and M. Mecella. Automatic Services Composition based on Behavioral Descriptions. *International Journal of Cooperative Information Systems (IJCIS)*, 2004.

[BCG$^+$03]   D. Berardi, D. Calvanese, G. De Giacomo, M. Lenzerini, and M. Mecella. Automatic composition of e-services that export their behavior. In *Proc. 1st Int. Conf. on Service Oriented Computing (ICSOC)*, volume 2910 of *LNCS*, pages 43–58, 2003.

[BCH05]   D. Beyer, A. Chakrabarti, and T.A. Henzinger. Web Service Interfaces. In *Proc. 14th Intl. World Wide Web Conf.* (WWW), pages 148-159, 2005.

[BGHM04]   D. Berardi, M. Grüninger, R. Hull, and S. McIlraith. Towards a first-order ontology for web services. In *W3C Workshop on Constraints and Capabilities for Web Services*, October 2004.

[BGL$^+$04]   D. Berardi, G. De Giacomo, M. Lenzerini, M. Mecella, and D. Calvanese. Synthesis of underspecified composite e-services based on automated reasoning. In *Proc. Second International Conference on Service-Oriented Computing*, pages 105–114, 2004.

[BPEL]   Business Process Execution Language for Web Services (BPEL), Version 1.1. `http://www.ibm.com/developerworks/library/ws-bpel`, May 2003.

[Bör03]   E. Börger and R. Stark. *Abstract STate Machines: A Method for High-LEvel System Design and Analysis.* Springer-Verlag, 2003.

[BFHS03]   T. Bultan, X. Fu, R. Hull, and J. Su. Conversation specification: A new approach to design and analysis of e-service composition. In *Proc. Int. World Wide Web Conf. (WWW)*, May 2003.

[DMS$^+$05]   A. Deutsch, M. Marcus, L. Sui, V. Vianu, and D. Zhou. A Verifier for Interactive, Data-Driven Web Applications. In *Proc. ACM Conf. on Mgmt. of Data* (SIGMOD), 2005.

[DSV04]   A. Deutsch, L. Sui, and V. Vianu. Specification and verification of data-driven web services. In *Proc. ACM Symp. on Principles of Database Systems*, 2004.

[FBS03]   X. Fu, T. Bultan, and J. Su. Conversation protocols: A formalism for specification and verification of reactive electronic services. In *Proc. Int. Conf. on Implementation and Application of Automata (CIAA)*, 2003.

[FBS04a]   X. Fu, T. Bultan, and J. Su. Analysis of interacting BPEL web ser-
            vices. In *Proc. Int. World Wide Web Conf. (WWW)*, May 2004.
[FBS04b]   X. Fu, T. Bultan, and J. Su. Model checking XML manipulating
            software. In *Proc. Int. Symposium on Software Testing and Analysis
            (ISSTA)*, July 2004.
[GM03]   M. Grüninger and C. Menzel. Process specification language: Princi-
            ples and applications. *AI Magazine*, 24:63–74, 2003.
[Grü03]   M. Grüninger. Applications of PSL to semantic web services. In *Pro-
            ceedings of SWDB'03, The first International Workshop on Semantic
            Web and Databases*, 2003.
[GHM05]   M. Grüninger, R. Hull, and S. McIlraith. A First-Order On-
            tology for Semantic Web Services. In *W3C Workshop on
            Frameworks for Semantic Web Services*, April, 2005, Innsbruck
            http://www.w3.org/2005/04/FSWS/Submissions/59/w3c05.pdf
[HBCS03]   R. Hull, M. Benedikt, V. Christophides, and J. Su. E-services: A look
            behind the curtain. In *Proc. ACM Symp. on Principles of Database
            Systems*, 2003.
[HNK02]   J. E. Hanson, P. Nandi, and S. Kumaran. Conversation support for
            business process integration. In *Proc. 6th Int. Enterprise Distributed
            Object Computing (EDOC)*, Ecole Polytechnic, Switzerland, 2002.
[HS05]   R. Hull and J. Su. Tools for Composite Web Services: A Short
            Overview. *SIGMOD Record*, Vol. 34, Number 2, June 2005. Available
            at http://www.sigmod.org/record/issues/0506/.
[MS02]   S. McIlraith and T. Son. Adapting Golog for composition of seman-
            tic web services. In *Proc. of the Eighth International Conference on
            Knowledge Representation and Reasoning (KR2002)*, pages 482–493,
            April 2002.
[MSZ01]   S. A. McIlraith, T. C. Son, and H. Zeng. Semantic web services. In
            IEEE Intelligent Systems, March/April 2001.
[NM02]   S. Narayanan and S. McIlraith. Simulation, verification and auto-
            mated composition of web services. In *Proc. Int. World Wide Web
            Conf. (WWW)*, 2002.
[OWL-S]   OWL Services Coalition. OWL-S: Semantic markup for web services,
            November 2003.
[Pin94]   J.A. Pinto. *Temporal Reasoning in the Situation Calculus*. PhD thesis,
            University of Toronto, 1994.
[PG03]   M.P. Papazoglou and D. Georgakopoulos. Service Oriented Comput-
            ing (special issue). *Communication of the ACM*, 46(10):24–28, 2003.
[PMBT05]   M. Pistore, A. Marconi, P. Bertoli, and P. Traverso. Automated Com-
            position of Web Services by Planning at the Knowledge Level. In *Intl.
            Joint Conf. on Artificial Intelligence* (IJCAI), 2005
[POSV04]   Abhijit Patil, Swapna Oundhakar, Amit Sheth, and Kunal Verma.
            METEOR-S Web service Annotation Framework. In *Proc. of the
            World Wide Web Conf.* (WWW), July 2004.
[PTBM05]   M. Pistore, P. Traverso, P. Bertoli, and A. Marconi. Automated Syn-
            thesis of Composite BPEL4WS Web Services In *Proc. 3rd IEEE In-
            ternational Conference on Web Services* (ICWS), Orlando, 2005.
[PSL]   PSL standards group. Psl home page. http://ats.nist.gov/psl/.
[Rei01]   R. Reiter. *Knowledge in Action: Logical Foundations for Specifying
            and Implementing Dynamical Systems*. MIT Press, Cambridge, MA,
            2001.

[SL03]   R. B. Scherl and H. J. Levesque. Knowledge, action, and the frame problem. *Artificial Intelligence*, 144:1–39, 2003.

[Spi03]   M. Spielmann. Verification of relational transducers for electronic commerce. *Journal of Computer and System Sciences*, 66(1):40–65, 2003.

[SWSI]   Semantic Web Serivces Initiative (SWSI). Home page at `http://www.swsi.org/`.

[SWSF]   SWSL Committee. Semantic Web Services Framework Overview (SWSF), 2005. Available in `http://www.w3.org/Submission/SWSF/`.

[SWSO]   SWSL Committee. Semantic web service ontology (SWSO), 2005. Available in `http://www.w3.org/Submission/SWSF-SWSO/`.

[SPAS03]   K. Sycara, M. Paolucci, A. Ankolekar and N. Srinivasan. Automated Discovery, Interaction and Composition of Semantic Web services. *Journal of Web Semantics*, Vol. 1, Issue 1, September 2003, pp. 27–46.

[TP04]   P. Traverso and M. Pistore. Automatic Composition of Semantic Web Services into Executable Processes. In *Proc. Intl. Semantic Web Conference* (ISWC), 2004.

[WSCDL04]   Web Services Choreography Description Language Version 1.0 (W3C Working Draft). `http://www.w3.org/TR/2004/WD-ws-cdl-10-20041217/`, December 2004.

[WSCL02]   Web Services Conversation Language (WSCL) 1.0. `http://www.w3.org/TR/2002/NOTE-wscl10-20020314/`, March 2002.

[WSDL]   Web Services Description Language (WSDL) 1.1. `http://www.w3.org/TR/wsdl`, March 2001.

[WSDL04]   Web Services Description Language (WSDL) Version 2.0 Part 2: Predefined Extensions (W3C Working Draft). `http://www.w3.org/TR/2004/WD-wsdl20-extensions-20040803/`, August 2004.

[WSMO]   Web Services Modeling Ontology (WSMO). Home page at `http://http://www.wsmo.org/`.

Peer-to-Peer Data Integration with Active XML*

Tova Milo

School of Computer Science,
Tel Aviv University, Tel Aviv 69978, Israel

Abstract. The advent of XML as a universal exchange format and of Web services as a basis for distributed computing, has fostered the emergence of a new class of documents that we call *Active XML documents* (AXML in short). These are XML documents where some of the data is given explicitly while other parts are given only intentionally by means of embedded calls to web services, that can be called to generate the required information. We argue that AXML provides powerful means for the modeling and integration of distributed dynamic Web data. AXML can capture various integration scenarios including peer-to-peer data mediation and warehousing, while providing support for new features of Web services such as subscription, service directories, and controlling data changes. Moreover, by allowing service call parameters and responses to contain calls to other services, AXML enables distributed computation over the web. We overview here the AXML project, considering the new possibilities that Active XML brings to Web data management and the fundamental challenges it raises.

1 Introduction

The increasing popularity of the Web and the diversity of information that it contains introduced several new trends in the management of Web data. From an architectural viewpoint, the Web promotes *peer-to-peer* based architectures, as sites typically have only limited knowledge about the overall Web content or its structure[21, 13]. From a model viewpoint, the information available at a given Web peer is typically defined as a mixture of *extensional data* stored at the peer and *intensional data* that the peer can extract from other remote peers[12, 16]. Finally, for structure, due to the great heterogeneity of Web data, information is often represented as *XML documents* rather than, e.g. relations in more centralized/homogeneous settings[25]. These three aspects set the basis of this work: we consider here the management and querying of *XML data*, both *extensional and intensional*, in a *peer-to-peer* environment.

More specifically, we consider *Active XML* data (AXML for short), a new generation of XML documents that is recently gaining popularity. AXML documents are XML documents where some of the data is given explicitly while other parts are given only intensionally by means of embedded calls to Web services

---

* The research has been partially supported by the European Project EDOS and the Israel Science Foundation.

S. Grumbach, L. Siu, and V. Vianu (Eds.): ASIAN 2005, LNCS 3818, pp. 11–18, 2005.

[5, 17, 14]. These services can be dynamically called to generate the required information when needed. Besides allowing for dynamic data access, Active XML also lead to the a new class of Web services defined declaratively by queries over AXML documents that return AXML data as answer [3, 20]. We call such Web services *AXML services*. The increasing acceptance of XML as a universal exchange format and of Web services as a basis for distributed computing promotes this new type of AXML documents and services as a powerful means for the modeling and integration of distributed dynamic Web data [5, 3, 14, 17].

To explain the potential that AXML holds and the fundamental new possibilities and challenges it brings to data management, we start by explaining (in Sections 2 and 3) the origin of this new class of documents and their particular properties. Next, (in Sections 4 and 5), we explain how they can be exchanged, and efficiently used, to facilitate distributed data integrations and processing.

2   What are AXML Documents?

As mentioned above, XML is becoming a standard format for data exchange between application on the Web. In the spirit of including code in HTML documents, one is lead naturally to the idea of embedding active fragments in XML documents. Indeed the idea of interpreting or running XML documents is already promoted by technologies such as XSL, JSP, Microsoft's ASP, and MacroMedia's DreamWeaver[17]. We are concerned here in particular with documents where the dynamic part is provided by *Web services*. Recent standards for Web services such as SOAP [22] and WSDL [24] normalize the way programs can be invoked over the Web, and are becoming the standard means of publishing and accessing valuable, dynamic, up-to-date sources of information. The increasing acceptance of these standards naturally leads to including into XML documents calls to Web services to capture the non-static parts of the documents. This approach is followed, for example, in the .Net framework, or in DreamWeaver, that recently changed its interface from a Java-based model of "components" to a web-service based one [17]. The aforementioned projects promote Active XML documents primarily for presentation purposes. Pushing the idea further, one can view more generally Active XML documents as a convenient tool for distributed data management, and in particular, for peer-to-peer data integration[3].

To see an example, consider the following application scenario. An AXML document can be used to describe the content of a music portal. The document contains some extensional information, e.g. a list of CD's referenced by the portal, as well as some intensional information, e.g. how more references may be obtained from other portals via some Web services. This intensional information may be materialized by invoking the services and the list of references of the portal thereby enriched. The portal also provides an AXML Web service that, given some search criteria (e.g. the name of a musician or the title of a CD), returns the required information. The answer is an AXML document that may contain (besides extensional information) embedded calls to other portals to obtain more information.

3   Why are AXML Documents Interesting?

It should be noted that the idea of embedding calls into data is not new in databases: (i) relational systems support procedural attributes, i.e., columns in relations that are defined by some code, and (ii) objects in object databases have attached methods. The novelty of AXML is in turning embedded calls into a powerful tool for data and services integration.

When dealing with data integration, typically the goal is to integrate information provided by a number autonomous, heterogeneous sources and to be able to query it uniformly. One usually distinguishes between two main alternatives in a data integration scenario: warehousing vs. mediation [12, 16]. The former consists in replication the data of interest from the external sources, and working on this data locally, whereas the latter relies on query rewriting mechanisms to fetch just the necessary data from the sources at query time.

AXML data allows to introduce flexibility in various ways. First, it can be employed in peer-to-peer architecture, so in particular, the integrator needs not be one particular server, i.e. many peers may participate to this task. Second, it allows to follow a hybrid path between data mediation and warehousing: By controlling which service calls are executed and when (e.g. every hours, only when the data is needed, etc.) one can warehouse part of the information while allow the rest be mediated on demand. Furthermore, by allowing data sources to return AXML data where part on the information is materialized and some is not (rather than always returning fully materialized XML data), the granularity of warehoused/mediated data can be refined. Finally, it considers Web services and service calls as first class entities, hence any new Web resource that uses Web services standards may be discovered and integrated. Thus, in some sense, AXML also allows "service integration".

Beyond data integration, AXML also facilitate the deployment of distributed applications based on distributed data sharing at large. To see this observe that AXML documents have a property that we view here as crucial: since Web services can be called from essentially anywhere on the Web, one does not need anymore to materialize all the intensional data before sending the document. Instead, a more flexible data exchange paradigm is possible, where the sender sends an intensional document and gives the receiver the freedom to materialize the data if and when needed. In general, one can use a hybrid approach, where some data is materialized by the sender before the document is sent, and some is materialized by the receiver. As a simple example, consider an AXML document for the home-page of a local newspaper. It may contain some extensional XML data, such as general information about the newspaper, and some intensional fragments, e.g. one for the current temperature in the city, obtained from a weather forecast Web service, and a listing of current art exhibits, obtained from the *TimeOut* local guide. A newspaper reader may receive the full materialized document, a smaller intensional one, or one where some data is materialized (e.g. the temperature) and some is left intensional (e.g. the art exhibits).

Note that this allows for some form of distributed computing. By sending data containing service calls (as parameters of a call), one can delegate some work to other peers. Also, by returning data containing service calls, one can give to the receiver the control of these calls and the possibility to obtain directly the information from its provider.

4   Exchange of AXML Data

One of the key aspects of AXML is the exchange of AXML data between peers. As mentioned before, when sending a piece of AXML data, one has the choice whether to evaluate the service calls embedded in it or not. Some of the considerations that may guide the choice of materializing or not some information are the following:

Performance. The decision whether to execute calls before or after the data transfer may be influenced by the current system load or the cost of communication. For instance, if the sender's system is overloaded or communication is expensive, the sender may prefer to send smaller files and delegate as much materialization of the data as possible to the receiver. Otherwise, it may decide to materialize as much data as possible before transmission, in order to reduce the processing on the receiver's side.

Capabilities. Although Web services may in principle be called remotely from anywhere on the Internet, it may be the case that the particular receiver of the AXML document cannot perform them, e.g., a newspaper reader's browser may not be able to handle the intensional parts of a document. And even if it does, the user may not have access to a particular service, e.g., by lack of access rights. In such cases, it is compulsory to materialize the corresponding information before sending the document.

Security. Even if the receiver is capable of invoking service calls, she may prefer not to do so for security reasons. Indeed, service calls may have side effects. Receiving intensional data from an untrusted party and invoking the calls embedded in it may thus lead to severe security violations. To overcome this problem, the receiver may decide to refuse documents with calls to services that do not belong to some specific list. It is then the responsibility of a helpful sender to materialize all the data generated by such service calls before sending the document.

Functionality. Last but not least, the choice may be guided by the application. In some cases, e.g. for a UDDI-like service registry, the origin of the information is what is truly requested by the receiver, hence service calls should not be materialized. In other cases, one may prefer to hide the true origin of the information, e.g., for confidentiality reasons, or because it is an asset of the sender, so the data must be materialized. Finally, calling services might also involve some fees that should be payed by one or the other party.

A uniform, flexible mechanism is needed for describing the various constraints and preferences and incorporating them dynamically into the computation.

For purely extensional data, schemas (like DTD and XML Schema) are used to specify the desired format of the exchanged data. Similarly, we have introduced the use of schemas to control the exchange of AXML data and, in particular, the invocation of service calls. The novelty here is that schemas also entail information about which parts of the data are allowed to be intensional and which service calls may appear where. Before sending information, the sender must check whether the data, in its current structure, matches the schema expected by the receiver and if not, the sender must perform the required calls for transforming the data into the desired structure, if possible.

In [20] we have provided a simple but flexible XML-based syntax to embed service calls in XML documents, and introduce an extension of XML Schema for describing the required structure of the exchanged data. This consists in adding new type constructors for service call nodes. In particular, our typing distinguishes between accepting a concrete type, e.g. a *temperature* element, and accepting a service call returning some data of this type, e.g., $() \to temperature$.

Given a document t and a data exchange schema, the sender needs to decide which data has to be materialized. We developed algorithms that, based on schema and data analysis, find an effective sequence of call invocations, if such a sequence exists (or detect a failure if it does not)[20, 4]. The algorithms provide different levels of guarantees of success for this rewriting process, ranging from "sure" success to a "possible" one. At a higher level, in order to check compatibility between applications, the sender may wish to verify that *all* the documents generated by its application may be sent to the target receiver, which involves comparing two schemas. We showed that this problem can be easily reduced to the previous one.

As explained above, our algorithms allow to find an effective sequence of call invocations, if one exists, and detect failure otherwise. In a more general context, an error may arise because of type discrepancies between the caller and the receiver. One may then want to modify the data and convert it to the right structure, using data translation techniques such as [8, 10]. As a simple example, one may need to convert a temperature from Celsius degrees to Fahrenheit. These aspects are clearly complementary and need to be added to the framework. Another challenging research direction is to develop a module that may act as a "negotiator" who could speak to other peers to agree with them on the AXML Schemas that should be used to exchange data.

In many applications, it is necessary to screen queries and/or results according to specific user groups [7]. More specifically for us, the embedding of Web service calls into documents that are exchanged may be a serious cause of security violation. Indeed, this was one of the original motivations for the above mentioned research. Security and access models for XML and Web services have been proposed in, e.g., [9, 19]. Our preliminary research shows that the use encryption and signature techniques provided as Web services, together with our schema-based mechanism to control when and by whom they are used, provides a generic framework for the enforcement of access and update constrains on the exchanged data.

5   Execution and Evaluation

The performance of a data integration platform and in particular of queries over the integrated data is of course a key issue in system design. The AXML model must be accompanied by an appropriate optimization technique in order to be feasible in practice. The challenge here is to analyze the declarative specification of AXML data and accordingly provide better data materialization and query/update processing,

To see an example, recall that in AXML, some portions of the documents are given intentionally by means of embedded calls to Web service. A brute force way to evaluate a query is to materialize the full document and then run the query. Naturally, for more efficient processing, one would like to materialize only the minimal "relevant" data. This can be achieved by (1) invoking only those service calls that may contribute such relevant data, and (2) when possible, "pushing" some of the query processing out, into the service, so that rather than returning its full answer only the relevant portions will be returned. While this resembles traditional query processing in relational/XML mediator systems, where the mediator identifies the relevant data sources and pushes some of the computation to them[12, 16, 18, 11], two particular difficulties arise in the context of AXML:

- Service calls may appear anywhere in the documents, and when invoked may return AXML data, namely XML fragments with new embedded service calls. These in turn may bring more data and more service calls. Consequently, in AXML, the detection of relevant data sources (i.e. service calls) is more involved and must be a dynamic continuous process.
- AXML documents may be defined in a recursive manner. For instance the a music portal may contain some materialized XML data describing the music listings available at the peer plus some intentional data obtained by querying (calling the Web services of) some other portals. Those may also contain some local materialized data and calls to other portals, possibly recursively. Consequently, the process of query "pushing" and data gathering becomes recursive.

To overcome thes problems we have proposed in [2] a set of efficient algorithms which, based on query rewriting combined with the analysis services signatures, detect set the of calls relevant to a given query and pushes some of the query processing to the relevant sites.

Before considering in more detail query processing in this setting, let us draw an analogy between query evaluation in AXML documents and in distributed deductive databases[15]. An AXML document can be modeled as a labeled tree where some of the nodes are *real* XML elements and some are *virtual*, defined intensional by service calls embedded in the document. When a call is invoked, the returned data is appended to the document as siblings of the service call. Think of each node in the document as a collection. *Real* nodes play the role of extensional relations and *virtual* ones of intensional relations from deductive databases. The embedded service calls play the role of rules in deductive databases, a call defining intensionally its parent node. The recursion if natural in this setting: some document d may depend intensionally (via service calls) on some document d' and conversely.

Two important and closely related optimization techniques for query evaluation in deductive databases have been studied, namely Query-Sub-Query (QSQ in short) [23] and Magic Set (MS in short)[6]. They are both based on minimizing the quantity of data that is materialized and we believe that they can serve as a sound foundation for optimization in the AXML context. To achieve that, they need to be enriched along two dimensions.

- The first one is distribution. The core of the QSQ and MS techniques is a rewriting of the datalog program given a query. In the AXML context, the "program" (i.e. the documents and services) is distributed over several peers. A main issue is thus to have each peer perform its own rewriting with only local information available, i.e., without using any global knowledge of the program.
- The second more challenging dimension is moving from relations to trees. As service calls may return AXML data, new intensional relations (nodes) and rules defining them (service calls) are dynamically added to the document tree. The rewriting has to continuously account for these new calls, detecting the ones involved in a particular query and rewriting them when needed.

The AQSQ (AXML QSQ) technique that we developed [1] extends QSQ along these two dimensions, providing what we believe to be a a uniform framework for distributed AXML query evaluation.

Beside the minimizing the quantity of materialized data one would like also to minimize communications or computational cost and other complementary techniques such as semijoins and indexing techniques may be used to this end. This complementary direction requires further research.

6   Conclusion

The research described here led to the development of the Active XML system [3, 5, 20, 2]. The AXML system provides persistent storage for XML documents with embedded calls to Web services, along with active features to automatically trigger these services and thus enrich/update the intensional documents. Furthermore, it allows users to declaratively specify Web services that support intensional documents as input and output parameters. The experience with the system demonstrated that this new type of AXML documents and services have the potential of forming a powerful means for the modeling and integration of distributed dynamic Web data.

Since XML and Web services are promised such a brilliant future, we believe it very important to develop a sound foundation for AXML so that this technology can be better understood and used. While the AXML system provides a convenient test bed for the ideas developed in this research, it should be emphasized that the techniques developed are aimed to be generic and be applicable to many other systems supporting Active XML data.

References

1. S. Abiteboul, Z. Abrams, S. Haar, and T. Milo. Diagnosis of asynchronous discrete event systems - datalog to the rescue! In *PODS*, 2005.
2. S. Abiteboul, O. Benjelloun, B. Cautis, I. Manolescu, T. Milo, and N. Preda. Lazy query evaluation for active xml. In *SIGMOD*, pages 227–238, 2004.
3. S. Abiteboul, O. Benjelloun, I. Manolescu, T. Milo, and R. Weber. Active XML: Peer-to-Peer Data and Web Services Integration (demo). VLDB, 2002.
4. S. Abiteboul, T. Milo, and O. Benjelloun. Regular and unambiguous rewritings for active xml. In *PODS*, 2005.
5. The Active XML homepage. http://activexml.net/.
6. F. Bancilhon, D. Maier, Y. Sagiv, and J. D. Ullman. Magic sets and other strange ways to implement logic programs. In *Proc. of SIGMOD*, pages 1–16, 1986.
7. K. Selcuk Candan, Sushil Jajodia, and V. S. Subrahmanian. Secure Mediated Databases. In *Proc. of ICDE*, pages 28–37, 1996.
8. Sophie Cluet, Claude Delobel, Jérôme Siméon, and Katarzyna Smaga. Your mediators need data conversion! In *Proc. of ACM SIGMOD*, pages 177–188, 1998.
9. E. Damiani, S. De Capitani di Vimercati, S. Paraboschi, and P. Samarati. Securing XML Documents. In *Proc. of EDBT*, 2001.
10. AnHai Doan, Pedro Domingos, and Alon Y. Halevy. Reconciling schemas of disparate data sources: a machine-learning approach. In *Proc. of ACM SIGMOD*, pages 509–520. ACM Press, 2001.
11. D. Draper, A. Y. Halevy, and D. S. Weld. The Nimble XML Data Integration System. In *Proc. of ICDE*, pages 155–160, 2001.
12. H. Garcia-Molina, Y. Papakonstantinou, D. Quass, A. Rajaraman, Y. Sagiv, J. Ullman, and J. Widom. The TSIMMIS Approach to Mediation: Data Models and Languages. *Journal of Intelligent Information Systems*, 8:117–132, 1997.
13. A. Halevy, Z. Ives, D. Suciu, and I. Tatarinov. Schema mediation in peer data management systems. In *Proc. of ICDE*, 2003.
14. Jelly: Executable xml. http://jakarta.apache.org/commons/sandbox/ jelly.
15. T. Jim and D. Suciu. Dynamically Distributed Query Evaluation. In *Proc. of ACM PODS*, pages 413–424, 2001.
16. A. Levy, A. Rajaraman, and J. Ordille. Querying Heterogeneous Information Sources Using Source Descriptions. In *Proc. of VLDB*, pages 251–262, 1996.
17. Macromedia Coldfusion MX. http://www.macromedia.com/.
18. I. Manolescu, D. Florescu, and D. Kossmann. Answering XML queries over heterogeneous data sources. In *Proc. of VLDB*, 2001.
19. Microsoft and IBM. The WS-Security specification.
    http://www.ibm.com/webservices/library/ ws-secure/.
20. T. Milo, S. Abiteboul, B. Amann, O. Benjelloun, and F. Dang Ngoc. Exchanging Intensional XML Data. In *Proc. of ACM SIGMOD*, 2003.
21. W. Siong Ng, B. Chin Ooi, and K. Lee Tan A. Zhou. Peerdb: A p2p-based system for distributed data sharing. In *Proc. of ICDE*, 2003.
22. Simple Object Access Protocol (SOAP) 1.1. `http://www.w3.org/TR/SOAP`.
23. L. Vieille. Recursive axioms in deductive database: the query/subquery approach. In *Proc. of the First Int. Conf. on Expert Database Systems*, pages 179–193, 1986.
24. Web Services Definition Language (WSDL). `http://www.w3.org/TR/wsdl`.
25. The W3C XML Activity. http://www.w3.org/XML.

Query Incentive Networks

Prabhakar Raghavan

Yahoo! Research, 701 First Avenue, Sunnyvale CA 94089, USA
pragh@yahoo-inc.com

Abstract. We formulate a model for *query incentive networks*, motivated by users seeking information or services that pose queries, together with incentives for answering them. This type of information-seeking process can be formulated as a game among the nodes in the network, and this game has a natural Nash equilibrium.

How much incentive is needed in order to achieve a reasonable probability of obtaining an answer to a query? We study the size of query incentives as a function both of the rarity of the answer and the structure of the underlying network. This leads to natural questions related to strategic behavior in branching processes. Whereas the classically studied criticality of branching processes is centered around the region where the branching parameter is 1, we show in contrast that strategic interaction in incentive propagation exhibits critical behavior when the branching parameter is 2.

This lecture is based on the paper [14] with Jon Kleinberg of Cornell University.

References

1. L. A. Adamic, O. Buyukkokten and E. Adar. A social network caught in the Web. *First Monday* 8:6(2003).
2. K.B. Athreya and P.E. Ney. Branching Processes. Springer, 1972.
3. A. Blanc, Y-K. Liu and A. Vahdat. Designing Incentives for Peer-to-Peer Routing. *2nd Workshop on Economics of Peer-to-peer systems*, 2004.
4. A. Broder, R. Krauthgamer and M. Mitzenmacher. Improved Classification via Connectivity Information. *Proc. 11th Annual ACM-SIAM Symposium on Discrete Algorithms*, 2000.
5. A. Brodsky and N. Pippenger. The Boolean Functions Computed by Random Boolean Formulas OR How to Grow the Right Function. UBC Computer Science Technical Report, TR-2003-02, 2003.
6. M. Charikar, R. Fagin, V. Guruswami, J. Kleinberg, P. Raghavan and A. Sahai. Query Strategies for Priced Information. *Proc. 32nd ACM Symposium on Theory of Computing*, 2000.
7. I. Clarke, O. Sandberg, B. Wiley and T. Hong. Freenet: A Distributed Anonymous Information Storage and Retrieval System. *International Workshop on Design Issues in Anonymity and Unobservability*, 2000.
8. O. Etzioni, S. Hanks, T. Jiang, R.M. Karp, O. Madani and O. Waarts. Efficient information gathering on the Internet. *Proc. IEEE Symposium on Foundations of Computer Science*, 1996.

S. Grumbach, L. Siu, and V. Vianu (Eds.): ASIAN 2005, LNCS 3818, pp. 19–21, 2005.

9. M. Granovetter. The strength of weak ties. *American Journal of Sociology*, **78**(6):1360-1380, 1973.

10. M. Jackson. A Survey of Models of Network Formation: Stability and Efficiency. In *Group Formation in Economics: Networks, Clubs and Coalitions.* G. Demange and M. Wooders, eds. Cambridge, 2004.

11. S. Kakade, M. Kearns, L. Ortiz, R. Pemantle and S. Suri. Economic Properties of Social Networks. *Proc. NIPS*, 2004.

12. S. Kamvar, B. Yang and H. Garcia-Molina. Addressing the Non-Cooperation Problem in Competitive P2P Systems. *1st Workshop on Economics of Peer-to-peer systems*, 2003.

13. H. Kautz, B. Selman and M. Shah. ReferralWeb: Combining Social Networks and Collaborative Filtering. *Communications of the ACM*, 1997.

14. J.M. Kleinberg and P. Raghavan. Query Incentive Networks. *IEEE Symposium on Foundations of Computer Science*, 2005.

15. R. Krishnan, M. Smith and R. Telang. The Economics of Peer-to-Peer Networks. SSRN Working Paper, September 2003.

16. C. Li, B. Yu and K. Sycara. An Incentive Mechanism for Message Relaying in Peer-to-Peer Discovery. *2nd Workshop on Economics of Peer-to-peer systems*, 2004.

17. E-K Lua, J. Crowcroft, M. Pias, R. Sharma and S. Lim. A Survey and Comparison of Peer-to-Peer Overlay Network Schemes, *IEEE Communications Survey and Tutorial*, March 2004

18. M. Luby, M. Mitzenmacher and A. Shokrollahi. Analysis of Random Processes via And-Or Tree Evaluation. *Proc. 9th Annual ACM-SIAM Symposium on Discrete Algorithms*, 1998.

19. C. H. Papadimitriou. Algorithms, Games, and the Internet. *Proc. 33rd ACM Symposium on Theory of Computing*, 2001.

20. B. Raghavan and A. Snoeren. Priority Forwarding in Ad Hoc Networks with Self-Interested Parties. *1st Workshop on Economics of Peer-to-peer systems*, 2003.

21. P. Resnick, R. Zeckhauser, E. Friedman and K. Kuwabara. Reputation Systems. *Communications of the ACM*, **43**(12):45-48, 2000.

22. A. Salkever, in *BusinessWeek*, 28 October 2003.

23. B.A. Sevastyanov. Asymptotic Behavior of the Extinction Probabilities for Stopped Branching Processes. *Theory Prob. Appl.* **43**(2):315-322, 1999.

24. É. Tardos. Network Games. *Proc. 36th ACM Symposium on Theory of Computing*, 2004.

25. L.G. Valiant. Short monotone formulae for the majority function. *Journal of Algorithms*, **5**:363-366, 1984.

26. V. Vishnumurthy, S. Chandrakumar and E.G. Sirer. KARMA : A Secure Economic Framework for P2P Resource Sharing. *1st Workshop on Economics of Peer-to-peer systems*, 2003.

27. A. Vivacqua and H. Lieberman. Agents to Assist in Finding Help. *Proc. ACM SIGCHI Conf. on Human Factors in Computing Systems*, 2000.

28. B. Wellman. The Three Ages of Internet Studies: Ten, Five and Zero Years Ago. *New Media and Society*, **6**(1):123-129, 2004.

29. B. Yu and M. P. Singh. Searching Social Networks. *Proc. 2nd International Joint Conference on Autonomous Agents and Multi-Agent Systems*, 2003.
30. B.Yu and M.P. Singh. Incentive Mechanisms for Peer-to-Peer Systems. *Proc. 2nd International Workshop on Agents and Peer-to-Peer Computing*, 2003.
31. J. Zhang and M. Van Alstyne. SWIM: fostering social network based information search. *Proc. ACM SIGCHI Conf. on Human Factors in Computing Systems*. 2004.

Database and Information Retrieval Techniques for XML

Mariano P. Consens[1] and Ricardo Baeza-Yates[2]

[1] University of Toronto, Toronto, Canada
consens@cs.toronto.edu
[2] ICREA – Univ. Pompeu Fabra Barcelona, Spain
ricardo.baeza@upf.edu

1 Overview

The world of data has been developed from two main points of view: the structured relational data model and the unstructured text model. The two distinct cultures of databases and information retrieval now have a natural meeting place in the Web with its semi-structured XML model. As web-style searching becomes an ubiquitous tool, the need for integrating these two viewpoints becomes even more important.

This tutorial[1] will provide an overview of the different issues and approaches put forward by the Information Retrieval and the Database communities and survey the DB-IR integration efforts with a focus on techniques applicable to XML retrieval. A variety of application scenarios for DB-IR integration will be covered, including examples of current industrial tools.

2 Tutorial Content

The tutorial consists of two parts: the first part will cover the problem space (basic concepts, requirements, models) and the second part the solution space (approaches and techniques).

The major topics covered together with specific bibliographic references are listed below.

Introduction. Types of data, DB & IR views, Applications, Tokenization, Web Challenges ([1, 2, 3]).

Requirements for DB-IR. Motivation, Data and Query Requirements, Sample Use Cases ([4, 5]).

Semi-structured text models. XPat and XQuery, Full-text extensions to XQuery, Structured text models, Query algebras ([6, 7, 8, 9, 10, 11, 12]).

DB Approaches. IR on Relational Data and IR on XML: keyword search, full query language with extensions, algebras and evaluation ([13, 14, 15, 16, 17, 18, 17, 19, 20, 21, 22, 23, 24, 25, 26, 27]).

---

[1] Earlier versions of this tutorial have been given at VLDB 2004 and SIGIR 2005.

S. Grumbach, L. Siu, and V. Vianu (Eds.): ASIAN 2005, LNCS 3818, pp. 22–27, 2005.

IR and Hybrid Approaches. Retrieval models, Ranking, Evaluation ([28, 29, 30, 31, 32, 33, 34, 35, 36, 37, 38]).

Query Processing. XML Processing Algorithms (summaries, indexes), Query Optimization ([39, 40, 41, 42, 43, 44, 45, 46, 47, 48, 49, 50, 51, 52, 53, 54, 55, 56, 57, 58, 59, 60, 61, 62, 63, 64, 65, 66, 67, 68, 69, 70, 71, 72, 73]).

Open Problems. A discussion of research problems in the area.

Additional Reading. The following proceedings are relevant to the tutorial material.

- Proceedings of the ACM SIGIR Workshops on XML and Information Retrieval (edited by Yoelle Maarek et al.), 2002 & 2002.
- Proceedings of the workshops of the Initiative for the Evaluation of XML Retrieval (INEX) (edited by N. Fuhr, G. Kazai, M. Lalmas et al), 2002-2004.
- Special JASIST issue on XML and IR, 53(6): 2002. Edited by Ricardo Baeza-Yates, David Carmel, Yoelle Maarek, and Aya Sofer.
- Proceedings of First International Workshop on XQuery Implementation, Experience and Perspectives (XIME-P 2004) (edited by Ioana Manolescu and Yannis Papakonstantinou), June 2004.
- Proceedings of First and Second International XML Database Symposium (XSym), 2003-2004.
- Proceedings of Joint Workshop on XML and DB-IR Integration (edited by Ricardo Baeza-Yates, Yoelle Maarek, Thomas Roelleke, and Arjen P. de Vries), SIGIR 2004, Sheffield, 2004.

References

1. Salton, G.: Automatic information organization and retrieval. McGraw-Hill, New York, USA (1968)
2. Baeza-Yates, R., Ribeiro-Neto, B.: Modern Information Retrieval. Addison-Wesley, Harlow, UK (1999)
3. Crestani, F., Lalmas, M., van Rijsbergen, C.J., Campbell, I.: Is this document relevant? . . . probably: A survey of probabilistic models in information retrieval. ACM Computing Surveys **30** (1998) 528–552
4. W3C: XQuery and XPath full-text requirements (2003) W3C Working Draft, http://www.w3.org/TR/xmlquery-full-text-requirements.
5. W3C: XQuery and XPath full-text use cases (2003) W3C Working Draft, http://www.w3.org/TR/xmlquery-full-text-use-cases.
6. Salminen, A., Tompa, F.W.: PAT expressions: An algebra for text search. Acta Linguistica Hungarica **41** (1993) 277–306
7. Consens, M., Milo, T.: Algebras for querying text regions. In: Proceedings of the Symposium on Principles of Database Systems, San Jose, California, USA (1995) 11–22
8. Clarke, C., Cormack, G., Burkowski, F.: An algebra for structured text search and a framework for its implementation. The Computer Journal **38** (1995) 43–56
9. Navarro, G., Baeza-Yates, R.: Integrating content and structure in text retrieval. SIGMOD Record **25** (1996) 67–79

10. Navarro, G., Baeza-Yates, R.: Proximal nodes: A model to query document databases by contents and structure. ACM Transactions on Information Systems **15** (1997) 401–435
11. Lee, Y.K., Yoo, S.J., Yoon, K., Berra, P.B.: Index structures for structured documents. In: Proceedings of the 1st ACM International Conference on Digital Libraries. (1996) 91–99
12. Navarro, G., Baeza-Yates, R.A.: Proximal nodes: A model to query document databases by content and structure. ACM Transactions on Information Systems (TOIS) **15** (1997) 400–435
13. Goldman, R., Shivakumar, N., Venkatasubramanian, S., Garcia-Molina, H.: Proximity search in databases. In: Proceedings of the 24th International Conference on Very Large Data Bases. (1998) 26–37
14. Florescu, D., Kossmann, D., Manolescu, I.: Integrating keyword search into XML query processing. In: Proceedings of International World Wide Web Conference. (2000)
15. Kanza, Y., Sagiv, Y.: Flexible queries over semistructured data. In: Proceedings of the Symposium on Principles of Database Systems. (2001) 40–51
16. Agrawal, S., Chaudhuri, S., Das, G.: DBXplorer: A system for keyword-based search over relational databases. In: Proceedings of International Conference on Data Engineering. (2002)
17. Bhalotia, G., Hulgeri, A., Nakhey, C., Chakrabarti, S., Sudarshan, S.: Keyword searching and browsing in databases using BANKS. In: Proceedings of International Conference on Data Engineering. (2002)
18. Hristidis, V., Papakonstantinou, Y.: DISCOVER: Keyword search in relational databases. In: Proceedings of the International Conference on Very Large Data Bases. (2002)
19. Amer-Yahia, S., Cho, S., Srivastava, D.: Tree pattern relaxation. In: Proceedings of Conference on Extending Database Technology. (2002) 496–513
20. Amer-Yahia, S., Fernandez, M., Srivastava, D., Xu, Y.: Pix: exact and approximate phrase matching in xml. In: Proceedings of the 2003 ACM SIGMOD International Conference on Management of Data. (2003) 664–664
21. Kabra, N., Ramakrishnan, R., Ercegovac, V.: The QUIQ engine: A hybrid IR-DB system. In: Proceedings of the 19th International Conference on Data Engineering. (2003) 741
22. Amer-Yahia, S., Koudas, N., Srivastava, D.: Approximate matching in xml. In: Proceedings of the 19th International Conference on Data Engineering. (2003) 803
23. Hristidis, V., Papakonstantinou, Y., Balmin, A.: Keyword proximity search on XML graphs. In: Proceedings of International Conference on Data Engineering. (2003)
24. Guo, L., Shao, F., Botev, C., Shanmugasundaram, J.: XRANK: Ranked keyword search over XML documents. In: Proceedings of ACM SIGMOD International Conference on Management of Data. (2003)
25. Cohen, S., Mamou, J., Kanza, Y., Sagiv, Y.: XSearch: a semantic search engine for XML. In: Proceedings of the 29th International Conference on Very Large Data Bases. (2003)
26. Hristidis, V., Gravano, L., Papakonstantinou, Y.: Efficient IR-style keyword search over relational databases. In: Proceedings of the International Conference on Very Large Data Bases. (2003)
27. Amer-Yahia, S., Lakshmanan, L.V.S., Pandit, S.: FleXPath: Flexible structure and full-text querying for XML. In: Proceedings of the 2004 ACM SIGMOD International Conference on Management of Data. (2004) 83–94

28. Luk, R.: A survey of search engines for XML documents. In: SIGIR Workshop on XML and IR. (2000)
29. Fuhr, N., Grobjohann, K.: XIRQL: An extension of XQL for information retrieval. In: ACM SIGIR Workshop on XML and Information Retrieval. (2000) 11–17
30. Theobald, A., Weikum, G.: Adding relevance to XML. In: Proceedings of International Workshop on the Web and Databases. (2000) 35–40
31. Fuhr, N., Grobjohann, K.: XIRQL: A query language for information retrieval in XML documents. In: Proceedings of ACM SIGIR International Conference on Research and Development in Information Retrieval. (2001) 172–180
32. Chinenyanga, T.T., Kushmerick, N.: Expressive and efficient ranked querying of XML data. In: Proceedings of International Workshop on the Web and Databases. (2001)
33. Theobald, A., Weikum, G.: The index-based XXL search engine for querying XML data with relevance ranking. In: Proceedings of Conference on Extending Database Technology. (2002) 477–495
34. Chinenyanga, T.T., Kushmerick, N.: An expressive and efficient language for XML information retrieval. Journal of the American Society for Information Science and Technology **53** (2002) 438–453
35. Grabs, T., Schek, H.J.: Flexible information retrieval from XML with PowerDB-XML. In: Proceedings of the Third INEX Workshop. (2003)
36. Mass, Y., Mandelbrod, M., Amitay, E., Carmel, D., Maarek, Y., Soffer, A.: JuruXML - an XML retrieval system at INEX 02. In: Proceedings of the First INEX Workshop. (2002)
37. Fuhr, N., Grobjohann, K.: XIRQL: An XML query language based on information retrieval concepts. ACM Trans. Inf. Syst. **22** (2004) 313–356
38. Schenkel, R., Theobald, A., Weikum, G.: Semantic similarity search on semistructured data with the XXL search engine. Information Retrieval **8** (2005) 521–545
39. Goldman, R., Widom, J.: Dataguides: Enabling query formulation and optimization in semistructured databases. In: Proceedings of the 23rd International Conference on Very Large Data Bases. (1997) 436–445
40. Nestorov, S., Ullman, J.D., Wiener, J.L., Chawathe, S.S.: Representative objects: Concise representations of semistructured, hierarchial data. In: Proceedings of the 13th International Conference on Data Engineering. (1997) 79–90
41. Milo, T., Suciu, D.: Index structures for path expressions. In: Proceedings of the 7th International Conference on Database Theory. (1999) 277–295
42. Cooper, B., Sample, N., Franklin, M.J., Hjaltason, G.R., Shadmon, M.: A fast index for semistructured data. In: Proceedings of the 27th International Conference on Very Large Data Bases. (2001) 341–350
43. Natsev, A., Chang, Y.C., Smith, J.R., Li, C.S., Vitter, J.S.: Supporting incremental join queries on ranked ranked inputs. In: Proceedings of the International Conference on Very Large Data Bases. (2001)
44. Fagin, R., Lotem, A., Naor, M.: Optimal aggregation algorithms for middleware. In: Proceedings of the Symposium on Principles of Database Systems. (2001)
45. Rizzolo, F., Mendelzon, A.O.: Indexing XML data with ToXin. In: Proceedings of 4th International Workshop on the Web and Databases. (2001) 49–54
46. Li, Q., Moon, B.: Indexing and querying XML data for regular path expressions. In: Proceedings of the 27th International Conference on Very Large Data Bases. (2001) 361–370
47. Kaushik, R., Bohannon, P., Naughton, J.F., Korth, H.F.: Covering indexes for branching path queries. In: Proceedings of the 2002 ACM SIGMOD International Conference on Management of Data. (2002) 133–144

48. Chung, C.W., Min, J.K., Shim, K.: APEX: An adaptive path index for XML data. In: Proceedings of the 2002 ACM SIGMOD International Conference on Management of Data. (2002) 121–132
49. Kaushik, R., Shenoy, P., Bohannon, P., Gudes, E.: Exploiting local similarity for indexing paths in graph-structured data. In: Proceedings of the 18th International Conference on Data Engineering. (2002) 129–140
50. Kaushik, R., Bohannon, P., Naughton, J.F., Shenoy, P.: Updates for structure indexes. In: Proceedings of the 28th International Conference on Very Large Data Bases. (2002) 239–250
51. Al-Khalifa, S., Jagadish, H.V., Patel, J.M., Wu, Y., Koudas, N., Srivastava, D.: Structural joins: A primitive for efficient XML query pattern matching. In: Proceedings of the 18th International Conference on Data Engineering. (2002) 141–
52. Chien, S.Y., Vagena, Z., Zhang, D., Tsotras, V.J., Zaniolo, C.: Efficient structural joins on indexed XML documents. In: Proceedings of the 28th International Conference on Very Large Data Bases. (2002) 263–274
53. Bruno, N., Koudas, N., Srivastava, D.: Holistic twig joins: Optimal XML pattern matching. In: Proceedings of the 2002 ACM SIGMOD International Conference on Management of Data. (2002) 310–321
54. Hristidis, V., Papakonstantinou, Y.: Algorithms and applications for answering ranked queeries using ranked views. In: Proceedings of the International Conference on Very Large Data Bases. (2003)
55. Ilyas, I.F., Aref, W.G., Elmagarmid, A.K.: Supporting top-k join queries in relational databases. In: Proceedings of the International Conference on Very Large Data Bases. (2003)
56. Bremer, J.M.: Next-Generation Information Retrieval: Integrating Document and Data Retrieval Based on XML. PhD thesis, Department of Computer Science, University of California at Davis (2003)
57. Bremer, J.M., Gertz, M.: An efficient XML node identification and indexing scheme. Technical Report CSE-2003-04, Department of Computer Science, University of California at Davis (2003)
58. Chen, Z., Jagadish, H.V., Lakshmanan, L.V.S., Paparizos, S.: From tree patterns to generalized tree patterns: On efficient evaluation of XQuery. In: Proceedings of the 29th International Conference on Very Large Data Bases. (2003) 237–248
59. Al-Khalifa, S., Yu, C., Jagadish, H.V.: Querying structured text in an XML database. In: Proceedings of ACM SIGMOD International Conference on Management of Data. (2003)
60. Qun, C., Lim, A., Ong, K.W.: D(K)-index: An adaptive structural summary for graph-structured data. In: Proceedings of the 2003 ACM SIGMOD International Conference on Management of Data. (2003) 134–144
61. Ramanan, P.: Covering indexes for XML queries: Bisimulation - simulation = negation. In: Proceedings of the 29th International Conference on Very Large Data Bases. (2003) 165–176
62. Zezula, P., Amato, G., Debole, F., Rabitti, F.: Tree signatures for XML querying and navigation. In: First International XML Database Symposium, XSym 2003. (2003) 149–163
63. Wang, H., Park, S., Fan, W., Yu, P.S.: ViST: A dynamic index method for querying XML data by tree structures. In: Proceedings of the 2003 ACM SIGMOD International Conference on Management of Data. (2003) 110–121
64. Jiang, H., Wang, W., Lu, H., Yu, J.X.: Holistic twig joins on indexed XML documents. In: Proceedings of the 29th International Conference on Very Large Data Bases. (2003) 273–284

65. Jiang, H., Lu, H., Wang, W., Ooi, B.C.: XR-Tree: Indexing XML data for efficient structural joins. In: Proceedings of the 19th International Conference on Data Engineering. (2003) 253–263
66. Li, Q., Moon, B.: Partition based path join algorithms for XML data. In: Proceedings of the 14th International Conference on Database and Expert Systems Applications, DEXA 2003. (2003) 160–170
67. Weigel, F., Meuss, H., Bry, F., Schulz, K.U.: Content-aware dataguides: Interleaving IR and DB indexing techniques for efficient retrieval of textual XML data. In: Proceedings of the 26th European Conference on IR Research, ECIR 2004. (2004) 378–393
68. Kaushik, R., Krishnamurthy, R., Naughton, J.F., Ramakrishnan, R.: On the integration of structure indexes and inverted lists. In: Proceedings of the 2004 ACM SIGMOD International Conference on Management of Data. (2004) 779–790
69. Amato, G., Debole, F., Rabitti, F., Savino, P., Zezula, P.: A signature-based approach for efficient relationship search on XML data collections. In: Second International XML Database Symposium, XSym 2004. (2004) 82–96
70. Rao, P., Moon, B.: PRIX: Indexing and querying XML using Prüfer sequences. In: Proceedings of the 20th International Conference on Data Engineering. (2004) 288–300
71. Vagena, Z., Moro, M.M., Tsotras, V.J.: Efficient processing of XML containment queries using partition-based schemes. In: Proceedings of the 8th International Database Engineering and Applications Symposium, IDEAS 2004. (2004) 161–170
72. Wang, H., Meng, X.: On the sequencing of tree structures for XML indexing. In: Proceedings of the 21st International Conference on Data Engineering. (2005)
73. Bremer, J.M., Gertz, M.: Next-generation information retrieval. VLDB Journal (2006) To appear.

Implementing a Tamper-Evident
Database System

Gerome Miklau[1] and Dan Suciu[2]

[1] University of Massachusetts, Amherst
`miklau@cs.umass.edu`
[2] University of Washington
`suciu@cs.washington.edu`

Abstract. Data integrity is an assurance that data has not been modified in an unknown or unauthorized manner. The goal of this paper is to allow a user to leverage a small amount of trusted client-side computation to achieve guarantees of integrity when interacting with a vulnerable or untrusted database server. To achieve this goal we describe a novel relational hash tree, designed for efficient database processing, and evaluate the performance penalty for integrity guarantees. We show that strong cryptographic guarantees of integrity can be provided in a relational database with modest overhead.

1 Introduction

Data integrity is an assurance that data has not been modified in an unknown or unauthorized manner.[1] In many settings (e.g. banking, medical information management, or scientific data) preventing unauthorized or inappropriate modification is essential.

In database systems, integrity is typically provided by user authentication and access control. Users are required to authenticate, and are limited in the operations they can perform on columns, tables, or views. Unfortunately, in real-world systems these mechanisms are not sufficient to guarantee data integrity. The integrity vulnerabilities in a modern database system stem from the complexity and variety of security-sensitive components, integration of database systems with application level code, underlying operating system vulnerabilities, and the existence of privileged parties, among others. Consequently, when a data owner uses a database to store and query data, she is forced to trust that the system was configured properly, operates properly, and that privileged parties and other users behave appropriately.

The goal of this paper is to allow a user to leverage a small amount of trusted client-side computation to achieve guarantees of integrity when interacting with a potentially vulnerable database server. We achieve this goal by adapting techniques from hash trees to a client-server relational database. In particular, we

---

[1] Throughout the paper we use this sense of the term *integrity*, appropriate to information security, as distinct from the notion of relational integrity maintained by constraints and familiar to database practitioners.

S. Grumbach, L. Siu, and V. Vianu (Eds.): ASIAN 2005, LNCS 3818, pp. 28–48, 2005.

describe a novel relational hash tree, designed for efficient database processing, and evaluate the performance penalty for integrity guarantees. Our implementation does not require modification of system internals and can therefore easily be applied to any conventional DBMS. While our implementation is oriented to a relational DBMS, the problem of efficiently generating proofs of integrity has many applications to the secure management of data on the web [3, 2, 15].

Threats to database system integrity. The variety of security-sensitive components and the complexity of the modern database system make it very difficult to secure in practice. Database systems figured prominently in a recent list [22] of the 20 most critical internet security vulnerabilities . We review next a range of vulnerabilities in modern database systems that could permit modification of stored data.

- *Authentication and access control.* The authentication mechanisms of a database system may be vulnerable to weak passwords, or passwords stored unencrypted in scripts and programs. Access control vulnerabilities include improper enforcement by the system, improper policy specification, or configuration of privileged users as well-known system defaults.

- *Application integration.* Many database systems are linked to front-end applications like web interfaces. Developers often add access control features at the application level because database systems lack fine-grained access control. This can lead to inconsistencies and new vulnerabilities. For example, *SQL injection* [23, 1] is an attack on databases accessible through web forms. A successful attacker can use a web form to inject SQL commands that modify data with the access rights of the web application (which are usually high) or to discover passwords. Command injection attacks including SQL injection were ranked as the top security vulnerability for web applications in [18]. SQL injection attacks have been reported for many of the most popular commercial database systems.

- *Database extensions.* Almost all modern database applications include extensions in the form of user-defined functions and stored procedures. Stored procedures may be written in general-purpose programming languages, by local users or third-party vendors, and may be executed with the access rights of the calling user or in some cases the program author. Since it is very difficult to evaluate a stored procedure for proper behavior, this constitutes a serious threat.

- *Inherited OS vulnerabilities.* Since relations are stored as files managed by the operating system, any threats to the integrity of the operating system and filesystem are inherited by the DBMS, and therefore constitute a threat to data integrity.

- *Privileged parties.* The user of a database system is always vulnerable to the incompetence or malicious intentions of certain privileged parties. A recent survey of U.S. institutions found that about half of computer security breaches are traced to members internal to the organization [8]. Database administrators always have sufficient rights to modify data or grant permissions inappropriately, while system administrators have root access to the filesystem and could modify records stored on disk.

The techniques presented in this paper are a safeguard against each these vulnerabilities because they provide the author of data with a mechanism for detecting tampering. When verification succeeds, the author has a strong guarantee that none of the vulnerabilities above has resulted in a modification in their data. Considering the range of vulnerabilities described, it makes sense to implement the protection mechanisms described here even when the database system is controlled by a single organization or institution.

Motivating scenario. Imagine Alice manages a software company and records the account information of her customers in a relation Account(acctId, name, city, current-balance). Alice would like to evaluate the following queries over Customer:

Q1 Retrieve the current balance for acctId=234.
    Alice would like an assurance that the query result is *correct*: that she authorized creation of the result tuple, and that the current-balance has not been modified by an unauthorized party.
Q2 Retrieve all customers with negative balances.
    Alice would like an assurance that the query result is *correct* and *complete*: that the attributes of each result tuple are authentic, and in addition, no customers with negative balances have been omitted from the query result.
Q3 Retrieve all customers located in New York City.
    Alice would like an assurance that the query result accurately reflects a *consistent* state of the database, meaning that tuples that were authentic with respect to a prior state of the database cannot be presented as part of the current database. Since customers may change city, this prevents mixing tuples that were correct at different points in time.

We formalize correctness, completeness, and consistency in Sec 2. To achieve these assurances of integrity, Alice will perform some computation locally using her own trusted computing resources, and store locally only a small bit string acting as a certificate of authenticity for her data. The local computation is performed by a middleware component which receives Alice's operations on her database (e.g. query, insert, update, delete), performs a straightforward translation, and submits them to the database server for processing.

The database server is largely oblivious to the fact that Alice is taking special steps to ensure the integrity of her data. The server stores a modified schema for the database which, in addition to the base data, also includes integrity metadata. The integrity metadata consists of one or more specially-designed tables each representing a hash tree [12, 13, 5]. Alice's database queries are rewritten by the middleware to retrieve the query answer along with some integrity metadata. The middleware performs an efficient verification procedure, returning to Alice the query answer along with notice of verification success or failure.

Contributions and Alternative methods. The primary contribution of this work is the design, implementation and performance evaluation of hash trees for use with a client-server relational database. We describe a novel relational representation of a hash tree, along with client and server execution strategies, and show that the *cost of integrity* is modest in terms of computational overhead as well as communication overhead. Using our techniques we are able to provide strong integrity guarantees and process queries at a rate between 4 and 7 times slower than the baseline, while inserts are between 8 and 11 times slower. This constitutes a dramatic improvement over conceivable methods of insuring integrity using tuple-level digital signatures, and also a substantial improvement over naive implementations of hash trees in a database. Since our techniques can easily augment any database system, we believe these techniques could have wide application for enhancing the security of database systems.

We describe hash trees in detail in Sec. 2.2, and our novel design in Sec. 3. Before doing so, we briefly review some alternative integrity strategies and their limitations.

Authenticating tuples. Digital signatures or message authentication codes at the level of tuples can prevent modification of data, but cannot resist deletion of tuples from the database or omission of tuples from query answers. Individually signed tuples may also permit inclusion of authentic but out-of-date tuples in the collection. (Using notions we will define shortly, *completeness* and *consistency* are not provided.) In addition, per-tuple signatures are likely to be prohibitively expensive.

Integrity by data duplication. Using two (or more) database replicas running on different systems, executing all operations in both systems, and comparing outcomes may increase one's confidence in data integrity since an adversary would be forced to compromise both systems simultaneously. In the worst case, this technique doubles the resource costs, which may be acceptable. However, such a strategy only addresses vulnerabilities related to privileged parties, requiring collusion between parties for successful attacks, and does not guarantee integrity. The other database vulnerabilities described above (authentication weaknesses, application integration, OS vulnerabilities, etc.) will tend to hold for each system and replication does not substantially decrease the risks. Maintaining consistency between replicas is also a challenge. In general, two weakly-trusted systems do not combine to offer a fully trusted system.

Adapting B-Trees to hash trees. All major database systems already contain B-tree implementations which efficiently store and update trees over sorted collections of tuples. If a strategy of server modification is followed, it could make sense to reuse this code at the server which is likely to be highly optimized. We are aware however of a number of challenges of adapting B-trees to hash trees. First, while reusing code at the server seems like an easy solution, the precise tree structure (different for each database system) needs to be reproduced at the client, and internal nodes of the tree must be returned by the server which is non-standard. In addition, transaction and locking semantics are substantially different between hash trees and B-trees. B-trees may be a viable option, and require further investigation.

Related Work

Hash trees were developed by Merkle and used for efficient authentication of a public file [11, 12] as well as a digital signature construction in [13]. Merkle's hash tree can be described as an authenticated dictionary data structure, allowing efficient proofs (relative to the root hash) of membership or non-membership of elements in the set. Authenticated dictionaries were adapted and enhanced to manage certificate revocation lists in [9, 16].

Authenticated dictionaries were adapted to relations in [5, 4], where algorithms based on Merkle trees and refinements in [16] are proposed for authenticating relations and verifying basic relational queries. In [20] the authors envision authenticated B-trees and the application of commutative hash functions to improve certain performance metrics, but abandon guarantees of completeness for queries, and provide no implementation. To our knowledge, no implementation and thorough performance evaluation of B-tree based techniques has been performed.

Our work draws on the above results (providing the integrity guarantees of [5]) but offers the first design and implementation of an authenticated database using a database management system. The algorithms in existing work were described with a main memory implementation in mind: the data structures are tree-based, and the algorithms require pointer traversals and modifications that are not appropriate for a relational DBMS. Further, the algorithms are evaluated merely in terms of worst case computational and communication complexity, which can hide critical factors in the implementation. For example, we show that minimizing the number of hashes is not a major concern, but a tree organization that minimizes index lookups is critical. Although the connection is not obvious, we propose here a novel structure for a hash tree inspired by techniques for managing intervals in database systems [6, 10].

Authenticating queries using the techniques above may require revealing some data items that are not in the query answer. It is the goal of [14, 17] to provide authenticated answers while also maintaining certain secrecy properties. We focus exclusively on integrity in this work. Recently, substantially different cryptographic techniques were proposed for verifying completeness of relational queries [19]. While promising, efficient performance in practice has not yet been demonstrated.

2   Background

2.1   Threat Model and Formalizing Integrity

We assume the data owner interacts as a client with an untrusted database server. The data owner operates a trusted computing base, but would like to store and process relational data using the untrusted resources of the server. The server may insert false tuples into relations, modify existing tuples, and remove or hide tuples from the database or from query answers. The communication medium between client and server is also untrusted. The adversary may impersonate the client and try to insert or modify tuples at the server. Alternatively, the adversary may impersonate the server and attempt to return spurious tuples as a query result. Our goal is resistance against each of these tampering threats: although we cannot prevent these actions, we can detect them with a negligible probability of failure.

We assume the client trusts the implementation of the techniques described in this work. In practice this is a reasonable assumption. Checking the correctness of our client procedure is much easier than attempting to certify the correctness of an entire database system.

We focus primarily on a single author who is the sole individual with rights to create and modify data. Many parties may issue queries, but integrity is judged with respect to the author. (We discuss extensions of our results to the multiparty case in Section 6.) To formalize integrity guarantees, we assume the author creates a relation R, stores it at the server (and not locally), and asks queries over the database. We further assume that the author updates the relation and that the sequential authentic states of the database are $R_1, R_2, \ldots R_n$. When a user asks a (monotone) query q over R, they receive ans. The key integrity properties we consider are:

Correctness. Every tuple was created or modified only by the author:

$$ans \subseteq \bigcup_{1 \leq i \leq n} q(R_i)$$

The union on the right consists of all tuples present in any state of the database. Correctness asserts that the answer set is composed of only these tuples.

Completeness. No qualifying tuples are omitted from the query result: for some i, $q(R_i) \subseteq ans$.

Consistency. Every tuple in the database or query result is current; i.e. it is not possible for the server to present as current a tuple that has been been removed, or to mix collections of data that existed at different points in the evolution of the database. Consistency means $ans \subseteq q(R_i)$ for some i.

If the author were to sign tuples individually, verification by the client would prove correctness only. Consistency is a stronger condition which implies correctness. The hash tree techniques to be described provide consistency (and thus correctness) upon verification. In some cases hash trees can provide completeness as well. The index i, which identifies particular states of the database, corresponds to a version of the authentication tag which is changed by the author with updates to the database. Proofs of consistency or completeness are relative to a version of the authentication tag.

2.2   Enforcing Integrity with Hash Trees

In this subsection we review the use of hash trees for authenticating relations [5, 12] by illustrating a simple hash tree built over 8 tuples from a relation R(score,name). We denote by f a collision-resistant cryptographic hash function (for which it is computationally-infeasible to find inputs x and x' such that $f(x) = f(x')$). We build the tree of hash values, shown in Fig. 1, as follows. First we compute the hash for each tuple t_i of the relation by hashing the concatenated byte representation of each attribute in the tuple. Then, to generate a (binary) hash tree, we pair these values, computing f on their concatenation

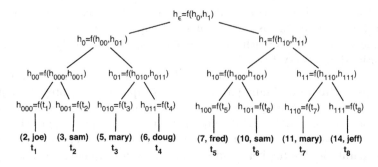

Fig. 1. Hash tree built over a relation containing tuples $t_1, t_2, ...t_8$. f is a cryptographic hash function; comma denotes concatenation when it appears in the argument of f.

and storing it as the parent. We continue bottom-up, pairing values and hashing their combination until a root hash value h_ϵ is formed. The root hash value, h_ϵ, is a short sequence of bytes that depends on each tuple in the database and on a chosen order for the tuples. (The value of the root hash can therefore be used to uniquely identify states of the database, as per the definition of consistency above.)

The computation of a hash tree uses the *public* hash function f and is deterministic, so for a given tree shape it can be repeated by anyone. Alice chooses an order for the tuples in her relation, computes the root hash h_ϵ and stores it locally and securely. She will then store the relation at the vulnerable server. In Fig. 1 the hash tree is perfectly balanced, but this is not required.

Verifying query results. The client verifies a query by checking that the query result is consistent with the root hash. To do so, the client must duplicate the sequence of hash computations beginning with the query result, and verify that it ends with the root hash. The tree structure allows the client to perform this computation without recovering the entire relation from the server. For a set of result tuples, the nodes in the tree the server must return are those on the *hash path*, which consist of all siblings of nodes on a path from a result tuple to the root. Successful verification proves integrity under the assumption that it is impossible for the server to find a collision in the hash function f. We illustrate with the example queries below which refer to the database R in Fig. 1 and we assume score is a key for R.

Example 1. Select tuples with score=5. The server returns the answer tuple, t_3. The client can compute h_{010}. In order to complete the computation to the root, the client needs more values from the database, or some nodes internal to the tree. The server returns in addition the hash path consisting of nodes h_{011}, h_{00} and h_1. From these values the client can compute up the tree a new root hash h'_ϵ. Verification succeeds if h'_ϵ equals the root hash h_ϵ stored at the client. Unless the server can find a collision in the hash function, this proves that tuples t_3 is an authentic element of the database, proving consistency and correctness of the query answer.

Example 2. Select tuples with score=8. Since 8 is not present in the database, the query result is empty and correctness holds trivially. To show completeness, i.e. that there are no tuples with score=8 omitted illegally, the server must return the predecessor tuple, t_5, and the successor, t_6, and the hash path $\{h_{11}, h_0\}$.

Example 3. Select tuples with *score* between 4 and 6. The server will return answer tuples t_3 and t_4 along with their hash path $\{h_{00}, h_1\}$ which allows the client to verify correctness and consistency, as above. However there could exist other tuples in the collection matching the search condition, *score* between 4 and 6. Evidence that the answer is in fact complete relies on the fact that the tree is built over sorted tuples. The server provides the next-smallest and next-largest items for the result set along with their hash path in the tree. To prove completeness, the result will consist of t_2, t_3, t_4, t_5 and the hash path is h_{000}, h_{101}, h_{11}.

Example 4. Select tuple with name='Mary'. This query is a selection condition on the B attribute, which is not used as the sort key for this hash tree. The server may return the entire result set $\{t_3, t_7\}$ along with the hash path nodes $\{h_{011}, h_{00}, h_{111}, h_{10}\}$, however in this case only consistency and correctness is proven. The server could omit a tuple, returning for example just t_3 as an answer along with it's verifiable hash path. The author will not be able to detect the omission in this case.

Modifying data: Insertions, deletions, updates. The modification of any tuple in the database changes the root hash, upon which the verification procedure depends. Therefore, the client must perform re-computation of the root hash locally for any insertion, deletion, or update. We illustrate with the following example:

Example 5. Insert tuple (12, jack). This new tuple t' will be placed in sorted order between tuples t_7 and t_8. More than one tree shape is possible, but one alternative is to make t' a sibling of t_7 and set $h_{110} = f(t_7, t')$. Since the value of h_{110} has changed, the hashes on the path to the root must be updated, namely h_{11}, h_1 and h_ϵ.

It is critical that the root hash be computed and maintained by a trusted party, and retrieved securely when used during client verification. If the server could compute or update the value of the root hash, it could perform unauthorized modifications of the database without violating the verification procedure. The root hash can be stored securely by the client, or it can be stored by the server if it is digitally signed. Since the root hash changes with any modification of the database, the latter requires re-signing of the root hash with each update operation.

3   The Relational Hash Tree

In this section we describe techniques for implementing a hash tree in a relational database system.

3.1 Overview of Design Choices

The simplest representation of a hash tree as a relation would represent nodes of the tree as tuples with attributes for parent, right-child, and left-child. With each tuple uniquely identified by its node id, the parent and child fields would contain node id's simulating pointers. There are a number of drawbacks of this simple organization. The first is that in order to guarantee completeness the server must return not just the result set, but the preceding and following elements in the sorted order (as in Ex. 3). Second, traversing the tree requires an iterative query procedure which progresses up the tree by following a sequence of node-ids, and gathers the nodes on the hash path. Finally, the performance of this scheme depends on the tree being balanced which must be maintained upon modification of the database. Even assuming perfect balancing, experiments indicate that the time at the server to execute a simple selection query using this organization is about 12 ms (a factor of 20 times higher than an standard query) and that query times scale linearly or worse with the size of the result.

To simplify the hash path computation, a basic optimization is to store the child hashes with their parent. Then whenever the parent is retrieved, no further database access is required for gathering the children. To simplify the identification of preceding and following elements, we translate our sorted dataset into intervals. The leaves of the hash tree are intervals, and we always search for the containing interval of a point, or the intersecting intervals of a range. This provides completeness as in Ex. 2 and 3. To remove the iterative procedure on the path to the root, we store intervals in the internal nodes of the tree representing the minimum and maximum of the interval boundaries contained in that node's descendants. The result is a relational representation of a hash tree with the only remaining challenges being (i) implementing interval queries efficiently and (ii) keeping the tree balanced.

Interval queries are not efficiently supported by standard indexes. One of the best methods for fast interval queries was presented in [21]. These techniques are a relational adaptation of an interval tree [6] and themselves require representing a tree as relations. Since any tree shape can work as a hash tree, our innovation is to adapt interval trees to design a hash tree, combining both trees into one structure. This serves dual purposes: in addition to supporting very efficient hash path queries, it also maintains a balanced tree for many data distributions.

3.2 Interval Trees

An interval tree [6, 21] is a data structure designed to store a set of intervals and efficiently support intersection queries. We review this data structure here, and then adapt it to a hash tree in the next subsection.

The *domain tree* T_k for positive[2] domain $\mathbf{dom} = [0..2^k - 1]$ is a complete binary tree whose nodes are labeled with the elements of $\mathbf{dom} - \{0\} = (0..2^k - 1]$.

---

[2] For illustration purposes only, we describe a relational hash tree over a positive domain, although it is easily generalized to signed integers, floats, or strings. We implemented a signed integer domain with $k = 32$.

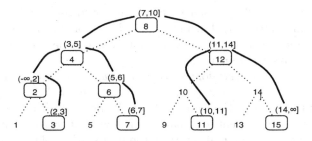

Fig. 2. The *domain tree* T_4 is the complete binary tree, rooted at 8, shown with dotted edges. The *value tree* is represented by circled nodes and solid edges, for intervals derived from **adom** $= \{2, 3, 5, 6, 7, 10, 11, 14\}$. The intervals shown in the tree are stored in the Auth table.

Its structure is precisely that of a perfectly balanced search tree built over the entire domain. The root of T_k is the midpoint of **dom** $- \{0\}$, 2^{k-1}, or in bits $1000...0$. It's children are $01000...0$ and $1100...0$. The tree has height $k - 1$ and its leaves are the odd elements of **dom**. Domain tree T_4 is shown in Fig. 2. We often refer to the nodes of T_k by their labels in **dom**.

Each node in T_k is the midpoint of its spanning interval, denoted $span(n)$, defined to be the interval containing every element in the subtree rooted at n, including itself. The span of the root is therefore $(0..2^k - 1]$; the span of node 2, shown in Fig. 2 is $(0, 3] = \{1, 2, 3\}$. For a given **dom**, we denote $-\infty = 0$, and $\infty = 2^k - 1$.

An interval with endpoints in **dom** is stored at a unique node in the domain tree as defined by its *fork node*. The fork is the lowest node n such that $span(n)$ contains the interval.

Definition 1 (Fork node of interval). *Let $I = (x, y]$ be an interval with $x, y \in$* **dom** *and $x < y$. The fork node $fork(I)$ is the unique node $n \in T_k$ such that:*

(i) $I \subseteq span(n)$, and
(ii) for all descendants n' of n, $I \not\subseteq span(n')$.

It follows immediately that $n \in I$, and that n is the highest node in the domain tree such that $n \in I$.

As an example, the fork node in T_4 of interval $(3, 5]$ is 4 as shown in Fig 2. The computation of the fork for interval $I = (x, y]$ can be performed efficiently using bitwise operations on x and y. Since $x < y$, x and y can be written as $x = z0x_0$ and $y = z1y_0$ for (possibly empty) bit strings z, x_0, y_0. Then $fork(I) = z10^{|x_0|}$. If $x = 3 = 0011$ and $y = 5 = 0101$ then $z = 0$ and $fork(I) = 0100 = 4$.

3.3 Disjoint Interval Trees

We now adapt interval trees to our setting. Let **adom** $= \{x_1 \ldots x_n\}$ be a set of data values from **dom**. We always assume the data values are different from $-\infty$ and ∞. Then they partition **dom** into a set U of $n + 1$ intervals:

$$I_0 = (-\infty, x_1], \quad I_1 = (x_1, x_2] \quad \ldots \quad I_n = (x_n, \infty]$$

for $-\infty = 0$ and $\infty = 2^k - 1$. Since the elements of **adom** are distinct, we have $x_i < x_{i+1}$ for all intervals I_i. Each interval of U is stored at its fork node in the domain tree, and we show next how the intervals can be connected to form a tree which overlays the domain tree.

We say a node w in the domain tree is *occupied* if there is an interval in U whose fork is w. The occupied nodes in Fig 2 are circled and labeled with the intervals that occupy them. Recall that the intervals of U are always non-overlapping and cover the entire domain.[3] It follows that each node in the domain tree holds at most one interval. Further, the root of T_k is always occupied, and we show next that for any such U, the occupied nodes can always be linked to form a unique (possibly incomplete) binary tree, called the *value tree* for U. Let SUBTREE(x) in T_k be the subtree rooted at x.

Property 1. For any node x in domain tree T_k, if there is at least one occupied node in SUBTREE(x), then there is always a unique occupied node y which is the ancestor of all occupied nodes in SUBTREE(x).

For example, in Fig 2, the unique occupied ancestor in SUBTREE(10) is node 11. Property 1 implies that nodes 9 and 11 could never be occupied while 10 remains unoccupied.

Definition 2 (Value tree). *For a set of disjoint intervals U derived from* **adom** *as above, and domain tree T_k, the value tree V_U is a binary tree consisting of the occupied nodes from T_k and defined inductively as follows:*

- *$root(V_U) = root(T_k)$*
- *For any value node x in V_U, its right (resp. left) child is the unique occupied ancestor of the right (resp. left) subtree of x in T_k, if it exists.*

x *is a leaf in V_U iff the right and left subtrees of a value node x are both unoccupied.*

In Fig. 2 the value tree is illustrated with solid edges connecting the occupied nodes of T_4.

Benefits of the value tree. In summary, the domain tree is static, determined by the domain, while the value tree depends on the set of values from which the intervals are derived. The value tree has a number of important properties for our implementation. First, by design, it is an efficient search structure for evaluating range intersection queries (i.e. return all stored intervals that intersect a given interval $I = (x, y]$). Such a query is evaluated by beginning at the root of the value tree, traversing the path in the value tree towards $fork(I)$ and checking for overlapping stored intervals. Secondly, it provides an organization of the data into a tree which we use as the basis of our hash tree. This avoids explicit balancing operations required by other techniques. Finally, the

---

[3] Ours is therefore a special case of the structure considered in [6, 10] which is designed to accommodate a general set of intervals.

relationship between the domain tree and value tree allows us to avoid expensive traversals of the tree at the server. Instead of traversing the path from a node in the value tree to the root, we statically compute a *superset* of these nodes by calculating the path in the domain tree. We then probe the database for the value tree nodes that exist. The sets defined below are used for query evaluation in Sec. 3.5, and compute all the forks of nodes in the value tree necessary for client verification.

$$\mathsf{Ancestors}(x) = \{n \mid x \in span(n)\}$$
$$\mathsf{rangeAncestors}(x, y) = \{n \mid (x, y] \cap span(n) \neq \emptyset\}$$

For example, $\mathsf{Ancestors}(13) = \{8, 12, 14, 13\}$ and $\mathsf{range\text{-}Ancestors}(6,9) = \{8, 4, 6, 7, 12, 10, 9\}$.

Properties of a disjoint interval tree. Each set **adom** determines a unique value tree. If **adom** is empty, then the resulting interval set contains only one interval $(-\infty, \infty]$, and the value tree consists of a single node: the root of T_k. At the other extreme, if **adom** = **dom** $- \{-\infty, \infty\}$ then every node of the domain tree will be occupied, and the value tree will be equal to the domain tree. We describe next some properties of the value tree which are implied by sets **adom** derived according to a known distribution.

The depth of a node $n \in T_k$ is the number of edges along the path from the root to n (hence 0 for the root). Recall that the fork node of an interval is the lowest node whose span contains the interval. Since the span of nodes in T_k decreases (by half) as you descend the domain tree, it follows that the width of an interval determines the maximum depth of the interval's fork.

Property 2 (Maximum depth of interval). Let $I = (x, x']$ be an interval and define $j = \lfloor \log_2(x' - x) \rfloor$. Then the depth of fork(i) is less than $k - j$.

This result implies that if **adom** consists of values spread uniformly, then the value tree fills T_k completely from the top down. Alternatively, if **adom** consists of consecutive values, then Prop 1 implies that the value tree fills T_k completely from the bottom up. Formally, this is captured by:

Property 3 (Value tree shape). Let **adom** be a set of $2^m - 1$ elements (for $m < k$). If (1) **adom** is spread uniformly or (2) it consists of consecutive values, then the value tree has height m.

We omit further formal analysis of the properties of the value tree for lack of space. The relevant issue for our implementation is the length of paths in the value tree. Both a uniform distribution and a set of consecutive values result in a minimal height of the value tree. The question of the worst case distribution in this setting remains open. We return to the impact of the data distribution, and domain size, k, in Sec. 5.

3.4   Relational Hash Tree

In this subsection we describe the relational representation of a hash tree based on interval trees. Fig. 3 contains table definitions, indexes, user-defined functions, as well as the important verification queries. Given a relation $R(A, B_1, ...B_m)$, we choose the sort attribute of the hash tree to be A and assume the domain of A can be represented using k bits. A is not necessarily a key for R, and we let $\mathbf{adom}_A$ be the set of distinct A-values occurring in R. We form disjoint intervals from this domain as described above, build a disjoint interval tree, and encode each node in the *value tree* as a tuple in table $\mathsf{Auth}_{R.A}$. The table Data_R stores each tuple of the original table R, with an added field fork which is a foreign key referencing $\mathsf{Auth}_{R.A}.\mathsf{fork}$. We drop the subscripts for Auth and Data when the meaning is clear. For tuple $t \in \mathsf{Auth}$, $t.\mathsf{fork}$ is the fork of the interval $(t.\mathsf{predA}, t.A]$. Hash values for the left child and right child of the node are stored in each tuple. In addition, the hash of the node *content* is stored in attribute $\mathsf{hashed\text{-}content}$. The *content* of a value tree node is a serialization of the pair (pred, A), concatenated with a serialized representation of all tuples in Data agreeing on attribute A, sorted on a key for the remaining attributes. The hash value at any node in the value tree is computed as $f(\mathsf{Lhash}, \mathsf{hashed\text{-}content}, \mathsf{Rhash})$. For internal nodes of the value tree, Lhash and Rhash are hash values of right and left children of the node. For leaf nodes, Lhash and Rhash are set to a public initialization value. All hash values are 20 bytes, the output of the SHA-1 hash function. Note that in a conventional hash tree data values only occur at the leaves while in our interval hash tree, data values are represented in all nodes.

TABLES

$\mathsf{Auth}_R(\underline{\mathsf{fork}}\ \mathsf{bit}(k), \mathsf{predA}\ \mathsf{bit}(k), A\ \mathsf{bit}(k),$
   $\mathsf{Lhash}\ \mathsf{byte}(20), \mathsf{hashed\text{-}content}\ \mathsf{byte}(20),$
   $\mathsf{Rhash}\ \mathsf{byte}(20)\ )$

$\mathsf{Data}_R(\mathsf{fork}\ \mathsf{bit}(k), A\ \mathsf{bit}(k), B_1 ... B_m)$

INDEXES

Auth-index CLUSTERED INDEX on (Auth.fork)
Data-index INDEX on (Data.fork)
(additional user indexes on Data not shown)

FUNCTIONS

Ancestors(x bit(x))   ⟨defined in Sec. 3.3⟩
rangeAncestors(x bit(x),y bit(x))

(Q1) Selection query on A: R.A = \$x
SELECT Auth.*
FROM Ancestors(\$x) as F, Auth
WHERE F.fork = Auth.fork   ORDER BY F.fork

(Q2) Range query on A: \$x < R.A ≤ \$y
SELECT Auth.*
FROM rangeAncestors(\$x,\$y) as F, Auth
WHERE F.fork = Auth.fork   ORDER BY F.fork

(Q3) Arbitrary query condition: cond(R.A, R.B1 .. R.Bm)
SELECT Auth.*
FROM Auth, Data, Ancestors(Data.A) as F
WHERE F.fork = Auth.fork AND
cond(Data.A,Data.B1 .. Data.Bm)   ORDER BY F.fork

Fig. 3. Table definitions, indexes, functions, and queries for relational hash tree implementation

3.5   Authenticated Query Processing

The client-server protocol for authenticated query and update processing is illustrated in Fig. 4. We describe next server query processing, client verification, and updates to the database.

Server query processing. The query expressions executed at the server are shown in Fig. 3. For selection and range queries on the sort attribute, $Q1$ and $Q2$, and arbitrary query conditions, $Q3$. They each retrieve from Auth the result tuples along with paths to the root in the value tree. We avoid iterative traversal in the value tree by computing the sets Ancestors(x) or rangeAncestors(x, y) and performing a semijoin. Note that the computation of the ancestors makes no database accesses. It is performed efficiently as an user-defined procedure returning a unary table consisting of nodes from the domain tree. The following examples illustrate the execution of $Q1$ and $Q2$.

Example 6. SELECT * FROM R WHERE R.A $= 13$ Referring to Fig. 2, we compute Ancestors(13) which is equal to $\{8, 12, 14, 13\}$. $Q1$ joins these nodes with the value tree nodes in Auth$_R$. The result is just two tuples representing nodes 12 and 8 in the value tree. Node 12 holds interval $(11, 14]$ which contains the search key 13, proving the answer empty but complete, and node 8 is included since it is on the path to the root.

Example 7. SELECT * FROM R WHERE $6 < A \leq 9$ Computing rangeAncestors $(6, 9)$ yields the set $\{8, 4, 6, 7, 12, 10, 9\}$ since each of these nodes in the domain tree has a span intersecting $(6, 9]$. Of these, only nodes $\{8, 4, 6, 7, 12\}$ are in the value tree, and are retrieved from the database. Note that some intervals stored at these nodes do not overlap the query range $(6, 9]$ (for example, $(3, 5]$ is retrieved with node 4). Nevertheless, node 4 is required for reconstructing this portion of the value tree since nodes 6 and 7 are its descendants. The client will perform a final elimination step in the process of verifying the answer.

Arbitrary queries. For queries that include conditions on attributes $B_1, ... B_m$ the interval hash tree cannot be used to prove completeness of the query answer, but can still be used to prove correctness and consistency. Any complex condition on $B_1, ... B_m$ can be evaluated on Data, resulting in a set of values for attribute A. These values will be distributed arbitrarily across the domain and therefore arbitrarily in the value tree. They are fed into the Ancestors function to retrieve all paths up to the root. Duplicates are eliminated, and then these nodes are joined with Auth (as in queries $Q1$ and $Q2$). The resulting query is shown in Fig. 3 as $Q3$.

Example 8. The query in Ex. 4 asked for all tuples from R with *name*='Mary'. The query result consists of tuples with *scores* 5 and 11. To authenticate this query, the fork ancestor set is computed to be Ancestors(5) $\cup$ Ancestors(11) $= \{8, 4, 6, 5\} \cup \{8, 12, 10, 11\} = \{8, 4, 6, 5, 12, 10, 11\}$.

Execution plan. For queries Q_1, Q_2 and Q_3 the favored execution strategy is to materialize the Ancestors table, and perform an index-nested loops join using the index on $Auth_R$. The query optimizers in the two database systems we tried chose this execution plan. For Q_1, the Ancestors set is quite small – it is bounded by parameter k of the domain tree (32 for most of our experiments). Thus evaluation of Q_1 consists of not more than k probes of the index on Auth. For range queries, the Ancestors set is bounded by the result size plus $2k$. The execution of range queries can be improved by utilizing the clustering of the index on Auth. This optimization is described in Sec. 4.3.

Client verification. In each case above, the server returns a subset of tuples from Auth which represent a portion of the value tree. The client verifies the query answer by reassembling the value tree and recomputing hashes up the tree until a root hash h'_ϵ is computed. To enable the client to efficiently rebuild the tree, the result tuples can be sorted by the server.

Insertion, deletion, and update. Updating any tuple in the database requires maintenance of the interval hash tree, namely addition or deletion of nodes in the value tree, and re-computation of hashes along the path to the root from any modified node. These maintenance operations are integrity-sensitive, and can only be performed by the client. Therefore, before issuing an update, the client must issue a query to retrieve the relevant portions of the hash tree, verify authenticity, and then compute the inserts or updates to the database. The insertion protocol between client and server is illustrated in Fig. 4. We focus for simplicity on inserts (deletes are similar, and updates are implemented as deletes followed by insertions).

Example 9. To insert a new tuple $(13, ..)$ the client issues the selection query for $A = 13$. This is precisely the query described in Ex. 6, and retrieves nodes 8 and 12 from the value tree. Node 12 contains interval $(11, 14]$ which must be split, with the insertion of 13, into two intervals: $(11, 13]$ and $(13, 14]$. This requires an update of the tuple representing value tree node 12, changing its interval upper bound from 14 to 13. Interval $(13, 14]$ will be stored at the formerly unoccupied node 14, which requires insertion of a new tuple in Auth representing the new value node. The hashes are recomputed up the tree from the lowest modified node in the value tree. In summary, this requires 1 insert into Auth, and a sequence of updates to the value tree tuples along the path from the inserted tuple to the root.

In general, executing an authenticated insertion involves the cost of an authenticated query, the insertion of one new Auth tuple, and updates to h Auth tuples, where h is the depth of the fork of the new interval created by the insertion. Although each update to Auth can be executed efficiently using the index on node, the large number of updates can cause a severe penalty. We address this problem next by bundling the nodes of the value tree.

4   Optimizations

4.1   Bundling Nodes of the Value Tree

The execution cost of queries and inserts depends on the length of paths in the value tree, which is determined by the data distribution and bounded by the maximum depth in the tree k. Reducing the length of paths in the value tree reduces the number of index probes executed for queries, and reduces the number of tuples modified for insertions. To reduce path length, we propose grouping nodes of the value tree into bundles, and storing the bundles as tuples in the database. For example, we can imagine merging the top three nodes $(8, 4, 12)$ in the tree of Fig. 2 into one node. We measure the degree of bundling by the height of bundles, where a bundle of height b can hold at most $2^b - 1$ value tree nodes ($b = 1$ is no bundling). The schema of the Auth table is modified so that a single tuple can hold the intervals and hashes for $2^b - 1$ nodes in the value tree. and the Ancestors and rangeAncestors functions are generalized to account for bundling.

4.2   Inlining the Fork Ancestors

Although the Ancestors set is efficiently computed for selection queries on the sort attribute, our experiments show that when evaluating arbitrary query conditions that return a large number of distinct A-values, computation of the Ancestors set can have a prohibitive cost. To remedy this, we have proposed trading off space for computation, and inlining the ancestor values for each tuple in Data. This requires that the schema of the Data table be modified to accommodate $\lceil k/b \rceil$ fork nodes, where k is the parameter of the domain tree and b is the bundling factor.

4.3   Optimizing Range Queries

The evaluation of range queries can be substantially improved by expressing rangeAncestors(x, y) as the disjoint union of three sets: leftAncestors, Inner, and rightAncestors. Inner(x, y) consists of all fork nodes inside $(x, y]$. leftAncestors(x, y) consists of all fork nodes not in Inner whose span upper boundary intersects $(x, y]$. Likewise, rightAncestors(x, y) contains all nodes not in Inner whose span lower boundary intersects $(x, y]$. The range query $Q2$ is then equivalent to the following union of three subqueries:

```
SELECT * FROM leftAncestors(x,y) as L, Auth
WHERE L.fork = Auth.fork    UNION ALL
SELECT * FROM rightAncestors(x,y) as R, Auth
WHERE R.fork = Auth.fork    UNION ALL
SELECT * FROM Auth
WHERE Auth.fork BETWEEN x AND y
```

The benefit is that the range query in the third SELECT can be evaluated using the clustered index on fork. This optimization is used in [10].

5   Performance Evaluation

In this section we present a thorough performance evaluation of the relational hash tree and our proposed optimizations. The client authentication code was written in Java, using JDBC to connect to the database server. Experiments were performed using both PostgreSQL, and Microsoft SQL Server databases.[4] No substantial differences were found between engines, and for each experiment we present numbers for only one system. Both the client and server machines were Pentium 4, 2.8Ghz machines with 2 GB memory. We used SHA-1 [7] as our hash function. SHA-1 is no longer considered secure. It was broken after these experiments were performed, but moving to SHA-224 is expected to have a negligible impact on the numbers presented here. The performance numbers below do not include the invariant cost of signing the root hash upon update (4.2 ms), and verifying the root hash for queries (0.2 ms). The numbers below represent the average execution time for 200 random query or insert operations, with the 5 lowest and highest values omitted, over a database of random values.

Overview of cost for selection query and insert. Our experiments were run on synthetic datasets containing 200-byte tuples. On a database of 1,000,000 tuples, without authentication, a selection query on an indexed attribute takes approximately 0.6ms while an insert takes about 1.0ms. These are the baseline values used for comparison in our analysis.

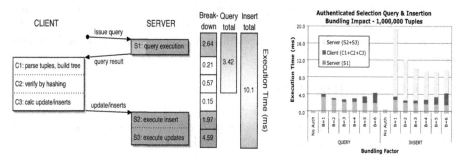

Fig. 4. (Left) Processing diagram for authenticated QUERY and INSERT. C_1, C_2, C_3 are client-side computations, S_1, S_2, S_3 are server-side computations (including communication cost), with execution times broken down by component cost (for bundling = 4). (Right) Impact of bundling on execution times for authenticated query and insert.

Figure 4 shows the processing protocol for a simple selection query and an insert, along with times for our best-performing method. An authenticated query consists of execution of the hash path query at the server (quantity S_1) followed by client-side parsing the result tuples and re-building tree structure (C_1) and verification by hashing up the tree and comparing the root hash (C_2). The total time is 3.42ms, of which 77% is server computation and 23% is client time.

---

[4] Moving between database systems was very easy; the only challenge was adapting to different SQL dialects.

This verified query therefore executes about 6 times slower than the baseline. Communication costs are included in the server-side costs for simplicity.

Execution of an authenticated insert includes the costs of the query *plus* the additional client computation of the updates and inserts to the relational hash tree (quantity C_3) and server execution of updates and inserts (S_2 and S_3). Overall, authenticated inserts run about 10 times slower than the baseline. The dominant cost is the execution of updates. Our bundling optimization targets this cost, bringing it down from $14ms$ to the value in Fig. 4 of 4.59ms (for bundle height 4). The cost is significant because for a relational hash tree of average height h, approximately h tuples in the Auth table must be updated since the hash values of the nodes have changed. This cost is targeted by our bundling optimization described next.

Impact of domain tree bundling. Recall that our bundling optimization was defined in terms of a bundle height parameter b, the tree height of bundles, which is 1 for no bundling. Fig. 4 (right) shows the impact of bundling on authenticated selection queries and inserts. Each bar in the graph also indicates the breakdown between client and server computation. Bundling primarily speeds up server operations by reducing the number of tuples retrieved and/or updated. The impact of bundling is dramatic for inserts, where the time for $b = 4$ is about half the time for $b = 1$. This is a consequence of fewer updates to the bundled value tree nodes in the Auth table (5 instead of about 16 without bundling).

Range and Arbitrary queries. The bundle height $b = 4$ is optimal not only for inserts (shown above) but for range and arbitrary queries studied next, and all results below use the bundling technique. Range queries (using the optimization described in Sec. 4.3) run very efficiently, just 2-3 times slower than the baseline case. Arbitrary queries are slower because disparate parts of the tree must be retrieved, and each node retrieved requires and index probe. They run about 20-30 times slower than the baseline, and scale roughly linearly with the result size. Inlining is a critical optimization, as shown in Fig. 5 (left) which improved processing time by about a factor of 5 in our experiments. The figure shows the per-tuple speed-up for processing an arbitrary query. That is, a value of 1 indicates that an arbitrary query returning 1000 tuples takes the same time as 1000 separate selection queries returning 1 tuple.

Scalability. Fig. 5 (right) shows that our techniques scale nicely as the size of the database grows. The table presents selection queries, range queries, and inserts for databases consisting of 10^5, 10^6, and 10^7 tuples. Authenticated operations are roughly constant as the database size grows. This is to be expected since at the client the execution time is determined by the result size, and at the server the execution time is largely determined by the length of paths in the relational hash tree which grow logarithmically with the database size.

Impact of domain size and data distribution. Recall that parameter k of the domain tree is determined by the number of bits required to represent elements in the domain of the sort attribute A, and was set to 32 in most of our experiments. Since k is the height of the domain tree, k bounds the length of paths in the value tree, and determines the size of the sets returned by Ancestors and rangeAncestors. This means that as k increases, the number of index probes increases with the average depth of nodes in the domain tree. This increases the server query time, but is mitigated by the bundling optimization. Further, the more important factor is the length of paths in the value tree because this determines the number of nodes returned by the server, as well as the number of updates/inserts to the database when hashes are recomputed upon update. The length of paths in the value tree is determined by the database instance size and distribution of values across the sort attribute. Prop. 3 proves an upper bound on the height for two cases. Our experiments confirmed that the value tree is well-balanced and these paths are short. For example, there is no measurable difference in query execution times between a uniform distribution, a database of consecutive values, or distributions derived from compound sort keys. Thus the shape of the interval tree is a very effective alternative to explicit balancing of the hash tree stored at the server.

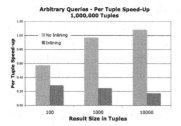 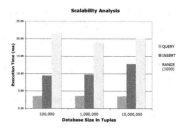

Fig. 5. (Left) Per-tuple speed up for arbitrary condition queries using inlining. (Right) Scalability graph showing execution time for selection queries, inserts, range queries for databases with size $10^5, 10^6$ and 10^7.

Storage and Communication overhead. Communication cost is included with the server-side query execution costs in all performance numbers above, and was not substantially increased by our techniques. Storage overhead was also modest: total size on disk (including indexes) for the authenticated database was 321MB compared to 249MB for the baseline.

We consider the costs presented modest, especially since the overhead of our techniques is measured by comparison to some of the fastest operations that can be performed in a database system (index lookups and updates). In a real application, the overhead of integrity could easily be dwarfed by a query that included even a simple table scan.

6   Multiple Party Integrity

Conventional notions of authenticity typically refer to a single author. There are therefore some basic underlying challenges to formalizing authenticity of data modified by many parties. A straightforward extension of the single party case we have studied so far permits multiple authors, who all trust one another, but do not trust the database server. In this case any author is permitted to update the root hash, and the authors use a shared signature to prevent the server from modifying the root hash. Such a scenario presents some challenges for concurrent processing of updates because there is contention for the root hash value.

Nevertheless, a more realistic model for multiple party integrity has n mutually untrusting authors contributing to a common database which is stored at an untrusted server. In this setting we partition the tuples of the database by author, and ownership of a tuple is indicated by the presence of an author field in our modified schema: R'(author, A, B1 ... Bm). A query over R can be evaluated over R' and the same integrity properties of correctness, consistency, and completeness are relevant in this setting. However, it should be impossible for author α_1 to add, modify, or delete tuples in the name of any other author. Our techniques can be used to provide these integrity guarantees by prepending the author field to whichever sort key is used for the authentication table Auth, and essentially maintaining separate hash trees for each author. This relieves contention for the root hash, and improves concurrency. This model can be extended to support transfer of ownership amongst users, but we leave this as future work.

7 Conclusion

We have described techniques that allow a client – with a modest amount of trusted computational overhead, and a reasonable cost at the server – to verify the correctness, consistency, and completeness of simple queries, even if the database system is vulnerable to tampering. Our work is the first to design and evaluate techniques for hash trees that are appropriate to a relational database, and the first to prove the feasibility of hash trees for integrity of databases. Our implementation shows that some of the metrics optimized in other works are inappropriate and will not lead to better performance in database system. In the future we would like to investigate probabilistic (rather than absolute) guarantees, and additional models of multiple party integrity.

References

1. C. Anley. Advanced SQL injection in SQL server applications. NGSSoftware Insight Security, available from www.ngssoftware.com, 2002.
2. E. Bertino, G. Mella, G. Correndo, and E. Ferrari. An infrastructure for managing secure update operations on xml data. In *Symposium on Access control models and technologies*, pages 110–122. ACM Press, 2003.
3. P. Devanbu, M. Gertz, A. Kwong, C. Martel, G. Nuckolls, and S. G. Stubblebine. Flexible authentication of XML documents. In *Proceedings of the 8th ACM conference on Computer and Communications Security*, pages 136–145. ACM Press, 2001.
4. P. Devanbu, M. Gertz, C. Martel, and S. G. Stubblebine. Authentic data publication over the internet. *J. of Computer Security*, 11(3):291–314, 2003.

5. P. T. Devanbu, M. Gertz, C. Martel, and S. G. Stubblebine. Authentic third-party data publication. In *IFIP Work. on Database Security*, 2000.
6. H. Edelsbrunner. Dynamic data structures for orthogonal intersection queries. Technical report, Technical University of Graz, Austria, 1980.
7. Secure hash standard (SHA). Federal Information Processing Standard Publication 180-2, 2000.
8. L. A. Gordon, M. P. Loeb, W. Lucyshyn, and R. Richardson. 2004 CSI/FBI computer crime and security survey. Computer Security Institute, 2004.
9. P. C. Kocher. On certificate revocation and validation. In *Fin. Cryptography*, pages 172–177, 1998.
10. H.-P. Kriegel, M. Potke, and T. Seidl. Managing intervals efficiently in object-relational databases. In *VLDB Conference*, pages 407–418, 2000.
11. R. C. Merkle. *Secrecy, authentication, and public key systems*. PhD thesis, Information Systems Laboratory, Stanford University, 1979.
12. R. C. Merkle. Protocols for public key cryptosystems. In *Symp. Security & Privacy*, 1980.
13. R. C. Merkle. A certified digital signature. In *CRYPTO*, pages 218–238, 1989.
14. S. Micali, M. O. Rabin, and J. Kilian. Zero-knowledge sets. In *FOCS*, 2003.
15. G. Miklau and D. Suciu. Managing integrity for data exchanged on the web. In A. Doan, F. Neven, R. McCann, and G. J. Bex, editors, *WebDB*, pages 13–18, 2005.
16. M. Naor and K. Nissim. Certificate revocation and certificate update. In *USENIX Security Symp.*, 1998.
17. R. Ostrovsky, C. Rackoff, and A. Smith. Efficient consistency proofs on a committed database.
18. The 10 most critical web application security vulnerabilities. OWASP http://aspectsecurity.com/topten/, Jan 2004.
19. H. Pang, A. Jain, K. Ramamritham, and K.-L. Tan. Verifying completeness of relational query results in data publishing. In *SIGMOD Conference*, pages 407–418, 2005.
20. H. Pang and K.-L. Tan. Authenticating query results in edge computing. In *ICDE*, 2004.
21. F. P. Preparata and M. I. Shamos. *Computational Geometry*. Springer-Verlag, New York, NY, 1985.
22. The 20 most critical internet security vulnerabilities. SANS Inst. http://www.sans.org/top20/, Oct 2004.
23. SQL injection: Are your web applications vulnerable? SPI Dynamics Inc. White Paper, Retrieved Oct 1, 2004 from: www.spidynamics.com, 2002.

Ontology Engineering from a Database Perspective
(Extended Abstract)

Bodo Hüsemann[1] and Gottfried Vossen[2]

[1] Informationsfabrik* GmbH, Scheibenstraße 117,
48153 Muenster, Germany
bhuesemann@informationsfabrik.com
[2] European Research Center for Informationsystems (ERCIS),
University Muenster, Leonardo Campus 3,
48149 Muenster, Germany
vossen@uni-muenster.de

Abstract. Ontologies have recently become popular in the context of the *Semantic Web* as an appropriate tool for developing a common reference terminology and language in specific application domains. However, the design and specification of an ontology still does not follow a generally accepted methodology, but is considered to be a task based on perception and intuition. This paper tries to remedy this situation by proposing a novel methodology for ontology engineering that is based on the phase model of traditional database design. Accordingly, the design process of an ontology consists of (1) requirements analysis, (2) conceptual design, (3) logical design, and (4) physical design. Detailed design guidelines are given which include continuous evaluation at the end of each phase. The exposition also provides a running example to ease the understanding of the core activities in each stage.

1 Introduction

Ontologies have recently become popular in the context of the *Semantic Web* as an appropriate tool for developing a common reference terminology and language in specific application domains. The development of an ontology is a non-trivial engineering task comparable to other complex design processes such as software engineering or database design. While many different ontology editors, languages, or processing systems are readily available to the Semantic Web community, the foundations of systematic ontology design and engineering is still a vastly open problem. In this paper, we try to remedy this situation by proposing a novel methodology for ontology engineering that is based on the four-phase model of traditional database design consisting of requirements analysis, conceptual design, logical design, and physical design.

At present, ontologies are typically created using intuitive design processes which depend on the functionality and restrictions of a specific ontology language or ontology editor. While this may be feasible for small projects with low monetary risks, it is necessary to base complex design tasks within enterprise-level projects on a clear methodological foundation.

---

* Work was done while the author was with the University of Muenster.

S. Grumbach, L. Siu, and V. Vianu (Eds.): ASIAN 2005, LNCS 3818, pp. 49–63, 2005.

To illustrate the approach we take in this paper, we will use a running example from the multimedia domain. To this end, we assume that private users want to manage their personal multimedia file collections, including music, images, movies, and ordinary files, using metadata extracted from the files in their collection. In this sample scenario we consider the metadata attributes given in Table 1. The aim is to develop a multimedia ontology for the description of this metadata as well as for relevant concepts of the application scenario.

Table 1. Metadata attributes of a sample multimedia scenario

music file	image file	movie file	file
music title, music album, music artist, music band, music genre, music cover	image title, image width, image height	movie title, movie series title, director, film genre, soundtrack, movie cover	file name, file type

We briefly look at previous work in the area next. To this end, we first note that the work on *conceptual* ontology design reported in this paper is orthogonal to ontology design approaches that are based on or exploit Description Logic [7]; the latter refers to *logical* design only. Various ontology design methodologies have been proposed in the literature which are based on different process models and design languages; overviews can be found in [11, 13, 2]. Earlier work, which includes [20, 19, 4, 5], mainly focuses on general design guidelines and often relies on specific ontology languages and systems used (e.g., [14]).

Essentially, the ontology design approaches reported in the literature can be put in two major categories, based on whether they adapt methodologies from *Knowledge Management* or from *Software Engineering*:

1. Knowledge Meta Process (KMP) [18]: KMP consists of the following main activities: (1) feasibility study, (2) kickoff, (3) refinement, (4) evaluation, and (5) application & evolution. The most prominent KMP design methodology is *On-To-Knowledge* [17, 18]. The authors discuss several design steps and methods in each development phase which present an overall engineering methodology based on traditional Knowledge Engineering methods such as KommonKADS [16].
2. Software Engineering Process (SEP): A simple SEP consists of three development steps: (1) specification, (2) design, and (3) implementation. The most detailed SEP design methodology is *Methontology* [12, 3]. The authors provide detailed design guidelines for the development of ontologies based on traditional software engineering methods, like classification diagrams, binary relation diagrams, or concept glossaries.

These methodologies are generally faced with a number of problems, including a lack of separation of ontology abstraction levels, no continuous ontology evaluation, and a lack of ontology context definition. With the ontology design methodology described in this paper, we strive to remedy this situation and to achieve the following major goals:

1. The methodology should provide structured guidelines and detailed methods for the ontology engineering process.
2. The methodology should provide a clear separation between the conceptual, logical, and physical schemas of an ontology.
3. The methodology should include quality management providing evaluation guidelines throughout all design stages.

The remainder of this paper is organized as follows: In Section 2, we survey our phase model for ontology design, which resembles traditional database design. In Section 3, we study the requirements analysis phase, and in Section 4 we look into conceptual design, these two stages being by far the most important ones. In Section 5 we sketch logical as well as physical design, and in Section 6 we summarize our findings. This paper is an extended abstract of [10], where further details of the approach can be found.

2   Ontology Design Methodology

Ontologies are frequently used to describe the semantic structure of related instance databases. Thus the extension of an ontology schema can technically be understood as a conventional database in which the concepts of an ontology describe different classes and properties of instances. Nevertheless, an ontology is not bound to a specific database or application context in general. Since we here focus on the application of ontologies in the context of data-centric information systems, we perceive ontology design as a specific form of database design and hence propose to adapt the traditional database design process to the development of ontologies. Nevertheless, we aim at developing an ontology which in general does not require the design of a related database. There exist semantic data models with corresponding database systems (e.g., SESAME) which can be used to manage and query instance data in correspondence to an ontology schema. The mapping of ontologies to databases without explicit support for ontologies (e.g., traditional relational database systems) can be a very complex task which is beyond the scope of this paper.

We emphasize that an ontology schema is an artificial model which may or may not be a reflection of a real-world concept or scenario. This is important to note, since many people confuse this terminology with its use in classical philosophy where we designate "ontology" (singular!) as the metaphysical study of existence. We do not follow this philosophical view here, so that it may be perfectly reasonable to design a consistent ontology for "Alice in Wonderland" which contradicts reality. In other words, there may be more than one "correct" but different ontology schema for a domain and these schemas may even contradict each other, yet consistently follow the specific requirements of their respective users.

Database design is well understood in the literature and is traditionally performed in the four sequential design steps [1] of requirements analysis, conceptual design, logical design, and physical design.

In general, the modeling of ontologies is a complex design task which should be decomposed into several sequential phases, where the output of each design phase delivers the input for the next phase. Every design phase ends with an evaluation activity in which specific validation and verification methods provide extensive quality assessment of the produced output. It turns out that the four major phases of a database design process are sufficient for the design of an ontology as well. These phases, already mentioned, are illustrated in Figure 1 as an iterative process, where documentation and evaluation are continuously done all along the process. If evaluation activities fail at some point, predefined quality measures need to apply and lead to iteration loops which improve modeling quality by returning to previous design phases as needed.

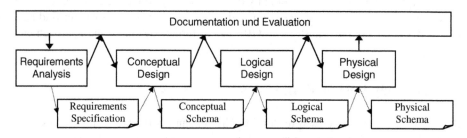

Fig. 1. Iterative phase model of the ontology design methodology

In the following sections we will look into each phase in detail, where we will use the multimedia setting introduced earlier as our running example.

3   Requirements Analysis

The design goal of the requirements analysis phase is to analyze and specify the requirements for the ontology under design. Therefore we divide this phase into requirements analysis, and requirements specification.

Requirements analysis of an ontology analyzes the relevant "information space" of an ontology. It consists of a *context analysis* via three different views in conjunction with a *value analysis* to scope all identified requirements in relation to a specific value for their use. These views are explained next.

- *Organization analysis.* The goal of organization analysis is the identification and analysis of relevant user groups, potential target hardware, and software systems for the ontology under design. Relevant organization elements of our running example include "multimedia creator", "multimedia user", or "multimedia device".
- *Process analysis.* The aim of process analysis is the identification and analysis of relevant application processes where the ontology will be used or which should be modeled with the ontology. Relevant processes of our running example include "play audio CD", "burn music collection", or "search music album".
- *Data analysis.* Data analysis is the identification and analysis of relevant data sources which will be described by the ontology or which are useful for determin-

ing relevant concepts in the application domain. In our example we identify, among others, the EXIF-specification [URL2] relevant to describe images of digital cameras, or the ID3V2-specification [URL1] relevant to describe metadata of MP3 audio files.

Requirements specification comprises a specification of all relevant concepts within the identified scope of an ontology obtained from requirements analysis. It integrates the output of the various views analyzed within the specification of use-case diagrams, competency questions, and a glossary of all concepts relevant to the ontology. Requirements specification is decomposed into the following sequential design steps:

1. Specification of use-case diagrams,
2. specification of competency questions,
3. specification of an initial glossary,
4. glossary refinement, and
5. evaluation.

1. Specification of use-case diagrams
We specify the general context of an ontology by modeling use-case diagrams using the simplified graphical use-case notation shown in Figure 2 (cf. [URL3]). We derive actors and systems in a use case diagram from the organizational analysis and model their relation with use-cases identified by the process analysis (cf. Figure 3).

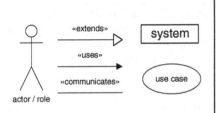

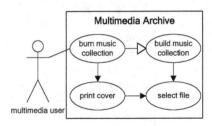

Fig. 2. Graphical notation used for use-case diagrams

Fig. 3. Use-case diagram U1 for the use-case "burn music collection"

2. Specification of competency questions
For each use case in the diagrams obtained we define competency questions that comprise all concepts relevant to the context of a use case. These competency questions can be used to evaluate the completeness of the resulting ontology at the end of the design process. The specification of competency questions can be done by using a tabular notation like the one shown in Table 2 for our sample scenario. Each item in the table is a relation between a competency question, its description, and all related use cases or information sources.

Table 2. Partial specification of competency questions for the running example

Competency question	Description	Information sources
ID: C1 use-case: U1	Which *music title, artist, album, band*, and *genre*, are related to a specific *music file*?	ID3V2
ID: C2 use-case: U1	Which *cover* is related to a *music file, music album, movie*, or *movie series*?	EXIF, ID3V2
ID: C3 use-case: U1	Which *files* of the database are *image files, music files*, or *movie files*?	-

3. Specification of an initial glossary

Given all relevant concepts for the specified competency questions, we can start building a glossary of all concepts in the scope of the ontology (cf. Table 3). The organization of the ontology should be done with respect to the semantic relation of its concepts in the glossary.

Table 3. Partial specification of the initial glossary for the running example

Concept	Description	Synonym, abbr.	Comp. question
File	A *file* represents a persistent digital information object.	-	C3
Music file	A *music file* is a *file* that contains audio contents.	audio file, track	C1, C3
Music title	A *music title* is a caption for a *music file* and frequently represents the official name of an audio track.	song title, audio title	C1
Cover	A *cover* is an *image file* that is associated with a *music file, movie file, music album*, or *movie series* for the official illustration of retail packages.	-	C2

4. Glossary refinement

For the refinement of the initial glossary we specify for each entry a sample value, a context, and generalized concepts. The specification of the refinement is used to relate similar or semantically related concepts within the glossary. A concept *value* is either a literal or an instance of another concept defined in the glossary. The *context* of a concept comprises concepts that may use a given concept as a valid description. All *general concepts* of a given concept relate to an abstract IS-A relation. In Table 4 we show the refined glossary for the initial glossary of the example.

5. *Evaluation*

The evaluation of the requirements specification is done in two steps:

- *Validation* of the requirements should review all produced diagrams and tabular listings. The aspects of correctness, completeness, minimalism, and clarity guide this review process.
- *Verification* of the requirements should assess all existing formal criteria for the requirements specification. As a guide we advise to take again the aspects of correctness and completeness into account.

As a result of the requirements analysis phase together with its "local" evaluation, we obtain a collection of input for the conceptual design of the ontology in question, which is described next. Note that what has been described above as the data to be collected during requirements analysis covers a variety of aspects and uses techniques from requirements *engineering* as proposed, for example, in [15].

Table 4. Glossary refinement of the initial example glossary

Concept name	Concept values	Concept context	Concept generalization
Collection	Collection	-	Concept
Cover	Cover	Movie file, Movie series, Music file, Music album	Image file
File	File	-	Concept
Image file	Image file	-	File
Movie file	Movie file	Movie series	File
Movie series	Movie series	-	Collection
Music album	Music album	-	Collection
Music file	Music file	Music album	File
Music title	Literal	Music file	Title
Title	Literal	-	Concept

4   Conceptual Design

The goal of the conceptual design phase is the modeling of the ontology according to all specified requirements at a conceptual level. Similar to what happens in database design, the output of conceptual design is the *conceptual schema* of the ontology. The conceptual schema is specified by using a conceptual notation to represent the requirements in a suitable semi-formal language. This language should include all elements necessary to model the requirements without restraining itself to potential logical processing restrictions.

We distinguish the following steps, explained next, within the phase-model for the conceptual modeling of an ontology:

1. Definition of naming conventions,
2. modeling of concept hierarchies,
3. modeling of concept roles,
4. modeling of class and property hierarchies,
5. extension of the conceptual property schema,
6. extension of the conceptual class schema,
7. evaluation.

1. Definition of naming conventions

The definition of naming conventions is reasonable to improve the readability of a conceptual schema. We propose to define modeling directives for capitalization, compounds, stemming, use of singular and plural, and language-specific characters; details can be found in [10].

2. Modeling of concept hierarchies

With the specification of concept hierarchies we apply the modeling abstractions *generalization* and *aggregation* to all specified concepts within the glossary of the requirements specification. The aim of doing so is to prepare the analysis of which conceptual roles apply to the concepts of the ontology.

Fig. 4. Graph notation of concept hierarchies

A concept-hierarchy is represented by a directed acyclic graph that allows for more than one parent for each node in its poly-hierarchy (so a concept hierarchy is not necessarily a tree). In a *generalization hierarchy* a subconcept is related to all superconcepts by a directed edged (the direction of edges is designated by a white arrow, cf. Figure 4) which points to the direction of the generalization. In an *aggregation hierarchy* each component is related to all aggregates by a directed edge (the direction of the edge is designated by a white circle, cf. Figure 4).

In Figure 5 we show the generalization hierarchy for the example scenario along with its aggregation hierarchy in Figure 6. The aggregation hierarchy can exploit the generalization hierarchy to simplify the modeled graph. A specified aggregation for a super-concept of the generalization hierarchy is also valid for all its sub-concepts.

3. Modeling of concept roles

For the definition of concept roles we distinguish two different conceptual role types: (1) class and (2) property. The instances of an ontology database are concrete entities of associated *classes*. The instances of a class are described by *properties* that have a data *value*. All instances of a class share a common set of properties which describe the schema of the class.

In this modeling step we analyze the roles of all concepts in the ontology. For this analysis we look at the modeled concept hierarchies and use markers (P := property and C := class) in the diagrams to show the roles of concepts in the hierarchies. To determine which concept roles are valid we use the following decision guidelines:

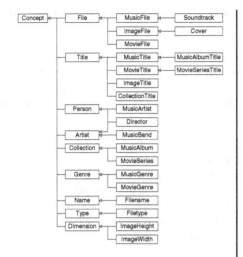

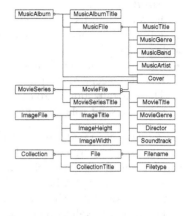

Fig. 5. Generalization concept hierarchy of the running example

Fig. 6. Aggregation concept hierarchy of the running example

Aggregation hierarchy. All aggregate concepts in the graph are marked as *classes*, and all component concepts in the graph are marked as *properties*. The marked aggregation hierarchy does not necessarily contain every concept of the glossary, because concept generalizations without their own components may be omitted in the graph (cf. Figure 7).

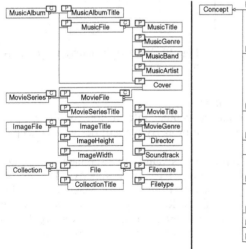

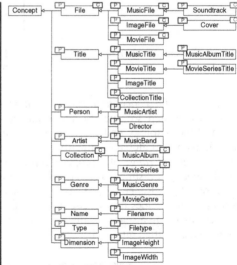

Fig. 7. Aggregation hierarchy of the example with concept-role markers

Fig. 8. Generalization hierarchy of the example with concept-role markers

Generalization hierarchy. To specify roles for all concepts in the glossary we carry over the roles from the aggregation hierarchy to the generalization hierarchy. In the next step we exploit the transitivity of the generalization relation using the following guidelines:

- Inherit concept roles from super-concepts to all subordinated sub-concepts.
- Inherit concept roles from sub-concepts to all super-ordinated superconcepts. The generalization of roles is consistent if all sub-concepts of a super-concept share the same role (cf. Figure 8).

4. Modeling of class and property hierarchies

Given the associated roles for each concept we separate classes from properties in the generalization concept hierarchy. Properties are first-class elements in the conceptual schema of an ontology, which is a difference to conventional object-oriented conceptual models like UML where attributes are bound to a specific class. Therefore we model separate generalization hierarchies for classes and properties in this design step using the marked generalization hierarchy as input (cf. Figures 9 and 10).

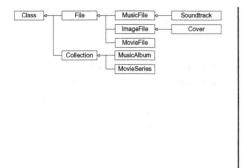

Fig. 9. Class hierarchy of the running example

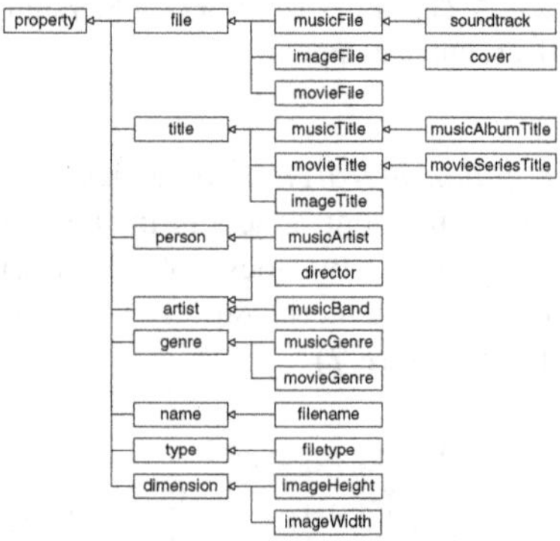

Fig. 10. Property hierarchy of the running example

5. Extension of the conceptual property schema

In this design step we specify additional conceptual information for the property schema of the ontology under design. For each property we will design a conceptual range, domain, and global cardinality.

The conceptual *range* of a property represents its value space (domain). In the conceptual model we distinguish three different range types of a property: (1) *Class*, (2) *Literal*, or (3) *All*. Range type "Class" specifies a set of classes of which all related instances are valid values for the associated property. Range type "Literal" represents any character-based value space for the associated property. Special range type "ALL" designates an unspecified range where the value space of a property is unrestricted.

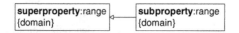

Fig. 11. Extended graph notation of the property schema

The conceptual *domain* of a property models its valid class context. A property can describe all instances which are elements of its domain. Special domain "ALL" designates an unspecified domain of a universal property which can be used in the context of every class. We specify the extension of the property schema with additional graphical notation as shown in Figure 11. In Figure 12 we indicate the extended property schema for the example. We use the glossary to determine the range and domain of each property in the diagram. Column "Concept values" of the extended glossary determines the global range of a property. The "Concept context" of each concept in the glossary determines its global domain.

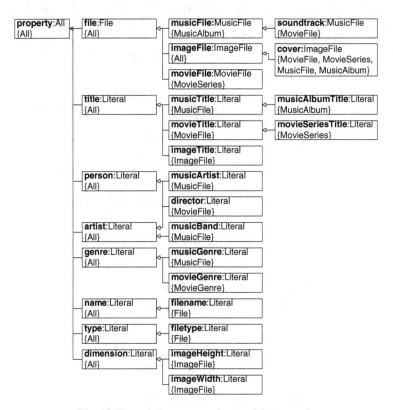

Fig. 12. Extended property-schema of the example

6. Extension of the conceptual class schema

In this design step we define property constraints in the local context of a specific class. For this extension we add class properties with local range and cardinality definitions to the class schema. Figure 13 shows the extended graph notation to model the class schema. All properties of a specific class are defined inside the class node followed by their class dependent range and cardinality. For the specification of the conceptual cardinality of a property we use common (min, max)-notation.

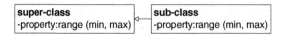

Fig. 13. Extended graph notation of the class-schema

To determine the local range of a property in the context of a specific class we start with its global range definition given by the property schema. The local range of a property is a (non-strict) restriction of its global range. Thus, to ensure schema consistency, the local range of a property must be a subset of its global range.

Figure 14 shows the extended class-schema of the example. The classes "Soundtrack" and "Cover" do not have local properties. All "title" properties in the schema are mandatory and existential to a specific class, thus they have the conceptual cardinality "(1,1)". The property "file" has the global range "File" which is restricted to "MusicFile" (resp. "MovieFile") in the context of the class "MusicAlbum" (resp. "MovieSeries").

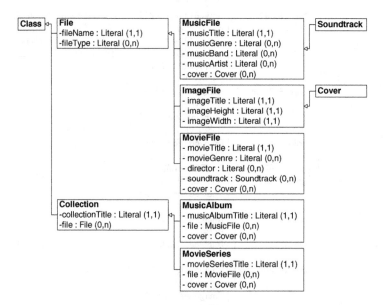

Fig. 14. Extended class-schema of the example

7. Evaluation

To evaluate the conceptual schema created during this design phase, we propose guidelines for validation as well as for verification regarding completeness, readability, naming conventions, and others; details can again be found in [10]. As a result, we have constructed a conceptual schema that can be handed over to the logical design phase of the ontology.

We finally mention that several of the steps described above can be enhanced by considerations such as the ones described in [6] regarding properties and annotations of *is-a* relationships.

5   Logical and Physical Design

The logical design step that follows next will express the conceptual schema in terms of a logical schema based on a formal ontology language. For this transformation we start by using construction rules to generate the base of the logical schema from the conceptual one. The transformation depends on the logical ontology language we use, and hence we have to choose one of many different ontology languages available today (e.g., RDF Schema (RDFS) [URL4], Web Ontology Language (OWL) [URL5]); see [7] for a tutorial exposition of the logical foundations of these languages.

In [10] as well as in [8], we show in detail how to use OWL for the construction of a logical ontology schema from its conceptual counterpart. To this end, we use the following sequential phase model for logical design:

1. Definition of namespaces,
2. transformation of the class hierarchy,
3. transformation of the property hierarchy,
4. transformation of global restrictions for properties,
5. transformation of local restrictions for properties,
6. evaluation.

We will not explain these steps any further here. In general, most of these transformations should be automated or supported by tools.

Last, but not least, the final *physical design* step of an ontology will adapt the logical schema to the specific needs of a target application system. It is quite common that application systems have specific requirements regarding the physical format of an ontology. We will provide some generic examples for such requirements that lead to the specification of a physical ontology schema. The general phase model for the physical design of an ontology includes the following sequential phases:

1. Target application-system selection,
2. physical design.
3. evaluation.

Physical design inherently depends on the chosen application system, but in [10] we give some general guidelines for typical physical design decisions regarding target application system selection, physical adaptation, and evaluation; details are omitted.

6   Summary and Lessons Learned

In this paper we have proposed an ontology engineering methodology that is based on the traditional four-phase model for database design. For each phase of the development process we have shown detailed design methods and continuous evaluation activities. In this approach we have combined approved design methods from knowledge engineering (e.g., competencies questions) with methods specific to software engineering (e.g., use case diagrams) and to database engineering (e.g., aggregation/generalization diagrams). Compared to existing methodologies, our approach strictly separates design decisions at their corresponding abstraction level, distinguishing between ontology requirements, the conceptual, the logical, and the physical schema of an ontology. Indeed, ontology design can now benefit from a well-established methodological approach that has proved stable over the years, and that has brought along criteria which distinguish a "good" from a "bad" result.

In summary, the proposed approach provides various benefits: First, there is a clear decoupling of conceptual, logical, and physical design decisions which leads to more flexibility with respect to future changes of used ontology languages or application systems. This separation also helps to adequately address different involved people using suitable modeling languages. Second, our goal-oriented requirements analysis and specification supports engineers to identify the *relevant* concepts of an ontology and to determine the right detail level and scope of the ontology. Finally, the methodology includes continuous evaluation support with increasing automation potential depending on the formalization of the used modeling languages. This minimizes evaluation costs and improves detection of design problems in early design phases.

The methodology introduced in this paper, which has originally been developed in [8], has meanwhile been successfully applied to the multimedia domain and resulted in a tool called OntoMedia, details of which can be found in [9]. We plan to extend the formal underpinning of our design methodology, in order to provide even more grounding for an area where an engineering type of approach has so far been the best that could be done.

Acknowledgement. The authors are grateful to the reviewers for various remarks that helped improve the original version of the paper.

References

[1] C. Batini, S. Ceri, S.B. Navathe: "Conceptual Database Design: An Entity-Relationship Approach," The Benjamin/Cummings Pub., 1992.

[2] O. Corcho, M. Fernandez, A. Gomez-Perez: "Methodologies, tools and languages for building ontologies: Where is their meeting point?" Data & Knowledge Eng. 46(1): 41-64 (2003)

[3] M. Fernandez, A. Gomez-Perez, N. Juristo: "METHONTOLOGY: From Ontological Art Towards Ontological Engineering." Ontological Engineering: Papers from the 1997 AAAI Spring Symposium. Technical Report SS-97-06, AAAI Press (1997)

[4] M. Grüninger, M.S. Fox: "Methodology for the Design and Evaluation of Ontologies," Proceedings of the IJCAI'95 Workshop on Basic Ontological Issues in Knowledge Sharing, 1995.

[5] T.R. Gruber: "A translation approach to portable ontologies," Knowledge Acquisition, 5(2), 1993.

[6] N. Guarino, C. Welty: "A Formal Ontology of Properties." Proc. 12th Int. Conf. on Knowledge Engineering and Knowledge Management, Springer LNCS 1937, 97-112.

[7] I. Horrocks, D.L. McGuinness, C.A.Welty: "Digital Libraries and Web-Based Information Systems," in F. Baader et al. (eds.), *The Description Logic Handbook*, Cambridge University Press 2003, 427-449.

[8] B. Hüsemann: "Design and Realization of Ontologies for Multimedia Applications;" Ph.D. dissertation (in German); University of Münster, May 2005.

[9] B. Hüsemann, G. Vossen: "OntoMedia - Semantic Multimedia Metadata Integration and Organization;" submitted for publication, May 2005.

[10] B. Hüsemann, G. Vossen: "Ontology Engineering from a Database Perspective;" Technical Report, ERCIS Münster, June 2005.

[11] D.M. Jones, T.J.M Bench-Capon, P.R.S. Visser: "Methodologies for Ontology Development," in Proc. IT&KNOWS Conference, XV IFIP World Computer Congress, Budapest, 1998.

[12] M.F. Lopez, A. Gomez-Perez, J.P. Sierra: "Building a Chemical Ontology Using Methontology and the Ontology Design Environment," IEEE Intelligent Systems, Vol. 14, No. 1, Special Issue on Ontologies, January/February 1999

[13] F. Lopez: "Overview of Methodologies for building ontologies," Proc. of IJCAI-99, workshop KRR5, Sweden, 1999.

[14] N. F. Noy, D. L. McGuinnes: "Ontology Development 101: A Guide to Creating Your First Ontology." Stanford Technical Report KSL-01-05 and SMI-2001-0880, March 2001.

[15] K. Pohl: "PRO-ART: A Process Centered Requirements Engineering Environment;" In: M. Jarke; C. Rolland; A. Sutcliffe (eds.): *The NATURE of Requiremtents Engineering*. Shaker Verlag, Aachen, Germany, 1999.

[16] G. Schreiber, H. Ackermanns, A. Anjewierden et al.: "Knowledge Engineering and Management: The CommonKads Methodology." The MIT Press, 1999.

[17] Y. Sure, R. Studer: "On-To-Knowledge Methodology - Final Version." Institute AIFB, University of Karlsruhe, On-To-Knowledge Deliverable 18, 2002.

[18] S. Staab et al.: "Knowledge processes and ontologies," IEEE IntelligentSystems, 16(1) 2001.

[19] M. Uschold: "Building ontologies: towards a unified methodology," in Proc. 16th Annual Conference of the British Computer Society Specialist Group on Expert Systems, Cambridge, UK, 1996.

[20] M. Uschold, M. King: "Towards a Methodology for Building Ontologies," IJCAI-95 Workshop on Basic Ontological Issues in Knowledge Sharing. Montreal, 1995.

Web Links

[URL1] ID3V2 specification. http://www.id3.org/develop.html, last accessed 05/22/05.

[URL2] Exchangeable Image File Format (EXIF). http://www.exif.org/specifications.html, last accessed 05/22/05.

[URL3] Unified Modeling Language, Version 2.0. Nov. 2004.
http://www.uml.org/#UML2.0/, last accessed 05/22/05.

[URL4] Web Ontology Language, http://www.w3.org/2004/OWL/, last accessed 06/03/05.

[URL5] RDF Schema, http://www.w3.org/TR/rdf-schema/, last accessed 06/03/05.

[URL6] XML Schema Part 2: Datatypes Second Edition:
http://www.w3.org/TR/xmlschema-2/, last accessed 06/03/05.

Shared Ontology for Pervasive Computing

Junfeng Man, Aimin Yang, and Xingming Sun

Computer Science Department,
Zhuzhou Institute of Technology, 412008 Zhuzhou, China
mjfok@tom.com

Abstract. In smart space applications, we usually adopt semantic Web technologies which possess pervasive context-aware ability to process many onerous tasks, e.g., knowledge sharing, context reasoning and interoperability. In order to achieve above purpose, it is necessary to exploit a Shared Ontologies for Pervasive Computing (SO4PC). These ontologies are expressed with standard Ontology Web Language (OWL) and include modular component vocabularies to represent intelligent agents which are associated with beliefs, desires, intentions, time, space, events, user profiles, actions, policies for security and private protection. We discuss how SO4PC can be extended and used to support the applications of Smart Meeting Rooms (SMR) which is a broker-centric agent architecture.

1 Introduction

Pervasive computing is a natural extension of the existing computing paradigm. In the pervasive computing vision, computer systems will seamlessly integrate into the everyday life of users and provide them with services and information in an "anywhere, anytime" fashion. In the dynamic environment, intelligent computing entities must be able to share knowledge, reason about their environment and interoperate.

In the past, many prototyping systems and architectures have been successfully developed, e.g., handheld devices are augmented with context-aware applications to create personalized tour guides for the museum visitors[1], the user interfaces and applications on a resource-poor mobile device can dynamically migrate to a nearby resource-rich stationary computer when the user enters the office[2]. However, they offer only weak support for knowledge sharing and reasoning.

Main weakness of the above systems and architectures is that they are not built on the foundation of common ontologies with explicitly semantic representation[3]. For example, the location information of a user is widely used for guiding the adaptive behavior of the systems[4]. However, none has taken advantageous of the semantics of spatial relations in reasoning about the location context of the users. Additionally, many systems use programming language objects (e.g., Java class objects) to represent the knowledge that the computer systems have about the situational environment. Because these representations require the establishment of a prior low-level implementation agreement between the programs that wish to share information, they cannot facilitate knowledge sharing in a dynamic environment.

S. Grumbach, L. Siu, and V. Vianu (Eds.): ASIAN 2005, LNCS 3818, pp. 64–78, 2005.

To address above issues, we believe shared ontologies[5] must be developed for supporting knowledge sharing, context reasoning and interoperability in pervasive computing systems. By defining such ontologies, we can help system developers to reduce their efforts on creating ontologies and to be more focused on the actual system implementations.

2 Background

In the previous systems, ontologies are often defined based on ad hoc representation schemes, such as a set of programming language objects or data structures. There are two problems with this approach: (i) the use of ad hoc representation schemes lacking shared vocabularies can hinder the ability of independently developed agents to interoperate(i.e., to share context knowledge), and (ii) the use of objects and data structures of low expressive power provides inadequate support for context reasoning.

In order to help agents to discover, reason about and communicate with contextual information, we must define explicit ontologies for context concepts and knowledge. In this paper, we present a set of ontologies that we have developed to support pervasive agents in the Context Broker Architecture (CBA) system. CBA is a broker-centric agent architecture for smart space applications. Being suit for CBA, we exploit a set of ontologies which is defined using OWL[5]. These CBA ontologies model basic concepts of people, agents, places and presentation events. It also describes the properties and relationships between these basic concepts including (i) relationships between places, (ii) roles associated with people in presentation events, and (iii) typical intentions and desires of speakers and audience members.

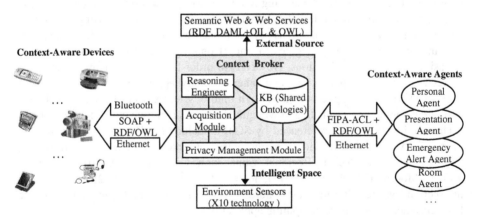

Fig. 1. CBA acquires context information from devices, agents and sensors in its environment and fuses it into a coherent model that is then shared with the devices and the agents. Here, Semantic Web and shared ontologies play very important role, they are used for concepts description, context reasoning and knowledge share.

In Fig.1, Central to CBA is an intelligent agent called the context broker. In a smart space, a context broker has the following responsibilities: (i) provide a centralized contextual model that all devices, services, and agents in the space can share, (ii) acquire contextual information from sources that are unreachable by the resource-limited devices, (iii) reason about contextual information that can't be directly acquired from the sensors, (iv) detect and resolve inconsistent knowledge stored in the shared context model, and (v) protect privacy by enforcing policies that users have defined to control the sharing and use of their contextual information.

In following sections, we will discuss how to create a set of ontologies expressed with OWL to support context modeling and knowledge sharing, detect and resolve inconsistent context knowledge.

3 SO4PC Ontologies

3.1 The Web Ontology Language OWL

The OWL language is a semantic web language used by computer applications that need to process the content of information instead of just present information to humans. This language is developed in part of the semantic Web initiatives sponsored by the World Wide Web Consortium (W3C).

OWL is a knowledge representation language for defining and instantiating ontologies. An ontology is a formally explicit description of concepts in a domain of discourse (or classes), properties of each class describing various features and attributes of the class, and restrictions on properties[6].

3.2 Related Ontologies

Part of the SO4PC vocabularies are adopted from a number of different consensus ontologies. The strategy for developing SO4PC is to borrow terms from these ontologies but not to import them directly. Although the semantics for importing ontologies is well defined, by choosing not to use this approach we can effectively limit the overhead in requiring reasoning engines to import ontologies that may be irrelevant to pervasive computing applications. However, in order to allow better interoperability between the SO4PC applications and other ontology applications, many borrowed terms in SO4PC are mapped to the foreign ontology terms using the standard OWL ontology mapping constructs (e.g., owl:equivalentClass and owl: equivalentProperty).

The ontologies that are referenced by SO4PC include the Friend-Of-A-Friend ontology (FOAF)[7], DAML-Time and the entry sub-ontology of time[8], the spatial ontologies in OpenCyc[9], Regional Connection Calculus (RCC)[10], COBRA-ONT[5], MoGATU BDI ontology[11], and the Rei policy ontology[12]. In the rest of this section, we describe the key features of these related ontologies and point out their relevance to pervasive computing applications.

FOAF. This ontology allows the expression of personal information and relationships, and is a useful building block for creating information systems that support online communities. Pervasive computing applications can use FOAF ontology to express and reason about a person's contact profile and social connections to other people in their close vicinity.

DAML-Time & the Entry Sub-ontology of Time. The vocabularies of these ontologies are designed for expressing temporal concepts and properties common to any formalization of time. Pervasive computing applications can use these ontologies to share a common representation of time and to reason about the temporal orders of different events.

OpenCyc Spatial Ontologies & RCC. The OpenCyc spatial ontologies define a comprehensive set of vocabularies for symbolic representation of space. The ontology of RCC consists of vocabularies for expressing spatial relations for qualitative spatial reasoning. In pervasive computing applications, these ontologies can be exploited for describing and reasoning about location and location context.

COBRA-ONT & MoGATU BDI Ontology. Both COBRA-ONT and MoGATU BDI ontology are aimed for supporting knowledge representation and ontology reasoning in pervasive computing environment. While the design of COBRA-ONT focuses on modeling contexts in smart meeting rooms (SMR), the design of MoGATU BDI ontology focuses on modeling the belief, desire, and intention of human users and software agents.

Rei Policy Ontology. The Rei policy language defines a set of deontic concepts (i.e., rights, prohibitions, obligations, and dispensations) for specifying and reasoning about security access control rules. In a pervasive computing environment, users can use this policy ontology to specify high level rules for granting and revoking the access rights to and from different services.

SO4PC consists of two parts: SO4PC Core and SO4PC Extension. The set of the SO4PC Core ontologies defines generic vocabularies that are universal for different pervasive computing applications. The set of SO4PC Extension ontologies extended from the core ontologies defines additional vocabularies for supporting specific types of applications and provide examples for the future ontology extensions.

3.3 SO4PC

This set of ontologies consists of vocabularies for expressing concepts that are associated with person, agent, belief-desire-intention (BDI), action, policy, time, space, and

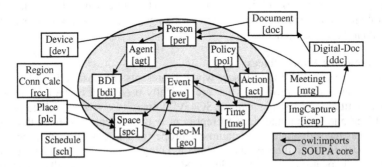

Fig. 2. SO4PC consists of two sets of ontology documents: SO4PC Core and SO4PC Extension. The OWL `owl:imports` construct is used to enable a modular design of the ontology. Different domain vocabularies are grouped under different XML namespaces.

CBA Ontology Classes		CBA Ontology Properties	
"Place" Related	Agents' Location Context	"Place" Related	Agents' Location Context
Place AtomicPlace CompoundPlace Campus Building AtomicPlaceInBuilding AtomicPlaceNotIn- Building Room Hallway Stairway OtherPlaceInBuilding	ThingInBuilding SoftwareAgentInBuilding PersonInBuilding ThingNotInBuilding SoftwareAgentNotInBuilding PersonNotInBuilding	latitude longitude hasPrettyName isSpatiallySubsumeBy spatiallySubsumes	locatedIn locatedInAtomicPlace locatedInRoom locatedInRestroom locatedInCompoundPlace LocatedInBuilding LocatedInCampus
	Agents' Activity Context	"Agent" Related	
	PresentationSchedule Event EventHappeningNow PresentationHappeningNow RoomHasPresentationHappen- ingNow		Agents' Activity Context
"Agent" Related		HasContactInformation hasFullName hasEmail hasHomePage hasAgentAddress	ParticipatesIn startTime endTime Location
Agent Person SoftwareAgent Role SpeakerRole AudienceRole IntentionalAction ActionFoundInPresenta- tion	ParticipantOf Presentation- HappeningNow SpeakerOfPresentationHap- peningNow AudienceOfPresentationHap- peningNow PersonFillsRoleInPresentation PersonFillsSpeakerRole PersonFillsAudienceRole	fillsRole isFilledBy intendsToPerform desiresSameoneTo- Achieve	hasEvent hasEventHappeningNow invitedSpeaker expectedAudience presentationTitle presentationAbstract presentation eventDescription eventSchedule

Fig. 3. A complete list of the classes and properties in SO4PC

event. The ontologies are grouped into nine distinctive ontology documents. Fig.2 shows a diagram of the ontology documents and their associated relations.

SO4PC is used in CBA in terms of class and property. Fig.3 shows a complete list of the classes and properties in SO4PC, which consists of many classes (i.e., RDF resources that are type of owl:class) and many properties (i.e., RDF resources that are type of either owl:ObjectProperty or owl:DatatypeProperty).

Our ontology is categorized into four distinctive but related themes: (i) ontologies about physical places, (ii) ontologies about agents (both human and software agents), (iii) ontologies about the location context of the agents, and (iv) ontologies about the activity context of the agents.

3.3.1 Ontologies About Places

A top level class in SO4PC is Place, which represents the abstraction of a physical location. It has a set of properties that are typically used to describe a location (e.g., longitude, latitude, and string name). SO4PC defines two special subclasses called AtomicPlace and CompoundPlace to represent two different classes of the physical locations that have distinctive containment property. The containment property of a physical location is defined as its model for being capable of spatially subsuming other physical locations. For example, in SO4PC, a campus spatially subsumes all buildings on the campus, and a building spatially subsumes all rooms that are in it.

The containment property in SO4PC is represented by the spatially-Subsumes and isSpatiallySubsumedBy class properties. The two class properties are defined as the inverse property of each other (i.e., if X spatially subsumes Y, then Y is spatially subsumed by X).

For the AtomicPlace class and its subclasses, the cardinality of their spatiallySubsumes property is restricted to zero, and the range of their is-SpatiallySubsumedBy property is CompoundPlace. The function of these constraints is to express the idea that all individuals of the type AtomicPlace do not spatially subsume other physical locations, and they can be spatially subsumed by individuals of the type CompoundPlace.

Like the AtomicPlace class, the CompoundPlace class is also defined with special constraints on its containment properties. For this class and its subclasses, the range of the spatiallySubsumes is Place, and the range of the isSpatiallySubsumedBy property is CompoundPlace. The function of these constraints is to express the idea that all individuals of the type CompoundPlace can spatially subsume other individuals of the type either AtomicPlace or CompoundPlace, and they can be spatially subsumed by other CompoundPlace individuals.

There are four subclasses of the "Place" class in this version of SO4PC. They are Campus, Building, Room and OtherPlaceInBuilding. The predefined subclasses of AtomicPlace are Room and OtherPlaceInBuilding. The OtherPlaceInBuilding class represents places in a building that are not usually categorized as a type of room (e.g., hallways and cafeteria). The predefined subclasses of CompoundPlace are Campus and Building.

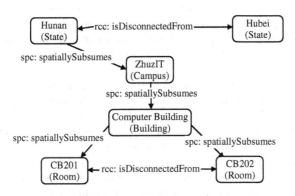

Fig. 4. A sample of the Place ontology in SO4PC

To help to describe a place is hosting an event (e.g., a meeting), we define the hasEvent property. This property has domain Place and range Event. Instances of the Event class are associated with time intervals.

3.3.2 Ontologies About Agents

The top level agent class in SO4PC is Agent. This class has two predefined subclasses, namely Person and SoftwareAgent. The former represents the class of all human agents, and the latter represents the class of all software agents. The two classes are defined to be disjoint. We have defined a number of properties for describing the profile of an agent (e.g., names, home pages, and email addresses). Each agent in SO4PC can have associated roles in an event (e.g., during a presentation event, the role of a person is a speaker, and after the presentation event, the role of the same person changes to a meeting participant). The role of an agent is defined by the fillsRole property, which has range Role. For convenience, we predefined two sub-classes of Role, SpeakerRole and AudienceRole. They represent different roles of a human agent in a meeting.

In SO4PC, the role of an agent can be used to characterize the intention of the agent. This allows the system to reason about the possible actions that a user intends to take after knowing the role of the user. To describe a user's intended action, we have defined the property intendsToPerform for the Role class. The range of this property is IntentionalAction. Sometimes an agent may desire other agents to achieve certain objectives on its behalf. For example, a speaker may desire services to set up the presentation slides before the meeting starts. To define what actions an agent desires other agents to take, we define a property called desiresSomeoneToAchieve. The range of this property is IntentionalAction.

3.3.3 Ontologies About an Agent's Location Context

By location context, we design a collection of dynamic knowledge that describes the location of an agent. The location property of an agent is represented by the property locatedIn. As the physical locations are categorized into AtomicPlace and CompoundPlace, it is possible to define the following context reasoning: (i) no agent can be physically present in two different atomic places during the same time interval, and (ii) an agent can be physically present in two different compound places during the same time interval just in case one spatially subsumes the other.

This type of reasoning is important because they can help the broker to detect inconsistent knowledge about the current location of an agent. For example, if two different sensor agents report a person is currently located in the CB201 and the CB202 respectively, then based on the first rule, the broker can conclude the information about the person's location is inconsistent because both instances that represent the CB201 and the CB202 are type of the atomic place.

To describe an agent is physically present in an atomic or a compound place, from the locatedIn property we define two sub-properties called locatedInAtomicPlace and locatedInCompoundPlace. The former is defined with the range restricted to AtomicPlace, and the latter is defined with the range restricted to CompoundPlace. From these two properties, we define additional properties that further restrict the type of the physical place that an agent can have physical presence in. For example, locatedInRoom and locatedInRestroom are sub-properties of locatedInAtomicPlace; locatedInCampus and locatedInBuiding are sub-properties of locatedInCompoundPlace.

For agents that are located in different places, we can categorize them according to their location properties. For example, we define PersonInBuilding to represent a set of all people who are located in a building, and SoftwareAgentInBuilding to represent a set of software agents that are located in a building. The complement of these classes is PersonNotInBuilding and SoftwareAgentNotInBuilding.

3.3.4 Ontologies About an Agent's Activity Context

The activity context of an agent, similar to the location context, is a collection of dynamic knowledge that describes the events in which an agent participates. We assume that Events have schedules. In SO4PC, the class PresentationSchedule represents the schedule of a presentation event. This class has associated properties that describe the start time, the end time, the presentation title, the presentation abstract, and the location of a presentation event. Additionally, in SO4PC we also provided a set of constructs for describing the audiences and speakers of a presentation event. We assume in each presentation, there is at least one invited speaker and one or many audiences. To describe a presentation that has a speaker or an audience, one can use the property invitedSpeaker and expectedAudience. Both of these properties have domain PresentationSchedule and range Person.

To describe currently happening event, we define a class called PresentationEventHappeningNow. The individuals of this class are assumed to have implicit association with the temporal predicate "now". Sometimes it is useful to reason about the temporal property of the people and places that are associated a presentation event. For example, the broker might want to reason about who is currently participating in a meeting, or which room is currently hosting a meeting. To support this type of reasoning, we define the class RoomHasPresentationEventHappeningNow to represent the rooms that are currently hosting meetings, the class SpeakerOfPresentationHappeningNow to represent the presentations of the speakers that are currently happening, and the class AudienceOfPresentationHappeningNow to represent the presentations of the audiences that are currently happening.

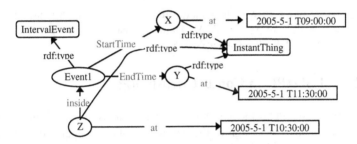

Fig. 5. The UML diagram for expressing temporal order between time instants and intervals

We use Time class to describe the temporal properties of different events in CBA. The basic representation of time consists of the TimeInstant and TimeInterval classes. The TimeInstant is type of time instant, and TimeInterval is type of time interval. The union of these two classes forms the TemporalThing class. In order to associate temporal things with date/time values (i.e., their temporal descriptions), the at property is defined to associate an instance with an XML xsd:dateTime datatype value(e.g., 2005-5-1 T10:30:00), and the StartTime and EndTime properties are defined to associate an instance with two different TimeInstant individuals. Fig.5 describes the relationship of temporal properties.

3.4 CBA Demo Toolkit

This toolkit is a set of software applications for demonstrating the key features of CBA. It is aimed to provide a proof-of-concept demonstration and stimulate future system design and development. This toolkit has three key components: (i) a stand-alone Context Broker implementation in JADE, (ii) a customizable JADE agent called ScriptPlay for facilitating demo scripts, and (iii) an Eclipse Plug-in called CBA Eclipse Viewer (CEV) for monitoring the knowledge base changes Context Broker.

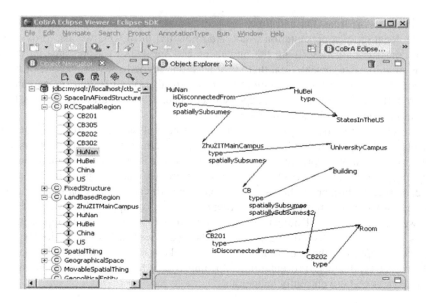

Fig. 6. A screenshot of the CBA Eclipse Viewer (CEV). On the left, CEV lists the ontology classes and instances that are part the CBA's knowledge base. On the right, CEV users can explore the properties of individual class instances.

4 The Use of SO4PC in Context Reasoning

The key feature of SO4PC is the ability to support ontology reasoning in a distributed dynamic environment. The design of the ontology makes an open-world assumption about how and where distributed information is described. This means that properties about a particular person, place and activity can be described by distributed heterogeneous sources, and the contexts of these individual entities can be dynamically inferred through classification. In this section, we will describe some rules used in CBA, and show how to use these rules to reason about contextual information and resolve the problem of inconsistent context.

4.1 The Rules Used in CBA

In previous context inference approaches[13], there are many deficiencies. Thus, we adopt rule-based inference approach. This approach can efficiently resolve the following problems: (i) it can deal with the problem of inconsistent context due to untrusty sensor or uncertain knowledge, (ii) it should possess description capacity because contextual information needs to describe properties and relations of entities. At the same time, the describing capacity makes context reasoning knowledge common, and (iii) it should have reasonable complexity because we want immediate results when apply contextual query.

This rule-based inference approach uses a number of different rule-based systems, which include the Jena rule-based reasoners[14], JESS (Java Expert System

Shell)[15], and Theorist (an assumption-based reasoner in Prolog)[16]. Different rule-based systems provide different logical inference support for context reasoning. The Jena rule-based reasoners are used for OWL ontology inferences, the JESS rule engine is used for interpreting context using domain specific rules, and the Theorist system is used for supporting the necessary logical inferences to resolve inconsistent knowledge. The implementation of context reasoning is illustrated in figure 7.

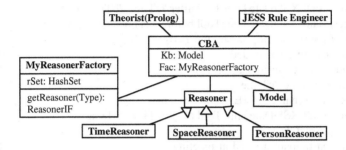

Fig. 7. A UML diagram that shows CBA's implementation of reasoning model

Here, we show part of the rules used to define a temporal reasoner in Jena, these rules are defined to reason about SO4PC time ontology vocabularies in a RDF graph.

(?x tme:before ?y) <-   (Rule 1)
 (?x rdf:type tme:IntervalThing), (?x tme:EndTime ?endsX),
 (?y rdf:type tme:IntervalThing), (?y tme:BeginTime ?beginsY),
 (?endsX tme:before ?beginsY).
(?x tme:inside ?y) <-   (Rule 2)
 (?x rdf:type tme:InstantThing),
 (?y rdf:type tme:IntervalThing),
 (?y tme:BeginTime ?beginsY), (?y tme:EndTime ?endsY),
 (?beginsY tme:before ?x), (?x tme:before ?endsY).

Here, we show part of the rules used to define a spatial reasoner, these rules are defined to reason about SO4PC space and RCC ontology vocabularies in a RDF graph.

(?x spc:spatiallySubsumes ?y) <-   (Rule 3)
 (?x rdf:type spc:GeographicalSpace), (?y rdf:type spc:GeographicalSpace),
 (?y spc:spatiallySubsumedBy ?x).
(?x spc:spatiallySubsumedBy ?z) <-   (Rule 4)
 (?x rdf:type spc:GeographicalSpace), (?y rdf:type spc:GeographicalSpace),
 (?x spc:spatiallySubsumedBy ?y), (?y spc:spatiallySubsumedBy ?z).
(?x rcc:isDisconnectedFrom ?y) <-   (Rule 5)
 (?x rdf:type spc:GeographicalSpace), (?y rdf:type spc:GeographicalSpace),
 (?x rdf:type rcc:RCCSpatialRegion), (?y rdf:type rcc:RCCSpatialRegion),
 (?x spc:spatiallySubsumedBy ?z), (?z rcc:isDisconnectedFrom ?y).

In our SMR system, reasoning about the meeting status is an important thing. The logic of the reasoning is as follows: (i) a scheduled meeting is in session if the current time instant is inside the beginning and the ending time of the meeting schedule, (ii) a scheduled meeting has ended if the current time instant is after the ending time of the meeting schedule, (iii) a participant (a presenter or an invited participant) is arrived at the meeting if he/she is located in the room of the schedule meeting, and there is no evidence suggesting that he/she is located in any other place, and (iv) a meeting can begin if no participants (a presenter or an invited participant) are missing. Here, we show the set of JESS rules that implement this logic inference process.

```
(defrule meeting-in-session                                    (Rule 6)
    (meeting (name ?x) (location ?l) (BeginTime ?bTime) (EndTime ?eTime))
    (current-time ?cTime)
    (test (call XSDDateTimeTool after ?cTime ?bTime))
    (test (call XSDDateTimeTool before ?cTime ?eTime))
    => (assert (meeting-in-session ?x)))
(defrule meeting-has-ended                                     (Rule 7)
    ?id <- (meeting-in-session ?x)
    (current-time ?cTime)
    (meeting (name ?x) (EndTime ?eTime))
    (test (call XSDDateTimeTool after ?cTime ?eTime))
    => (retract ?id))
(defrule participant-arrived-at-meeting                        (Rule 8)
    (meeting-in-session ?m)
    (meeting (name ?m) (location ?loc) (BeginTime ?bTime) (EndTime ?
eTime))
    (arrival (person ?p) (location ?loc) (at-time ?t))
    (test (call XSDDateTimeTool after ?t ?bTime))
    (test (call XSDDateTimeTool before ?t ?eTime))
    (not (not-located-in ?p ?loc))
    => (assert (arrived ?p ?m)))
```

4.2 Examples of Context Reasoning

Here, we will present some examples to testify the reasoning ability of SO4PC.

4.2.1 Examples of People Presence Reasoning

In pervasive computing environment, sensors are often used to detect the presence of people in a building. For example, Bluetooth sensors can detect the proximity presence of the Bluetooth-enabled personal devices and conclude the presence of the device owners.

Using the SO4PC, these people presence sensors can effectively share people presence information with the broker in the system and enable the broker to reason about the situational contexts of these people. For example, (i) whether a person is in the building, (ii) whether a person is in school today, and (iii) whether a person is not in a room (e.g., in hallway or in a cafeteria).

Assuming the scenario, when Tom enters Room CB201 and swipes his RFID badge at the door, the RFID sensor informs the broker of his presence in the room. On receiving this information, the broker will reason about Tom's context. The following two examples describe how the broker may reason about his contexts.

Example 1: To determine if Tom is in the Computer Building.

A1: Person("Tom") has property LocateIn("CB201").

A2: According to Rule 4, consulting Fig.4, we know that Room("CB201") is spc:spatiallySubsumedBy Building("Computer Building").

A3: For any person who has the property LocateIn() with rdfs:range limited to any Place that spc:spatiallySubsumedBy building, that person must be a type of Person-InBuilding (i.e., that person is in a building).

A4 <= A2+A3: Person("Tom") is a type of the PersonInBuilding class (i.e., Tom is currently in a building). The broker can deduce Tom is currently in the Computer Building.

Example 2: To determine if Tom is NOT in room CB202.

B1: Person("Tom") has property LocateIn("CB201").

B2: According to Rule 5, consulting Fig.4, we know that Room("CB201") is rcc:isDisconnectedFrom Room("CB202").

B3: A person is not located in two disjoint places at the same time.

B4 <= B1+B2+B3: Person("Tom") is NOT in Room("CB202").

We use JADE's agent development toolkit to design a demonstration of presence reasoning(Fig.8).

4.2.2 An Examples of Room Agent Reasoning

In SMR, room agents will play an important role in maintaining and sharing room-specific contexts with devices and agents. Let's assume in each room, there is a room agent maintains a set of specific contexts of the room, for example (i) whether the room is currently hosting a meeting, (ii) the temperature, noise level, and light intensity level in the room, (iii) the close/open states of the doors and windows in the room, and (iv) the type of devices/services that are available as the context of the room changes, the room agent will inform the broker of the updated contexts.

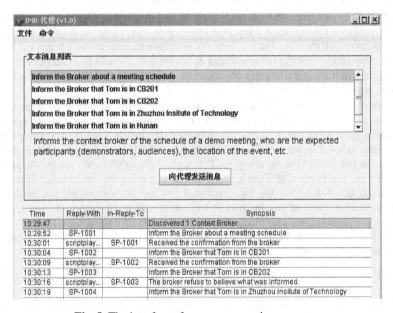

Fig. 8. The interface of presence reasoning program

Assuming the scenario, according to conference arrangement, there will be a meeting in CB201 from 09:00:00 am to 11:30:00 am today. Now, it is 10:30:00 am.

Example 3: To determine if Tom is attending a meeting in room CB201 (i.e., is Tom a meeting participant?).

C1: Person("Tom") has property LocateIn("CB201") (from Example 1: A1)

C2: For any room that has the property hasEvent() with rdfs:range limited to Meeting, the room must be a type of MeetingPlaceInBuilding.

C3: Room("CB201") has the property hasEvent("Meeting239") from 09:00:00 am to 11:30:00 am today.

C4: According to Rule 2, the TimeInstance("10:30:00 am") is tme:Inside TimeInterval("09:00:00 am", "11:30:00 am").

C5<= C2+C3+C4: According to Rule 6, the Meeting239 is meeting-in-session in CB201.

C6: If a person has the property LocateIn() with a value that is a type of Room class and the meeting in this room is in session, the person is a type of MeetingParticipant.

C7<= C1+C5+C6: Person("Tom") is a meeting participant.

4.2.3 An Examples of Person Agent Reasoning

Person agents are specialized as agents that provide personalized services for individual users[17]. In smart space, these agents will keep track of users' profiles, preferences, desires and intentions. For example, the person agent of a speaker will automatically set up presentation slides when the speaker arrives at the meeting and adjust room lighting when the presentation starts. In order for the person agent to provide these services, it must acquire contextual knowledge about the person from the broker. This knowledge may include the following: (i) the role of the person in the meeting, (ii) the type of services that the person has access to, (iii) the type of the devices that the person carries, (iv) the type of non-computing objects the person's vicinity (e.g., the type of clothes the person wears & the type of objects that the person holds), (v) the time when the person enter the room or joins the meeting, and (vi) the identity of people whom the person is talking to.

One source from which person agents can acquire information about their users is through user behavior monitoring. For example, Tom is scheduled to talk about ontology development at Meeting239. Days before the meeting, while Tom prepares his PowerPoint slides, his personal agent learns his intention to give presentation at the meeting. On the day of the meeting, as Tom enters the conference room, the personal agent informs the broker of Tom's intention and queries the broker for Tom's situational contexts. On receiving information from the person agent, the broker will reason about the context of the user. Sometimes ontology reasoning may involve uncertainty. For example, knowledge about the context of a person may not always be completely accurate. The following examples show how reasoning about the role of a person can involve varied degree of certainty.

Example 4: To determine the role of a person (e.g., is Tom is the speaker of Meeting239?).

D1: Person("Tom") is the same person as MeetingParticipant("Tom") (from Example 3: C7)

D2: MeetingParticipant("Tom") is associated with Meeting239. (from Example 3).

D3: Person("Tom") has the intention to GiveSlideShowPresentation (Informed by Tom's person agent).

D4: If a person is a type of MeetingParticipant and that person has the SpeakerIntention, then that person is LIKELY to be a speaker.

D5 <= D1+D2+D3+D4: Person("Tom") is likely to be a speaker.

Now, let's assume the broker has some prior knowledge about the invitations that are given to meeting participants. For example, from a talk announcement server (e.g., ITTalks.ORG[18]), the broker learns that some person who is a type of TalkEventHost has invited Tom to the Meeting239.

D6: Person("Tom") is invited by a TalkEventHost.

D7 <= D5+D6: Person("Tom") must be a speaker.

5 Summary

In this paper, we have described a broker-centric architecture for an agent based pervasive computing environment. This broker accepts and integrates context related information from devices and agents in the environment as well as from other sources to maintain a coherent model of the space, the devices, agents and people in it, and their associated services and activities. A key to realizing this architecture is the use of a set of common ontologies that the devices, agents and people use to describe their context information and query the broker's context model. For this reason, we exploit a set of ontologies – SO4PC which is helpful for concepts description, context reasoning and knowledge share. In future, we plan to prototype an ontology reasoning component for implementing CBA.

Acknowledgement

The financial support from the National Natural Science Fund of China under the grant No.60373062 is gratefully acknowledged.

References

1. Kindberg T., Barton J.: A web-based nomadic computing system. Computer Networks, 35(4) (2001) 443-456.
2. Bennett F., Richardson T., Harter A.: Teleporting – making applications mobile. In Proceedings of 1994 Workshop on Mobile Computing, (1994) 120-127
3. Man J.F., Liu Q., Yang D.: Research on the Representation Method of Spatial Data. Computer Application, 28(11) (2004) 97-100
4. Priyantha N. B., Chakraborty A., Balakrishnan H.: The cricket location-support system. In Mobile Computing and Networking, (2000) 32-43.
5. Chen H., Finin T., Joshi A.: An ontology for context-aware pervasive computing environments. Special Issue on Ontologies for Distributed Systems, Knowledge Engineering Review, 18(2004) 197-207
6. Noy N. F., McGuinness D. L.: Ontology development 101: A guide to creating your first ontology. Technical Report KSL-01-05, Stanford Knowledge Systems Laboratory, (2001) 20-50

7. Brickley D., Miller L.: FOAF vocabulary specification. In RDF Web Namespace Document, (2003) 48-56
8. Pan F., Hobbs J. R.: Time in OWL-S. In Proceedings of AAAI-04 Spring Symposium on SemanticWeb Services, Stanford University, California, (2004) 50-64.
9. Lenat D. B., Guha R. V.. Building Large Knowledge-Based Systems: Representation and Inference in the Cyc Project. Addison-Wesley, 2(1990) 12-20.
10. Randell D. A., Cui Z., Cohn A.: A spatial logic based on regions and connection. Morgan Kaufmann, San Mateo, California, (1992) 165-176.
11. Perich F.: MoGATU BDI Ontology. http://www.BDI-Ont.com/MoGATU/, (2004).
12. Kagal L., Finin T., Joshi A.: A Policy Based Approach to Security for the Semantic Web. In 2nd International Semantic Web Conference (ISWC2003), September (2003) 210-219.
13. Schilit B., Adams N., Want R.: Context-aware computing applications. In IEEE Workshop on Mobile Computing Systems and Applications, Santa Cruz, CA, US, (1994)102-110
14. Dave R.: Jena 2 Inference Support. http://jena.sourceforge.net/inference/, (2004).
15. Ernest J., Hill F.: The Expert System Shell for the Java Platform. Sandia National Laboratories. http://herzberg.ca.sandia.gov/jess/docs/index.shtml, (2004)
16. David P.: Compiling a default reasoning system into prolog. New Generation Computing, 9(1991) 3–38
17. Finin T., Joshi A., Kagal L.: Information Agents for Mobile and Embedded Devices. International Journal on Cooperative Information Systems, (2003) 30-35.
18. Cost S., Finin T., Joshi A.: A Case Study in the Semantic Web and DAML+OIL. IEEE Intelligent Systems, (2002) 40-47.

Practical Ontology Systems for Enterprise Application[*]

Dongkyu Kim[1], Sang-goo Lee[2], Junho Shim[3],
Jonghoon Chun[4], Zoonky Lee[5], and Heungsun Park[6]

[1] CoreLogiX, Inc., Seoul, Korea
dkkim@corelogix.co.kr
[2] Center for e-Business Technology, Seoul National University, Seoul, Korea
sglee@snu.ac.kr
[3] Department of Computer Science, Sookmyung Women's University, Seoul, Korea
[4] Department of Computer Engineering, Myongji University, Kyongkido, Korea
[5] Graduate School of Information & Communications, Yonsei University, Seoul, Korea
[6] Department of Statistics, Hankook University of Foreign Studies, Kyongkido, Korea

Abstract. One of the main challenges in building enterprise applications has been to balance between built-in functionality and domain/scenario-specific customization. The lack of formal ways to extract, distill and standardize the embedded domain knowledge has been a barrier to effective and efficient customization. Ontology may provide, as many would hope, the much needed methodology and standard to achieve the objective of building flexible enterprise solutions. This article examines the uses, issues and challenges of using ontology in enterprise applications. We believe that we are seriously lacking in modeling methodology, domain user tools, and lifecycle management methodology for the creation and maintenance of ontology on a large deployable scale. We present the issues based on an ongoing project to build a product ontology for a public procurement system. Through real life scenarios, we are hoping to convey important research directions to better enable ontology.

1 Introduction

One of the main challenges in building enterprise applications has been to balance between built-in functionality and domain/scenario-specific customization. The successful extraction, distillation and standardization of functional requirements in storage, messaging, workflow and business rules has lead to the flourishing successful middleware software segment. This approach, however, has not really been applied to enterprise applications with similar success. The primary reason, as the authors conjecture, is due to the vast amount of knowledge embedded in these applications. The lack of formal way to extract, distill and standardize the embedded domain knowledge has prevented application builders from enriching the functionality while minimizing the cost of customization.

---

[*] This work was support in part by the Ministry of Information & Communications, Korea, under the ITRC program.

S. Grumbach, L. Siu, and V. Vianu (Eds.): ASIAN 2005, LNCS 3818, pp. 79–89, 2005.
© Springer-Verlag Berlin Heidelberg 2005

Creating ontology for a domain provides an opportunity to analyze domain knowledge, make domain assumptions explicit, separate domain knowledge from operational knowledge, provide common understanding of the information structure, and enable reuse of domain knowledge [1]. The created ontology provides a reference domain model that human and software can refer to for various purposes such as search, browsing, interoperability, integration, and configuration [2]. There have been studies in recent years for realizing this vision of ontology-based technologies to serve the purposes. Also, there has been active work on building foundation for ontology (e.g., standard semantic markup languages such as RDF and OWL), especially in the context of W3C's Semantic Web [3].

Although there have been a rich amount of research in ontology, there are still gaps to be filled in actual deployment of the technology/concept in a real life commercial environment. The problems are hard especially in those applications that require well-defined semantics in mission critical operations. We believe that we are seriously lacking in modeling methodology, domain user tools, and lifecycle management methodology for the creation and maintenance of ontology on a large deployable scale. We present the issues based on an ongoing project to build a product ontology for a public procurement system.

Product information seems to be the most adequate domain within e-commerce where ontology can play a vital role for a number of reasons, including relatively clear and well defined semantics compared to process oriented domains, and the availability of a number of product classification standards. Product information, in the form of e-catalogs, makes up a key component in e-commerce. A base of precisely and clearly defined products and services is a necessary foundation for collaborative business processes. With the sharing of precise product model containing rich semantics, diverse e-business systems with high-level interoperability can be offered. One possibility is dramatically improved supply chain management. With more accurate and up-to-date information on current inventories and demands, more accurate production plans can be formed with significant savings in costs. A strong support for semantics of product data and processes will allow for dynamic, real-time data integration, and also real-time tracking and configuration of products, despite differing standards and conventions at each stage.

The rest of this paper is structured as follows: Section 2 introduces our product ontology system with motivation our experience on using ontology for a product information management project. In sections 3, 4, and 5, we present in groups the practical issues that hinder widespread use of ontology-based applications in enterprise settings; modeling and design, creation and lifecycle management, and project management and human factors. We provide sample solutions and approaches taken in our project for reference. The paper is concluded in section 6.

2   Product Ontology

2.1   Motivation

There are several significant difficulties in content construction for e-commerce applications. A good example would be the product registration process common to most e-procurement systems. When new products are entered into the system, a tremendous amount of (human) work is required to compare and then properly categorize them. If an attribute set significantly different from those already in use is needed for describing a product or if the vocabulary used cannot be translated in a straightforward manner, then the task becomes more complicated and further work is required.

Product information seems to be the most adequate domain within e-commerce where ontology can play a vital role for a number of reasons.

First, the semantics required for product information is complex enough to benefit from an ontological approach, yet not too daunting as to prevent the development of an effective solution for practical applications.

Second, although semantically limited, current classification standards, such as UNSPSC[1] [4] and eCl@ss[2] [5], and legacy product databases residing in hundreds of e-procurement systems collectively form a rich and strong basis to start from. An added bonus is that these references (or instances) are not embedded in application program codes (as is the case with much of the process related contents) but are declaratively available as database tables or spreadsheets.

Third, product information is a key fundamental component of e-commerce, the richness of which will enable enhancement of different parts of collaborative business processes. The benefits can be realized throughout the system.

Forth, from a project management point of view, because of the aforementioned characteristics, we can build successful cases relatively quickly and use them as stepping stones to expand our models and solutions into more challenging areas of business process integration.

Several systems for standardizing the information of products and services already exist. Examples include UNSPSC, eCl@ss, and UCCnet[3] [6]. These standards (or standard bodies) provide content standards such as product class hierarchy used for data synchronization and product classification. However product categorization is but one piece of data among the rich set of information that are required for machines to operate on products intelligently (or without too much human intervention); such as the product's attributes and its relationship to other products (related products, similar alternatives). Current standards in the form of technical dictionaries [7, 8] and/or classification codes are simply too restricted to properly represent the complex relationships among millions of classes, properties, and semantics of (or constraints on) properties. One needs to take a more holistic view of a product instead. Rich semantics must be captured and represented in machine-processable form for [9]:

- Enabling data exchanges between business entities that use different product standards
- Mapping different classification schemes to support catalog search and purchasing
- (Semi) Automating the classification of incoming catalogs

---

[1] United Nations Standard Products and Services Code is a product classification scheme developed and managed by the United Nations Development Programme (UNDP).

[2] eCl@ss is a product classification scheme developed and managed by a consortium of European companies.

[3] UCCnet, lead by UCC and EAN, is a both a user group and a program run by the user group for promoting the development and use of standards for global commerce.

- Enhancing reusability of current business processes against changing standard models
- Sharing established business concept standards while allowing variation due to specific requirements of individual industries
- Reducing the resources required for building a new catalog database through reuse and sharing of the product structures

To fulfill these requirements, product information should be enriched with intentional knowledge describing its exact and detail specifications using a set of agreed upon concepts and axioms. Ontology provides an approach fulfilling the needs, where such information can be represented in a product ontology that can be understood and processed by machines.

2.2   The Product Ontology System

We have built an ontology system helping data integration for business processes for the Public Procurement Services (PPS) of Korea, which is responsible for procurement for government and public agencies. The main focus is the development of a system of ontologies representing products and services, which includes the definitions, properties, and relationships of the concepts that are fundamental to products and services. The system functions as a standard reference system for e-catalog construction providing tools and operations for managing catalog standards. The ontology is a knowledge base, not only for the design and construction of product databases but also for search and discovery of products and services. [10]

The ontology system consists of the ontology database and two subsystems; the ontology construction & maintenance system and the ontology search system (Fig. 1).

The Ontology database consists of five basic components; the vocabulary, classification, attributes, UOM (unit of measure), product instance, and four relationship components; classification-product, classification-attribute, attribute-UOM, and vocabulary-vocabulary. Each component is further divided into subcomponents which in turn are composed of multiple tables. Further discussion is given in section 3.

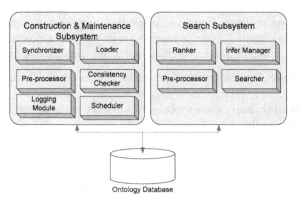

Fig. 1. The ontology system

Ontology construction and maintenance subsystem populates the product ontology database from the existing product database, and manages updates while maintaining consistency of the ontology database. Ontology search subsystem helps users to navigate through or search the domain knowledge stored in the ontology database.

3 Modeling and Design

Even though the ontology-based information infrastructure sets up the framework for our purposes, we cannot easily apply the algorithms, technology, theories in enterprise scale applications for a number of reasons. In this and the next two sections (sections 3 ~ 5), we present the practical issues that hinder widespread use of ontology-based applications in enterprise settings. Certain solutions and approaches taken in our project are presented as references.

3.1 Modeling

The challenge here would be to find the right level of abstraction for an ontology, defining the adequate model, and presenting the model in a readily comprehendible form to practitioners in the field. Is "red pen" a separate class of items deserving a separate concept in the ontology, or should it be modeled as a "pen" with certain properties? In the latter case, a red pen would only be realized in the system when instances of red pen are present.

The ontology model must be robust enough to accommodate possibly different perspectives of potential users and be easily modifiable to adapt to changing trends and products. Multiple views and taxonomies, often with conflicting semantics, present another challenge for the field engineer. Users tend to insist on using their view of the domain space (i.e., vocabulary, taxonomy, etc.), and the system is required to serve a number of different user groups with differing views all at the same time.

In a product ontology, an important component of the model will be the semantic model for product classification scheme, since that alone can be used to enrich the current classification standards to include machine-readable semantic descriptions of products. The model will provide a logical structure in which to express the standards. The added semantics will enhance the accuracy of mappings between classification standards. A clearly understood mapping semantics must be provided along with the supporting algorithms.

Fig. 2-a) illustrates our view for product ontology using the meta-model approach [11, 12]. The meta-modeling approach enables a product ontology model to be more extensible and flexible. Our product model [13] follows the basic meta-model which employs three modeling-levels: M0 meta-class level, M1 class level, and M2 instance level. Within the M0 level which describes a high level conceptual product ontology, we have the key concepts as the meta-classes. As illustrated in the figure, the meta-classes may have relationships (meta-relationships). The relationships are shown in Fig. 2-b). They include semantic relationships from general domain; such as class inclusion (isa), meronymic inclusion (component, substance, and member), attribution, and synonym. In addition, product domain specific relationships such as substitute, complement, purchase-set, mapped-to are also considered.

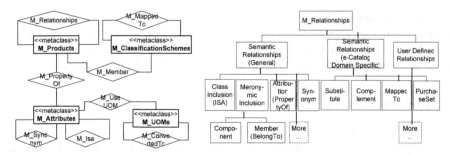

a) Product ontology model in meta-level   b) Meta-relationships hierarchy

Fig. 2. The Ontology Data Model

Our modeling goal is not only to design a 'conceptual' product ontology model but also to implement it as an operational ontology database model. One way to achieve this goal may be through using an ontology language such as OWL and building an OWL knowledgebase that represents the intentional and extensional concepts and relationships. This approach was not taken because we were not able to find a robust enough OWL engine to practically handle a large knowledgebase as ours (over 10 million entries in voc-voc component alone). In addition, we only needed a limited-set of reasoning capabilities such as transitivity and inverse. The general purpose reasoning capability of an OWL engine was considered an over-kill. We have created an object-relational product ontology database consisting of more than 40 base tables to reflect the conceptual schemas and class schemas.

3.2 Ontology-DB Integration

One way of defining the role of ontology in an information system is to consider the ontology as meta data for the database; the database represents the information content of the system and the ontology is a secondary facility. Queries and operations are defined on the database and the ontology is used only as an aid to facilitate and enrich the operations. This approach is easier to implement since the ontology can be built as an add-on facility to an existing system without requiring fundamental changes.

Another way is to model the information content of the system as an integration of ontology and database, i.e., the ontology is an integral part of the database. The database alone does not represent the complete information content. In this case, ontology must be part of all queries and operations. The implementation is complex since the information foundation of the system is changed, and hence, all parts of the system must be changed to reflect this. However, the system is now able to fully utilize the expressive power and flexibility of ontology, and is that much richer in semantics.

For our product ontology, we took the first approach because of its non-intrusiveness (to the everyday operation of the organization) and low-risk nature (if the ontology has flaws, we can simply decide not to use it). However, because the ontology database and the product database are run on separate systems, performance is becoming a problem (3 months after deployment, the system must handle over 4,000 ontology-based-searches per day).

3.3 Search and Navigation

Various visualization techniques have been introduced for exploring ontology entangled with relations and concepts. For the majority of ontologies where taxonomy is the predominant content, hyperbolic style diagram with few cross-taxonomical links and with very few relationships is mostly suitable for navigating data structures. However, it may not be suitable in product ontology since a concept related with multiple relationships may have a large number of instances, and those instances may participate in different types of relationships. Instead we employ a navigation approach to provide paths for searching other information. A path associated with a concept means that the concept has a relationship (path) with other concepts. In our navigation interface, each concept is associated with a set of links each of which represents paths to other concepts.

Searching in an ontology system requires a different model than those available for conventional IR (information retrieval) systems. In IR, "document-keyword" mapping information is stored and used for finding which documents are relevant to the given keywords. In ontology, relationship information between concepts, in addition to the concepts themselves, play important roles in determining relevance. We have developed a location/frequency model where an object's rank is determined by keyword frequency and location of occurrence (product name or classification name, etc.). The model provides flexibility and allows more natural matching in a product environment.

4 Creation and Lifecycle Management

4.1 Creation

Populating the ontology is a daunting task which can make or break the project. The job is complicated by multiple formats, semantic mismatches, errors or dirty data in pre-existing information sources. The problem is similar to the ETL (extract-transform-load) task for data warehouses. Our product ontology database is built in a batch fashion by bulk-loading and transforming the data from the existing product catalog database. The transformation at this phase is done automatically by the system. The product descriptions are decomposed into terms which make up the vocabulary component and those terms are linked to represent ontology concepts or relationships.

Since entities that have references to other entities should be built later than the referenced entities, transformations should be performed in a specific order to preserve the reference dependency of each entity. In our case, the order is classification schemes, attributes, UOMs, and products. At the end of the construction process, we performed the quality checking and cleaning manually. Then, technical dictionaries are built upon the product ontology database.

4.2 Consistency of Ontology Database

As with any other information systems, the contents of the ontology change over time. Change management (versions, mergers, decompositions, etc.) is another complicated issue that must be addressed. The system must ensure consistency of the ontology during through the changes. Consistency refers to the logical coherence of the contents along such decomposing and linking process.

We consider two kinds of consistency, intra-concept consistency and inter-concept consistency. Intra-concept consistency describes the correspondence between the concept and its decomposed vocabularies. For example, if the class name of "LCD-monitor" is changed to "Computer monitor", the corresponding concepts should be altered accordingly. Inter-concept consistency describes the correspondence among the concepts and relationships. A relationship has to change as its participating concepts change. For example, when a product class is dropped from the catalog, any relationship which the class has should be removed from the database. Our system supports both types of consistencies by adding built-in consistency managing modules into every update operations. The modules are triggered by update operations: insert, delete or update, and different modules are built for each concept, relationship and update operation type.

4.3 Synchronization Between the Ontology Database and the Product Database

A separate issue that is specific to our architecture is synchronization between the ontology database and the product catalog database. Since our ontology draws its information from the product database and search through ontology must point back to the product database, it is essential that the two databases be kept in sync, i.e., all updates on the source catalog database should be propagated towards the ontology database as soon as they are detected. We considered two approaches for implementing the online synchronization; a database-level approach and an application-level approach.

In a database-level approach, as an update occurs on a source table, the DBMS automatically triggers the corresponding maintenance module. This approach provides a simple and easy way of implementing synchronization process since the process is mainly supported by the DBMS functionalities. It is, however, inappropriate due to the performance degradation as the database schema grows and more number of maintenance modules are required.

In an application-level approach, specially designed logging modules are implemented to cover every update cases. It gives flexibilities on the system design by allowing database schema evolving, efficient scheduling of batch updates and distributing servers over the network. The application-level architecture suggested was suggested in [14] for maintaining replica's consistency while minimizing the performance degradation due to the synchronization of refresh transactions. We have adopted the consistency criteria and the system architecture from [14] and optimized the algorithm to work in a single copy environment.

Fig. 3 illustrates the architecture of our synchronization system. As the catalog database changes, the Propagator sends the ontology system Java RMI messages that describe the types of changes and changed contents. The RMI messages are in XML format. The Receiver stores the reception logs in a database table. The Refresher schedules the synchronization process considering the system load accordingly.

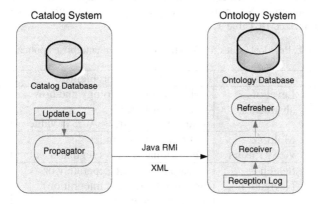

Fig. 3. Architecture of synchronization subsystem

5   Project Management and Human Factors

5.1   Accountability and Control

For system managers and IT managers, one of the biggest concerns against ontology is its lack of control. When is an ontology complete, in the sense that it holds sufficient content to support all mission critical operations? What if the inference produces an unintended result at a critical moment? Is the behavior/performance predictable? These questions are legitimate concerns for any enterprise application. A system that is seemingly intelligent but not predictable is not acceptable. It is better to do simple things fast and reliably. In order to use ontology in an enterprise setting with mission critical tasks, these issues must be addressed.

  Because our ontology model is relatively simple, the contents are drawn from the pre-existing product database, and with visualization supported by the navigation tool, users and operators were comfortable with the comprehension and control level they had over the structure of the ontology.

5.2   Human Factors

Building and maintaining the ontology requires much more than software engineers. Domain experts must define the concepts and relationships for the domain model. They must populate and maintain the contents of the ontology system. The ontological information model is not a concept easily understood by non-computer/ontology experts. Thus, a set of intuitive (and non-technical) guidelines and manuals for these uses must be provided. Easy-to-use tools are also essential. Other end users such as analysts and merchandiser are users of the ontology, and they must understand the subtle differences of how the system behaves compared to conventional systems.

6 Conclusion

We have presented our ongoing product ontology project. Even with a well-defined architecture and theory, there are practical problems galore when trying to build a system around ontology. Some of the problems that we encountered were presented. These are summarized in Table 1.

Table 1. Practical issues for adopting ontology in enterprise applications

Area	Issue	Specific problems	Remarks
Modeling	Level of abstraction	- How much is ontology and how much is instance? - Subclass vs attr. / Attr. vs value	
	Multiple views / users	- Different taxonomies - Functional spec. vs regular users	
Ontology / DB Integration	Search & Navigation	- Search/Navigate separately or as one (need seamless integration)? - Search semantics	Related to model
	Tight vs Loose coupling	- Is ontology part of DB or just an aid for search and navigation?	
	Mapping	- Seamless mapping between ontology and schema - Auto-generation of schema	
Lifecycle Management	Creation / Bootstrapping	- Multiple formats of pre-existing source for ontology - Syntactic, semantic problems - Cleansing	Related to ETL
	Change management	- Versions of ontology - Merging of ontology - How this affects underlying DB	
Accountability & Control	Ambiguity & imprecision	- Incomplete information in ontology - Conflicts in ontology - Dirty data in DB - Who's to blame for wrong information?	Related to tight/loose coupling
	Automation	- Blackbox inference are not acceptable - Want firm control comparable to relational DB with SQL	Related to tight/loose coupling
Human Factors	Operations manual	- Guideline for the ontology builder (domain expert) - Guideline for the end user (analyst, merchandiser, system integrator, etc.)	
	Training	- Consultants - End users	

We do not try to present solutions to these problems but wish to share our experiences and raise awareness. The solutions to these problems are most likely to come as disciplines and guidelines, and tools that implement these guidelines. There is a proliferation of technologies on ontology. A logical next step for our research would be to examine how each of these technologies addresses the integration issues and practical issues presented in the previous sections. We plan to build a map that links individual ontological requirements to ontology issues, and then to applicable ontology technology. We believe the maturity of "ontological engineering" [15] is a pre-requisite to a successful deployment of ontology and ontology based solutions in business applications.

References

1. N. F. Noy, & D. L. McGuinness: Ontology Development 101: A Guide to Creating Your First Ontology.
   http://protege.stanford.edu/publications/ontology_development/ontology101.html.
2. D. L. McGuinness: Ontologies Come of Age. In: D. Fensel, et al (eds.): The Semantic Web: Why, What, and How. MIT Press (2001)
3. W3C: Semantic Web. http://www.w3.org/2001/sw/.
4. UNSPSC, United Nations Standard Products and Services Code. UNDP, http://www.unspsc.org/
5. eCl@ss - New Standardized Material and Service Classification. Cologne Institute for Business Research, http://www.eclass-online.com/
6. UCCnet, http://knowledgebase.uccnet.org/
7. eOTD, ECCMA Open Technical Dictionary, ECCMA, http://www.eccma.org/eotd/index.html
8. GDD, Global Data Dictionary, http://www.ean-ucc.org/global_smp/global_data_dictionary.htm
9. D. Kim, S. Lee, J. Chun: A Semantic Classification Model for e-Catalogs. IEEE Conference on E-Commerce (2004)
10. S. Lee: Design & Implementation of an e-Catalog Management System. Tutorial at DASFAA (2004)
11. J. Shim, S. Lee, C. Wu: A Unified Approach for Software Policy Modeling: Incorporating Implementation into a Modeling Methodology. 22nd International Conference on Conceptual Modeling (2003)
12. C. Atkinson, T. Kühne: The Essence of Multilevel Metamodeling. 4th International Conference on The Unified Modeling Language, Modeling Languages, Concepts, and Tools, Springer-Verlag (2001)
13. J. Shim, H. Lee, S. Lee: Conceptual and Formal Modeling of Product Ontology. Technical Report, Center for e-Business Technology, Seoul National University (2004) (submitted to Journal of Organizational Computing and Electronic Commerce).
14. E. Pacitti, E. Simon: Update Propagation Strategies to Improve Freshness in Lazy Master Replicated Databases. The International Journal on Very Large Data Bases, Vol.8, No.3-4, (2000)
15. F. Gandon: Ontology Engineering: A Survey and a Return on Experience. Research Report No. 4396, INRIA (2002)

Multi-labeled Graph Matching - An Algorithm Model for Schema Matching

Zhi Zhang[1], Haoyang Che[2], Pengfei Shi[1], Yong Sun[3], and Jun Gu[3]

[1] Institute of Image Processing and Pattern Recognition,
Shanghai Jiaotong University, Shanghai 200030, China
{zzh, pfshi}@sjtu.edu.cn
[2] Institute of Software, The Chinese Academy of Sciences,
Beijing 100080, China
hyche@hotmail.com
[3] Department of Computer Science, Science & Technology
University of Hong Kong, Hong Kong, China

Abstract. Schema matching is the task of finding semantic correspondences between elements of two schemas, which plays a key role in many database applications. In this paper, we treat the schema matching problem as a combinatorial problem. First, we propose an internal schema model, i.e., the multi-labeled graph, and transform schemas into multi-labeled graphs. Secondly, we discuss a generic graph similarity measure, and propose an optimization function based on multi-labeled graph similarity. Then, we cast schema matching problem into a multi-labeled graph matching problem, which is a classic combinational problem. Finally, we implement a greedy algorithm to find the feasible matching results.

1 Introduction

The goal of schema matching is to find semantic correspondences between the elements of two schemas. It plays a key role in many database applications such as schema integration, data warehousing, e-business, XML message mapping, and semantic query processing [15]. However schema matching still remains largely a manual, labor-intensive, and expensive process.

In this paper, we cast the schema matching problem (SMP) into a combinatorial optimization problem. First, we propose an internal schema model: multi-labeled graph. We represent schemas by multi-labeled graphs. Second, we discuss a generic graph similarity measure, and propose an optimization function based on multi-labeled graph similarity. Then, we transform the schema matching problem into a multi-labeled graph matching problem, which is a classic combinational problem. Finally, we implement a greedy algorithm to find the feasible matching results.

The outline of this paper is as follows: In Section 2 we discuss related work on schema matching. Section 3 presents the internal schema model: multi-labeled graph. Section 4 introduces the definition of SMP based on multi-labeled graph. We call SMP as multivalent matching, which is composed of multivalent correspondences.

S. Grumbach, L. Siu, and V. Vianu (Eds.): ASIAN 2005, LNCS 3818, pp. 90–103, 2005.

Section 5 gives a real-life example to expound our matching framework. First, we present the definition of matching space. Second, we investigate a generic graph similarity method, and propose an objective function to SMP. Then, Section 6 studies a greedy algorithm in detail. In Section 7, we make some concluding remarks and discuss our future work.

2 Related Work

Numerous solutions have been proposed in specific applications to solve SMP. Madhavan et al. [9, 14] implemented a Cupid system to achieve semi-automatic schema matching, which uses a hybrid matching algorithm comprising linguistic and structural schema matching techniques, and computes similarity coefficients with the assistance of a precompiled thesaurus; The LSD system [7] uses machine-learning techniques for individual matchers to match a pair of schemas. In addition to a name matcher, they use several instance-level matchers, which discover during the learning phase different characteristic instance patterns and matching rules for single elements of the target schema [6]; Melnik et al. [10, 11] used the graph matching algorithm – Similarity Flooding to achieve schema matching, which can measure the similarity between vertices of two schemas. The similarity between pairs of vertices, described by a nonnegative vector, is computed iteratively until convergence to a fixed point; Berlin and Motro [1] devised Automatch system for database schema matching which uses machine learning techniques, bases primarily on Bayesian learning, to achieve automate schema matching; Bouquet [2] viewed each semantic schema as a context, and proposed an algorithm based on SAT solver to matching two schemas; Furthermore, based on [2], Giunchiglia et al. [8] developed S-Match algorithm to solve semantic matching between schemas. S-Match takes two trees, and for any pair of nodes from these two trees, it computes the strongest semantic relation holding between them. Miller proposed a semi-automated mapping tool Clio to obtain mappings between a given target schema and a new schema [12]. The algorithm regards schema mapping as query discovery, which uses query search method to match the schemas; Do and Rahm [5] devised the COMA schema matching system. It follows a composite approach, which provides an extensible library of different matchers and supports various ways for combining match results. For the details of SMP, we can refer to two surveys of schema matching [6, 15].

Graphs are versatile representation tools, which have been used and studied in schema matching [9, 10, 11]. In [17], Zhang et al. proposed a *meta-meta structure* based on universal algebra, which is named *multi-labeled schema*. In this paper, we use a *multi-labeled graph model* as the internal schema model, which is an instance of *multi-labeled schema*. As a result, SMP can be reduced to a graph matching problem. The graph matching problem (i.e., graph homomorphism) is one of the classic combinatorial optimization problems.

To retrieve similar case in a CBR system, Champin and Solnon [3] proposed a generic similarity measure model to compare multi-labeled graphs. Based on their work, we use the labeled graph similarity method as objective function, so that we can design optimization methods to solve SMP.

3 Multi-labeled Graph Model (Internal Schema Model)

3.1 Multi-labeled Graph Model

As we all know, there are many kinds of schemas, such as relational model, object-oriented model, ER model, conceptual graph, DTD, XML schema, and UML, etc. In [17], Zhang et al. proposed a meta-meta model of schema: multi-labeled schema, which views schemas as finite structures over the specific signatures. Moreover, since graphs are versatile representation tools, which have been used and studied in a wide range of application domains. In this paper, we present a model, namely multi-labeled graph, an instance of multi-labeled schema, to describe various schemas, where each vertex and edge can be associated with a set of labels describing its properties.

Definition 1. A schema S can be represented by a labeled graph structure $S = (V, E, Lab, r_V, r_E)$.

1. *V is the finite set of vertices. Vertices are prepared-matching objects, and each of them is uniquely identified by an object identifier (OID).*
2. *$E \subseteq V \times V$ is the finite set of edges. Each of edges denotes the relation between two vertices.*
3. *$Lab = \{Lab_V, Lab_E\}$ is the finite constant collection of labels. The labels are strings for describing the properties of vertices and edges. Lab_V is the finite collection of vertex labels; Lab_E is the finite collection of edge labels.*
4. *$r_V \subseteq V \times Lab_V$ is a relation associating labels to verteices, i.e., r_V is the set of couples (v_i, l) such that vertex v_i is labeled by l. r_V is called vertex feature of S.*
5. *$r_E \subseteq E \times Lab_E$ is a relation associating labels to edges, i.e., r_E is the set E of triples (v_i, v_j, l) such that (v_i, v_j) is labeled by l. r_E is called edge feature of S.*
6. *$descr(S) = r_V \cup r_E$ is the set of all vertex and edge features of a schema S that completely describes the schema S.*
7. *$|V| \models n$ is the cardinality of schema S.*

3.2 Encode Schemas into Labeled Graphs

For encoding relational schemas, XML schemas, SQL views, etc. as multi-labeled graphs, we use the following rules:

1. *A vertex of graph represents the prepared matching object of schema. V is the vertex set that comprises all prepared matching objects of a schema;*

2. *The labels of a vertex are composed of properties of a prepared matching object;*

3. *An edge represents the relation between two prepared matching objects of schema. E is the edge set that comprises all relations of schema ($E \subseteq V \times V$);*

4. *The labels of one edge comprise properties of two prepared matching objects, such as is-a, part-of, etc.*

For example, at first, we show the approach how to convert the relational schema into multi-labeled graph. The elements of a relational schema comprise tables, columns, and constraints; a table contains an ordered list of columns, each of which has a type; tables and columns carry names; the constraints are specialized into primary key, unique key, non-null, or referential constraints; a referential constraint refers to two columns, one of which is a foreign key and the other is a primary key; etc. Therefore, we can obtain the multi-labeled graph of relational schema by the approach as follows:

a. The prepared matching objects are tables, columns, which constitute the vertices of multi-labeled graph;

b. The labels of vertices are composed of name of tables and columns, types of columns, and constraints of columns, such as primary key, unique key, non-null, etc.

c. Because the table contains an ordered list of columns, then the columns and their table constitute the edges of multi-labeled graph;

d. The labels of edges is is-a, etc.

In addition, for XML schema, we can use OEM, and DOM to represent it. OEM and DOM are all directed labeled graph model [10]. In section 4.2, we show an example to explain how to encode BizTallk XML schemas into the multi-labeled graphs.

4   Schema Matching

To measure the similarity of labeled graph, Solnon *et al.* [3, 16] proposed multivalent mapping, which is used to characterize the many-to-many matching between the vertices of two labeled graphs. Similarly, we introduce multivalent matching for SMP, i.e., a vertex of source schema may be associated with a set of vertices of target schema. The matching results are called multivalent correspondences.

Definition 4. If S is the source schema, T is the target schema, the matching result of two schemas is a set $m \subseteq V^S \times V^T$ that contains every matched couple $(s, t) \in V^S \times V^T$.

Multivalent correspondences are binary relationships that aiming to establish many-to-many correspondences between the vertices of two schemas.

Therefore, the schema matching problem is transformed into the multi-labeled graph matching.

4.1 Motivating Scenario

The SMP is a critical problem for interoperability in heterogeneous information sources, which plays a key role in many database applications. In this section, we introduce a real-life scenario happens in e-business to illustrate our algorithm framework.

For a multinational company, there are two subsidiary companies locate at different countries (company A in S area and company B in another T area), and the companies want to share and interoperate their customers' information by Web Service. The XML description schemas are deployed on their own XML web services. However, the XML schemas used by the company undergoes periodic changes due to the dynamic nature of its business. If do the schema matching by manual operate, it is a tiresome and costly work. Moreover, if the company A changes its customer information database structure, and the XML schema is changed synchronously, but they do not notice the company B to update its Web Service correspondingly, under this conditions, if the interoperate wants to carry out successfully, the two web agents have to automatic matching their schemas again, and need not manual acting. The automatic schema matching can improve the reliability and usability of Web services. Now, the two XML schemas are shown in Fig.1, which are based on BizTalk Schema specification, where, Schema AccountOwner S is used by company A, and Customer T is deployed by company B.

```
<Schema name="Schema S"                        <Schema name="Schema T"
   xmlns="urn:schemas-microsoft-com:xml-data">     xmlns="urn:schemas-microsoft-com:xml-data">
   <ElementType name="AccountOwner">               <ElementType name="Customer">
      <element type="Name"/>                          <element type="CFname"/>
      <element type="Address"/>                       <element type="CLname"/>
      <element type="Birthdate"/>                     <element type="CAddress"/>
      <element type="TaxExempt"/>                   </ElementType>
   </ElementType>                                   <ElementType name="CustomerAddress">
   <ElementType name="Address">                       <element type="Street"/>
      <element type="Street"/>                        <element type="City"/>
      <element type="City"/>                          <element type="Province"/>
      <element type="State"/>                         <element type="PostalCode"/>
      <element type="ZIP"/>                         </ElementType>
   </ElementType>                                 </Schema>
</Schema>
```

Fig. 1. XML schema AccountOwner S and Customer T

4.2 Multi-labeled Graph Model of Schemas

From the schemas in Fig.1, we can obtain the vertices and edges of them, which are shown in Fig.2, $V^S = \{s_1, s_2, \cdots, s_{11}\}$, $V^T = \{t_1, s_2, \cdots, t_{10}\}$.

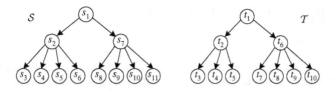

Fig. 2. Vertices and edges of S and T

By Definition 1, Table 1 shows the labels of vertices. Lab_V includes the name set Lab_{Vname}, the concept set $Lab_{Vconcept}$ or the type set Lab_{Vtype}. In the same way, Lab_E can include the labels for edges. Here, $Lab_E = \{\text{part-of}\}$.

Table 1. The labels of vertices

OID	Labels of schema S			Labels of schema T		
	Lab_{Vname}^S	$Lab_{Vconcept}^S$	Lab_{Vtype}^S	Lab_{Vname}^T	$Lab_{Vconcept}^T$	Lab_{Vtype}^T
1	Schema S	schema	Schema	Schema T	schema	Schema
2	AccountOwner	account + owner	ElementType	Customer	customer	ElementType
3	Name	name	element	CFname	first name	element
4	Address	address	element	CLname	last name	element
5	Birthdate	birthdate	element	CAddress	address	element
6	TaxExempt	tax-exempt	element	CustomerAddress	address	ElementType
7	Address	address	ElementType	Street	street	element
8	Street	street	element	City	city	element
9	City	city	element	Province	province	element
10	State	state	element	PostalCode	postal code	element
11	ZIP	ZIP	element			

Based on Fig. 2 and Table 1, we show the vertex and edge features of S and T:

1. Features of S: $descr = \{r_{V^S}, r_{E^S}\}$

$r_{V^S} = \{(s_1, \text{Schema } S), (s_1, \text{schema}), (s_1, \text{Schema});$

$\qquad (s_2, \text{AccountOwner}), (s_2, \text{account + owner}), (s_2, \text{ElementType});$

$\qquad (s_3, \text{AccountOwner.Name}), (s_3, \text{name}), (s_3, \text{element}); \ldots$

$\qquad (s_{11}, \text{Address.ZIP}), (s_{11}, \text{ZIP}), (s_{11}, \text{element})\}$

$r_{E^S} = \{(s_1, s_2, \text{part-of}), (s_2, s_3, \text{part-of}), \ldots, (s_7, s_{11}, \text{part-of})\}$

2. Features of T: $descr = \{r_{V^T}, r_{E^T}\}$

$r_{V^T} = \{(t_1, \text{Schema } T), (t_1, \text{schema}), (t_1, \text{Schema});$

$\qquad (t_2, \text{Customer}), (t_2, \text{customer}), (t_2, \text{ElementType}); \ldots$

$\qquad (t_{10}, \text{PostalCode}), (t_{10}, \text{postal code}), (t_{10}, \text{element})\};$

$r_{E^T} = \{(t_1, t_2, \text{part-of}), (t_2, t_3, \text{part-of}), \ldots, (t_6, t_{10}, \text{part-of})\}$

5 Similarity of Multi-labeled Graphs

5.1 Matching Space

By Definition 2, the matching result can be represent as a relation set m, here, we introduce an equivalent concept: matching matrix, to denote the solution of schema matching.

Definition 3. (*Matching Matrix*) If S is the source schema, T is the target schema, where, $V^S = \{s_1, s_2, \cdots, s_n\}$ and $V^T = \{t_1, t_2, \cdots, t_k\}$ denote vertex sets of S and T respectively. A matching matrix m is a $n \times k$ 0-1 matrix:

$$m = \begin{bmatrix} m_{1,1} & m_{1,2} & \cdots & m_{1,k} \\ m_{2,1} & m_{2,2} & \cdots & m_{2,k} \\ \vdots & \vdots & \cdots & \vdots \\ m_{n,1} & m_{n,2} & \cdots & m_{n,k} \end{bmatrix}, \; m_{i,j} \in \{0, 1\}, \; n = |V^S|, \; k = |V^T| \quad (1)$$

where, $m_{i,j} = 1$ denotes s_i and t_j are matched and $m_{i,j} = 0$ denotes s_i and t_j are unmatched. All the matching couples compose the result of schema matching.

While given an assignment for matching matrix, we obtain a possible matching result of two schemas. All of these mapping matrixes constitute the whole matching space.

Definition 4. (*Matching Space*) All the assignments of m (matching matrix) constitute a matching space M, also named a *mapping space*, where,

$$M := \left\{ m \; \middle| \; m_{i,j} \in \{0, 1\}, \; \begin{matrix} i \in \{1, 2, \cdots, n\} \\ j \in \{1, 2, \cdots, k\} \end{matrix} \right\} \quad (2)$$

Namely, every assignment of the matching matrix obtains a state in the matching space, and the state is a possible solution of schema matching. The scale of matching space is the number of the matching states: $|M| = 2^{n \times k}$.

While we obtain a mapping state, we can check whether this state satisfies the mapping constraints. In virtue of different labels, we discuss similarity measure of multi-labeled graphs.

5.2 Similarity with Respect to a Matching State

There are many methods to compare the similarity of two graphs, such as graph isomorphism, subgraph isomorphism, graph edit distance, maximum common subgraph, etc. Champin and Solnon [3] proposed a generic method to measure similarity of directed multi-labeled graph, which is based on graph edit distance. A schema S is described by the set $descr(S)$ of all its vertex and edge features. Hence, the similarity of two different schemas S and T depends on both the common features of $descr(S)$ and $descr(T)$, and the set of all their features. Given a matching state $m \in M$, we can calculate the common features of $descr(S)$ and $descr(T)$:

$$descr(S) \cap_m descr(T) \doteq$$

$$\left\{ (s_a, l) \in r_{V^S} \middle| \begin{array}{l} \exists m_{aj} = 1, \ (t_j, l) \in r_{V^T} \\ a \in \{1, 2, \cdots, n\}, \ j \in \{1, 2, \cdots, k\} \end{array} \right\}$$

$$\cup \left\{ (t_b, l) \in r_{V^T} \middle| \begin{array}{l} \exists m_{ib} = 1, \ (s_i, l) \in r_{V^S} \\ b \in \{1, 2, \cdots, k\}, \ i \in \{1, 2, \cdots, n\} \end{array} \right\}$$

$$\cup \left\{ (s_c, s_{c'}, l) \in r_{E^S} \middle| \begin{array}{l} \exists m_{cj} = 1, \ \exists m_{c'j'} = 1, \ (t_j, t_{j'}, l) \in r_{E^T} \\ c, \ c' \in \{1, 2, \cdots, n\}, \ c \neq c' \end{array} \right\}$$

$$\cup \left\{ (t_c, t_{c'}, l) \in r_{E^T} \middle| \begin{array}{l} \exists m_{ic} = 1, \ \exists m_{i'c'} = 1, \ (s_i, s_{i'}, l) \in r_{E^S} \\ c, \ c' \in \{1, 2, \cdots, k\}, \ c \neq c' \end{array} \right\}$$

$$(3)$$

If given a multivalent mapping m (i.e., $n{:}k$ matching), we also have to identify the set of split vertices, i.e., the set of vertices that are mapped to more than one vertex, each split vertex v being associated with the set p_v of its mapped vertices:

$$splits(m) := \left\{ (s, p_s) \middle| \begin{array}{l} s \in V^S, \ |p_s| \geq 2 \\ p_s = \left\{ t \in V^T \middle| \begin{array}{l} m_{s,t} = 1 \\ t \in \{1, 2, \cdots, k\} \end{array} \right\} \end{array} \right\}$$

$$\cup \left\{ (t, p_t) \middle| \begin{array}{l} t \in V^T, \ |p_t| \geq 2 \\ p_t = \left\{ s \in V^S \middle| \begin{array}{l} m_{s,t} = 1 \\ s \in \{1, 2, \cdots, n\} \end{array} \right\} \end{array} \right\}$$

$$(4)$$

The similarity of S and T with respect to a matching state m is then defined by:

$$sim_m(S, \ T) = \frac{f(descr(S) \cap_m descr(T)) - g(splits(m))}{f(descr(S) \cup descr(T))} \tag{5}$$

where f and g are two functions that are introduced to weigh features and splits, depending on the desired application. Here, f and g are cardinality functions:

$$f(descr(S)) = w_{name} \cdot \left| r_{V^S\,name} \right| + w_{concept} \cdot \left| r_{V^S\,concept} \right| + w_{type} \cdot \left| r_{V^S\,type} \right| + w_E \cdot \left| r_{E^S} \right| \tag{6}$$

$$g(splits(m)) = w' \cdot \left| splits(m) \right| \tag{7}$$

Finally, the maximal similarity $sim(S, \ T)$ of two schemas S and T is the greatest similarity with respect to all possible matching state:

$$sim(S, T) = \max_{m \subseteq M} \frac{f(descr(S) \cap_m descr(T)) - g(splits(m))}{f(descr(S) \cup descr(T))} \tag{8}$$

The denominator $f(descr(S) \cup descr(T))$ of Eq.8 does not depend on the matching states, which is introduced to normalize the similarity value to the 0-1 range [3].

Hence, to compute the maximum similarity between two graphs S and T, one has to find the matching state m that maximizes the score function:

$$score(S, T) = f(descr(S) \cap_m descr(T)) - g(splits(m)) \tag{9}$$

5.3 An Example

To illustrate the similarity computation, we take a matching state for example. For two schemas in Fig. 1, based on Fig. 2 and Table 1, we can obtain all the features of two schemas:

$$descr(S) \cup descr(T) = descr(S) \cup descr(T)|_{concept} \cup descr(S) \cup descr(T)|_{name}$$
$$\cup \ descr(S) \cup descr(T)|_{type} \cup descr(S) \cup descr(T)|_{edge}$$

$$f(descr(S) \cup descr(T)) = |r_{V\,name}| + 4 \cdot |r_{V\,concept}| + |r_{V\,type}| + |r_E|$$
$$= 21 + 4 \times 21 + 21 + 19 = 145$$

Remark: For Eq.6, $w_{concept} = 4$, because the semantic matching is stronger than other label matchings [17].

Suppose that there is a mapping state of S and T:

$$m_1 = \begin{bmatrix} 1 & 0 & 0 & 0 & 0 & 0 & 0 & 0 & 0 & 0 \\ 0 & 1 & 0 & 0 & 0 & 0 & 0 & 0 & 0 & 0 \\ 0 & 0 & 1 & 1 & 0 & 0 & 0 & 0 & 0 & 0 \\ 0 & 0 & 0 & 0 & 1 & 0 & 0 & 0 & 0 & 0 \\ 0 & 0 & 0 & 0 & 0 & 0 & 0 & 0 & 0 & 0 \\ 0 & 0 & 0 & 0 & 0 & 0 & 0 & 0 & 0 & 0 \\ 0 & 0 & 0 & 0 & 0 & 1 & 0 & 0 & 0 & 0 \\ 0 & 0 & 0 & 0 & 0 & 0 & 1 & 0 & 0 & 0 \\ 0 & 0 & 0 & 0 & 0 & 0 & 0 & 1 & 0 & 0 \\ 0 & 0 & 0 & 0 & 0 & 0 & 0 & 0 & 1 & 0 \\ 0 & 0 & 0 & 0 & 0 & 0 & 0 & 0 & 0 & 1 \end{bmatrix}$$

i.e., $m_1 = \{(s_1, t_1), (s_2, t_2), (s_3, t_3), (s_3, t_4), (s_4, t_5), (s_7, t_6), (s_8, t_7), (s_9, t_8), (s_{10}, t_9), (s_{11}, t_{10})\}$.

1. We compare the name labels of schemas to obtain the name features. There are many methods to measure similarity of names [4, 9, 14]. For example we use the Levenshtein distance (i.e., edit distance) to compare the name string of vertices [5], $sim_{name}(s_1, t_1) = 0.875$. Suppose the threshold of name matching $th_{name} = 0.4$, the name common features of $descr(S)$ and $descr(T)$:

$descr(S) \cap_{m_1} descr(T)|_{name} = \{(s_1,$ Schema $S), (s_2,$ AccountOwner$), (s_3,$ AccountOwner.Name$), (s_4,$ AccountOwner.Address$), (s_7,$ Address$), (s_8,$ Address.Street$), (s_9,$ Address.City$), (t_1,$ Schema $T), (t_2,$ Customer$), (t_3,$ Customer.Cfname$), (t_4,$ Customer.Clname$), (t_5,$ Customer.CAddress$) (t_6,$ CustomerAddress$), (t_7,$ CustomerAddress.Street$), (t_8,$ CustomerAddress.City$)\}$

2. To obtain the common concept features, we need compare the concept label of two vertices. We can use some semantic distances to compare similarity of two con-

cepts [13], such as *hso*, *wup*, *res*, *lin*, and *jcn*, etc. By *wup*, $sim_{concept}(s_2, t_2) = 0.67$. If $th_{concept} = 0.55$, for m_1, the intersection features of $descr(S)$ and $descr(T)$:

$descr(S) \cap_{m_1} descr(T)|_{concept} = \{(s_1,$ schema$), (s_2,$ account + owner$), (s_3,$ name$), (s_4,$ address$), (s_7,$ address$), (s_8,$ street$), (s_9,$ city$), (s_{10},$ state$), (s_{11},$ ZIP$), (t_1,$ schema$), (t_2,$ customer$), (t_3,$ first name$), (t_4,$ last name$), (t_5,$ address$) (t_6,$ address$), (t_7,$ street$), (t_8,$ city$), (t_9,$ province$), (t_{10},$ postal code$)\}$

3. The common type labels of two schemas:

$descr(S) \cap_{m_1} descr(T)|_{type} = \{(s_1,$ Schema$), (s_2,$ ElementType$), (s_3,$ element$), (s_4,$ element$), (s_7,$ ElementType$), (s_8,$ element$), (s_9,$ element$), (s_{10},$ element$), (s_{11},$ element$), (t_1,$ Schema$), (t_2,$ ElementType$), (t_3,$ element$), (t_4,$ element$), (t_5,$ element$) (t_6,$ ElementType$), (t_7,$ element$), (t_8,$ element$), (t_9,$ element$), (t_{10},$ element$)\}$

4. If we concern type features of the schemas, the intersection features of $descr(S)$ and $descr(T)$ are shown as follows:

$descr(S) \cap_{m_1} descr(T)|_{edge} = \{(s_1, s_2,$ part-of$), (s_2, s_3,$ part-of$), (s_2, s_4,$ part-of$), (s_1, s_7,$ part-of$), (s_7, s_8,$ part-of$), (s_7, s_9,$ part-of$), (s_7, s_{10},$ part-of$), (s_7, s_{11},$ part-of$), (t_1, t_2,$ part-of$), (t_2, t_3,$ part-of$), (t_2, t_4,$ part-of$), (t_2, t_5,$ part-of$), (t_1, t_6,$ part-of$), (t_6, t_7,$ part-of$), (t_6, t_8,$ part-of$), (t_6, t_9,$ part-of$), (t_6, t_{10},$ part-of$)\}$

5. If we use all of the vertex and edge labels of schemas together, such as names, concepts, types, and edge labels, we can get the intersection features of $descr(S)$ and $descr(T)$ as follows:

$$descr(S) \cap_{m_1} descr(T) =$$
$$descr(S) \cap_{m_1} descr(T)|_{concept} \cup descr(S) \cap_{m_1} descr(T)|_{name} \cup$$
$$descr(S) \cap_{m_1} descr(T)|_{type} \cup descr(S) \cap_{m_1} descr(T)|_{edge}$$
$$f(descr(S) \cap_{m_1} descr(T)) = 15 + 4 \times 19 + 19 + 17 = 127$$

6. The matching state m_1 has the following splits:

$$splits(m_1) = \{(s_3, \{t_3, t_4\})\} \quad g(splits(m_1)) = | splits(m) | = 3$$

7. The score and similarity of two schemas S and T based on m_1 is:

$$score_{m_1}(S, T) = 127 - 3 = 124 \quad sim_{m_1}(S, T) = 124/145 = 0.855$$

6 Greedy Algorithm

6.1 Algorithm Description

It is well known that, the greedy strategy is a fundamental technique to solve NP-hard problem. Since the labeled graph matching is a classic NP-hard optimization problem, the greedy strategy can apply naturally to SMP. Therefore, we design a greedy algorithm to find the matching results. The algorithm is shown in Fig. 3.

```
function Greedy(S, T) return a mapping m
begin
    m_cand ← V^S × V^T ; m ← 0 ; m' ← 0 ; m" ← 0 ; m_best ← 0 ;
    loop
        score_best ← score(m) ;
        m' ← m_cand − m ; m" ← m ; cand ← ∅ ;
        for i = 1, i < |V^S|, i ++
            for j = 1, j < |V^T|, j ++
                if m'_{i,j} = 1 and score(m" | m"_{i,j} ← 1) is maximal then
                    cand ← cand ∪ {(s_i, t_j)} ;
                end if
            end for
        end for
        cand' ← {(s_i, t_j) ∈ cand | f(look_ahead(s_i, t_j)) is maximal}
        where , look_ahead(s_i, t_j) =
                {(s_i, s, l) ∈ r_{E^S} | ∃t ∈ V^T, (t_j, t, l) ∈ r_{E^T}} ∪
                {(t_j, t, l) ∈ r_{E^T} | ∃s ∈ V^S, (s_i, s, l) ∈ r_{E^S}} ∪
                {(s, s_i, l) ∈ r_{E^S} | ∃t ∈ V^T, (t, t_j, l) ∈ r_{E^T}} ∪
                {(t, t_j, l) ∈ r_{E^T} | ∃s ∈ V^S, (s, s_i, l) ∈ r_{E^S}} −
                descr(S) ∩_{m∪{(s_i, t_j)}} descr(T)

        exit loop when ∀(s_i, t_j) ∈ cand' ,
            score(m" | m"_{i,j} ← 1) ≤ score(m") , and look_ahead(s_i, t_j) = ∅ ;
            choose randomly one couple ∀(s_i, t_j) ∈ cand' ;
            let m_{i,j} ← 1 ;
            if score(m) > score(m_best) then m_best ← m
    end loop
    return m_best ;
end
```

Fig. 3. Greedy algorithm for schema matching

The basic greedy strategy of our algorithm has been first proposed in [3]: iteratively pick the couple that most increase the score function and has the greatest looked-ahead common edge features. The algorithm stops iterating when every couple neither directly increases the score function nor has looked-ahead common edge features.

For example, we show the matching process of two schemas S and T. At the beginning, the current mapping m is a zero matrix. The possible matching set: $m_{cand} = V^S × V^T$.

During the first iteration, the set of couples $cand$ that most increase the score function contains (s_1, t_1), (s_2, t_2), (s_3, t_3), (s_3, t_4), (s_4, t_5), (s_7, t_6), (s_8, t_7), and (s_9, t_8), whose scores all equal to 6+6 (e.g. $|r_{V^S}| + |r_{V^T}|$). Here, (s_7, t_6) has 5+5 potential common edge features, so that $look\_ahead(s_7, t_6) = 10$, other candidates all have a smaller number of potential common edge features. Hence, $cand' = \{(s_7, t_6)\}$, the greedy algorithm will obtain $m_{7,6} = 1$. At the second iteration, $cand$ will contain (s_1, t_1), (s_8, t_7), and (s_9, t_8), which increase the score function of 7+7. $cand'$ will only contain (s_1, t_1) as it has more potential common edge features (1+1=2) than other couples (0). Hence, the next couple to enter the mapping will be (s_1, t_1), i.e., $m_{1,1} = 1$. At the third iteration, *cand* will contain (s_2, t_2), (s_8, t_7), and (s_9, t_8), which increases the score function of 7+7. *cand'* will contain (s_2, t_2) as it has more potential common edge features ($look\_ahead(s_2, t_2) = 7$) than other couples. At the fourth iteration, *cand* and *cand'* will contain (s_3, t_3), (s_3, t_4), (s_4, t_5), (s_8, t_7), and (s_9, t_8), because those matched couples increase the score function of 7+7 and all have zero common edge feature. Now, the algorithm selects couple randomly, suppose that the couple $m_{3,3} = 1$. At the fifth iteration, *cand* and *cand'* will contain (s_4, t_5), (s_8, t_7), and (s_9, t_8), suppose (s_4, t_5) is the next couple that enter m_{best}. At the sixth and seventh iteration, we will obtain $m_{8,7} = 1$ and $m_{9,8} = 1$, because (s_8, t_7) and (s_9, t_8) increase the score function of 7+7. At the eighth and ninth iteration, the algorithm will obtain $m_{10,9} = 1$ and $m_{11,10} = 1$ because (s_{10}, t_9) and (s_{11}, t_{10}) increase the score function of 6+6. At the tenth iteration, since (s_3, t_4) increases the score function of 3+4 and other couples have fewer scores, we will obtain $m_{3,4} = 1$. Now, the algorithm stops iterating because the rest couples neither directly increase the score function nor have looked-ahead common edge features.[1]

After ten iterations, we will obtain the matching state $m_{best} = m_1$, which is the best matching state of S and T. The algorithm has been implemented in Visual C++. For this example, the algorithm outputs the matching result by ten iterations and cost average 0.10 sec. (Experiment settings: P4 2.4G, Window 2000, 256M DDR).

6.2 Discussion

If we do not use extended knowledge about schemas, i.e., we do not use concepts of schemas to match, and only use name and type labels, we will obtain the matching result: $m_2 = \{(s_1, t_1), (s_2, t_2), (s_3, t_3), (s_4, t_5), (s_5, t_4), (s_7, t_6), (s_8, t_7), (s_9, t_8), (s_{10}, t_{10})\}$.

The optimization function (Eq.8) is very important to achieve the optimal matching result. To be more specific, for functions f and g, which impact the matching result directly. First, for function f, the concept feature has greater weight than name and type feature. If the concepts of two vertices are matchable, then the matching probability of two vertices is higher than only name or type matchable. For example, if $w_{concept} = 4$, $w' = 1$, the greedy algorithm will obtain the couples (s_3, t_3) and (s_3, t_4), however, if $w_{concept} \leq 2$, $w' = 1$, the algorithm cannot obtain both (s_3, t_3) and (s_3, t_4), and will obtain (s_5, t_4).[2] Second, the function g determines the number of multivalent mappings. The greater weight of g is, the more difficult to obtain multivalent mapping. For example, if $w_{concept} = 4$, $w' = 3$, then the algorithm cannot obtain many-to-many matching, and will obtain one-to-one mapping result.[3]

---

[1] We can see that the greedy matching can achieve many-to-many matching, because in m_1, $m_{3,3}=1$ and $m_{3,4}=1$.

[2] The matching results will be $m_3 = \{(s_1, t_1), (s_2, t_2), \mathbf{(s_3, t_3)}, (s_4, t_5), \mathbf{(s_5, t_3)}, (s_7, t_6), (s_8, t_7), (s_9, t_8), (s_{10}, t_9), (s_{11}, t_{10})\}$ or $m_4 = \{(s_1, t_1), (s_2, t_2), \mathbf{(s_3, t_4)}, (s_4, t_5), \mathbf{(s_5, t_3)}, (s_7, t_6), (s_8, t_7), (s_9, t_8), (s_{10}, t_9), (s_{11}, t_{10})\}$, etc.

[3] The matching results will be $m_5 = \{(s_1, t_1), (s_2, t_2), (s_3, t_3), (s_4, t_5), (s_7, t_6), (s_8, t_7), (s_9, t_8), (s_{10}, t_9), (s_{11}, t_{10})\}$ or $m_6 = \{(s_1, t_1), (s_2, t_2), (s_3, t_4), (s_4, t_5), (s_7, t_6), (s_8, t_7), (s_9, t_8), (s_{10}, t_9), (s_{11}, t_{10})\}$.

For this greedy algorithm, the computations of the f function has a polynomial time complexity of $O((|V^S|\times|V^T|)^2)$; g functions has a linear time complexities with respect to the size of the schemas $O(\text{Max}(|V^S|,|V^T|)$; The computation of "look ahead" sets has a polynomial time complexity of $O(|V^S|\times|V^T|)$, and can be computed in an incremental way [3]. Therefore, the greedy algorithm has a polynomial time complexity of $O((|V^S|\times|V^T|)^2)$.

We also use four real-life schemas that are provided in [10] to evaluate our algorithm: Purchase order, Biztalk, University (XML), and Property schemas. The average Precision is 98.3%, and the average Recall is 96.6%. To compare with Similarity Flooding, the search time of greedy algorithm is less than SF, and the average "accurate" is higher than SF.

7   Conclusion and Future Work

In this paper, we propose an internal schema model: multi-labeled directed graph, where vertices and edges may have more than one label. Then, we transform SMP into a labeled graph matching problem. We study a similarity measure on such graphs, and design a greedy algorithm to obtain the feasible matching results. The experimental results confirm that the greedy algorithm is an effective matching method.

By tuning the parameters of optimization function, the matching algorithm can obtain different matching result. To obtain more accurate matching result, we will design some meta-heuristic strategies to tune the weights of functions during the search process. Therefore, we can integrate all the possible matching methods to find an optimal matching state. In the near future, we also can use other search methods to refine the matching result based on greedy matching algorithm, such as local search, genetic algorithm, and approximate matching methods, etc. Based on these methods, we will design fast algorithms for large-scale schema matching.

Acknowledgment

This work was supported by the National 973 Information Technology and High-Performance Software Program of China under Grant No.G1998030408.

References

1. Berlin, J., Motro, A.: Autoplex: Automated Discovery of Content for Virtual Databases. CoopIS 2001, LNCS 2172:108-122.
2. Bouquet, P., Magnini, B., Serafini, L., Zanobini, S.: A SAT-Based Algorithm for Context Matching. LNAI 2680: 66-79.
3. Champin, P.-A., Solnon, C.: Measuring the similarity of labeled graphs. Springer-Verlag, ICCBR 2003, LNAI 2689: 80–95.
4. Cohen, W. W., Ravikumar, P., Fienberg, S. E.: A Comparison of String Distance Metrics for Name-Matching Tasks. 2003, IJCAI-03: 3-78.

5. Do, H. H., Rahm, E.: COMA - A system for flexible combination of schema matching approaches. VLDB 2002.
6. Do, H. H., Melnik, S., Rahm, E.: Comparison of schema matching evaluations. Web Databases and Web Services 2002, LNCS 2593: 221–237.
7. Doan, A., Domingos, P., Halevy, A.: Learning to Match the Schemas of Data Sources: A Multistrategy Approach. Machine Learning. Kluwer Academic Publishers Manufactured in The Netherlands, 2003 (50):279-301.
8. Giunchiglia, F., Shvaiko, P., Yatskevich, M.: S-Match: An algorithm and an implementation of semantic matching. In Proceedings of ESWS'04.
9. Madhavan, J., Bernstein, P. A., Rahm, E.: Generic Schema Matching with Cupid. 27th VLDB Conference.
10. Melnik, S.: Generic model management - concepts and algorithms, Springer, 2004, LNCS 2967.
11. Melnik, S., Garcia-Molina, H., Rahm, E.: Similarity Flooding: A Versatile Graph Matching Algorithm. ICDE 2002
12. Miller, R. J., Haas, L.M., Hernández, M.A.: Clio: Schema Mapping as Query Discovery. Proc. VLDB 2000.
13. Pedersen, T., Patwardhan, S., Patwardhan, S.: WordNet::Similarity - Measuring the Relatedness of Concepts. Proceedings of the Nineteenth National Conference on Artificial Intelligence, 2004, San Jose, CA.
14. Rahm, E., Bernstein, P. A.: On matching schemas automatically. Microsoft Research, Redmon, WA. Technical Report MSR-TR-2001-17, 2001.
15. Rahm, E., Bernstein, P. A.: A survey of approaches to automatic schema matching, The VLDB Journal, 2001(10): 334-350.
16. S. Sorlin, C. Solnon.: Reactive Tabu Search for Measuring Graph Similarity. GbRPR 2005: 172-182
17. Zhang, Z., Che, H. Y., Shi, P. F., Sun, Y., Gu, J.: An algebraic framework for schema matching. WAIM 2005, LNCS 3739.

Dynamic Hybrid DVE Architecture

Yanhua Wu, Yunze Cai, and Xiaoming Xu

Dept. of Compute Science, Shanghai Jiaotong University,
Shanghai 200030, P.R. China
{wyhross, yzcai, xmx}@sjtu.edu.cn

Abstract. A dynamic hybrid DVE architecture is presented in this paper. It's an extension of client-server architecture. It combines the advantages of client-server architecture and peer-to-peer architecture. By utilizing users' hardware resources system can support more users. Compaired with the traditional multi-server architecture it holds lower system cost. Theory analysis and simulation results prove its correctness and validity. The flaws of this architecture are also checked and the settlement is discussed.

1 Introduction

With the development of network technology and 3D image accelerate technology distributed virtual environment (DVE) has attracted more and more attention in recent years. One possible definition of DVE is given by Singhal and Zyda: "...a software system in which multiple users interact with each other in real time, even though those users may be located around the world" [1]. There are many DVE application systems have been developed during the past decade in many fields such as: military simulation [2], 3D on-line game [3][4], interactive e-learning [5], electronic business [6], etc.

There are mainly two architectures adopted by DVE system: client-server architecture [7] and peer-to-peer architecture [8], shown as Fig.1 and Fig.2.

Peer-to-peer architecture does not need expensive center server any more, which can reduce the system cost effectively. However to a peer-to-peer system, N users associated with o(N^2) message packets appearing in the network in a refresh cycle, which cause the network transmission congestion and high delay. It will become more serious with the increasing of user number.

It is probably true that the client-server architecture is more commonly nowadays. The architecture is very simple to implement. At the same time the center server gives the commerce companies an absolutely control power to the whole system, which will guarantees the company's benefits. With this architecture a client sends an update packet to the server, which is then propagated it to other clients. All communications pass the server, which cause both a bottleneck and a single point failure. That is to say a single center server hardly support a large number of users.

To solve this problem, as an amendment of client-server architecture, multi-server architecture is proposed in [9], shown as Fig.3. Its main idea is paralleling

S. Grumbach, L. Siu, and V. Vianu (Eds.): ASIAN 2005, LNCS 3818, pp. 104–112, 2005.

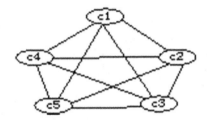

Fig. 1. Peer-to-Peer Architecture

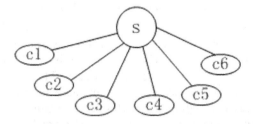

Fig. 2. Client-Server Architecture

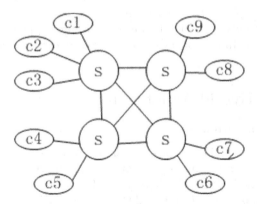

Fig. 3. Multi-server Architecture

a group of servers to support large use scale. Based on this architecture several load balance algorithms are proposed in [10][11][12][13]. Though this architecture can offer unlimited scalability for DVE system, it still exits a lack that a large number of expensive servers are needed, which lead to high cost. At the same time the static server topology of Multi-server architecture is not suitable for the dynamic user network topology.

Based on this problems we present dynamic hybrid architecture (DHA) in this paper, shown as Fig.4. The main idea of DHA is borrowing idea from peer-to-peer and merging it into client-sever architecture, which can be described as fellow: in a client-server DVE system, when its user scale gets to a predefined threshold a

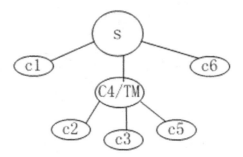

Fig. 4. Dynamic Hybrid Architecture

few users are selected with some predefined rules to work as temp-servers(TM). A certain number of users will be chosen to migrate to TM from center server. To the migrating users the TM acts as a server. The migrating users don't communicate directly with the center server any more and they just connect with TMs. TM technology can reduce the center server's bandwidth and computing load effectively while need not add any expensive servers. For the client's dynamic character, TMs are selected dynamically which adapt to the dynamic of the system topology.The rest of our paper is organized as follows: section II gives out the theory analysis of DHA. In section III we do some simulation experiments basing on our self-developed simulation software prototype and the experiment results is discussed. In section IV we draw the conclusion and talk about the future works.

2   Dynamic Hybrid Architecture

2.1   Architecture Analysis

DHA is extended from the client-server architecture. The network topology in this system changes from time to time at the running time. At the initial state when the user scale is small the system equal client-server architecture. When user increases to a predefined threshold the architecture will change dynamically to adapt the problem: firstly a user is selected as a temp-server (TM) with a predefined rule. Secondly the center server migrates a few users to it. Once this process finish the TM and its 'children' make up of a group. TM manages all its children and substitutes all the child clients to communicate with server. When TM receives its children's message packets, it aggregates them into a large packet and forwards it to center server. When the server's message packet arrives the TM broadcasts it to all its children. From the point of sever the whole group is equal to a single user. So the user directly linked to server is reduced effectively, which saves center server's computer and bandwidth resource. However TM is a free client in nature so it can exit randomly. When a TM exits system its children will have to link to center server again and become center server's direct users. This process may cause a pulse on the server's load curve in some degree. This problem will be discussed detailed in section IV.

2.2 System Model

Firstly, we define N_1 as the number of user which are directly linked to center server but are not include TMs. We define m as the number of TM and N_s as the total number of users which are linked directly to center server(include TMs). Then we can easily get formula (1):

$$N_s = N_1 + m \quad (1)$$

For example in Fig.4: $N_1=2$, $m=1$ and $N_s=3$.

Secondly we define N as the total user number in the system, γ_i as the user number of the ith TM. Then we can get the formula (2);

$$N = N_s + \sum_{i=N_s+1}^{N_s+m} \gamma_i \quad (2)$$

To simplify the model if a user is not a TM we ignore center server's load caused by its exiting act in a refresh cycle. We define L_s as the total load of center server in a refresh cycle, L_i as the server's load caused by user i, p_i as the exiting probability of user i in a refresh cycle, δ as server's load caused by migrating a user from TM to center server. Basing on DHA we can get formula (1):

$$L_s = \sum_{i=1}^{N_s} L_i(1 - P_i) + \sum_{i=N_s+1}^{N_s+m} P_i \gamma_i \delta \quad (1)$$

Basing on client-server architecture we can get formula (2):

$$L_s = \sum_{i=1}^{N} L_i(1 - P_i) \quad (2)$$

Formula (2) can be rewritten as:

$$L_s = \sum_{i=1}^{N_s} L_i(1 - P_i) + \sum_{i=N_s+1}^{N} L_i(1 - P_i) \quad (3)$$

We define θ be the server load difference between DHA and client-server architecture. From (1) and (3) we can get (4).

$$\theta = \sum_{i=N_s+1}^{N} L_i(1 - P_i) - \sum_{i=N_s+1}^{N_s+m} P_i \gamma_i \delta \quad (4)$$

As we all know the probability of a user exiting system in a short cycle time is very small. That is mean: $P_i \ll 1$, even $P_i \approx 0$. So formula (4) can be rewritten as:

$$\theta \approx \sum_{i=N_s+1}^{N} L_i(1 - P_i) \quad (5)$$

Not lost generality, we think all the users have the same leaving probability marked as P. We also think all the users, which are linked to the center server, lead to the same server load when they run well in system, which is defined as L.

So formula (5) can be rewritten as:

$$\theta \approx L(1 - P)(N - N_s) \tag{6}$$

From formula (1), (2), (6) we can get:

$$\theta \approx L(1 - P) \sum_{N_s+1}^{N_s+m} \gamma_i \tag{7}$$

We know that $\sum_{N_s+1}^{N_s+m} \gamma_i$ is the sum of TMs' children users. Because $L(1 - P)$ is a constant we can get: $\theta \propto \sum_{N_s+1}^{N_s+m} \gamma_i$ (10)

From formula (10) we can find that the decreased value of center server's load is in direct proportion to the sum of TMs' child user number.

3   Simulation Experiments

We have developed a simulation program prototype in c++ and done a group simulation experiments. We logged simulation results and gave out the discussion. Fig.5 list a snapshot of our program prototype, in which the big ball denotes TM and the smell balls around it with the same color denotes its child users.

3.1   Simulation Process

Not lose generality we set up a special simulation process. In the process the system's user added linearly form 0 to 50 and then reduced linearly from 50 to 0, shown as Fig.6.

3.2   Center Server Load

Center server load can be denoted as the packet number the server received in a synchronization period. Variable φ is defined as the total packet number the center server receives and sends in a period. Variable η is defined as the user threshold of the center server. If $N_s¿\eta$ we think the server is overload and the over users will be migrated to an unsaturated TM. Term β is defined as max user scale a TM can support. If $\gamma = \beta$ we think the TM is saturated or otherwise we think it's unsaturated. We defined a triplet V= $[\eta, \beta, \varphi]$ to denote our simulation experiments. To simplify analyses TM is selected randomly. With the define of triplet we can easily find that client-server architecture is a special case of DHA. It can be described with $V_1=[\infty, 0, \varphi]$.

We chose another two cases of DHA architecture: $V_2=[17, 3, \varphi]$, $V_3=[11, 5, \varphi]$. Basing on the simulation process talked above we have done simulation experiments with the three cases and logged φ. Simulation results are shown

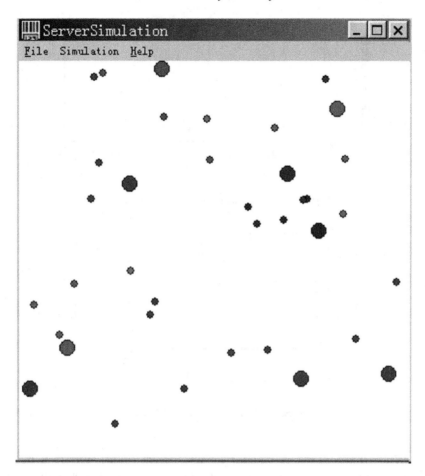

Fig. 5. A snapshot of simulation prototype

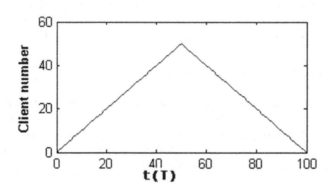

Fig. 6. User number change process

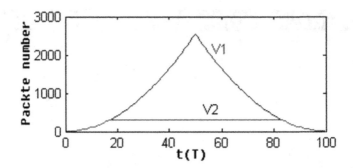

Fig. 7. Server's packet number curves:V_1,V_2

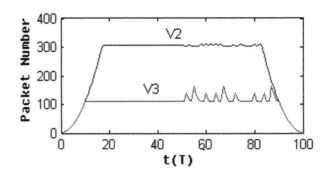

Fig. 8. Server's packet number curves:V_2,V_3

as Fig.7 and Fig.8. Let's talk about the experiment results. Firstly If $N = \eta\beta$ we think center server is saturated. $N¿\eta\beta$ marks the overload of center server. Considering the process we have talked above we know that center server is not overload in the whole simulation process. From Fig.7 we can easily find V_2 holds a lower server load than V_1. That's means even$\beta = 2$ the DHA can reduce the center server's load remarkably compared to client-server architecture.

3.3   TM Exiting Impact

As we all know a TM is just a user in nature. So it can exit system at any time. In our strategy if a TM exits its children will be migrated to center server. Some interactive message packets need to be sent among TM, users and center server, which increases center server's load. We define$\chi_i$as the increasing load of center server when TM_iexits system. From formula (1) we can get:

$$\chi_i \quad = \quad P_i\gamma_i\delta. \tag{8}$$

As we all know the exiting probability of TM is a stochastic variable. It depends on user's behavior character. We don't discuss its influence here. As to

δ it is determined by an objective factor -system interactive communicate model. It can't be changed as the programmer's will. So we ignore it here yet. We pay most our attention to the effect of γ_i-TM's children number. For$\gamma_i \le \beta$ we useβ instead γ_i to study its influence onχ_i.

Firstly we can find form Fig.8 that there are a few pulses in the tails of the two curves. As we have discussed above they are caused by the exiting acts of TM. An overload of center server may appear when a TM's children migrated to it and a new TM must be selected and the redundant users will be migrated to the new TM. This progress adds the server's communicate and compute load.

Secondly we can find form Fig.8 that the pulse of curve V_3 is higher than curve V_2. It comes form the difference ofβ-the TM's children scale. Because$\beta_{v_3}=$ 5 so there are total 5 children migrate to center server when a saturate TM leave the system. However$\beta_{v_2}=3$ so the migrating users number is only 3 in V_2. So the V_3's pulse is higher thanV_2.

4   Conclusion and Future Works

The dynamic hybrid architecture has more advantages than the traditional client-server architecture and multi-server architecture, which is certified by the theory analysis and simulation results. It can be looked as an extension of traditional client-server architecture. DHA can supports greater user scale comparing to client-server architecture and lower cost comparing to multi-server architecture. Big group size can reduce the server load effectively but causes the big disturb impulse. So to a system designer a proper tradeoff must be taken between them.

In the future work we will pay attention to the TM's exiting behavior study. For the unstableness of TM a good TM select rule can reduce its negative effect on server load. Children migrating strategy after a TM exiting is another question for the future.

Acknowledgements

This work is supported by the National Key Fundamental Research Program of China (2002cb312200), and in part by the National High Technology Research and Development Program of China (2002AA412010) and the Natural Science Foundation of China (60174038).

References

1. S.Singhal and M.Zyda, "Network Virtual Environments: Design and Iplementation", Addison-Wesley, (1999).
2. D.C.Miller, J.A.Thorpe. "SIMNET: The advent of simulator networking". Proceedings of the IEEE, 83(6): 1114-1123. August (1995).
3. M.Abrash. "Quake's game engine: The big picture". Dr.Dobb's. Journal.Spring. (1997).

4. Michael Lewis and Jeffrey Jacboson. "Game Engines in Scientific Research". Communication of the ACM. Vol 45,N1, January (2002)
5. Tohei Nitta, Kazuhiro Fujita, Sachio Cono. "An Application of Distributed Virtual Environment To Foreign Language". Kansas City, Missouri. IEEE Education Society. October (2000).
6. Jun Zhang, Fengsen Li, Hua Li. "Multi-user Shared Virtual Reality in the Exhibition of Chinese Nationalities-Virtual Museum of Chinese Nationalities". Computer Supported Cooperative Work in Design,The Sixth International Conference on, (2001) ,P:83 – 88
7. Larocque, J. "Client-server trends". Spectrum, IEEE, Volume: 31 , Issue: 4 , P:48 – 50, April (1994)
8. Schollmeier. R. "A definition of peer-to-peer networking for the classification of peer-to-peer architectures and applications". Peer-to-Peer Computing,2001. Proceedings. Aug. (2001), p: 27-29
9. W.Cai,p.Xavier,S.Turnr and B.S.Lee, "A Scalable Architecture to Support Interactive Games on the Internet", Proc. of the 16th workshop on Parallel and Distributed Simulation, May (2002)P: 60-67
10. J.C.S. Lui, M.F.Chan. "An Efficient Partitioning Algorithm for Distributed Virtual Environment systems". IEEE Transactions on parallel and distributed systems. Vol.12, No 3, March (2002).
11. Ta nguyen Binh Duong, Suiping Zhou, "A Dynamic Load Sharing Algorithm for Massively Multiplayer Online games". Networks, 2003. ICON2003. The 11th IEEE International Conference on, 28 Sept.-1 Oct. (2003), P: 131 - 136
12. R.Lau, B.Ng, Antonio Si, Frederick Li. "Adoptive Partitioning for multi-Server Distributed virtual Environments". Proceedings of the ACM International Multimedia Conference and Exhibition, (2002), P: 271-274
13. G.Shivaratri, P. Krueger and M. Singhal, "Load Distributing for Locally Distributed Systems", IEEE Computer, 25(2), December (1992)P: 33-44

ACB-R: An Adaptive Clustering-Based Data Replication Algorithm on a P2P Data-Store*

Junhu Zhang, Dongqing Yang, and Shiwei Tang

Department of Computer Science,
Peking University, Beijing, China 100871
Phone: 861062755440, Fax: 861062755822
jhzhang@db.pku.edu.cn, {dqyang, tsw}@pku.edu.cn

Abstract. Replication on geographically distributed, unreliable, P2P interconnecting nodes can offer high data availability and low network latency for replica access. The challenge is how to take good control of the number of replicas and their distribution over well-chosen nodes to get a good replica access performance. We observe that, there exists such a *logical node cluster overlay* over any P2P data-store's underlying network topology that the replica transmission delay of *inter-cluster* is much greater than that of *intra-cluster* because of geographical distance or bandwidth sharing between nodes in different *clusters*. Based on *nodes-clustering*, we propose a decentralized algorithm *ACB-R* to direct the data replication, which can adapt dynamically to the changing replica access patterns or network topologies. The experiment shows that *ACB-R* can benefit much of the access requests at the price of negligible *intra-cluster* replica transmission and consequently achieves a good average replica access performance.

1 Introduction

In P2P data-stores([1, 2, 3, 4, 5]), data objects are replicated and distributed on a number of P2P cooperating nodes. As depicted in Fig. 1(a), Clients and nodes of a P2P data-store are both distributed geographically, where a client can connect to any node and requests any data object in the P2P data-store no matter whether a replica of the data object is stored locally or not. When no replica of the data object is stored locally on the node connected by the client, the node has to get a replica of the data object from the node having a replica of the data object stored, which will pose extra replica transmission delay to the replica access.

We observe that, there exists the *logical node cluster overlay*(see Fig. 1(a)) over any P2P data-store's underlying network topology, which divides the replica transmission on a P2P data-store into two classes:

* This work is supported by the NKBRSF of China (973) under grant No.G1999032705, the National '863' High-Tech Program of China under grant No. 2002AA444140.

S. Grumbach, L. Siu, and V. Vianu (Eds.): ASIAN 2005, LNCS 3818, pp. 113–126, 2005.

Class 1. The replica transmission of *iter-cluster* — the replica transmission between two nodes in different clusters respectively.

Class 2. The replica transmission of *intra-cluster* — the replica transmission between two nodes in a same cluster.

As outlined in Fig. 1(b), there exists such a *logical node cluster overlay* over any P2P data-store's underlying network topology that the replica transmission delay of *inter-cluster* is much greater than that of *intra-cluster* because of geographical distance or bandwidth sharing between nodes in different *clusters*.

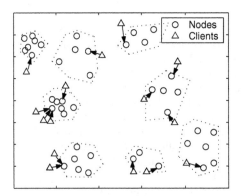
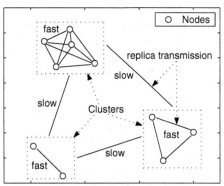

(a) Clients request data replica to nodes on a P2P data-store.(the dotted polygons suggest a possible *logical node cluster overlay*)

(b) The replica transmission of *inter-cluster* run much slower than that of *intra-cluster* because of geographical distance or bandwidth sharing between nodes in different *clusters*

Fig. 1. Characteristics of *inter-cluster* vs. *intra-cluster* of a *logical node cluster overlay* on a P2P data-store

We take good advantage of the characteristics of *inter-cluster* vs. *intra-cluster* to propose *ACB-R*, an adaptive clustering-based data replication algorithm on a P2P data-store.

The rest of this paper is organized as follows. Section 2 presents the design of our *ACB-R* — the initiation and dynamic maintenance of the node cluster overlay, and the adaptive data replication on the clusters. In Section 3, we compare the replica access performance of *ACB-R* with other two dynamic replication algorithms in an emulated P2P environment. We present related work in Section 4 and make conclusion in Section 5.

2   The Design of *ACB-R*

In the following, we propose *ACB-R* to direct the initiation and maintenance of the above node cluster overlay and the replica redistribution on clusters, for getting a good replica access performance by decreasing the amount of *inter-cluster* replica transmission delay as possible as it can. *ACB-R* is composed of two crucial *parallel-executed* procedures — *Nodes-clustering* and *Replica-redistributing* (serviced by *Nodes-clustering*), which are described as follows.

2.1   Nodes-Clustering Procedure

As the P2P data-store's underlying network topology is always changing because 1)Any node may request its adding into or leaving from a cluster at any time; 2)Any node in a cluster may fail at any time; 3)The replica transmission delay of *inter-cluster* or *intra-cluster* may vary due to the network congestion or node overburden, *Nodes-clustering* is designed to initiate and maintain the node cluster overlay accordingly, which is directed by the characteristics of the two classes of replica transmission, *inter-cluster* versus *intra-cluster*, of a *logical node cluster overlay* on a P2P data-store.

Assume,

- $S = \{s_1, s_2, \cdots, s_n\} \triangleq$ the nodes-set of a P2P data-store.
- $\mathbb{C}_S = \{C_1, C_2, \cdots, C_m\} \triangleq$ the logical node cluster overlay on S. It should be noticed that $\mathbb{C}_S$ is a division on S, and $S = C_1 \bigcup C_2 \bigcup \cdots \bigcup C_m$ as well.
- $delay(s_i, s_j) \triangleq$ the replica transmission delay per kilobyte between the node s_i and s_j, for $s_i \neq s_j \in S$.
- $intraDelay(c_k) \triangleq \max\{delay(s_i, s_j) \,|\, \forall s_i, s_j \in c_k\}$, for $c_k \in \mathbb{C}_S$.
- $interDelay(c_i, c_j) \triangleq \max\{delay(s_i, s_j) \,|\, \forall s_i \in c_i, \forall s_j \in c_j\}$, for $c_i \neq c_j \in \mathbb{C}_S$.
- $\theta = \max_{1 \leqslant k \leqslant m} intraDelay(c_k) \triangleq$ the *intra-cluster* replica transmission delay per kilobyte.
- $\alpha = \min_{1 \leqslant i \neq j \leqslant m} interDelay(c_i, c_j) \triangleq$ the *inter-cluster* replica transmission delay per kilobyte.

Due to the geographical distance or bandwidth sharing between nodes in different *clusters*, the *inter-cluster* replica transmission delay is much greater than the *intra-cluster* replica transmission delay, that is, $\alpha \gg \theta$.

We call the above inequation the **Clustering Principle**, which is the principle for initiating and maintaining dynamically the node cluster overlay on a P2P data-store, based on which, we propose the procedure *getClusters* to be called in *nodes-clustering*. As depicted in Table. 1, the fundamental idea of *getClusters* is to split all the nodes into clusters according to the replica transmission delays between them and then merge some "too-small" clusters into one if necessary(see Fig. 2 for demonstration).

With the two input parameters: $\mathbb{C}$ as the node cluster overlay to be initiated or maintained, θ as the *intra-cluster* replica transmission delay per kilobyte, the sub-procedure *getClusters* generates the clusters-set of the node cluster overlay through the following two phases(in Table. 1):

1) **Splitting phase.** As demonstrated in Fig. 2(a), the **Nodes-clustering** of *ACB-R* splits each cluster(C) whose maximum replica transmission delay per kilobyte is larger than θ.

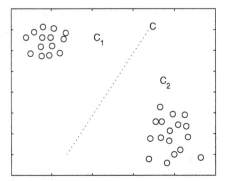 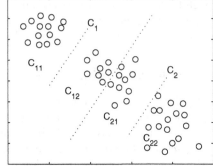

(a) Splitting the cluster C into two clusters C_1 and C_2 in the *Splitting phase* of the procedure $getClusters(\mathbb{C}, \theta)$

(b) Having split C_1 into C_{11}, C_{12}; C_2 into C_{21}, C_{22} respectively, C_{12} and C_{21} are to be merged in the *Merging phase* of the procedure $getClusters(\mathbb{C}, \theta)$

Fig. 2. A paradigm of the *getClusters* procedure

2) **Merging phase.** As demonstrated in Fig. 2(b), the **Nodes-clustering** of *ACB-R* checks each pare of the clusters-set($\mathbb{C} = \{C_{11}, C_{12}, C_{21}, C_{22}\}$) obtained in the "splitting phase", and merges some of them if necessary. Here C_{12} and C_{21} are to be merged because the maximum replica transmission delay per kilobyte in $C_{12} \bigcup C_{21}$ is equal to or larger than θ.

Initiation and dynamic maintenance of node cluster overlay. For the P2P data-store consisting of $S = \{s_1, s_2, \cdots, s_n\}$ as its nodes-set, *Nodes-clustering* calls $getClusters(S, \theta)$ to initiate the node cluster overlay on it by taking S as the initial sole cluster and θ as the expected *intra-cluster* transmission delay per kilobytes.

Assume we get $\mathbb{C} = \{C_1, C_2, \cdots, C_n\}$ as the initial node cluster overlay when the above cluster initiation is over, *Nodes-clustering* calls $getClusters(\mathbb{C}, \theta)$ periodically(say, at each end of a specified time interval t_c) to maintain up-to-date node cluster overlay adaptive to the changing network topology.

2.2   Replicas-Redistributing Procedure

With the help of the parallel-executed procedure *Nodes-clustering*, *Replicas-redistributing* procedure of *ACB-R* is responsible for redistributing an appropriate number of replicas on clusters. To get a satisfied data availability and a good replica access performance as well, it has to determine the minimum number of replicas for achieving the expected data availability, adapt dynamically the replication scheme to the current replica access pattern, and perceive the variational node cluster overlay (maintained by its parallel-executed procedure *Nodes-clustering* of *ACB-R*) as well.

In the following, we first propose the **Availability Principle** on how to hold the necessary data availability and then introduce the adaptive data replication with the help of it.

Guarantee the expected data availability. Due to the characteristics of a P2P data-store that failures may occur anytime anywhere at any node or connections of the underlying network topology([6, 7]), the quantity of replicas for a data object should be chosen with care — Too small number of replicas may not achieve expected data availability while too many replicas may bring overburden on the concurrency control and consistency maintenance([8, 9]). Thus our adaptive clustering-based data replication algorithm need firstly to maintain sufficient quantity of the replicas for a data object to achieve the expected data availability.

Ranganathan et al[10] presents a function to calculate the number of replicas needed for a certain availability threshold. It assumes all the nodes have the same probability of being up (we call it the *reliability percentile* in the following description) and the computed number of replicas is fixed regardless of the dynamic change of the reliability percentile of the nodes. Actually, each node on a P2P data-store has its own distinct reliability percentile. In the following, we propose a revised function in *ACB-R* giving the more precise lower bound of the replica quantity for a data object.

Assume $R = \{r_1, r_2, \cdots, r_m\}$ the replication scheme for o; a_e the expected availability for o; p_k the reliability percentile of the node r_k. We define the function $Avail(R)$ to get the lower bound of the replica quantity(m) of o:

$$Avail(R) \triangleq 1 - \prod_{k=1}^{m}(1 - p_k) \geqslant a_e$$

We call the above inequation the **Availability Principle**. It should be noticed that the function $Avail(R)$ is indispensable in the following proposed data replication procedure *getRepScheme*(see Table. 2 for detail).

Adapt to the replica access pattern and the node cluster overlay. Before replicating over clusters, we examine the following three cases on clients' requesting a replica of the data object o to the node s which is in the cluster C.

Case 1. There is a replica of o stored locally.

Case 2. There is no replica of o stored locally, but there is a nearest replica of o stored on the node which is also in C.

Case 3. There is no replica of o stored locally, but there is a nearest replica of o stored on the node which is not in C.

Recall the **Clustering Principle** addressed in Section 2.1, decreasing the probability of case 3 can improve the replica access efficiency in the greatest extent. That is to say, we should try best to place replicas in different clusters to improve the replica access efficiency of *ACB-R*.

Table 1. Sub-procedure *getClusters* with two inputs:1) $\mathbb{C}$ — the node cluster overlay to be initiated or maintained; 2) θ — the *intra-cluster* replica transmission delay per kilobyte

---

Procedure *getClusters*$(\mathbb{C}, \theta)$

---

  begin
    1). Splitting phase
    for each $(C_i \in \mathbb{C})$ & $(intraDelay(C_i) > \theta)$
      Find $s_1, s_2 \in C_i$ satisfying $delay(s_1, s_2) = intraDelay(C_i)$;
      $[\ R_1 \leftarrow \{s \in C_i \mid delay(s_1, s) < delay(s_2, s)\};\ R_2 \leftarrow C_i - R_1\ ]$;
      $\mathbb{C} \leftarrow \mathbb{C} - \{C_i\} + \{R_1, R_2\}$;
    endfor;
    2). Merging phase
    for each pair of $(C_i \neq C_j \in \mathbb{C})$ & $(interDelay(C_i, C_j) \leqslant \theta)$
      $R \leftarrow R_1 \bigcup R_2$;
      $\mathbb{C} \leftarrow \mathbb{C} - \{C_i, C_j\} + \{R\}$;
    endfor;
  end.

Given the expected object availability and the reliability percentile of the nodes on a P2P data-store, we can initially replicate minimal number of replicas into clusters by referring to the **Availability Principle**, then dynamically redistribute them in response to the replica access pattern and the node cluster overlay (maintained by *Nodes-clustering*) for getting a good replica access performance.

At each end of a specified time interval t_a, *Replicas-redistributing* procedure does the following steps to get a new replication scheme and do the corresponding replica creation or deletion if necessary.

1. Get o's replica access pattern(say, F) recorded during the last time interval. Here F is the set of nodes which requested a replica of o during the last time interval.
2. Get the old replication scheme(say, R) in the last time interval. Here R is the set of nodes which stored a replica of o in the last time interval.
3. Get the current clusters-set of the node cluster overlay(say, $\mathbb{C}$) over all the nodes of a P2P data-store. Recall that $\mathbb{C}$ is initiated and dynamically maintained by *getClusters*(Table. 1);
4. Get the clusters-set of the node cluster overlay(say $\mathbb{C}_R$) on R. This can be achieved by simply mapping the nodes in R into the clusters in $\mathbb{C}$;
5. Get the new replication scheme adaptive to the replica access pattern(F) and the node cluster overlay($\mathbb{C}$) by executing the sub-procedure *getRepScheme*(as described in Table. 2).

Different from current research on the dynamic replication algorithms such as [11, 12, 13, 14], we create or delete replicas not on nodes but on clusters, as depicted in Table. 2. For example, if we observe a cluster necessary to store a replica to improve the access efficiency, we don't create the replica immediately.

Table 2. Procedure *getRepScheme* with six inputs (some of them are dependent) and one output:1)o — the data object for replication; 2)a_e(user-specified) — the expected data availability; 3)F — the o's replica access pattern in the last time interval; 4)R — the o's old replication scheme in the last time interval; 5)$\mathbb{C}_R$(dependent on R and $\mathbb{C}$) — the clusters-set of node cluster overlay over the nodes in R; 6)$\mathbb{C}$(with the help of **Nodes-clustering**) — the node cluster overlay over all the nodes in a P2P data-store; 7)R' — the o's new replication scheme we get with necessary replica creation or deletion at the beginning of the next time interval.

Sub-procedure $R' = getRepScheme(o, a_e, F, R, \mathbb{C}_R, \mathbb{C})$

Assume $R = \bigcup r_i$, $\mathbb{C}_R = \bigcup R_i$, where $r_i \in R_i, \forall i = 1, \cdots, \|R\|$;
Assume $\mathbb{C} - \mathbb{C}_R = \{D_1, D_2, \cdots\}$;
Assume $F = \bigcup f_i$;
begin
  $R' \leftarrow \emptyset$;
  $\mathbb{C}_{R'} \leftarrow \emptyset$; the node cluster overlay on R'
  for $i = 1, 2, \cdots, \|F\|$, **do**
    if $(f_i \in R_x) \& (R_x \overline{\in} \mathbb{C}_{R'})$ **then**
      [$R' \leftarrow R' \bigcup \{r_x\}$; $\mathbb{C}_{R'} \leftarrow \mathbb{C}_{R'} \bigcup \{R_x\}$];
    if $(f_i \in D_y) \& (D_y \overline{\in} \mathbb{C}_{R'})$ **then**
      [Create a replica of o on f_i; $R' \leftarrow R' \bigcup \{f_i\}$; $\mathbb{C}_{R'} \leftarrow \mathbb{C}_{R'} \bigcup \{D_y\}$];
  endfor;
  ; Achieve the expected replica availability(a_e).
  if $(Avail(R') < a_e) \& (R - R' \neq \emptyset)$ **then**
    Assume $R - R' = \bigcup \{u_i\}$, $\mathbb{C}_U = \bigcup \{U_i\}$, where $u_i \in U_i, \forall i = 1, \cdots, \|U\|$;
    for $i = 1, 2, \cdots, \|U\|$, **do**
      [$R' \leftarrow R' \bigcup \{u_i\}$; $\mathbb{C}_{R'} \leftarrow \mathbb{C}_{R'} \bigcup \{U_i\}$];
      if $Avail(R') \geq a_e$ **then Return** R';
    endfor;
  endif;
  if $Avail(R') < a_e$ **then**
    Assume $\mathbb{C} - \mathbb{C}_{R'} = \{T_1, T_2, \cdots\}$;
    for $i = 1, 2, \cdots$, **do**
      Randomly find a node $t_i \in T_i$;
      [Create a replica of o on t_i; $R' \leftarrow R'_o \bigcup \{t_i\}$; $\mathbb{C}_{R'} \leftarrow \mathbb{C}_{R'} \bigcup \{T_i\}$];
      if $Avail(R') \geq a_e$ **then Return** R';
    endfor;
  endif;
  ; Delete the unneeded replicas.
  if $(R - R' \neq \emptyset)$ **then**
    Assume $R - R' = \bigcup \{u_i\}$, $\mathbb{C}_U = \bigcup \{U_i\}$, where $u_i \in U_i, \forall i = 1, \cdots, \|U\|$;
    for $i = 1, 2, \cdots, \|U\|$, **do**
      Delete the replica of o on u_i
    endfor;
  endif;
end.

Instead, we first check to see if there is already a replica in the cluster, if it is, we leave the cluster as before without creating new replicas. With the characteristics of the node cluster overlay (maintained by *Nodes-clustering*), we can save the space for storing necessary replicas, the unnecessary replica creation or deletion operation, and the cost of consistency maintenance for unnecessary replicas at the price of negligible *intra-cluster* replica transmission delay per kilobyte.

Here it should be pointed out again that the procedures, *Nodes-clustering* and *Replicas-redistributing*, are two crucial *parallel-executed* procedures in *ACB-R*, where *Nodes-clustering* procedure is responsible for maintaining up-to-date node cluster overlay adapting to the nodes' adding into or leaving from the network or the current status of the network traffic, while *Replicas-redistribution* procedure controls the number of replicas and distribute them into clusters of the node cluster overlay (initiated and maintained by *Nodes-clustering*) in response to the changing node cluster overlay and the changing data access pattern.

Through the above adaptive access-pattern driven replication, the replication scheme is converging to the access-pattern statistically. At the same time, with the help of the separate, parallel-executed procedure *Nodes-clustering*, *ACB-R* can also adapt to the changing status of the underlying node cluster overlay.

3   Experiments

To see the performance of *ACB-R*, we take the other two dynamic replication algorithms(*Simple-R* and *Ideal-R*) as comparison, which are depicted as follows.

- *Simple-R* We present this algorithm to be contrasted with *ACB-R* to see how much the clustering-based replication algorithm can benefit the effectiveness of dynamic replication. The *Simple-R* is a representative of simple dynamic replication algorithms unaware of the existence of the node cluster overlay, with the common characteristics of converging to a replication scheme adaptive to the replica access pattern.
- *Ideal-R* It is analogous to the *LOWER BOUND(LB)* algorithm presented in [11], which provides a lower bound for dynamic replication algorithms. The *Ideal-R* knows a priori the replica access schedule on nodes, which makes it the optimal dynamic replication algorithm among others. Thus, it is not applicable in a real network environment but an ideal algorithm for comparison with other dynamic replication algorithms.

Table 3. The other two parameters in our experiment

Parameter	Comment
$nRepS$	the number of replicas in the replication scheme for o
$nActC$	the number of the "active clusters" requesting o in a time interval

Recall the definitions of α and θ(see Section 2.1), we introduce other two crucial parameters in Table 3 for measuring the performance of the three dynamic replication algorithms in our experiment.

In our experiment, We make use of the tool provided by BRITE[15] for emulating the node placements and the initial bandwidth distribution among them for the following performance test.

3.1 The Characteristics of the Convergence to the Variational Replica Access Pattern and Network Topology

In Fig. 3(a), we assume the replica access for a data object(say, o) on a node(say, s) comply with the "Poisson Distribution" with the parameter λ_s as the expected number of requests for o issued by s in a time interval. At the beginning of each time interval, we apply "Poisson Series" on each node s generated by the "Poisson Distribution" with the parameter λ_s to simulate the replica requests on the 100 nodes emulated by BRITE[15] with the parameters specified in Table. 4. In *ACB-R* we specify θ=0.01s, α=1.2s to maintain the node cluster overlay. From the result of the experiment depicted in Fig. 3(a), we can see that the average replica transmission delay of the three replication algorithms goes stable with the increase of time intervals. When the number of time intervals equals to 100, the standard deviations are 0.32% for *Simple-R*, 0.53% for *ACB-R* and 0.06% for *Ideal-R*, which are all relative small. Thus, we can use 100 since then as the appropriate amount of time periods for evaluating the replica access performance for the three replication algorithms.

In Fig. 3(b), we vary the bandwidths of the 100 nodes to simulate the variational network topology. As shown in the figure, the average replica transmission delays of the three algorithms go stable with the changing status of the network topology while that of *Simpe-R* fluctuates greater than the other two. When the status number of the network topology equals to 40, the standard deviations are relatively stable at 9.86% for *Simple-R*, 4.28% for *ACB-R*, 4.16% for *Ideal-R* respectively. Thus in the following experiments, manage to get the average replica access performance on a network topology with 40 changing status.

Table 4. The parameters specified in BRITE[15] to generate 100 node-placements and the initial bandwidth distribution

Parameter	Comment
Name=1	Router Waxman = 1, AS Waxman = 3
N=100	Number of nodes in graph
HS=1000	Size of main plane (number of squares)
LS=100	Size of inner planes (number of squares)
NodePlacement=2	Random = 1, Heavy Tailed = 2
GrowthType=1	Incremental = 1, All = 2
m=2	Number of neighboring node each new node connects to.
alpha=0.15	Waxman Parameter
beta=0.2	Waxman Parameter
BWDist=3	Constant = 1, Uniform =2, HeavyTailed=3, Exponential=4
BWMin=10.0	The minimum bandwidth
BWMax=10000.0	The maximum bandwidth

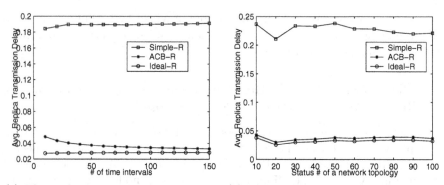

(a) The replica access performance con- (b) The replica access performance converges to the replica access pattern statis- verges to the network topology statistically
tically

Fig. 3. The average replica transmission delay varies with the cumulation of time
intervals and the variation of the node cluster overlay

Having the number of time intervals and status number of the network topology been configured to 100 and 40 respectively, we continue our experiment on
the following factors that influencing system performance greatly.

3.2   The Factors Influencing the Replica Access Performance

In Fig. 4(a), we evaluate the replica access performance of the three replication algorithm with an increasing $nActC$ and a fixed $nRepS = 4$. As shown in
Fig. 4(a), with the increase of $nActC$, the average replica transmission delay of
Simple-R increases proportionally, while *ACB-R* behaves in a particular manner:
the average replica transmission delay of *ACB-R* stays at almost the same level
until $nActC$ become larger than $nReps$. We can explain above as follows.

Assume R the replication scheme for o, $\mathbb{C}_R$ the clusters-set of node cluster
overlay on R, the replica access requests for o initiated from the $nActC$ clusters
can be assorted into two classes: 1)the requests initiated from a node in a cluster
in $\mathbb{C}_R$; 2)the requests initiated out of $\mathbb{C}_R$. It is then obvious that the first class of
requests can be satisfied at the cost of θ — the *intra-cluster* replica transmission
delay per kilobyte, while the second class of requests can only be satisfied at the
cost of α — the *inter-cluster* replica transmission delay per kilobyte.

Recall that $nRepS$ is the number of replicas in the replication scheme for
o(Table. 3). *ACB-R* distributes the $nRepS$ replicas for o in its replication into
$nRepS$ clusters in $\mathbb{C}_R$. When $nActC \leqslant nRepS$, the replica access requests for o
are all the first class so that the replica transmission delay stays at the magnitude
of θ. When $nActC > nRepS$ with the increase of $nActC$, the second class of the
replica access requests for o become present, posing more replica transmission
delay at the magnitude of α. As for *Simple-R* unaware of the *clusters*, the $nRepS$
replicas maybe in one cluster in the worst case so that most of the replica access
requests in its replication for o fall in the second class.

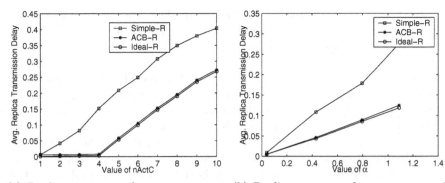

(a) Replica access performance compari- (b) Replica access performance compari-
ison with the increase of $nActC$ while son with the increase of α while $nActC >$
$nRepS = 4$ $nRepS$

Fig. 4. The replica access performance varies with the increase of $nActC$ or α

From Fig. 4(a), we know that the replica transmission delay stays at the magnitude of θ when $nActC \leqslant nRepS$. In the experiment depicted in Fig. 4(b), we examine the influence of α on the replica access performance when $nActC > nRepS$. From Fig. 4(b) we can see that with the larger α, *ACB-R* saves more replica transmission delay than *Simple-R*. But when the value of α is close to *intra-cluster* replica transmission delay(θ), the performance advantage of *ACB-R* is not remarkable — almost the same as *Simple-R*. Actually, *ACB-R*'s outperforming *Simple-R* is based on the substrate of the **Clustering Principle**(see Section 2.1) — *inter-cluster* replica transmission delay per kilobyte(α) far larger than *intra-cluster* replica transmission delay per kilobyte (θ).

4   Related Work

Wolfson et al[11] propose an *ADR* protocol that replicates objects dynamically to adapt to the changing access pattern. However, *ADR* doesn't pay attention to the problem of reliability constraints on objects, which is indispensable in an unreliable P2P environment. In addition, *ADR* replicates objects only among neighboring nodes, which would result in high delays and overheads for creating distant replicas. Our *ACB-R* hasn't that limitation.

Rabinovich et al[16] propose a protocol suite for dynamic replication and migration of Internet objects, the dynamic replication protocol attempts to place replicas in the vicinity of a majority of requests while ensuring that no nodes are overloaded. Unlike *ADR* protocol in [11], their protocol performs replication among distant nodes directly, without replicating at all intermediate nodes on the path. However, the replica placement algorithm concentrate on the load balance without considering the different replica transmission delay influencing the replica access performance much.

OceanStore[1] is a global-scale storage system. The same as our architecture, its replication are in the environment of unreliable P2P nodes. OceanStore proposes a replica management mechanism to adjust the number and location of its floating replicas for serving access requests more efficiently. It creates additional replicas to alleviate load and eliminates replicas that have fallen into disuse. But the neighbors in OceanStore is based on a logical topology not on geographical topology. A "nearby" replica to a client may be far away from the client.

There are also other current research on replicating data objects in a distributed environment such as ([6, 7, 17]), which didn't pay much attention to the geographical network topology and the consequent difference of replica transmission delay between nodes. Actually, it is significant for a good replication algorithm to take the replica transmission delay between nodes before replicating objects onto them.

5   Conclusion

The most important feature that distinguishes *ACB-R* from other replication strategies is that we take into account the difference of replica transmission delay between various nodes distributed geographically, which is done by posing *Nodes-clustering* on the nodes in a P2P data-store. The *Nodes-clustering* for the initiation and maintenance of the node cluster overlay addresses the difference of replica transmission delay between nodes by grouping nodes into clusters, where the *intra-cluster* replica transmission delay is statistically far less than the *inter-cluster* replica transmission delay. Thus, *ACB-R* shows a high access efficiency by dynamically converging the appropriate number of replicas to the clusters which represents the optimum replication scheme.

Compared with other replication algorithms unaware of the existence of the node cluster overlay, our adaptive cluster-based data replication algorithm *ACB-R* has the following features and advantages.

- It does the replication onto clusters not directly on nodes, which gives a replication scheme having much less number of replicas than others only at the price of negligible *intra-cluster* replica transmission per kilobyte. Having less number of replicas in the replication scheme can
  - save the space for storing necessary replicas
  - save the unnecessary replica creation or deletion operation
  - decrease the cost of consistency maintenance for unnecessary replicas ([8, 9])
- It can perceive the change of underlying network topology in addition to the replica access pattern for replication scheme adaption.
- It can adapt the replication scheme to the changing replica access pattern while guaranteeing the expected data availability at the same time.
- It parallels the procedure *Replica-redistribution* with the procedure *Nodes-clustering* to make the data replication more efficient.

References

[1] John Kubiatowicz, David Bindel, Yan Chen, Patrick Eaton, Dennis Geels, Ramakrishna Gummadi, Sean Rhea, Hakim Weatherspoon, Westly Weimer, Christopher Wells, and Ben Zhao. Oceanstore: An architecture for global-scale persistent storage. In *Proceedings of ACM ASPLOS*. ACM, November 2000.

[2] P. Druschel and A. Rowstron. PAST: A large-scale, persistent peer-to-peer storage utility. In *HotOS VIII*, pages 75–80, Schloss Elmau, Germany, May 2001.

[3] Ian Clarke, Oskar Sandberg, Brandon Wiley, and Theodore W. Hong. Freenet: A distributed anonymous information storage and retrieval system. In H. Federrath, editor, *Designing Privacy Enhancing Technologies: International Workshop on Design Issues in Anonymity and Unobservability, Berkeley, CA, USA, July 2000, Proceedings*, volume 2009, pages 46–66. Springer, 2001.

[4] M. Ripeanu. Peer-to-peer architecture case study: Gnutella network. Technical Report TR-2001-26, University of Chicago, 2001.

[5] Michael J. Carey, David J. DeWitt, Michael J. Franklin, Nancy E. Hall, Mark L. McAuliffe, Jeffrey F. Naughton, Daniel T. Schuh, Marvin H. Solomon, C. K. Tan, Odysseas G. Tsatalos, Seth J. White, and Michael J. Zwilling. Shoring up persistent applications. In *SIGMOD '94: Proceedings of the 1994 ACM SIGMOD international conference on Management of data*, pages 383–394, New York, NY, USA, 1994. ACM Press.

[6] Edith Cohen and Scott Shenker. Replication strategies in unstructured peer-to-peer networks. *SIGCOMM Comput. Commun. Rev.*, 32(4):177–190, 2002.

[7] Qin Lv, Pei Cao, Edith Cohen, Kai Li, and Scott Shenker. Search and replication in unstructured peer-to-peer networks. In *ICS '02: Proceedings of the 16th international conference on Supercomputing*, pages 84–95, New York, NY, USA, 2002. ACM Press.

[8] Jim Gray, Pat Helland, Patrick O'Neil, and Dennis Shasha. The dangers of replication and a solution. In *Proceedings of the 1996 ACM SIGMOD International Conference on Management of Data*, pages 173–182, 1996.

[9] Bharat K. Bhargava. Concurrency control in database systems. *Knowledge and Data Engineering*, 11(1):3–16, 1999.

[10] Kavitha Ranganathan, Adriana Iamnitchi, and Ian Foster. Improving data availability through dynamic model-driven replication in large peer-to-peer communities. In *CCGRID '02: Proceedings of the 2nd IEEE/ACM International Symposium on Cluster Computing and the Grid*, page 376, Washington, DC, USA, 2002. IEEE Computer Society.

[11] Ouri Wolfson, Sushil Jajodia, and Yixiu Huang. An adaptive data replication algorithm. *ACM Transactions on Database Systems*, 22(2):255–314, 1997.

[12] Azer Bestavros. Demand-based document dissemination to reduce traffic and balance load in distributed information systems. In *Proceedings of SPDP'95: The 7th IEEE Symposium on Parallel and Distributed Processing*, San Anotonio, Texas, 1995.

[13] Swarup Acharya and Stanley B. Zdonik. An efficient scheme for dynamic data replication. Technical Report CS-93-43, 1993.

[14] James Gwertzman. Autonomous replication in wide-area internetworks. Technical Report TR-17-95, Cambridgem Massachusetts, 1995.

[15] Alberto Medina, Anukool Lakhina, Ibrahim Matta, and John Byers. BRITE: Universal topology generation from a user's perspective. Technical Report 2001-003, 1 2001.

[16] Michael Rabinovich, Irina Rabinovich, Rajmohan Rajaraman, and Amit Aggarwal. A dynamic object replication and migration protocol for an internet hosting service. In *International Conference on Distributed Computing Systems*, pages 101–113, 1999.

[17] Francisco Matias Cuenca-Acuna, Richard P. Martin, and Thu D. Nguyen. Autonomous Replication for High Availability in Unstructured P2P Systems. In *The 22nd IEEE Symposium on Reliable Distributed Systems (SRDS-22)*. IEEE Press, October 2003.

TOP-k Query Calculation in Peer-to-Peer Networks

Qian Zhang, Yu Sun , Xia Zhang, Xuezhi Wen, and Zheng Liu

National Engineering Research Center for Computer Software,
Northeastern University, Shenyang 110004, China
zhangqian@neusoft.com

Abstract. This paper addresses the efficient top-k queries in pure peer-to-peer (P2P) networks. Top-k receives much attention in the search engine and gains great success. However, processing top-k query in pure P2P network is very challenging due to unique characteristics of P2P environments, for example, skewed collection statistics, and higher communication costs. Inspired by the success of ranking algorithms in Web search engine, we propose a decentralized algorithm to answer top-k queries in pure peer-to-peer networks which makes use of local rankings, rank merging, and minimizes both answer set size and network traffic among peers.

1 Introduction

Increasing the number of peers in unstructured peer-to-peer network may lead to vast result sets to a given query as well. So we need to restrict the number of results to minimize traffic among peers. Additionally, users are usually only interested in a few most relevant results to their query, which makes it necessary to investigate how to rank results and return only the best ones in such a distributed environment. Since users are usually only interested in a few most relevant results to their query, the goal in top-k retrieval techniques is to return result sets consisting of those most relevant results. However, processing top-k query in pure P2P network is very challenging because a P2P system is a dynamic system. Inspired by the great success of top-k retrieval algorithms in Web search engines, this paper presents a decentralized top-k ranking algorithm for unstructured peer-to-peer networks.

2 Related Works

Peer-to-peer networks have generated great research interests recently, but only very few authors have explored retrieval algorithms taking top-k ranking into account.

[1] proposes a decentralized top-k ranking algorithm for schema-based peer-to-peer networks, which is based on dynamically collected query statistics and no continuous index update processes are necessary. But the algorithm is just suitable for hybrid structured P2P systems and requires cooperation from peers, which we would prefer to avoid. [2] presents a hierarchical top-k query algorithm based on histogram, but it assumes that every peer throughout the network uses the same methods to score documents with respect to a query, though input data to compute these scores may be different. On the other hand, the algorithm discussed by [2] also requires cooperation

S. Grumbach, L. Siu, and V. Vianu (Eds.): ASIAN 2005, LNCS 3818, pp. 127 – 135, 2005.

from participants. [3] proposes a novel top-*k* query algorithm, but it is only suitable for hybrid P2P networks. [4] presents KLEE, a novel algorithmic framework for distributed top-k query processing. KLEE achieves performance gains in query response times, network bandwidth, and local peer load. However, KLEE assumes that each of peers throughout the network uses the same methods to score documents with respect to a query.

There have been many studies on results merging in the context peer-to-peer environment. About the related work, in PlanetP[5], it first ranks peers according to each peer's goodness for the submitted query and then ranks the documents returned by these peers, so its schema is heuristic but not deterministic and requires cooperation from peers. In[6], Zhiguo Lu have proposed a deterministic strategy, but it requires full cooperation from participants. [7] also presents a deterministic strategy, but it is just suitable for pure structured P2P systems and need global statistics such as the inverse document frequency, which can only be obtained in completely cooperative environments where each node share its document and corpus statistics. Jie Lu [8] adapted Semi-Supervised Learning (SSL) result merging algorithm to hybrid P2P networks with multiple directory nodes. A directory node that uses SSL learns a query-dependent score normalizing function for each of its neighboring nodes. This function transforms neighbor-specific documents to directory-specific document scores. However, the modified SSL requires downloading documents from neighboring nodes to serve as training data, which means higher communication costs. Jie Lu also proposed another result merging algorithm, which is called SESS. SESS is a cooperative algorithm that requires neighboring nodes to provide statistics information for each of their top-ranked documents. [9] investigates how to incorporate distributed information retrieval techniques into peer-to-peer systems. The basic idea is to filter the results as they are forwarded back to the query originator. The algorithm implemented by [9] does not require cooperation from participants, but it assumes that every participant uses the same methods to score documents for answering a given query.

Top-*k* retrieval algorithm in unstructured P2P networks is not a simple adaptation of existing approaches [10,11] due to unique characteristics of P2P environments, for example, skewed collection statistics, and higher communication costs. In this paper, we propose a novel top-*k* ranking algorithm for unstructured peer-to-peer networks, which is called *TRNC*（ top-*k* ranking with no cooperation）. *TRNC* does not require cooperation from participants and assumes that every peer throughout the network uses different methods to score documents with respect to a query, which makes it different from other algorithms that require cooperation from participants.

The remainder of the paper is organized as follows. Section 3 describes our new approach to top-*k* ranking. Section 4 proposes one method for ranking the neighboring nodes based on the relevance for answering a given query. The scores of the neighboring nodes with respect to a given query are important for top-*k* ranking. Section 5 and Section 6 explain our experimental methodology. Section 7 concludes.

3   Top-*k* Ranking

Our system model follows the unstructured P2P networks such as Gnutella. The query is flooded from the one peer node (called initiator peer) to its neighboring nodes until the TTL decreases to 0. The forwarding process forms a tree rooted at the initiator peer. Nodes that have a TTL value of 0 are the leaves of the tree. Each node on the query forwarding tree is responsible for collecting summary statistics about its sub-tree, and also for merging results from each of its child and selecting top *k* results. Each node uses different methods to process the query and sends the top *k* results to its parent node down the inverse query path.

As illustrated in Figure 1, the arrows on the edges indicate the directions to send back retrieval results to the query initiator. Node a is the query initiator and called root of the spanning tree, and node b is the child node of node a, while node b is the parent node of node c, d and e. The results that need to be merged at a node (e.g. *b*) may include not only the results from the node himself, but also the results sent back by the child nodes (e.g. *c*) down the query path. Each node selects the top *k* results from its merged results and returns it to its parent node. In the final stage, node *a* collects top *k* results from each of its child nodes and the best *k* or *k*+ results are retrieved.

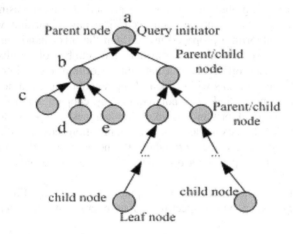

Fig. 1. Query processing tree

Our *TRNC* algorithm is base on a function that maps local document *ranks* obtained from a child node into global document *scores* which can then be merged together with document ranks from other child nodes. The local document ranks means the ranks of the documents at a child node resulted from relevance scoring computed locally by the node. The global document scores mean parent-specific scores, which are the new scores of the documents after being merged. In order to explain the algorithm, we suppose a set of child nodes $P = \{P_1, P_2,...,P_{|P|}\}$ with goodness scores $S_{1,q}, S_{2,q}, S_{|P|,q}$ has been selected for query *q*, and their parent node is called *h* with goodness scores $S_{|P|+1,q}$ for query *q*. Each of the child nodes returns top *k* documents(Probably the number of relevant documents returned by child node is less than *k*), called result set, ranked by their relevance scores with respect to the given query *q*. Node *h* merges these result sets and select top *k* results. $O_{u,v,q}$ denotes the rank of document *u* in child node *v* for a given query *q*.

In order to select top *k* results from child nodes, we assume that the following is good relevance indicating. The number of documents N_v contributed by node *v* to the merged result is proportional to its goodness score. One peer node would contain more relevant documents for a given query q, if its relevance score with respect to a given query q is high. N_v is defined as follows.

$$N_V = k \times \frac{S_{v,\ q}}{\sum_{p=1}^{|P|+1} S_{p,\ q}} \tag{1}$$

Based on the intuition mentioned above, we define the following local document rank to parent-specific relevance score mapping.

$$G_{u,v,q} = k \times \frac{S_{v,q}}{O_{u,v,q} \times S_{max,q}} \tag{2}$$

Where $O_{u,v,q}$ is the rank of document u in child node v, $G_{u,v,q}$ is the global relevance score of document u in child node v, and $S_{max,q}=max\{ S_{m,q} \mid m=1,2,....|P|+1\}$. In the final stage, the resulting global relevance scores are sorted in a decreasing score order, and the best k or $k+$ documents are retrieved. The new algorithm we propose is inspired in part by algorithm proposed in [12]. On the other hand, our algorithm is similar to that in [13], which only considers the number of results returned by collection servers. The difference is that our algorithm takes into account the distribution of document ranks within each of the neighboring child nodes. Also, our algorithm is deterministic and does not require any cooperation from participants, which means that our algorithm has many advantages compared to other result merging algorithms, for example, less communication costs. Additionally, our algorithm assume that every peer throughout the network uses different methods to score documents with respect to a query, which is similar to most real world file sharing systems.

The only information needed to compute $G_{u,v,q}$ used by Equation 2 is the relevance scores of nodes with respect to a given query q. Next we will identify the problem.

4 Neighboring Nodes Ranking

Many nodes ranking algorithms require cooperation from neighboring nodes, which we would prefer to avoid. On the other hand, neighboring nodes ranking in P2P networks is not a simple adaptation of existing approaches [12-15] due to unique characteristics of P2P environments, for example, skewed collection statistics, and higher communication costs. It is a more difficult problem especially in uncooperative P2P environments. In this paper, we extract correlations between query terms and peer nodes by analyzing past query logs, which can be used to score peer nodes. Similar observation has been made in [16]. The difference is that our algorithm takes into account the correlations between query terms and peer nodes. Parent nodes learn neighboring child nodes' content by observing which queries each neighboring child node responds to. The query logs we extract from parent node v are defined as follows:

$$Log_v := <query\ q>\ [(NUM_{j,q,v},\ ID_{j,v})]\ *$$

Where $ID_{j,v}$ is the jth child node and $NUM_{j,q,v}$ is the number of documents contributed by node $ID_{j,v}$ to the merged result for query q. Thus, some correlations between query terms and peer nodes can be established based on query logs. As illustrated in Figure 2, weighted links can be created between the query space (all query terms) and the query logs, as well as between the peer space (node v and its child nodes) and the query logs. If there is at least one path between one query term and one peer node, a link is created between them. Thus, we measure the correlations between the query terms and peer nodes by investigating the weights of links between them.

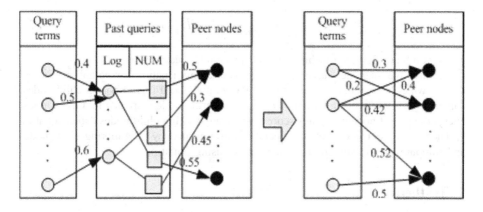

Fig. 2. Establishing correlation between query terms and peer nodes

We define the degrees of correlation as the conditional probabilities between query terms and peer nodes. The probability $P(B \mid ID_{j,v})$ (where $ID_{j,v}$ is the peer node for queries containing the query term B):

$$P(B \mid ID_{j,v}) = \frac{P(B, ID_{j,v})}{P(ID_{j,v})} \tag{3}$$

$P(ID_{j,v})$ can be estimated from the frequency of occurrences of nodes in query logs as follows:

$$P(ID_{j,v}) = \frac{count(ID_{j,v})}{count(ID)} \tag{4}$$

Where $count(ID)$ is the total frequency of occurrences of nodes in query logs, and $count(ID_{j,v})$ is the frequency of occurrences of node $ID_{j,v}$ in query logs.

$$P(B, ID_{j,v}) = \frac{count(B, ID_{j,v})}{count(\log_v)} \times \frac{\underset{B \in q}{NUM_{j,q,v}}}{count(B, ID_{j,v}) \times k} \tag{5}$$

Where $count(\log_v)$ is total number of query logs maintained by node v, and $count(B, ID_{j,v})$ is the number of query logs in which the query term B and the peer node $ID_{j,v}$ appear together.

By combining (3),(4), and (5), we obtain the following formula for $P(B \mid ID_{j,v})$:

$$P(B \mid ID_{j,v}) = \frac{count(ID)}{count(ID_{j,v})} \times \frac{\sum_{B \in q} NUM_{j,q,v}}{count(\log_v) \times k} \qquad (6)$$

In the final stage, we need to determine the correlation of a peer node to the whole query in order to rank it. For this, we use an idea similar to that of [15]. The relationship of a peer to the whole query is measured by the following cohesion calculation:

$$P(Q \mid ID_{j,v}) = \frac{1}{|Q|} \sum_{B \in Q} P(B \mid ID_{j,v}) \qquad (7)$$

which combines the relationship of the peer to all the query terms.

Initially, parent nodes have empty past queries information for neighboring child nodes, which means that $G_{u,v} = K / O_{u,v}$. Parent nodes learn neighboring child nodes' content by observing which queries each neighboring node responds to. Given a new query, the parent node computes scores for its neighboring child nodes using Equation 7. Then the parent node collects query results returned by neighboring child nodes and computes parent-specific relevance scores using Equation 2.

5   Testbed

There has been no standard data for evaluating the performance of top k results merging in P2P networks, so we developed one test set, which is a 5 gigabyte, 1 million document set downloaded from internet. The test data was divided into 2,000 collections based on document URLs. The HTML title fields of the documents were used as document names. Each of the 2,000 collections defined a peer node in a unstructured P2P network. Each peer throughout the networks uses different methods to process the local query, for example, the CORI algorithm[14], and Xu's language modeling approach[17].

Prior research shows that 85% of the queries posted at web search engines have 3 or less query terms [18], so for most documents, we only extract a few key terms as queries. Here we extract key terms from document names. Most queries had 2-3 terms and no query had more than 7 terms. 10,000 queries were randomly selected from the automatically-generated queries to be used in our experiments. For each query, a node was randomly chosen to issue the query on the condition that the node didn't have the document used to generate that query. Next we will discuss how to construct the topology of unstructured P2P network.

We use the Power-Laws method described by [19] to generate the connections between nodes. A node had on average 5 neighboring nodes. As in the Gnutella protocol [20], each message had a time-to-live (TTL) field that causes the query to expire and is not further propagated to other nodes. The initial TTL was set to 5 for query messages. When the query messages were routed to leaf nodes, the TTL was set to 0 since leaf nodes were not supposed to further route query messages.

Table 1. Parameter and settings

Parameter name	Default value	Description
Network topology	power-law	The topology of network, with out-degree of 4.6
Network size	20 00	The number of peers in the network
TTL	5	The time-of-live of a query message

6 Evaluation Methodology

We implement the top *k* ranking algorithms (called *TRC*) discussed by He [2] in order to have a comparison with our *TRNC* algorithm. *TRC* algorithm assumes that each node uses the same method to process the query. Recall and Precision are two classical metrics to evaluate the information retrieval technology. Here we use 11-point recall-precision to evaluate the merged retrieved results from the P2P networks.

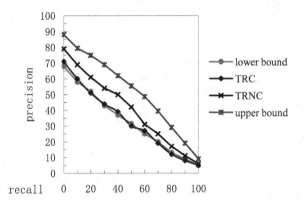

Fig. 3. The 11-Point Recall-Precision Curves for Different top *k* ranking Algorithms when 10,000 queries have been randomly issued

Figure 3 shows the 11-point recall-precision curves for different top *k* ranking algorithms when 10,000 queries have been randomly issued. The lower bound was generated by directly merging documents from different neighboring child nodes using their local document scores. The upper bound was generated by the documents according to their corresponding scores in the retrieval results from the whole single collection. The *TRNC* algorithm improved the average precision compared with *TRC* algorithm. On the other hand, our algorithm does not require cooperation from neighboring child nodes and assumes that every node throughout the network uses different methods to score documents with respect to a query, which makes it different from *TRC* algorithm that requires cooperation from neighboring child nodes, which means higher communication costs. *TRC* also assumes that every peer throughout the network uses the same methods to score documents with respect to a query, though input data to compute these scores may be different. So *TRNC* is similar to most real world file sharing systems.

7 Summary and Conclusions

In this paper, we propose a novel top-k ranking algorithm in unstructured P2P networks. Our algorithm does not require cooperation from neighboring child nodes and assumes that every node throughout the network uses different methods to score documents with respect to a query, which makes it different from other algorithms. Experimental results demonstrate that our algorithm is effective and has better optimal performance compared with top-k ranking algorithm described by [2].

References

1. Wolfgang Nejdl,Wolf Siberski,Uwe Thaden,Wolf-Tilo Balke. Top-k Query Evaluation for Schema-based Peer-to-Peer Networks. In *Proceedings of third International Semantic Web Conference*, Hiroshima, Japan, Springer-Verlag, Berlin Heidelberg New York. (2004) 137-151
2. HE Ying-Jie, WANG Shan, DU Xiao-Yong. Efficient Top-k Query Processing in Pure Peer-to-Peer Network. *Journal of Software*, Vol(16),(2005)540~552
3. Balke, W.-T., Nejdl, W.; Siberski, W.; Thaden, U.: Progressive Distributed Top-k Retrieval in Peer-to-Peer Networks. In *Proceedings of International Conference on Data Engineering (ICDE'05)*, Tokyo, Japan, 2005.
4. Sebastian Michel, Peter Triantafillou, and Gerhard Weikum. KLEE: A Framework for Distributed Top-k Query Algorithms. In *Proceedings of the 31th International Conference on Very Large Databases (VLDB)*.Norway,(2005)637-648
5. F. M. Cuenca-Acuna, C. Peery, and R. P. M. T. D. Nguyen. Plantet: Infrastructure support for p2p information sharing. In *Technical Report DCS-TR-465*, Department of Computer Science, Rutgers University, 2001.
6. Zhiguo Lu1, Bo Ling1, Weining Qian1,etc, A Distributed Ranking Strategy in Peer-to-Peer Based Information Retrieval Systems. In *Proceedings of the Sixth Asia Pacific Web Conference (APWeb'04)*, Springer-Verlag, Berlin Heidelberg New York. (2004)279-284
7. M. M. Chunqiang Tang, Zhichen Xu. Peersearch: Efficient information retrieval in structured overlays. In *Proceedings Of HotNets-1'02, ACM SIGCOMM.* (2002)
8. J. Lu and J. Callan. Merging retrieval results in hierarchical peer-to-peer networks (poster description). In *Proceedings of the 27th Annual International ACM SIGIR Conference on Research and Development in Information Retrieval.*(2004)472-473
9. Yu, B., Liu, J., Ong, C.S.: Scalable P2P information retrieval via hierarchical result merging.*Technical report*, Dep. of CS, University at Urbana-Champaign (2003)
10. Pei Cao, Zhe Wang,_Efficient top-K query calculation in distributed networks. In *Proceedings of the twenty-third annual ACM symposium on Principles of distributed computing.*.Canada:ACM Press,(2004)206-215
11. Martin Theobald, Gerhard Weikum, Ralf Schenkel. Top-k Query Evaluation with Probabilistic Guarantees. In *Proceedings of the 30th VLDB Conference (VLDB)*, Toronto, Canada, (2004)248-659
12. B. Yuwono and D.L.Lee. Server ranking for distributed text retrieval systems on the internet. In *proceedings of the 5th international conference on database systems for advanced applications*,Victoria,Australia,(1997)41-49
13. Rasolofo, Y., Abbaci, F. and Savoy, J.: Approaches to collection selection and results merging for distributed information retrieval. In *Proceedings of the tenth international conference on Information and knowledge management*, ACM Press, (2001)191-198

14. Callan, J.P., Lu, Z., and Croft, W. B. Searching Distributed Collections with Inference Networks. In *Proceedings of the 18th Annual International ACM SIGIR Conference on Research and Development in Information Retrieval*, ACM Press, (1995) 21-28

15. Gravano, L., and Garcia-Molina, H. Generalizing GLOSS to vector-space databases and broker hierarchies. In *Proceedings of the 21th International Conference on Very Large Databases (VLDB)*, (1995)78-89

16. Hang Cui, Ji-Rong Wen, Jian-Yun Nie, and Wei-Ying Ma. Query Expansion by Mining User Logs. *IEEE transactions on knowledge and data engineering*, Vol. 15, No. 4, IEEE Press, (2003)1-11

17. Xu, J. and Croft, W. B. Cluster-based Language Models for Distributed Retrieval. In *Proceedings of the 22th International Conference on Research and Development in Information Retrieval*, (1999) 254-261

18. M. Jansen, A. Spink and T. Saracevic. Real Life, real users, and real needs: A study and analysis of user queries on the web. *Information Processing and Management*, 36, 2 (2000)207-227.

19. C.R. Palmer and J. G. Steffan. Generating Network Topologies That Obey Power Laws. In *Proceedings of Global Internet Symposium*, (2000)

20. The Gnutella protocol specification v0.6. http://rfcgnutellasourceforge.net.

An Optimistic Fair Protocol for P2P Chained Transaction

Yichun Liu[1], Jianming Fu[2], and Huanguo Zhang[2]

[1] Hangzhou Dianzi University, Hangzhou 310018, P.R. China
liuyichun@126.com
[2] School of Computer Science, Wuhan University, Wuhan 430072, P.R. China
liss@whu.edu.cn

Abstract. As a decentralized technology, P2P architecture arises as a new model for distributed computing and transaction in the last few years, consequently there is a need for a scheme to incorporate payment services to enable electronic payment via P2P systems. In this paper, a new optimistic fair scheme is proposed for multi-party chained P2P transaction, which can ensure that every middleman and digital content owner can obtain the payments due to them. The disputes that might occur are analyzed and handling solution is proposed. The trusted third party need not be involved unless disputes have occurred. The optimistic payment scheme is fair, efficient, practical and suitable for multi-party chained P2P transaction.

Keywords: P2P transaction; chained transaction; onion payment; fairness.

1 Introduction

P2P networks are network where peer nodes communicate and transport information directly each other. Unlike the conventional client-server model, a peer node of P2P networks may act as both a client and a server simultaneously to share files or computing powers. It can request, serve, or relay services as needed. A major differentiating factor of P2P from traditional models is the lack of central management and control. This very important characteristic offers the ability to create efficient, scalable, and persistent services by taking advantage of the fully distributed nature of the systems.

In traditional electronic commerce transaction, some parties serve as vendors, who only sell goods, and the others act as buyers, who only purchase goods. However, in P2P transaction environment, peers serve as both vendors and buyers. A peer who has bought digital content might sell it to other for earning middleman commission.

An optimistic payment protocol does not need the trusted third party involved in transaction unless dishonest peers do not follow the protocol. The optimistic protocol is used for implementing lightweight payment, and the trusted third party is avoided becoming the bottleneck of transaction.

In this paper, we introduce a new P2P payment protocol which provides a secure and optimistic scheme on multi-party chained transaction, in which transactions are guaranteed to play fairly, possible disputes are effectively handled, and the trustee are not online involved.

S. Grumbach, L. Siu, and V. Vianu (Eds.): ASIAN 2005, LNCS 3818, pp. 136–145, 2005.

The paper is organized as follows: In the following section, we give an overview of related work in this field. An optimistic protocol for chained payment is proposed in section 3. Conclusions are drawn in section 4.

2 Related Work

A number of research projects have engaged in P2P computing and most have been focused on efficient resource location and load balancing; very few have addressed the need of payments in P2P environment.

An early P2P payment scheme is provided in [1], which relies on a fully trusted on-line escrow server. In this scheme, an escrow server deals with the protocol commitment, transmission of decryption key and payment. The escrow server bears too much burden and it might become the bottleneck of payment system, so the scheme has poor scalability.

Some P2P payment system introduces the stamped digital note as token of transaction [2,3], which can only be received and cashed by its issuer or specified agents, so the scheme has still poor scalability.

In the P2P payment protocol provided in [4], the buyer obtains the digital coin *BrokerScrip* from the broker, and the digital coin *VendorScrip* is produced by the vendor. The buyer and the vendor exchange their digital coins, and then buyer obtains the digital content from the vendor. The protocol is neither practical nor convenient because the buyer must obtain special coin from different vendor before per transaction.

Ppay is a micropayment scheme for P2P exchange [5], which presents the concept of floating and self-managed currency to greatly reduce broker involvement. This currency is practical and efficient, but the related payment protocol is not presented.

G. Arora, M. Hanneghan and M. Merabti propose the structure of the P2P content exchange application and the requirements for the cascading payment framework [6].

The chained transaction model is provided in [7], where provide a complex transaction model that describes the complex transaction as a transaction tree. The paper proposed some important requirement for chained transaction model, but the payment protocol has not been presented.

An exchange is fair if at the end, either each player receives the item it expects or neither player receives any additional information about the other's item. N. Asokan et al. present optimistic fair protocols for electronic commerce exchange by introducing trusted third party handling the disputes [8, 9].

3 Optimistic Payment Scheme for Chained Transaction

3.1 Preliminaries

In a chained P2P model, theoretically unlimited peers can participate in the whole transaction. Among these peers, there should be a customer who is an end buyer and a royalty owner who is an end seller. The other peers are intermediary, who buys the digital content and then resells it to another peer. Payment system should ensure the accurate distribution of payments to the appropriate peers, where the owner of the digital content receives a fixed amount of payment value (i.e. royalty) every time his digital content are propagated and each intermediary peer receives a middleman's fee (i.e. commission). The set of all peers is treated as a P2P group.

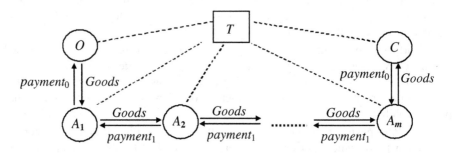

Fig. 1. Chained payment model

A chained P2P transaction system contains multiple peers in P2P group G: An end buyer who receives the digital content as a client, denoted by C; A digital content owner, denoted by O; multiple middleman peers who buy the digital content and then resell it, denoted by $A_1, A_2, A_3, ...A_{m-1}, A_m$. A trustee, denoted by T, is introduced to arbitrate the disputes and guaranteed the fairness of payment protocol, whose arbitrations are always respected and abided by all peers, brokers and law officers.

3.2 Cash System

Let us assume that each member of a P2P group has bank account in the broker (usually, a broker is a bank or other money issuer), and the broker prepares a key pair for the P2P group. The broker's public's key and all public keys of peers are published in the group. When a peer wants to obtain tokens for payment, he first sends a digital notes and his bank account to the broker. The broker will add a stamp on the digital note to form a stamped digital note as a token and then send it back to the peer. The broker stamp is utilized to authenticate the validity of a token. Simultaneously, the broker draws equal amounts of money out of the peer's account. The peer is the token owner now.

$DigitalNote=\{SerialNo, BrokerID, GroupID, value, IssueDate, Expiration\}$

$BrokerStamp=Sig_{Broker}(DigitalNote)$

$Token=\{DigitalNote, BrokerStamp\}$

The digital note $DigitalNote$ consists of the serial number $SerialNo$, the broker identifier $BrokerID$, the P2P group identifier $GroupID$, par value $value$ of the token, the date $IssueDate$ issuing the token and the expiration date $Expiration$ for the token circulation. The broker stamp on the digital note is *BrokerStamp*. The item *SerialNo* is chosen randomly with constant length and it is unique in the P2P group. The digital note *DigitalNote* should be ensured unique globally.

3.3 Onion Payment

Here, a new payment idea, i.e. onion payment, is presented to ensure that only the owner can obtain the royalty and each middleman can obtain the commission due to him. Now we consider the situation: the buyer C pays the peers $A_0, A_1, ...,A_m$ with the payments $payment_0, payment_1, ..., payment_m$, and these payments are transferred and distributed by the route $A_m \rightarrow A_{m-1} \rightarrow ... \rightarrow A_1 \rightarrow A_0$. The onion payment package is defined as follows:

$Onion\_Payment_0 = PK_{A_0}(payment_0)$

$Onion\_Payment_i = PK_{A_i}(payment_i, A_{i-1}, Onion\_Payment_{i-1})$ for $i=1,2, ...m$

The buyer C generates the onion payment package $Onion\_Payment_m$, and sends it to peer A_m. Peer A_m shucks off its surface layer, i.e. decrypting the onion payment package by his private key, to obtain the payment $payment_m$ due to him and the identifier A_{m-1} of next middleman, then peer A_m sends the onion payment package $Onion\_Payment_{m-1}$ to A_{m-1}. Each peer A_m does so until A_1 sends the onion payment package to A_0. All of peers $A_0, A_1, A_2, ...A_{m-1}, A_m$ can obtain the payment due to them, and none of them can illegally intercept or snatch the payment due to other peer.

The privacy of tokens for payment can be kept by using onion payment technology. Each middleman can only know the information of those tokens due to him, and he may not obtain the information of tokens due to other middlemen. The onion payment scheme can help to chained payment problem in complex transaction.

In our scheme, the token for payment consists of two parts, the item *DigitalNote* and item *BrokerStamp*, described as section 3.2. The item $DigitalNotes_i$ is the digital notes of tokens for paying peer A_i and the item $BrokerStamps_i$ is the broker stamps of those tokens. The goods producer A_0 will be paid digital notes $DigitalNotes_0$ and broker stamps $BrokerStamps_0$. The relevant onion payment package consists of two parts, onion digital notes package and onion broker stamp package.

$Onion\_DigitalNotes_0 = PK_{A_0}(DigitalNotes_0, Ts, Sig_C(DigitalNotes_0, Ts), C, Pid)$

$Onion\_DigitalNotes_i = PK_{A_i}(DigitalNotes_i, Ts, Sig_C(DigitalNotes_i, Ts),$

$$A_{i-1}, Onion\_DigitalNotes_{i-1}),   i=1,2, ...,m$$

$Onion\_BrokerStamps_0 = PK_{A_0}(BrokerStamps_0, C)$

$Onion\_BrokerStamps_i = PK_{A_i}(BrokerStamps_i, A_{i-1}, Onion\_BrokerStamps_{i-1}),$
$$i=1,2,...,m$$

The time stamp item *Ts* is applied to protect the protocol from replay attack.

3.4 Protocol Description

We assume that the buyer peer C decides to buy the digital content *item* within P2P group. Peer C searches the vendor peers of the digital content by P2P lookup services system and chooses suitable vendor peers. When a buyer peer requests the purchase of digital content by P2P content lookup mechanism, he is informed about the payment details which include the digital content owner's details along with the charge for owner royalty and the identifier of the intermediary along with the charge for middleman commission.

Detailed transaction protocol is as follows:

---

1. $C \rightarrow M$: C, T, B, Pid, bid

2. $M \rightarrow C$: $[Pid, desc]_O, price\text{-}list$

3. $M \rightarrow C$: $[Pid, E_s(item)]_O$

4. $C \rightarrow M$: $C, Tid, Onion\_DigitalNotes_m$

5. for $i=m\sim1$:

   $A_i \rightarrow A_{i-1}$: $Tid, C, Pid, Onion\_DigitalNotes_{i-1}$

6. for $i=1\sim m$:

   $A_{i-1} \rightarrow A_i$: $Tid, Sig_O(Tid, C, O, Pid, Ts), [Pid, PK_C(s)]_O$

7. $M \rightarrow C$: $Tid, [Sig_O(Tid, C, O, Pid, Ts)]_M$

8. $C \rightarrow M$: $Tid, Onion\_BrokerStamps_m$

9. M : if $valid(BrokerStamps_m)$ then

   $M \rightarrow C$: $[Pid, PK_C(s)]_O$

   else $abort$

10a. C: if $[timeout]$ or $unfit((Pid, PK_C(s)), Sig_O(Pid, PK_C(s)))$

   then $resolve\_C\_2$

   elseif $unfit(E_s(item), s)$ then $resolve\_C\_1$

10b. for $i=m\sim1$ do

   $A_i \rightarrow A_{i-1}$: $Tid, C, Onion\_BrokerStamps_{i-1}$

   A_{i-1} : if $invalid(BrokerStamps_{i-1})$ then $resolve\_A(i\text{-}1)$

Fig. 2. The exchange sub-protocol for chained payment

The peers $A_1, A_2, \dots A_m$, are the intermediary peers between the buyer C and the digital content owner O. They deliver the digital content and payment one by one. The peer A_0 denotes the digital content owner, and the peer A_m denotes the vendor M. B denotes the broker identifier, and the identifier T denotes the trustee.

$[message]_X$ includes the item $message$ and peer X's signature on it. $PK_X(message)$ is the ciphertext of item $message$ encrypted by peer X's public key. The session key s denotes the symmetric key for encrypting the digital content. The item $price\_list= PK_C(A_m, [commission_m]A_m, PK_C(A_{m-1}, [commission_{m-1}]A_{m-1}, \dots PK_C(O, [royalty]_O)\dots)$, which incudes both the commissions prices for all middlemen and the royalty prices. Because the item *commission$_i$* have been endorsed by peerA_i and the item *royalty* has been endorsed by the content owner O, any intermediary peer might not counterfeit the value of royalty or commission due to other peers.

In step 1, the buyer peer C sends his identifier C, the content request information, and bid *bid* for the digital content to a multicast subgroup of P2P group, whose members may resell content services.

In step 2, the member of multicast group reply with peer identifier P_i, digital content identifier *Pid*, digital content description *desc* and quoted price list *price-list*. The buyer peer C compares the price and services that are provided by vendors and then chooses a suitable vendor M.

In step 3, C downloads the content ciphertext $E_s(item)$ endorsed by the good owner.

In step 4, the buyer sends peer M with the onion digital notes package *Onion_DigitalNotes$_m$*. Only the content owner O can decrypt the payment for royalty. The payment for commission can only be decrypted by the corresponding middleman peer. Any peers might not illegally snatch the payments due to other peers.

In step 5, the vendor M shucks the onion payment after having received it and obtains the commission *DigitalNotes$_m$* endorsed by the buyer, and then transfers the onion payment package *Onion_DigitalNotes$_{m-1}$* to the middleman A_{m-1}. Each middleman $A_i(i=m-1\sim1)$ shucks the onion payments and obtains the commission *DigitalNotes$_i$* endorsed by the buyer C, and then transfers the onion payment package *Onion_DigitalNotes$_{i-1}$* to the middleman A_{i-1}, until the digital content owner has received the payment for the content royalty.

In step 6, the digital content owner forms the payment receipt $Sig_O(Tid, C, O, Pid, Ts)$, then sends peer A_1 with the receipt and the session key s encrypted by the buyer C 's public key.

For $i=1\sim m-1$, each middleman A_i verifies the validity of the endorsement $Sig_O(Pid, PK_C(s))$. If it is valid, peer A_i transfers the item $[Pid, PK_C(s)]_O$ and the receipt $Sig_O(Tid,C,O,Pid,Ts)$ to peer A_{i+1}; or else the protocol will be aborted.

In step 7, the vendor M sends the buyer C with the payment receipt $[Sig_O(Tid, C, O, Pid, Ts)]_M$ endorsed by himself to confirm that the digital content owner and all middleman have received the payment digital notes.

In step 8, the buyer sends peer M with the onion broker stamps package *Onion_Brokerstamps$_m$*. The onion package of broker stamps will make it possible that the digital content owner and all intermediaries can successively shucks the onion package by their private key and obtain the broker stamps of tokens due to them, but they might not snatch the tokens due other peers.

In step 9, M obtains the commission *BrokerStamps$_m$* due to him by peeling off the onion package *Onion_Brokerstamps$_m$.* If the broker stamps fit the digital notes, the vendor M sends the session key s to the buyer C, or else the protocol will be aborted.

In step 10a, the buyer tries to decrypt the encrypted digital content by the key s. If the buyer fails, he will call dispute the resolve protocol *resolve_C_1*. If the buyer has no received the key s or the key has not been endorsed validly by the content owner O, the buyer can call the resolve protocol *resolve_C_2*.

In step 10b, for each $i=1\sim m$, peer A_i obtains the items *Brokerstamps_i* by shucking the surface layer of the onion payment with decryption algorithm, and then hands on the onion digital notes package to peer A_{i-1}.

If a peer A_i cannot obtain the valid items *Brokerstamps_i* due to him by shucking off a layer of the onion payment package, he will resort to the dispute solution shown as section 3.5.

The step 10a and step 10b can be processed independently.

In the common P2P market, incentive mechanism is emphasized and adopted broadly. The more digital content the intermediary peer has sale, the more prize he will gain from the owner of the digital content. So when the intermediary peer has received the token encrypted by the owner's public key and he is unable to redeem it, he is willing to transfer them to the content owner.

3.5 Dispute Resolve

In the chained payment scheme, the three classes of dispute may occur and a trusted third party is introduced to resolve the disputes.

Dispute I. Peer C claims that he has received decryption key s endorsed validly by the owner O, but the content cipher text can not be decrypted successfully by the key.

Resolve protocol *resolve_C_1* for this dispute is as follows:

```
1.  C→T:  M, O, [Tid, Pid, desc]_O, [Tid, C, O, Pid, Ts]_O, [Pid, PK_C(s)]_O
2.  T→O:  C, Tid, Pid
3.  O→T:  item
4.  if fit(item, desc) then
         T→C:  item
    else
             T→C:  affidavit(C, O, Tid, Pid)
```

Fig. 3. The resolve sub-protocol for dispute I

Peer C sends the key s and other transaction information endorsed by owner O to the trustee T. T asks the owner O to transfer the digital content. If the digital content fits the description desc, it will be sent to the buyer peer C, or else the affidavit *affidavit(C, O, Tid, Pid)* will be sent to prove that the digital content owner has received the royalty but no digital content is transferred.

Dispute II. Peer C claims that he has paid for the content, but he has never received decryption key, or decryption key s has not been endorsed validly by the owner O.

Resolve protocol *resolve_C_2* for dispute II is as follows:

---

1. $C{\rightarrow}T$: $M, O, Ts, [Sig_O(Tid, C, O, Pid, Ts)]_M, Brokerstamps_m,$
   $\qquad Onion\_Brokerstamps_{m-1}$
2. $T{\rightarrow}M$: C, Tid, Pid
3. $M{\rightarrow}T$: $[Pid, PK_C(s)]_O, [DigitalNotes_m, Ts]_C$
   $\qquad$ if *unfit*$([Pid, PK_C(s)]_O)$ && *unfit*$([DigitalNotes_m, Ts]_C)$ then
   $\qquad\qquad T{\rightarrow}C$: *affidavit*$(C, M, Tid, Pid)$
   $\qquad$ elseif *fit* $(DigitalNotes_m, Brokerstamps_m)$ then
   $\qquad\qquad T{\rightarrow}C$: $[Pid, PK_C(s)]_O$
   $\qquad\qquad T{\rightarrow}M$: $Brokerstamps_m, Onion\_Brokerstampsm-1$

Fig. 4. The resolve sub-protocol for dispute II

In this sub-protocol, the buyer C sends the trustee T with the broker stamps due to the vendor M, the onion broker stamps package $Onion\_Brokerstamps_{m-1}$, and the payment receipt $Sig_O(Tid, C, O, Pid, Ts)$ endorsed by the vendor M. The trustee T asks the vendor M resends the session key and the digital notes for commission due to M. If the signature on item $[Pid, PK_C(s)]_O$ or item $[DigitalNotes_m, Ts]_C$ is not valid, the affidavit is sent to the buyer C so as to prove that the vendor should pay for his misbehavior; if the payment from the buyer is valid, the session key is transferred to the buyer C and the payment is transferred to the vendor M.

Dispute III. The digital content owner O or peer A_i complain that he cannot obtains the valid items *BrokerStamps* by shucking off a layer of the onion payment package.

Resolve protocol *resolve_A(i)* for dispute III sponsored by A_i is as follows:

---

1. $A_i \rightarrow T$: $Tid, C, [DigitalNotes_i, Ts]_C, Sig_O (Tid, C, O, Pid, Ts), [Pid, PK_C(s)]_O$
2. $T \rightarrow C$: Tid, A_i
3. $C \rightarrow T$: $Tid, A_i, Brokerstamps_i, Onion\_Brokerstamps_{i-1}$
4. if *fit*$(DigitalNotes_i, Brokerstamps_i)$ then
   $\qquad T \rightarrow A_i$: $Tid, Brokerstamps_i, Onion\_Brokerstamps_{i-1}$
   $\qquad T \rightarrow C$: $Tid, [Pid, PK_C(s)]_O, Sig_O (Tid, C, O, Pid, Ts)$
   $\quad$ else
   $\qquad T \rightarrow A_i$: *affidavit*(A_i, C, Tid, Pid)

Fig. 5. The dispute resolve sub-protocol for dispute II

In the sub-protocol *resolve_A(i)* sponsored by A_i, the middleman A_i sends trustee T with the digital notes *DigitalNotes$_i$* for commission due to A_i endorsed by the buyer C, the payment receipt Sig_O (*Tid, C, O, Pid, Ts*) and the item $[Pid, PK_C(s)]_O$. T verifies the signature on the digital notes *DigitalNotes$_i$*, the payment receipt and the endorsement on the key. If verification passes, the buyer is asked to resend the broker stamps due to peer A_i and the onion package *Onion_Brokerstamps$_{i-1}$*. If item *Brokerstamps$_i$* fits the item *DigitalNotes$_i$*, the broker stamps *Brokerstamps$_i$* and the onion package *Onion_Brokerstamps$_{i-1}$* are sent to the peer A_i, and the session key is sent to the buyer C; or else the affidavit is sent to the peer A_i to give witness that the peer A_i should obtain the payment. In the case $i=0$, the party A_i denotes the digital content owner O.

By far, the possible disputes on this scheme are discussed and feasible games for these disputes are proposed. The trusted third party can be off line and need only be called when disputes have occurred.

3.6 Security Analysis

Now we informally analyze the security properties of our payment scheme:

Confidentiality: The session key is encrypted by the buyer's public key and can only be disclosed by the buyer C. The payment due to each party A_i is encrypted by A_i's public key and can only be cashed by A_i. Any party cannot obtain the payment due to other parties.

Fairness: In the exchange sub-protocol, fairness will not be lost until step 6 since the buyer has not gotten the key and any other peers have not obtained the broker stamps of payment. After step 7, if some party misbehaves, the honest can obtain what he expects by starting the dispute resolve sub-protocol. No peers have advantage over other peers.

Non-repudiation: The onion digital notes package includes the buyer's signatures on digital notes for royalty and commissions, so it is impossible for a buyer to deny having sending a digital notes payment. The cipher text of the digital content and session key are endorsed by the digital content owner, and the owner can not deny having sent digital content after a successful digital content transfer. The payment receipt is used to confirming that the content owner and all middlemen have received the payment. Otherwise, middlemen and digital content owners cannot deny the quote price signed by them, and digital content owner can deny for having sent a digital content description endorsed by him.

Off-line: If both participants of transaction follow protocol, the trustee need not be involved in the protocol. The trustee only participates in the protocol when a dispute occurs. When a peer is judged a fraud peer, legal action should be taken and the malicious peer should be punished severely. The necessary punishment will effectively decrease the fraud so that trustee need be involved infrequently in disputes and efficiency of P2P transaction is improved. It is avoided that the trusted party might become the bottleneck of transaction.

4   Conclusion

P2P computing technology has become the focus of research on distributed computing and it will be used for electronic commerce. It is necessary to design a suitable payment scheme for P2P transaction system. In this paper, the optimistic payment protocol for the P2P chained transaction is presented. The disputes that might occur are analyzed and handling solution is proposed. The trusted trustee need not be involved on-line unless the dispute has occurred. Every party can obtain what they expect, or no one can. The optimistic payment scheme is fair, efficient, practical and suitable for P2P transaction.

References

1. Horne, B., Pinkas, B., Sander, T.: Escrow Services and Incentives in P2P Networks. Proceedings of the 3rd ACM Conference on Electronic Commerce (2001) 85-94
2. Anantharaman, L., Bao, F.: An Efficient and Practical P2P E-payment System. Manuscript (2002)
3. Onieva, J. A., Zhou , J., Lopez, J.: Practical Service Charge for P2P Content Distribution. Lecture Notes in Computer Science, Vol. 2836. Springer-Verlag, Berlin Heidelberg (2003) 112-123
4. Daras, P., Palaka, D. , Giagourta, V., Bechtsis, D., Petridis, K., Strintzis, M. G.: A Novel P2P Payment Protocol. Proceedings of the EUROCON '2003 (2003) 2-6
5. Yang, B., Garcia-Molina, H.: Ppay: Micropayments for P2P Systems. Proceedings of the 10th ACM Conference on Computer and Communication Security. ACM Press (2003) 300-310
6. Arora, G., Hanneghan, M., Merabti, M.: CasPaCE: A Framework for Cascading Payments in P2P Digital Content Exchange. PGNet Symposium 2003, Liverpoll John Unicversity, USA
7. Wang, G., Das, A.: Models and Protocol Structures for Software Agent Based Complex E-Commerce Transactions. Journal of Electronic Commerce (2001)
8. Asokan, N., Schunter, M., Waidner, M.: Optimistic Protocols for Fair Exchange. Proceedings of 4th ACM Conference Computer and Communication Security. ACM Press (1997) 6-17
9. Asokan, N., Schunter, M., Waidner, M.: Optimistic Protocols for Multi-Party Fair Exchange. Research Report RZ 2892 (# 90840), IBM Research (1996)

A Practical Approach to
Automatic Parameter-Tuning of Web Servers

Akiyoshi Sugiki[1], Kenji Kono[2], and Hideya Iwasaki[1]

[1] Department of Computer Science,
The University of Electro-Communications,
1-5-1 Chofugaoka, Chofu, Tokyo, Japan
sugiki@zeus.cs.uec.ac.jp, iwasaki@cs.uec.ac.jp
[2] Department of Information and Computer Science,
Keio University, 3-14-1 Hiyoshi,
Kohoku-ku, Yokohama, Japan
kono@ics.keio.ac.jp

Abstract. This paper presents a practical approach to automatically tuning the parameters of the Apache Web server. In particular, two significant parameters, KeepAliveTimeout and MaxClients, are dealt with. The notable features of our approach are twofold. First, it is easy to deploy because no modifications to Apache or the underlying operating system are required. Second, our approach is based on the detailed analysis on how each parameter affects the server's behavior. Experimental results demonstrate that our prototype works well on different workloads; it can discover almost optimal values and quickly adapt to workload changes.

1 Introduction

Modern Internet servers are growing rapidly in size and complexity. To maintain good performance and availability, an administrator is confronted with a huge amount of time consuming tasks to tune the server's ever-changing parameters. Performance parameters are especially difficult to tune *manually* for three reasons. First, it is not obvious what value is proper for each performance parameter. This is because the proper value largely depends on the execution environment. Second, it is time-consuming to find the proper values because tedious trials and errors must be repeated. Third, the proper value may change over time because the execution environment changes.

In this paper, we present a practical approach to automatically tuning the parameters of the famous Apache Web sever [1]. In particular, this paper deals with two major performance parameters, KeepAliveTimeout and MaxClients, because much of the literature [2, 3] has pointed out these greatly influence on Apache performance. Although we present our methodology within the context of Apache, we believe it could be applied to other Web servers.

The notable features of our methodology can be summarized as follows:

- **Easy to deploy:** Our mechanism does not require any modifications to Apache and the underlying operating system. To incorporate our mechanism, it is sufficient

S. Grumbach, L. Siu, and V. Vianu (Eds.): ASIAN 2005, LNCS 3818, pp. 146–159, 2005.

to restart Apache after defining a special environment variable. Since Apache is so widely used, it would help many administrators to tune their Web servers and thus have a practical impact.

- **Based on parameter analysis:** We exploit parameter-specific features to adjust KeepAliveTimeout and MaxClients. We analyzed the effects each parameter had on the behavior of Web servers to develop the tuning algorithm, and derived it to discover the proper value for each parameter. To derive both algorithms, HTTP-request intervals were assessed for KeepAliveTimeout, and resource contention was investigated for MaxClients.

Our approach based on parameter-specific analysis is effective for the performance-influenced parameters of widely used servers such as Apache. Although some might think our approach is not generic, our claim is that KeepAliveTimeout and Max Clients deserve to special consideration.

Our prototype system was implemented on Linux 2.4.20 and ran with Apache Web server 2.0.49. Experimental results demonstrated that our approach could successfully tune both KeepAliveTimeout and MaxClients to nearly optimal and manually tuned values. By automatically tuning KeepAliveTimeout, the throughput was improved by 27.5 – 368.5% compared to the default setting. Automatically tuning MaxClients also resulted in throughput close to the nearly optimal, hand-tuned level of Apache.

The rest of this paper is organized as follows. Section 2 analyzes the effects performance parameters had on the Apache. Section 3 introduces our mechanism. Section 4 describes the implementation of our prototype system. Section 5 presents the experimental results. Section 6 discusses related work. Finally, we conclude with a summary in Sect. 7.

2   Performance Effects on Parameters

It is important to adjust both KeepAliveTimeout and MaxClients properly, since they significantly affect server performance. To confirm whether this was the case, we measured the performance of the Apache Web server [1] using a standard Web benchmark (for details, refer to Sect. 5). Figure 1 plots the server throughput and average response time for various MaxClients and KeepAliveTimeout values.

We can see that KeepAliveTimeout dramatically affects server performance. When KeepAliveTimeout is set to 400 ms, the throughput improves up to 150.2% and the response time improves up to 13.3%, compared to the default KeepAlive Timeout value (i.e. 15 sec) of the Apache Web server. When this value is changed to 200 ms or 600 ms, the server throughput and response time both degrade down to 20.3% and 23.0% respectively, compared to 400 ms. This implies that KeepAlive Timeout is difficult to adjust manually; a slight difference in KeepAliveTimeout affects server performance.

Figure 1(b) shows that MaxClients also affects server performance. With this benchmark workload, the server yields the best throughput and moderate response time if its MaxClients is set to 700. Compared to the default MaxClients (150), the server throughput improves up to 297.9%. When the MaxClients is changed to 600

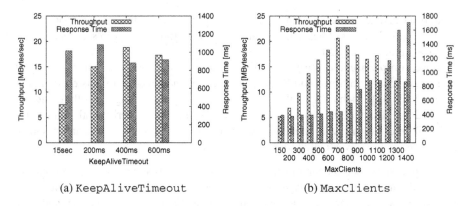

(a) KeepAliveTimeout   (b) MaxClients

Fig. 1. Performance Effects of KeepAliveTimeout and MaxClients

or 800, the server throughput degrades by 11.3% and 7.0% respectively. The response time suddenly increases when MaxClients is greater than 700. Again, as a slight difference in MaxClients affects server performance, it is very difficult to tune Max Clients manually.

3   Parameter-Tuning of Web Server

We will present the design for our tuning mechanism for Web servers. Our mechanism automatically tunes KeepAliveTimeout and MaxClients independently to the nearly optimal values for manual tuning. In Sect. 3.1, we will first show how Keep AliveTimeout is tuned, and then show how MaxClients is tuned in Sect. 3.2.

3.1   Tuning KeepAliveTimeout

Analysis on KeepAliveTimeout

Keep-alive connections [4] are beneficial for network efficiency, and server and client performance [5]. But, improperly setting KeepAliveTimeout may degrade server performance because of the low utilization of TCP connections, especially with heavy workloads.

Low utilization of TCP connections is caused by *idle* connections. Idle connections are TCP connections which no data was sent recently. For most Web servers that support keep-alive connections, idle connections are unavoidable, because most popular Web browsers (e.g. Internet Explorer, Firefox, and Opera) maintain connections as long as the server allows, for shorter response times and a better user experience.

However, most Web servers, including Apache, limit the maximum number of clients that can be connected to the server at the same time to avoid overloading the server. When the number of clients reaches MaxClients, a newly participating client cannot connect to the server due to MaxClients limitations, even though many idle connections are still maintained. As a result, the server capacity cannot be fully utilized and server throughput and response time are both degraded.

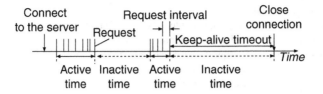

Fig. 2. Request cycles from client

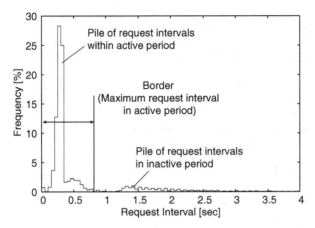

Fig. 3. Time Distribution for Request Intervals

Tuning Mechanism for `KeepAliveTimeout`

To avoid low server utilization without closing active connections, we reduce idle connections by adjusting `KeepAliveTimeout`.

Figure 2 outlines request cycles between a client and server. We can see two different periods of time, i.e, *active* and *inactive period* [6, 7, 3, 8]. During the active period, the client sends successive requests to retrieve Web page together with embedded objects such as JPEG images. During the inactive period, the client does not send any requests because the user is browsing the current, just retrieved Web page to determine which link to follow for the next page.

Request interval is closely related to `KeepAliveTimeout`. The request interval is the time between requests (Fig. 2). If a request interval exceeds `KeepAlive Timeout`, the connection is closed.

The request interval is closely related to these two periods of time. Figure 3 is a histogram of request intervals measured with the same benchmark as was discussed in Sect. 2. This histogram is based on the request time distribution of SURGE [6] which generates a representative workload for real traffic. We can see two distribution piles in Fig. 3; the left pile is built up with requests from the active period, and the right pile with requests from the inactive period. The intervals for successive requests in an active period are relatively small, since they were automatically issued by Web browsers. The request intervals in the inactive period on the other hand are much larger than those within the active period, since they include the user's thinking time.

```
 1: function tune_ka();
 2: // arr: an array to store request intervals (the size is N)
 3: // index: an index to the arr (the initial value is 0)
 4: // hist: histogram of request intervals (the size is T)
 5: // KeepAliveTimeout: the current KeepAliveTimeout
 6: // t_border: the border of active period
 7: begin
 8:     // Recording all request intervals
 9:     arr[index] := elapsed time from the last request processing;
10:     index := index + 1;
11:     if index < N then return;
12:     // Making up histogram of request intervals
13:     Making up the hist from the arr;
14:     index := 0;
15:     // Calculating the the border
16:     for t := 0 to T − 1 do begin
17:         ratio := hist[t]/∑_{j≤t} hist[j];        // (1)
18:         if t ≥ KeepAliveTimeout then begin
19:             err := (ratio − target)/target;    // (2)
20:             t_border := t + adj ∗ err;
21:             break
22:         end;
23:         if ratio < target then begin
24:             t_border := t; // It updates the border.
25:             break
26:         end
27:     end;
28:     // Updating KeepAliveTimeout
29:     KeepAliveTimeout := α · KeepAliveTimeout + (1 − α) · t_border    // (3)
30: end.
```

Fig. 4. Pseudo-Code for Tuning KeepAliveTimeout

We attempt to find the right verge, called *border*, for the active period and set Keep AliveTimeout to the border. By doing this, we can keep active connections and close inactive connections. As a result, the idle connections will be reduced and server utilization will be improved. If these two piles are mixed due to large round-trip-time between a client and server, we have only to determine the border to include majority of all the request intervals. Even in this case, most active connections are maintained.

Figure 4 shows the pseudo-code for our mechanism. Our mechanism tunes the single KeepAliveTimeout parameter across all clients connecting to the server. Every time a server accepts a request, the function tune_ka() is called. It first stores the request interval to the array *arr* (lines 8–11) and if *arr* is full, it prepares a histogram of request intervals (*hist*) (lines 12–14). The *hist* stores the frequency for each request interval t. It then finds the border by sweeping the histogram and calculating the ratio for the frequency of each interval (lines 15–27). Finally, it updates KeepAliveTimeout (lines 28–29). Our mechanism adjusts KeepAliveTimeout periodically, since a proper value for KeepAliveTimeout changes due to workload fluctuations.

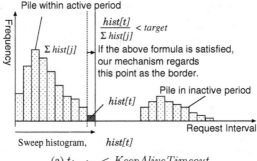

(a) $t_{border} < KeepAliveTimeout$

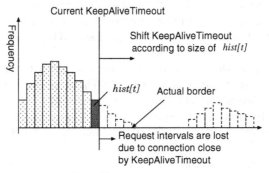

(b) $KeepAliveTimeout < t_{border}$

Fig. 5. Calculation of Border

There are several points that need to be noted. First, let us calculate

$$ratio := hist[t]/\sum_{j \leq t} hist[j] \qquad (1)$$

(line 17) and compare it to the threshold (*target*) to find the border (line 23, Figure 5(a)). The *ratio* is close to 1.0 when we start sweeping the histogram by incrementing the value of t. When t gets closer to the border, the *ratio* gets smaller and finally becomes less than *target*. At this point, we regard t as the border. The *target* is not difficult to determine because it is independent of workload.

Second, as we can see from Fig. 5(b), if the current value of `KeepAliveTimeout` is smaller than the border for active period, we cannot obtain the distribution of request intervals larger than `KeepAliveTimeout`. To cope with this, let us calculate

$$err := (ratio - target)/target \qquad (2)$$

and shift the border to a larger value determined by *err* (lines 19-20). The *err* is the metric how the *ratio* is different from the *target*. According to the difference *err*, we set t_{border} to a larger value. If t_{border} is set to a value larger than a proper `KeepAlive Timeout` value, it is made smaller by the method described above.

Third, to avoid the effect of request bursts frequently observed on the Internet [9, 10, 11], our mechanism updates `KeepAliveTimeout` using the well known weighted exponential moving average technique (line 29).

$$KeepAliveTimeout := \alpha \cdot KeepAliveTimeout + (1 - \alpha) \cdot t_{border} \qquad (3)$$

3.2 Tuning `MaxClients`

Analysis of `MaxClients`

`MaxClients` determines the maximum number of clients connecting to the server at the same time. Too large `MaxClients` leads to resource contention between server processes. On the other hand, too small `MaxClients` leads to poor server utilization. Resource contention occurs when many processes compete to acquire a shared resource (e.g. CPU, memory, disk and lock). `MaxClients` should be set at the maximum point that severe resource contention will not occur.

We detect severe resource contention by observing server throughput. If resource contention has occurred, throughput will degrade. The proper value for `MaxClients` achieves the peek throughput and its curve is convex. When `MaxClients` is less than the proper value, throughput improves if `MaxClients` is increased. When `Max Clients` is larger than the proper value, throughput degrades if `MaxClients` is increased.

To measure throughput, several points must be noted. First, because `MaxClients` determines the maximum number for server processes, Apache may increase or decrease the number of processes within `MaxClients`. Second, we must measure the throughput when all the processes are used, because many processes may be idle when the workload is light. Therefore, we must measure the throughput when the number of processes is close to `MaxClients` and all of these processes are used.

Tuning Mechanism for `MaxClients`

Our mechanism automatically tunes the `MaxClients` without administrator's intervention. If the throughput is improved by increasing `MaxClients`, our mechanism regards the proper `MaxClients` is larger than the current value and increases `Max Clients`. Contrary, if throughput degrades by increasing `MaxClients`, our mechanism regards the proper `MaxClients` is smaller than the current value and decreases `MaxClients`.

Figure 6 shows the pseudo-code for our mechanism. To tune `MaxClients`, this code runs when 95% of `MaxClients` processes are used (line 10). If the throughput is improved by increasing `MaxClients`, our mechanism increases `MaxClients` (line 16). If the throughput degrades by increasing `MaxClients`, it decreases `Max Clients` (line 17). Our mechanism works similarly to decrease `MaxClients`. If the throughput improves by decreasing `MaxClients`, our mechanism regards the proper `MaxClients` is smaller and reduces `MaxClients`. If the throughput degrades by decreasing `MaxClients`, our mechanism regards the current `MaxClients` is too small and increases `MaxClients`. Finally, if our mechanism changed `MaxClients`, it saves the current `MaxClients` and throughput for the next run (lines 24–27).

```
 1: function tune_mc(measured);
 2: // measured: measured throughput
 3: // throughput: smoothed throughput
 4: // MaxClients: MaxClients
 5: // prev: throughput at the previous control point
 6: // prevclients: MaxClients at the previous point
 7: // err_p, err_m: thresholds for adjustments
 8: // adj: const. for adjustments
 9: begin
10:    if not 95% of the server processes are utilized then return;
11:    throughput := α * throughput + (1 − α) * measured;
12:    err := (throughput − prev)/prev;
13:
14:    savedclients := MaxClients
15:    if MaxClients ≥ prevclients then begin
16:      if err > err_p then MaxClients := MaxClients + adj
17:      elif err < −err_m then MaxClients := MaxClients − adj
18:    end;
19:    elif MaxClients < prevclients then begin
20:      if err > err_p then MaxClients := MaxClients − adj
21:      elif err < −err_m then MaxClients := MaxClients + adj
22:    end;
23:
24:    if MaxClients <> savedclients then begin
25:      prev := throughput;
26:      prevclients := savedclients
27:    end
28: end.
```

Fig. 6. Pseudo-Code for Tuning MaxClients

4 Implementation

We implemented our algorithm for Apache Web server 2.0.49 running on Linux 2.4.20. We built our mechanism as a dynamic link library that was inserted at runtime between Apache and Linux. All that administrators have to do is to define our tuning library in a special environment variable LD_PRELOAD and start Apache. Our mechanism adjusts the parameters by hooking the system calls which relate to KeepAliveTimeout and MaxClients, and rewriting these system calls' arguments. If Apache started, reboot is never required even if our mechanism adjusts the parameters.

Before describing how to tune these parameters, we explain how Apache works. By default, Apache generates MaxClients processes at most to handle requests. Apache calls fork()/exit() to generate/terminate processes. We focus on the default prefork model. But our mechanism is easy to adapt to other models based on threads if we hook thread-related system calls instead of fork() and exit().

When Apache accepts a connection, it assigns a request handling process for this connection. The handling process invokes poll() to monitor request arrivals with the poll()'s timeout parameter set to KeepAliveTimeout. If no request arrives and timeout occurs, the handling process closes the connection.

Tuning `KeepAliveTimeout` is achieved by hooking `poll()` and rewriting the timeout parameter of `poll()` with the calculated `KeepAliveTimeout`. We can record request intervals by measuring the time between the call and exit of `poll()`.

Tuning `MaxClients` is achieved as follows. First, to enable our mechanism to change `MaxClients` freely, we set `MaxClients` in the Apache configuration file to a large value. To monitor the number of processes, our mechanism hooks `fork()` and `exit()`. If Apache tries to generate a process that exceeds the current `MaxClients` of our mechanism, our mechanism forces `fork()` to return an error code. Apache gracefully handles the error as if nothing happened. To reduce `MaxClients`, our mechanism sends the HUP signal to an excessive process to force it to exit, when the process completes the request handling.

5   Experiments

In this section, we demonstrate our mechanism can tune the server performance for several workload patterns. We will first present performance improvement obtained by tuning `KeepAliveTimeout`. We will then present the results by tuning `MaxClients`.

5.1   Experimental Setup

Our testbed consisted of a single server and 16 client nodes. Each node was equipped with a Pentium 4 2.8 GHz CPU, 512 MB memory, 7200 rpm HDD connected by an SCSI and 32 bit/33 MHz PCI bus. All of these were interconnected by a single switch via a 1000 Base-T Ethernet. The server software is Apache Web server 2.0.49 running on Linux 2.4.20. We did not modify any parameters of Apache from the default values except for `MaxClients`.

5.2   Experimental Workloads

We used the SPECWeb99 benchmark [12] to generate workloads. To emulate the client-side user behavior, we introduced request intervals to obey a Pareto distribution. It is generally known that the Pareto function emulates the client-side user behavior closely. We borrowed the same constant values for the Pareto function from SURGE [6]. In this experiment, we generated requests for static content.

We used two different workloads as shown in Tab. 1: (a) the SPECWeb99 Standard and (b) the SPECWeb99 Large. The SPECWeb99 Standard followed the standard file distribution specified in SPECWeb99 rules and the SPECWeb99 Large emulated a Web site including larger files such as JPEG images.

Table 1. Experimental workloads

Name	Description	File Distribution $\leq$1KB	$\leq$10KB	$\leq$100KB	$\leq$1MB	Total Size
(a) SPECWeb99 Standard	SPECWeb99 compliant	35%	50%	14%	1%	3.6 GB
(b) SPECWeb99 Large	Modified SPECWeb99 to generate requests for large files	1%	14%	50%	35%	3.6 GB

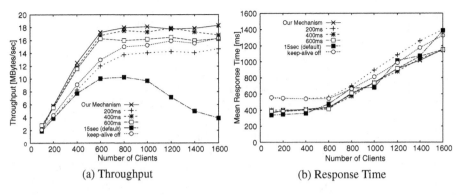

(a) Throughput

(b) Response Time

Fig. 7. Tuning `KeepAliveTimeout` for SPECWeb99 Standard

5.3   Results of Tuning `KeepAliveTimeout`

By tuning `KeepAliveTimeout`, server throughput and response time both improved. We fixed the `MaxClients` to 512 during this experiment to exclude the effect generated by `MaxClients`.

SPECWeb99 Standard
The results of server throughput and mean response time are plotted in Fig. 7. With manual tuning, the best `KeepAliveTimeout` value is 400 ms, since it yields the best throughput and a moderate response time.

Our mechanism automatically tuned `KeepAliveTimeout` to 450 ms, which is close enough to the best value. The throughput improved by 27.5 – 368.5% compared to the results for the default value of `KeepAliveTimeout` (15 sec).

SPECWeb99 Large
Figure 8 plots the results for the server throughput and the mean response time. The effect of tuning `KeepAliveTimeout` can be seen in the results for response time. With manual tuning, 800 ms is the best value for `KeepAliveTimeout`. Our mechanism automatically tuned `KeepAliveTimeout` to 850 ms and shortened response time. Server-side throughput is almost constant. The reason for this is it took a long time to

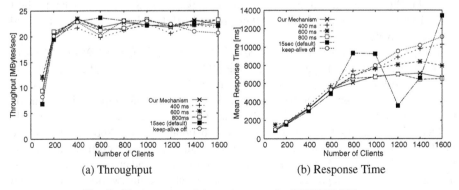

(a) Throughput

(b) Response Time

Fig. 8. Tuning `KeepAliveTimeout` for SPECWeb99 Large

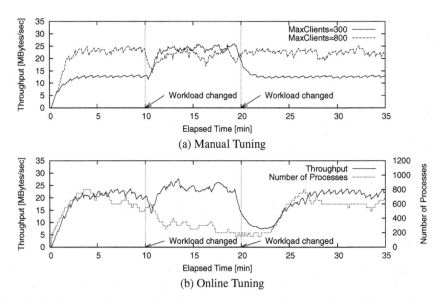

Fig. 9. Tuning `MaxClients`. The plot shows the server-side throughput and `MaxClients`. Workload changed at 10 min and 20 min.

transfer files, and the time needed to establish a connection becomes negligible. So the improvement in throughput is amortized.

5.4   Results of Tuning `MaxClients`

We demonstrate our mechanism automatically adjusts `MaxClients` and can adapt to workload changes. Figure 9(a) plots server throughput when `MaxClients` is fixed to 300, 800. Figure 9(b) plots server throughput and number of processes using our `Max Clients` mechanism. During this experiment, we used the unmodified SPECWeb99 to exclude the effect generated by `KeepAliveTimeout`. The offered load was fixed to 1000 clients. We intentionally changed the workload at 10 and 20 minutes to confirm how adaptable our mechanism was. We used the SPECWeb99 Standard workload until the 10 minutes, and SPECWeb99 Large from 10 to 20 minutes, and finally SPECWeb99 Standard again. In our preliminary experiment, we confirmed that the best `MaxClients` for the SPECWeb99 Standard and SPECWeb99 Large were 800 and 300, respectively.

In Fig. 9(a), the throughput for the 800 `MaxClients` for the SPECWeb99 Standard workload was twice as large as that for the 300 `MaxClients` for the SPECWeb99 Standard workload. But, the throughput for the 300 `MaxClients` outperformed that for the 800 `MaxClients` for the SPECWeb99 Large workload. During this period, the throughput for the 800 `MaxClients` fluctuated and degraded due to server overload.

Our mechanism took about three minutes to obtain almost proper value for the SPECWeb99 Standard workload. From 3 to 10 minutes, our mechanism maintained the `MaxClients` at around the proper value. When the workload changed at 10 minutes, throughput started to degrade, but our mechanism detected this workload change and started to decrease `MaxClients`. Around 12 minutes, `MaxClients` stabilized and throughput recovered. At 20 minutes, workload changed again. After that, throughput was recovered at around 28 minutes.

6 Related Work

We classify the existing approaches to automatic parameter-tuning for Internet servers into three categories: parameter-specific, parameter-generic, and control-theoretical.

6.1 Parameter-Specific Approach

The parameter-specific approach leverages the knowledge about parameter-specific features. From the detailed analysis of real HTTP traffic, Barford et al. [8] pointed out that Web servers should close keep-alive connections before the clients fall into the inactive period. This method is called *early close* in their paper. However, they did not show how to implement early close. Our tuning mechanism for `KeepAliveTimeout` can be regarded as an implementation of early close based on the analysis of connection activities.

Mogul [13] proposed the LRU (least recently used) policy to close idle connections. But, because it does not discern active period and inactive period, the server may start to close active connections to make room for newly coming connections when the workload is heavy. In contrast, our mechanism sets `KeepAliveTimeout` at the point where only inactive connections are closed, and thus avoids performance degradation caused by frequent requests for reconnections from the active clients whose connections have been just closed.

6.2 Parameter-Generic Approach

The parameter-generic approach formulates the parameter-tuning problem as a mathematical optimization problem and some heuristic search techniques are used to discover proper values of parameters. The Active Harmony project [14] uses traditional simplex downhill method for a cluster-based Web server, and Xi et al. [15] uses a smart hill-climbing algorithm using the importance sampling and the Latin hypercube sampling for an application Web server.

While this approach needs no knowledge about target parameters and internal server states, it has the following limitations. First, this approach does not always find optimal values since it may choose local minimum values or it may need long time to find optimal values. Second, it supposes that workload must not fluctuate until it finds proper values, which is impossible in actual environments. Finally, it is possible that the server's performance might be severely degraded, because this approach tries randomly selected values.

In contrast, our mechanism is able to tune the `KeepAliveTimeout` and `Max Clients` parameters without terrible performance degradation even if workload fluctuates. This is because our mechanism continually adjusts the parameters based on the observations of the server's performance.

6.3   Control-Theoretical Approach

In this approach, the Web server is mathematically modeled to apply the control theories. Control theory is well studied and applied to many engineering, especially in machinery systems. Diao et al. [3] proposed a mechanism that controls the Apache Web server according to user-specified policies in the CPU and memory utilization. Their mechanism mapped the policies into MaxClients and KeepAliveTimeout parameters, using the Multiple Input Multiple Output model. Doyle et al. [16] studied a resource provisioning tool for a co-hosted Web server. They focused on storage and memory, and built up the model that consists of these resources. Abdelzaher et al. [17] addressed the admission control of Web servers using traditional control theory techniques.

These studies simplified actual systems too much despite the fact that today's Internet servers are quite complex. For example, Diao et al. assume a model that can be represented by a linear combination of CPU and memory. In addition, these studies assume constant coefficients in the models whose values depend on the server's hardware and environments.

7   Conclusion

This paper presented a mechanism for tuning the parameters of Web servers. We focused on two significant parameters, KeepAliveTimeout and MaxClients. We developed the tuning algorithms for these two parameters based on the detailed analysis on how each parameter affected the server's behavior. Our mechanism is easy to deploy, because it requires no modification to the server and the underlying operating system. We implemented a prototype system for the Apache Web server. Experimental results revealed that our mechanism works well with different workloads and can adapt to workload changes.

Though our mechanism tunes KeepAliveTimeout and MaxClients independently, it may be possible that these two parameters interfere each other. For future directions, we are going to combine two tuning mechanisms into a single, more sophisticated mechanism.

References

1. The Apache Software Foundation: Apache HTTP server (1995)
   http://www.apache.org/.
2. The Apache Software Foundation: Performance notes - Apache tuning (2002)
   http://www.apache.com/.
3. Diao, Y., Gandhi, N., Hellerstein, J., Parekh, S., Tilbury, D.: Using MIMO feedback control to enforce policies for interrelated metrics with application to the Apache Web server. In: 7th IEEE/IFIP Symposium on Integrated Network Management. (2001)
4. Fielding, R., Gettys, J., Mogul, J., Frystyk, H., Masinter, L., Leach, P., Berners-Lee, T.: RFC 2616 Hypertext Transfer Protocol – HTTP/1.1 (1999)
5. Nielsen, H.F., Gettys, J., Baird-Smith, A., Prud'hommeaux, E., Lie, H.W., Lilley, C.: Network performance effects of HTTP/1.1, CSS1, and PNG. In: ACM SIGCOMM'97. (1997)

6. Barford, P., Crovella, M.: Generating representative Web workloads for network and server performance evaluation. In: ACM SIGMETRICS'98. (1998) 151–160
7. Crovella, M.E., Bestavros, A.: Self-similarity in World Wide Web traffic: evidence and possible causes. IEEE/ACM Transactions on Networking **5** (1997) 835–846
8. Barford, P., Crovella, M.: A performance evaluation of hyper text transfer protocols. ACM SIGMETRICS Performance Evaluation Review **27** (1999) 188–197
9. Jung, J., Krishnamurthy, B., Rabinovich, M.: Flash crowds and denial of service attacks: Characterization and implications for CDNs and Web sites. In: WWW Conference 2002. (2002)
10. Fox, A., Gribble, S., Chawathe, Y., Brewer, E., Gauthier, P.: Cluster-based scalable network services. In: 16th ACM Symposium on Operating System Principles. (1997) 78–91
11. Welsh, M., Culler, D.: Adaptive overload control for busy Intenet servers. In: 4th USENIX Symposium on Internet Technologies and Systems. (2003)
12. Standard Performance Evaluation Corporation: The SPECweb99 benchmark (1999) http://www.spec.org/osg/web99/.
13. Mogul, J.C.: The case for persistent-connection HTTP. In: ACM SIGCOMM'95. (1995)
14. Chung, I.H., Hollingsworth, J.K.: Automated cluster-based Web service performance tuning. In: 13th IEEE Int'l Symposium on High Performance Distributed Computing. (2004)
15. Xi, B., Liu, Z., Raghavachari, M., Xia, C.H., Zhang, L.: A smart hill-climbing algorithm for application server configuration. In: WWW Conference 2004. (2004)
16. Doyle, R.P., Chase, J.S., Asad, O.M., Jin, W., Vahdat, A.M.: Model-based resource provisioning in a Web service utility. In: 4th USENIX Symposium on Internet Technologies and Systems. (2003)
17. Abdelzaher, T.F., Shin, K.G., Bhatti, N.: Performance guarantees for Web server endsystems: A control-theoretical approach. IEEE Transactions on Parallel and Distributed Systems **13** (2002) 80–96

Media-Based Presentation with Personalization in a Web-Based eLearning System

Elvis Wai Chung Leung[1], Qing Li[1], and Yueting Zhuang[2]

[1] City University of Hong Kong
{iteleung, itqli}@cityu.edu.hk
[2] Zhejiang University, China
yzhuang@zjuem.zju.edu.cn

Abstract. A dramatic increase in the development of technology-based teaching and learning has been witnessed in the past decade. Many universities and corporations started rethinking the design and implementation of the learning systems. Due to the network infrastructure limitations in the traditional systems, it is difficult to provide an efficient and effective approach for delivering personalized course materials to individual student anytime anywhere. To take advantage from the emergence of the Internet, it provides an inexpensive and flexible infrastructure that can greatly enhance the communication among e-Learning system and students. In this paper, we introduce a SMIL-based approach to manage text, graphics, audio, and video for presenting the personalized media-based lesson on the Web. The facilities and capabilities of Web-based architecture, user profiles, XML, and SMIL are incorporated and utilized in a prototype system in our discussion.

1 Introduction

To meet with the increasing trend of learning demand, a dramatic increase in the development of technology-based teaching and learning has been witnessed in the past decade. To take advantage from the emergence of the Internet, it provides an inexpensive and flexible infrastructure that can greatly enhance the communication among e-Learning system and students. Nowadays, many universities and corporations started rethinking the design and implementation of learning systems [10, 12].

Among the multimedia-based projects for eLearning, *Classroom 2000* [1] is designed to automate the authoring of multimedia documents from live events. The researchers have outfitted a classroom at Georgia Institute of Technology with electronic whiteboards, cameras, and other data collection devices that collect data during the lecture, and combined these facilities to create a multimedia document to describe the class activities. *Cornell Lecture Browser* from Cornell University [2] captures a structured environment (a university lecture). It automatically produces a document that contains synchronized and edited audio, video, images and text, so as to synchronize the video footage in the live classroom with pre-recorded slides used in the class. Last but not the least, *MANIC,* from University of Massachusetts [3], discusses the ways of effectively utilizing WWW-based, stored materials and presentation para-

S. Grumbach, L. Siu, and V. Vianu (Eds.): ASIAN 2005, LNCS 3818, pp. 160–171, 2005.
© Springer-Verlag Berlin Heidelberg 2005

digms. In particular, *MANIC* proposes that students should be given the opportunity to browse the materials, stopping and starting the audio at their own pace.

Although online course materials have many advantages over traditional textbooks and lecture notes, they still have a number of generic deficiencies as follows.

- Distribution of media-based course materials on the Internet is comparatively slow.
- Development of course materials does not cater for individual student's needs.
- Pre-programming for combination of text and multimedia in a presentation is required.

Currently, a high student dropout rate and low satisfaction with the learning processes remain to be the drawbacks. Not surprisingly, failing to consider students' attributes and instructional strategies seems to cause ineffectiveness even with the technologically advanced e-Learning system being developed. In response to the above-mentioned issues in the technology-based learning, we have engaged in developing a *Personalized eLearning System* (**Peels**) over the last couple of years [4, 6].

1.1 Paper Objectives and Organization

To easily manage, store and retrieve course materials and generate media-based course materials that are interoperable, we propose an innovative mechanism that incorporates *user profile, dynamic conceptual network,* and *SMIL-based wrapper* to manipulate course materials. The proposed mechanism adopts user profiles to determine the characteristics of the students such as background knowledge, learning goals, level of difficulty for the course materials and so on. To provide a framework for course materials manipulation, a Dynamic Conceptual Network (DCN) is introduced. DCN is a *hierarchy tree* in association with *learning concepts*. Each learning concept is stored in a DCN *node*. Apart from the learning concept, each node also contains some *attributes* for constructing the relationships among the nodes and self-description of each node. For distributing the course materials to individual student, personalized course materials (e.g. text, graphic, audio, and video) are put together by the proposed SMIL wrapper. This paper aims to advocate the concept of *reusable and personalized course materials* mechanism through the hybrid use of Web-based architecture, user-profiles, XML, SMIL, and Java technologies.

Through designing the conceptual framework and algorithms, we aim to address the following main topic in this paper: *How to effectively distribute the media-based course materials to serve individual student needs on the Web?* The rest of this paper is organized as follows: The related works for reviewing the current applied technologies are discussed in section 2. The specific features of the proposed framework and algorithms are detailed in sections 3. The final section concludes this paper and makes suggestions for further research.

2 Background of Research

To address the problem of slow access to the online course materials on the Internet, *decentralizing approach for the multimedia application* [13, 14] is a possible solution.

In particular, we adopt a distributed approach for delivering course materials in Peels. More specifically, the overall course materials management in Peels is centrally controlled and the course materials (e.g. text, graphic, audio, and video) are distributed directly to individual students on demand [5, 11]. To advocate the concept of distributed course materials, standardized methodologies and languages for annotation of hypermedia information are required. The following are such technologies employed by Peels.

XML (Extensible Markup Language) is designed for content publishing on the Internet. The ambition of XML provides some advantages that are not available in HTML, such as DTD (Document Type Definition). XML is adopted for storing the course materials in the server-side of our proposed Peels. In XML documents processing, DOM (Document Object Model) and SAX (Simple API for XML) are employed to manipulate the XML files through Java technologies. To make it successful, standardization for course materials development becomes a critical factor.

In order to encourage the standardization and interoperating course materials, a common standard is required in building the eLearning course materials. One possibility is the IEEE's Standard for Learning Object Metadata (LOM) [7] that describes data structures for providing interoperability content. In the course materials development, XML metadata has become the de-facto standard for indexing, defining and searching learning objects and all of the repositories mentioned above use metadata standards developed under LOM.

In fact, a learning object (LO) contains learning units, and learning object metadata is data about learning objects and resources. The general functions served by metadata are description, structure, and administration. It also allows educators to evaluate whether the resources meet their specific requirements and those of their learners. The benefits of LOs are categorized below.

On teachers side	On students side
Save time in the development of lessons, course components and curriculum by reusing resources already in existence.	Able to find learning resources that are guaranteed to be accurate and up-to-date.
Save money by not having to develop resources that already exist.	All resources contain precise citation information.
Share interdisciplinary expertise.	Allow users to search across disciplines by key words, author, institution, etc.

To provide interactive learning environments, SMIL (Synchronized Multimedia Integration Language) is a suitable solution to facilitate media-on-demand for individual student. SMIL is recommended by W3C for designing Web-based multimedia presentations which combine text, graphic, audio, and video in real-time. It uses a simple XML-based markup language, similar to HTML, which enables an author to describe the temporal behavior of a multimedia presentation, associate hyperlinks with media objects and describe the layout of the presentation on screen. Also, the development of the SMIL template is quite easy for the teaching staff. No matter what course contents (e.g. text, graphic, audio, and video) are included, the template can be applied if the presentation layout is suitable. Thus, the development time and pre-programmed multimedia presentation by technical staff can be minimized.

Through SMIL, multimedia data can be played on the Internet in a synchronized manner. Moreover, the *Prefetch* feature allows having many different videos pre-set, and then displayed one by one. The waiting time can be minimized, and thus makes learning more efficient and enjoyable. SMIL allows the videos and lecture notes displayed simultaneously on the same screen, either in the same window or under sub-windows. This greatly facilitates students' learning and stimulates their interests.

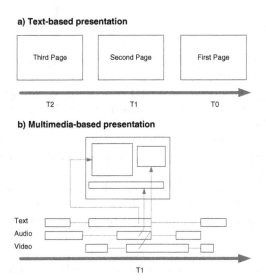

Fig. 1. Presentation layout

One important reason for developing SMIL-based course materials presentation is that the needs for the multimedia spatial layout model are different from the text-based documents. As shown in Figure 1a, the layout of text-based documents (e.g. HTML) is based on one-dimensional text-flow. The transformation from one to two dimensions is typically through scrolling. In Figure 1b, multimedia spatial layout is inherently two dimensional with little or no transformation from the document structure to the final display space. It helps student to manage the text and multimedia presentation simultaneously and simulates the classroom environment. As a result, the attraction of the lesson will be increased and thus, continuous learning on the Internet can be maintained, which may directly help improve the student dropout problem to a great extent.

3 System Components and Functionalities

The overall process of our system for generating the personalized course materials on the Web is as shown in Figure 2. The major components include the *Dynamic Conceptual Network* (DCN), *Analytic Hierarchy Process* (AHP), and *SMIL Wrapper*.

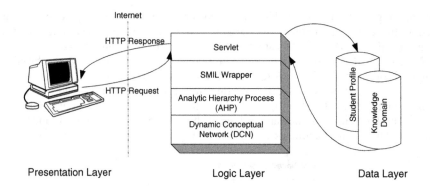

Fig. 2. Web-based architecture for media-based course materials generation

At the initial stage, students make HTTP requests to the logic layer through the browser. The servlet as a facilitator, located in logic layer, is waiting for such requests. Once a request is received, it will coordinate the request with other components for further action. Finally, it will gather the result from the SMIL Wrapper so as to send the course materials to the student. The responsibilities of each component are summarized next.

Basically, the Dynamic Conceptual Network (DCN) [4] is to manage course materials by a hierarchical tree and to generate the personalized course materials through some pre-defined rules and mechanism. As for the *Knowledge Domain*, it is the primary repository for all course materials and multimedia lessons. The relevant course materials are extracted from the Knowledge Domain in providing a suitable lesson to the student. The retrieval operation is based on the index server to locate the expected multimedia lessons/course materials for a given lesson.

To provide the best course materials to individual student, an Analytic Hierarchy Process (AHP) [9] is used as the selection mechanism based on student profiles. In particular, the *Student Profile* is the primary storage for all student-specific information such as study history, personal information, and study status. It provides the relevant information for determining the related concepts for a lesson. Normally, a user profile can provide the latest student's information on demand.

To implement the interactive learning environment, the media-based course materials are distributed by the SMIL wrapper. The function of the SMIL wrapper is to manage all the provided course materials from AHP and identify the most suitable SMIL presentation template to generate the multimedia presentation to individual student. The detailed mechanisms for each component will be discussed in subsequent sections.

3.1 Dynamic Conceptual Network

Definition: The Dynamic Conceptual Network (DCN) is a *hierarchical tree* to develop *dependent-relationships* among *learning concepts*. Each learning concept is stored as a *concept node* (Figure 3(a)) of the dynamic conceptual network.

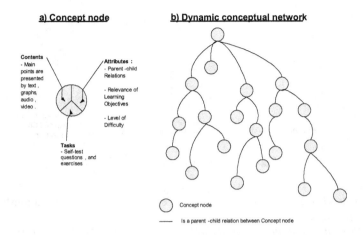

Fig. 3. Dynamic conceptual network

As depicted in Figure 3(b), the DCN is composed of concept nodes. Each concept node has a unique identity for easy reference. As shown, the concept node in Figure 3(a) includes *contents, tasks, and attributes*. The contents are represented by text, graph, audio, and video. Tasks include self-test questions and exercises. In order to provide facilities for building up the relationships among the concept nodes, three attributes are defined in each concept node, namely, *parent-child relations*, *relevance of learning objectives*, and *level of difficulty*. The semantics of each attribute are explained as follows.

- Parent-child Relations. These inter-concept links are for building up the dynamic conceptual network. Each relation contains a *parent link* and *child link*, which refer to the identities of the other concept nodes.
- Relevance of Learning Objectives. This is the information for identifying the relevant concepts of a particular learning objective.
- Level of Difficulty. As a means to serve the concept of personalization, this attribute is a parameter to determine whether the course materials are suitable for a targeted student group.

Based on the above attributes, we now explain the process of concept node mapping for generation of the DCN. Figure 4 shows three possible scenarios among the concept nodes, i.e., no relationship between concepts, concepts A and B have a relationship on an equal level (level of difficulty), and concepts A and B have a relationship and concept B is based on concept A. A rule-based mechanism [8] is employed for the concept node mapping according to the following rules.

- **Rule I:** // Figure 4a shows that no relation exists between concepts A and B.
  IF <no equal of parent-child attributes for the concept nodes A and B>
  THEN <No relation between A and B>

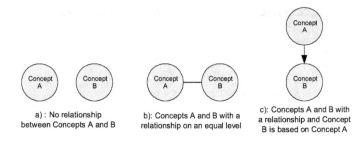

Fig. 4. Inter-concept-node relationships

- **Rule II:** // Figure 4b shows that concepts A and B are of a relationship on an equal level.
  IF <the parent links of concepts A and B in their parent-child attributes are of the same object reference>
  THEN <A and B are of the relation on an equal level>

- **Rule III:** // Figure 4c shows that concepts A and B are of relationship and concept B is based on concept A.
  IF <the parent link of concept node B is of the same object reference as that of concept node A's child link >
  THEN <A and B are of the parent-child relation; concept node A is the parent and concept node B is the child>

Based on these mechanisms, the course materials can be built up by a hierarchical framework for manipulation. To implement the DCN, XML is adopted to construct the course materials. The detailed course materials development is explained in [4]. The determination of the best-fit materials for a particular student through AHP will be explained in the following section.

3.2 Analytic Hierarchy Process

The Analytic Hierarchy Process (AHP) [9], developed at the Wharton School of Business by Thomas Saaty, allows decision makers to model a complex problem in a hierarchical structure showing the relationships of the goal, objectives (criteria), sub-objectives, and alternatives. AHP is a decision-making method that helps find the candidate out of a set of alternatives to best satisfy a set of criteria. The criteria may be divided into sub-criteria and so on, thus forming a hierarchical criteria tree. Basically, the first step of AHP is to define the objective of the task and then select some criteria to judge the alternatives for achieving the objective.

For illustration, we assume that *the objective is to identify the best course materials for student A in a particular subject.* The selected criteria to judge the alternatives (course materials) include related subject knowledge, current study workload, and learning initiative. This information can be extracted from the individual student profile for evaluation [6]. The alternatives contain Course Materials A (CMA), Course Materials B (CMB), and Course Materials C (CMC). These course materials are stored in XML files through the DCN.

CMA includes some revisions for the past learning concepts and additional examples/illustrations to explain the new learning concept. Meanwhile, the provided number of new learning concepts is less than the standard course materials (e.g. CMC) in order to fit for a student who needs more assistance. CMB includes some additional advanced topics and challenging exercises to cater for a student with good learning ability. CMC is a standard course material which is suitable for the middle-level ability students. According to the profile of individual student (say, student Tom) and Saaty's scale of relative importance table (Table 1), the criteria matrix and alternative matrix are calculated, as shown in Tables 2 and 3, for judging the alternatives.

Table 1. Saaty's scale of relative importance table

Comparative Importance	Definition	Explanation
1	Equally important	Two decision elements (e.g., indicators) equally influence the parent decision element.
3	Moderately more important	One decision element is moderately more influential than the other.
5	Strongly more important	One decision element has stronger influence than the other.
7	Very strongly more important	One decision element has significantly more influence over the other.
9	Extremely more important	The difference between influences of the two decision elements is extremely significant.
2, 4, 6, 8	Intermediate judgment values	Judgment values between equally, moderately, strongly, very strongly, and extremely.

By calculating priority weights for each matrix and linearly combining them, the following priority vector is developed: CMA is 0.363, CMB is 0.69, and CMC is 0.498. Referring to the AHP's definition, the alternative with the highest priority weight is the best choice. resulting this case, course material B is the best choice (for student Tom) with an overall priority weight of 0.69. Thus, course materials B should be provided for Tom. Once the relevant course materials are identified, it will be transferred to the SMIL wrapper for constructing and distributing to the student. The SMIL wrapper is discussed in coming section.

Table 2. Criteria matrix

Selection criteria	Related subject knowledge	Current study workload	Learning initiative		Selection criteria after normalization	Related subject	Current study workload	Learning initiative	Average
Related subject knowledge	1	1/3	1/5		Related subject knowledge	0.111	0.063	0.138	0.104
Current study workload	3	1	1/4		Current study workload	0.333	0.188	0.172	0.231
Learning initiative	5	4	1		Learning initiative	0.556	0.750	0.690	0.665

Table 3. Alternative matrix

Related subject knowledge	CMA	CMB	CMC		Related subject knowledge after normalization	CMA	CMB	CMC	Average
CMA	1	1/2	1/3		CMA	0.111	0.095	0.109	0.105
CMB	2	1	1/2		CMB	0.222	0.188	0.137	0.182
CMC	3	2	1		CMC	0.333	0.375	0.690	0.466

Current study workload	CMA	CMB	CMC		Current study workload after normalization	CMA	CMB	CMC	Average
CMA	1	1/3	1/9		CMA	0.111	0.045	0.157	0.104
CMB	3	1	1/6		CMB	0.333	0.188	0.196	0.239
CMC	9	6	1		CMC	1.000	1.125	0.690	0.938

Learning initiative	CMA	CMB	CMC		Learning initiative after normalization	CMA	CMB	CMC	Average
CMA	1	1/2	1/5		CMA	0.111	0.061	0.138	0.103
CMB	2	1	1/4		CMB	0.222	0.188	0.172	0.194
CMC	5	4	1		CMC	0.556	0.750	0.690	0.665

3.3 SMIL Wrapper and Its Implementation

As shown in Figure 5, the SMIL wrapper is to coordinate all the data sources (i.e. text, graphic, audio, and video) from AHP and the related SMIL-based presentation template to generate the media-based course materials to individual student. SMIL wrapper contains 4 layers which are *Presentation Layer* (PL), *Generation Layer* (GL), *Spatial Layer* (SL), and *Input Layer* (IL). The abstraction of each layer is described immediately below.

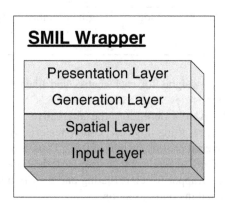

Fig. 5. SMIL Wrapper

Input Layer (IL). It is the input layer that communicates with Analytic Hierarchy Process (AHP) to get the course materials. The related parameters of each course material will be captured and transferred to each of the upper layers for further processing.

Spatial Layer (SL). To identify the sequence relationship among the course materials in a synchronized presentation, it is required to extract the spatio-temporal parameters of each course material. The sequence relation between the text and video in a presentation is an example.

Generation Layer (GL). This layer is required to identify which SMIL template can fit for the presentation based on the timeline information from SL. The pre-defined SMIL template is stored in a repository. Meanwhile, the SMIL template is required to update the presentation. For example, the *seq tag* and *URL* will be updated to capture both the sources of course materials and the presentation sequence, based on the timeline information and the parameters from the input layer.

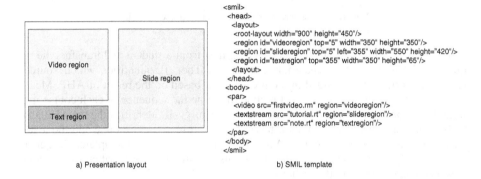

a) Presentation layout   b) SMIL template

Fig. 6. Sample of presentation template

A sample presentation layout is shown in Figure 6a. The presentation (screen) includes 3 regions which are video, slide, and text. Video region is designed for video presentation, slide region is for displaying text-based course materials, and text region is for displaying the supplement information. In the SMIL template (Figure 6b), the media and synchronization information is defined in the *body* tag. The temporal structuring can be specified by *seq* and *par* tags. In this example, all media components are contained in a par tag. Likewise, the media type and related URL are specified inside the temporal structuring tags.

Presentation Layer (PL). It includes a presentation interface through which a student can input some parameters (e.g. course code, topic) to request the lesson content through HTTP on the Internet. If PL receives the related result, then it will deliver the media-based course materials via the SMIL file which defines all the presentation schedule of each course material. Otherwise, the student is required to re-input the request.

Fig. 7. Sample screen of personalized course materials

In the overall processing, PL receives a request from a student and transfers the request to DCN for course materials generation. Then IL identifies which sources (course materials) are included in the presentation based on the result of AHP. Meanwhile, SL generates a presentation timeline to define the sequence of each course material based on each source's parameter. Subsequently, GL identifies the most suitable SMIL template for this presentation based on the presentation timeline and the available SMIL presentation templates. According to the timeline and template, GL generates a SMIL file to present the course materials. Finally, the PL distributes the media-based course materials to the student.

Based on the result from section 3.2, the media-based course materials are constructed as a SMIL file by SMIL wrapper. A sample screen as shown in Figure 7 is captured from the media-based presentation. In particular, student is only click on a hyperlink to start the media-based presentation. This screen is in conformance with Figure 6's template of three elements (viz., video region, slide region, and text region). In this example, course title information is displayed in the text region. The text-based learning materials are provided in the slide region. In order to enhance the learning effectiveness, the multimedia contents displayed in the video region are also incorporated to simulate the face-to-face learning environment.

4 Conclusions and Future Research

In this paper, we have presented a SMIL-based approach to manage multimedia data for course materials generation. Through the hybrid use of Dynamic Conceptual Network, Analytic Hierarchy Process, user-profiles, XML, SMIL, and Java technologies, our personalized e-learning system (Peels) aims at generating personalized media contents to meet individual student needs. Among the many desirable features offered by Peels, the following building blocks are worth mentioning:

- Dynamic Conceptual Network. It provides a hierarchical tree for developing the inter-relations among individual course materials. Through the student user profile, the best course materials can be determined by the Analytic Hierarchy Process.
- SMIL-based multimedia course materials. The suggested media-based course materials are generated based on individual student's expectation and learning goals, which support the ideas of personalization and interactive learning effectively. As a result, the attraction of the lessons can be increased and, thus, continuous learning on the Internet can be maintained satisfactorily.

Currently, the presented mechanism of SMIL-based approach for distributing multimedia course materials is being incorporated into our Peels prototype system. In our subsequent work, we plan to collect real user comments and perform user analysis and evaluation on the Internet for consolidated research.

References

[1] Pimentel, M.G.C., Abowd, G.D. and Ishiguro, Y., Linking by Interacting: a Paradigm for Authoring Hypertext, Proceedings of ACM Hypertext, May 2000
[2] Mukhopadhyay, S. and Smith, B., Passive Capture and Structuring of Lectures, Proceedings of ACM Multimedia, pp.477-487, October 1999
[3] Stern, M., Steinberg, J., Lee, H. I., Padhye, J. and Kurose, J.F., MANIC: Multimedia Asynchronous Networked Individualized Courseware, Proceedings of Educational Multimedia and Hypermedia, pp.1002-1007, 1997
[4] Leung, E. and Li, Q., Dynamic Conceptual Network Mechanism for a Web-based Authoring System, Proceeding of the Second International Conference on Human Society and the Internet (HIS'03), LNCS 2713, pp.442-453, Korea, 2003.
[5] Leung, E. and Li, Q., XML-based Agent Communication in a Distributed Learning Environment. Proceedings of the Third International Conference on Web-based Learning (ICWL'04), LNCS 3143, pp.136-146, China, Aug 2004
[6] Leung, E. and Li, Q., Towards a Personalized eLearning System. Encyclopedia of International Computer-Based Learning (to be published in spring of 2005).
[7] IEEE Standard 1484.12.1 for Learning Object Metadata, http://ltsc.ieee.org/wg12
[8] Riley, G., CLIPS, A Tool for Building Expert Systems.
    http://www.ghg.net/clips/CLIPS.html
[9] Saaty, T.L., The Analytic Hierarchy Process, New York, N.Y., McGraw Hill, 1980.
[10] Jonassen, D.H., Supporting Communities of Learners with Technology: A Vision for Integrating Technology with Learning in Schools. Educational Technology, 35(2). 60-63, 1995
[11] Lesser, V. R., Cooperative Multiagent Systems: A Personal View of the State of the Art, IEEE Transactions on Knowledge and Data Engineering, vol. 11, no.11, Jan –Feb 1999
[12] Johnson, D.W. and Johnson, R.T. Cooperative learning: where we have been, where we are going. Cooperative Learning and College Teaching. Vol 3, No.2, Winter, 1993.
[13] Duffield, N., Ramakrishnan, K., and Reibman, A. S., An Algorithm for Smoothed Adaptive Video over Explicit Rate Networks. IEEE Transactions on Networking 6, 717–728, 1998.
[14] Goncalves, P. A. S., Rezende, J. F., and Duarte, O. C. M. B., An Active Service for Multicast Video Distribution. Journal of the Brazilian Computer Society 7, 43–51, 2000.

Searching Patterns in Digital Image Databases

Fei Shi and Ahmad AlShibli

Computer Science Department, Suffolk University,
Beacon Hill, Boston, MA 02114, USA
{shi, alshibli}@mcs.suffolk.edu

Abstract. We present a method for the multiple two-dimensional pattern matching problem and its application in image database systems. In this problem, we are given a set $S = \{T_1, T_2, \cdots, T_N\}$ of two-dimensional matrices and another two-dimensional matrix P, called the pattern, and we want to find all occurrences of the pattern P in the set S. The main idea behind our method is to represent two-dimensional matrices with one-dimensional strings (called *fingerprint strings* or simply *fingerprints*) thus reducing the two-dimensional matrix matching problem into a one-dimensional string matching problem. We use a data structure, called *the generalized suffix array*, as our index structure to organize the fingerprints of the set S. The construction of the index (including converting the matrices in the set S into fingerprint strings) takes $O(M \log n)$ time and the index occupies $O(M)$ space ,where M denotes the total number of elements in all matrices in S and n the width of the widest matrix in S. Once the index is available, a query for the occurrences of an $m \times m$ pattern in the set S can be answered in $O(m^2 + \log M)$ time. The reduction of the two-dimensional matrix problem into a one-dimensional string problem, however, can introduce errors, called *false matches*. A false match occurs if the algorithm claims a "match" between the pattern P and some submatrix of some matrix in the set S while they are actually not equal. But as will be seen, the probability that a false match can occur is negligible. For instance, suppose our patterns are 512×512 images. Then the probability that a "match" that is claimed by our algorithm is a false one is less than 2.39×10^{-7}.

1 Introduction

In the multiple two-dimensional pattern matching problem, we are given a set $S = \{T_1, T_2, \cdots, T_N\}$ of two-dimensional matrices (each T_i is called a text) and another two-dimensional matrix P (called the pattern) over some alphabet Σ, our task is to find all occurrences of the pattern in the set S. This problem is an extended version of the *simple* two-dimensional pattern matching problem, which is to find all occurrences of a two-dimensional matrix P in another (larger) two-dimensional matrix T.

Example 1. $\Sigma = \{a, b, c\}$. $S = \{T_1, T_2\}$.

S. Grumbach, L. Siu, and V. Vianu (Eds.): ASIAN 2005, LNCS 3818, pp. 172–181, 2005.
© Springer-Verlag Berlin Heidelberg 2005

$$T_1 = \begin{pmatrix} a\ c\ a\ b\ c \\ a\ b\ b\ c\ b \\ a\ b\ c\ a\ c \\ a\ a\ c\ a\ b \end{pmatrix},$$

$$T_2 = \begin{pmatrix} a\ c\ a\ c\ a \\ a\ c\ c\ b\ b \\ a\ c\ a\ c\ c \end{pmatrix}.$$

$$P = \begin{pmatrix} a\ c \\ a\ b \end{pmatrix}.$$

The pattern P appears twice in T_1: at the upper-left corner and at the lower-right corner of T_1. But P does not appear in T_2 at all.

Since a digital image can be represented as a two-dimensional matrix, efficient techniques for the multiple two-d matching problem can be very useful in a web search engine that manages a huge number of digital images (photos) – the user of the search engine may want to find digital images on the web that contain a special image (pattern) issued by the user. Unfortunately, as of today, even the popular *Google Image Search* (http://images.google.com/advanced_image_search), can only find those images on the web whose description (including associated message, coloration, etc.), which is in *text* form, matches the key-words issued by the user, which also *must* be in *text* form, *not an image*.

An email server should also be able to quickly determine if the newly arrived email message contains an image that matches one of the images in the database – if yes, this new message should be blocked as a spam email. While most email programs can block email messages that match certain criterion specified in *text* form, the author is not aware of any email server that is able to block email messages that contain specified *images*.

With such applications in mind, we assume that the set $S = \{T_1, T_2, \cdots, T_N\}$ is given in advance. Hence we are allowed to preprocess the set S so that subsequent searches with different patterns can be performed very quickly.

The method we are going to present for the multiple two-d matching problem is an extension of the method we developed for the *simple* two-d matching problem [7]. The main idea behind our method is that the matrices in the set S are represented as one-dimensional strings using some hash function and the pattern is also converted into a one-dimensional string. Thus, the two-dimensional pattern matching problem is reduced to the one-dimensional (string) pattern matching problem. This reduction, however, can introduce errors, called *false matches*. A false match occurs if the algorithm claims a "match" between the pattern P and some submatrix of some text in the set S while they are actually not equal. However, as will be seen, the probability that a false match can occur is negligible.

In Section 2, we give a high-level description of our method. We then show in detail how to represent two-dimensional matrices with one-dimensional strings, called *fingerprint strings*, using some hash function in linear time in Section 3. Since fingerprint strings may introduce *false matches*, we study the probability that a false match may occur under some specific hash function in Section 4. We have implemented our method and used it to search a digital image database for images that contain given patterns. Extensive experimental results will be reported in Section 6.

2 Outline of the Approach

For notational convenience, we take the matrices to be square although our approach applies to rectangular matrices as well. Let T be a matrix in the set S:

$$T = \begin{pmatrix} t_{0,0} & t_{0,1} & \cdots & t_{0,n-1} \\ t_{1,0} & t_{1,1} & \cdots & t_{1,n-1} \\ \cdots & \cdots & \cdots & \cdots \\ t_{n-1,0} & t_{n-1,1} & \cdots & t_{n-1,n-1} \end{pmatrix} \tag{1}$$

Elements of any matrix T in S and the pattern P are drawn from some sorted finite alphabet $\Sigma = \{c_1, c_2, \cdots, c_a\}$. Suppose our pattern P has size $m \times m$ (m rows and m columns) and T has size $n \times n$ ($m \leq n$).

2.1 Fingerprints of Matrices

For any string $X = x_0 \cdots x_{m-1}$ over Σ, define a function

$$H_p(X) = \sum_{i=0}^{m-1} \bar{x}_i \times a^{m-i-1} \bmod p \tag{2}$$

where $\bar{x}_i = j$ if $x_i = c_j$ (that is, $\bar{x}_i = j$ if x_i is the j-th letter in Σ), a is the size of the alphabet, and p is some positive integer to be specified later. We call $H_p(X)$ the *fingerprint* of string X.

Let B_i denote the $m \times n$ submatrix of T whose first row is the i-th row of T ($0 \leq i \leq n - m$). That is,

$$B_i = \begin{pmatrix} t_{i,0} & t_{i,1} & \cdots & t_{i,n-1} \\ \cdots & \cdots & \cdots & \cdots \\ t_{i+m-1,0} & t_{i+m-1,1} & \cdots & t_{i+m-1,n-1} \end{pmatrix} \tag{3}$$

Let $B_i(j)$ denote the j-th column of B_i. We represent each column $B_i(j)$, viewed as a string, by its fingerprint $H_p(B_i(j))$. Thus, each $m \times n$ submatrix B_i of T is represented by a string $V_i = H_p(B_i(0)) \cdots H_p(B_i(n-1))$ of length n. Let $v_{i,j}$ denote $H_p(B_i(j))$. We then have $V_i = v_{i,0} \cdots v_{i,n-1}$. We call V_i the *fingerprint string* of the $m \times n$ submatrix B_i.

The $m \times m$ matrix P (the pattern) is processed in the same way. Let $P(i)$ denote the i-th column of P, viewed as a string. P is represented by a string $W = H_p(P(0)) \cdots H_p(P(m-1))$ of length m. Let w_j denote $H_p(P(j))$. We then have $W = w_0 w_1 \cdots w_{m-1}$. We call W the *fingerprint string* of the pattern P.

The function $H_p(\cdot)$ is said to be *unique* if for any two strings X and Y if $X \neq Y$ then $H_p(X) \neq H_p(Y)$.

Lemma 1. *If the function $H_p(\cdot)$ is unique, then P occurs in some submatrix B_i of T starting at position (i, j) if and only if W (the fingerprint string of P) occurs in V_i (the fingerprint string of B_i) starting at position j.*

Lemma 2. *If $H_p(\cdot)$ is not unique, then an occurrence of W in V_i starting at position j implies only a possible match between P and the $m \times m$ submatrix of T whose upper left corner lies at position (i, j) of T. We need further test whether this leads to a real match or false match.*

Definition 1. *Let $V_i = v_{i,0}v_{i,1} \cdots v_{i,n-1}$ be the fingerprint string of an $m \times n$ submatrix B_i of T $(0 \le i \le n - m)$ and $V_i(j)$ denote the substring of V_i of length m that starts at position j (i.e., $V_i(j) = v_{i,j}v_{i,j+1} \cdots v_{i,j+m-1}$). Let W be the fingerprint string of P. A false match is said to occur if $W = V_i(j)$ but P is not equal to the submatrix of T represented by its fingerprint $V_i(j)$ (This $m \times n$ submatrix's upper left corner is at position (i, j) of T).*

Thus, after we have represented every $m \times n$ submatrix of every T in the set S with its fingerprint string and the pattern P with its fingerprint string W, our problem is reduced to the problem of finding all occurrences of W in the set of fingerprint strings for S.

Though this reduction can introduce false matches, as will be shown in Section 4, the probability that a false match can occur is negligible if the integer p in the function $H_p(.)$ is chosen as a sufficiently large prime.

We will use a data structure, called the generalized suffix array, to store all the fingerprint strings for the set S.

2.2   The Generalized Suffix Array

The generalized suffix array of a set of strings [6] is an extension of Manber and Myers' suffix array of a single string [4]. Informally, a generalized suffix array of a given set V of strings consists of three arrays, *Pos*, *Llcp* and *Rlcp*. *Pos* is a lexicographically sorted array of all suffixes of strings in V. *Llcp* and *Rlcp* are two arrays of the information about the lengths of the longest common prefixes of the suffixes in *Pos*.

Let M denote the sum of the lengths of all strings in V and n the length of the longest string in V. Then the generalized suffix array of V can be constructed in $O(M \log n)$ time in the worst case using $O(M)$ storage. Given the suffix array, a query like

"*Is W a substring of any strings in V? If so, where does it occur within strings of V?*"

can be answered in $O(m + \log M)$ time where m is the length of W.

For more detailed information on the generalized suffix array, see [4, 6].

2.3   The Method

Our method has two phases:

1. Constructing index.
   (a) Represent every $m \times n$ submatrix of every text T in the set S with its fingerprint string. The result is a set V of fingerprint strings of all $m \times n$ submatrices of S.
   (b) Build a suffix array for V.
2. Searching.
   (a) Represent the pattern with its fingerprint string W;
   (b) Search the suffix array for the occurrences of W. Each occurrence of W in V represents an occurrence of the pattern P in some text T in the set S, possibly with some false matches.

Let M denote the total number of elements in all matrices in S and n the number of rows in the largest matrix in S.

In Phase 1, Step 1.a takes $O(M)$ time (see Section 3) and Step 1.b takes $O(M \log n)$ time occupying $O(M)$ space (see [6]).

In Phase 2, Step 2.a takes $O(m^2)$ time (see Section 3) and Step 2.b takes $O(m + \log M)$ time (see [6]).

In the next section, we show how to represent two-dimensional matrices with one-dimensional fingerprint strings.

3   Computing Fingerprint Strings

Let $\Sigma = \{c_1, c_2, \cdots, c_a\}$ be a finite sorted alphabet. Let $X = x_0 x_1 \ldots x_{m-1}$ be a string over Σ. Define $H(X)$ of string X as follows:

$$H(X) = \sum_{i=0}^{m-1} \bar{x}_i \cdot a^{m-i-1} \tag{4}$$

where $\bar{x}_i = j$ if $x_i = c_j$ (That is, $\bar{x}_i = j$ if x_i is the j-th letter in Σ), $i = 0, 1, \cdots, m - 1$ and $a = |\Sigma|$. Then, $H(X)$ represents string X uniquely.

Define

$$H_p(X) = H(X) \bmod p \tag{5}$$

for some positive integer p to be specified later. We call $H_p(X)$ the fingerprint of string X. $H_p(X)$ may not represent string X uniquely, as it is possible that $H_p(X_1) = H_p(X_2)$ for two different strings X_1 and X_2.

Let T be any matrix in the set S. Let T_j denote the j-th column of T. We may think of T_j as a string; that is, $T_j = t_{0,j} t_{1,j} \cdots t_{n-1,j}$. Denote by $T_j(i)$ the substring of length m of string T_j that starts at position i, i.e., $T_j(i) = t_{i,j} t_{i+1,j} \cdots t_{i+m-1,j}$. Then

$$H(T_j(i+1)) = (H(T_j(i)) - t_{i,j} \cdot a^{m-1}) \cdot a + t_{i+m,j} \tag{6}$$

Thus

$$H_p(T_j(i+1)) = (H_p(T_j(i)) \cdot a + \xi \cdot t_{i,j} + t_{i+m,j}) \bmod p \qquad (7)$$

where $\xi = -a^m \bmod p$.

Let $v_{i,j}$ denote $H_p(T_j(i))$. Then

$$v_{i+1,j} = (v_{i,j} \cdot a + \xi \cdot t_{i,j} + t_{i+m,j}) \bmod p \qquad (8)$$

We first compute

$$v_{0,j} = \sum_{i=0}^{m-1} t_{i,j} \cdot a^{m-i-1} \bmod p \qquad (9)$$

(To compute $v_{0,j}$ we can use Horner's method; it may also be worthwhile to save $a \bmod p$, $a^2 \bmod p$, ..., $a^{m-1} \bmod p$ into an array since we need to apply Eq(9) many times).

We then compute $v_{i+1,j}$, for $i = 0, 1, \ldots, n - m - 1$, by applying Eq(8). In this way, we obtain the fingerprints of all length m substrings of column j of T.

When implementing Eq(8) and Eq(9), care should be taken to avoid possible overflows. We should take advantage of arithmetic properties of the mod operation; such properties include:

$$(a + b) \bmod p = (a \bmod p + b \bmod p) \bmod p,$$

$$(a + b) \bmod p = (a \bmod p + b) \bmod p,$$

$$(a * b) \bmod p = ((a \bmod p) * (b \bmod p)) \bmod p, \text{ and}$$

$$(a * b) \bmod p = ((a \bmod p) * b) \bmod p.$$

Let $V_i = v_{i,0} v_{i,1} \ldots v_{i,n-1}$. That is, V_i is the fingerprint string of the $m \times n$ submatrix B_i of T whose first row is the i-th row of T (see Eq(3)).

Assuming that each application of Eq(8) takes constant time (we can keep constants ξ, p and the last computed fingerprint in fast registers), the time needed to compute the fingerprints of all length m substrings of column j of T is $O(n)$.

Thus the total time needed to compute the fingerprint strings $V_0, V_1, \ldots, V_{n-m}$ of all $m \times n$ submatrices of one matrix T in the set S is $O(n^2)$.

The total time to compute the fingerprint strings of all $m \times n$ submatrices of *all* matrices in the set S is therefore $O(M)$ where M denote the total number of elements in all matrices in S.

4   False Matches

Let X and Y be any two $m \times m$ matrices. Let $X(i)$ denote the i-th column of X, viewed as a string and $Y(i)$ the i-th column of Y, also viewed as a string.

Let

$$U = H_p(X(0)), H_p(X(1)), \ldots H_p(X(m-1))$$

and

$$W = H_p(Y(0)), H_p(Y(1)), \ldots, H_p(Y(m-1))$$

where $H_p(\cdot)$ is the fingerprint function defined before.

We say that a match found by our algorithm is a *false match* if

$$U = W$$

but

$$X \neq Y.$$

It's easy to see the following:

Lemma 3. *The probability that a match found by our algorithm is a false match is*

$$1 - (1 - 1/p^2)^m.$$

Proof. The probability that when $X(i) \neq Y(i)$, $H_p(X(i)) = H_p(Y(i))$ is $1/p^2$ ($i = 0, 1, \ldots, m-1$). Hence, the probability that when $X(i) \neq Y(i)$, $H_p(X(i)) \neq H_p(Y(i))$ is $1 - 1/p^2$ ($i = 0, 1, \ldots, m-1$).

For example, suppose our patterns are 512×512 images and $p = 2^{31} - 1$. Then the probability that a match that is found by our algorithm is a false one is less than

$$2.39 \times 10^{-7}.$$

Note that in this example, since we choose $p = 2^{31} - 1$ each character in our fingerprint string can be represented by a 4-byte integer.

5   A Filtering Approach

For an $m_1 \times m_2$ matrix $P[0 .. m_1 - 1, 0 .. m_2 - 1]$, the value m_1 is said to be the height of P. One restriction of our approach presented in the previous sections is that the height of patterns must be known to the preprocessing portion of the algorithm before the preprocessing begins.

There are many ways to lift this restriction in practice. For example, in a reasonable digital image processing system, we know in advance the range of the heights of the patterns.

Suppose this range is $[l, h]$. We preprocess every $n_1 \times n_2$ matrix $T[0 .. n_1 - 1, 0 .. n_2 - 1]$ in the set S in the same manner as was described in the previous sections for a series of values of m: $m = l, 2 * l, , 2^2 * l, \ldots 2^{\lfloor \log_2 h/l \rfloor} * l$, respectively. Then when presented with an $m_1 \times m_2$ matrix $P[0..m_1-1, 0..m_2-1]$ (the pattern), we choose $m_1' = 2^i * l$ such that $2^i * l \leq m_1 < 2^{i+1} * l$. We pick any $m_1' \times m_2$ submatrix P' from P. We first look for occurrences of P' in the set S in the same way as was described before. Then, for each such match found, we extend the match to see if it really leads to an occurrence of P in some matrix T in the set S or not using character by character comparisons.

6   Experimental Results

In this section we report experimental results on the performance of the presented algorithm. Our implementation is written in Pascal and was tested on a (old and slow) PC with Intel Pentium III 450 MHz and 512 MB RAM that runs MS Windows.

The texts and patterns used in our test were digital images of 256 color values (i.e., $|\Sigma| = 256$). The prime number used in our fingerprint function was $p = 2^{31} - 1$. The images database used in the test contains images of sizes: 320×240, 640×480 and 800×600. The size of the pattern was 100×100. Three different types of patterns were used, the first does not appear in the database, the second appears only once, and the third has ten matches in the database.

Table 1 shows the time used to construct the index for different database sizes. The total construction time is broken down into the time for converting the text into fingerprint strings (hashing) and the time for building the suffix array.

In our implementation we used a simple and easy-to-implement algorithm to construct the suffix array for the database which takes $O(N^2)$ time in the worst case – we did not use more efficient but more-difficult-to-implement algorithms that take only $O(N \log n)$ time, where N denotes the total size of images in the database (in number of pixels) and n the width of the widest image in the database.

Table 2 shows the average time used to search for a pattern in the database.

In the above experiments, no false matches occurred. In our program a double-check function was used to catch possible false matches.

Our experiments show that the time we have to spend on building the index is acceptable in most cases; once the index is available searches in a database of 500 images can be done very quickly – almost instantly.

Table 1. Index Construction (in seconds)

Image Size	#Images in DB	Index Construction		
		Hashing	Suffix Array	Total
320×240	10	0.001	0.012	0.013
320×240	100	0.005	0.500	0.506
320×240	250	0.007	4.932	4.940
320×240	500	0.008	9.783	9.791
640×480	10	0.003	0.106	0.109
640×480	100	0.019	4.224	4.244
640×480	250	0.026	50.091	50.117
640×480	500	0.028	229.137	229.165
800×600	10	0.004	0.149	0.153
800×600	100	0.024	8.351	8.375
800×600	250	0.033	80.229	80.262
800×600	500	0.036	639.411	639.447

Table 2. Searching the Database (in milliseconds)

Image Size	#Images in DB	#Matches in DB		
		0	1	10
320 × 240	10	0.00	0.00	0.01
320 × 240	100	0.00	0.00	0.01
320 × 240	250	0.00	0.00	0.01
320 × 240	500	0.00	0.01	0.01
640 × 480	10	0.00	0.01	0.01
640 × 480	100	0.01	0.01	0.02
640 × 480	250	0.01	0.02	0.02
640 × 480	500	0.02	0.02	0.03
800 × 600	10	0.01	0.01	0.02
800 × 600	100	0.03	0.04	0.05
800 × 600	250	0.07	0.07	0.09
800 × 600	500	0.12	0.13	0.15

7 Future Work

In the problem we studied in this paper we were looking for matrices in the database that contain an *exact* occurrence of the pattern. We plan to study a more general version of the problem: we want to find all matrices in the database that contain an *approximate* occurrence of the pattern (That is, we look for matrices in the database that contain a submatrix that is "similar" to the pattern).

In our current implementation, our index structure is stored on the computer's main memory. This will restrict the size of the image database that can be handled by our program. We plan to extend our implementation so that it can store the index structure on the secondary storage devices (such as disks) to allow us to handle larger image databases.

References

1. R. Giancarlo, The Suffix of a Square Matrix, with Applications. *Proc. Fourth Symposium on Discrete Algorithms.* ACM-SIAM, 1993, pp. 402-411.
2. R. Giancarlo and R. Grossi, Suffix Tree Data Structures for Matrices, in *Pattern Matching Algorithms*, A. Apostolico e Z. Galil Eds.,Oxford University Press, (1997), pp. 293-340.
3. K. Fredriksson, G. Navarro, and E. Ukkonen. Optimal exact and fast approximate two dimensional pattern matching allowing rotations. In *Proc. 13th Annual Symposium on Combinatorial Pattern Matching (CPM)*, Vol. 2373, LNCS, Springer, 2002, pp. 235-248.
4. U. Manber and G. Myers, Suffix Arrays: A New Method for On-Line String Searches. *SIAM Journal on Computing 22* (1993), pp. 935-948.
5. Euripides G. M. Petrakis, Christos Faloutsos, Similarity Searching in Medical Image Databases. *IEEE Trans. Knowl. Data Eng. 9(3)*: 435-447 (1997)

6. Fei Shi, Suffix arrays for multiple strings: a method for on-line multiple string searches, in *Concurrency and Parallelism, Programming, Networking and Security: Proceedings Second Asian Computing Science Conference (ASIAN'96)*, Vol. 1179 of LNCS, Springer-Verlag, Berlin, 1996, pp. 11-22.
7. Fei Shi and Ahmad AlShibli: An indexing method for two-d pattern matching, *Proc. of the 7th Asia Pacific Web Conference*, in Lecture Notes in Computer Science, Springer Verlag, March 2005, pp. 875-884.
8. R.F. Zhu and T. Takaoka, A Technique for Two-Dimensional Pattern Matching. *Communications of the ACM* 32 (9), 1989, 1110-1120.

DualRank: A Dual-Phase Algorithm for Optimal Profit Mining in Retailing Market[*]

Xiujuan Xu, Lifeng Jia, Zhe Wang, and Chunguang Zhou

College of Computer Science, Key Laboratory of Symbol Computation and
Knowledge Engineering of the Ministry of Education,
Jilin University, Changchun 130012, China
xuxiujuan666@yahoo.com.cn, cgzhou@jlu.edu.cn

Abstract. We systematically propose a dual-phase algorithm, DualRank, to
mine the optimal profit in retailing market. DualRank algorithm has two major
phases which are called mining general profit phase and optimizing profit phase
respectively. In the first phase, the novel sub-algorithm, ItemRank, integrates
the random distribution of items into profit mining to improve the performance
of item order. In the other phase, two novel optimizing sub-algorithms are proposed to ameliorating results generated in the first phase. According to the
cross-selling effect and the self-profit of items, DualRank algorithm could solve
the problem of item order objectively and mechanically. We conduct detailed
experiments to evaluate DualRank algorithm and experiment result confirms
that the new method has an excellent ability for profit mining and the performance meets the condition which requires better quality and efficiency.

1 Introduction

Many different algorithms for mining association rule [1] have been proposed in previous literatures. Furthermore, studies about the retailing market [2] have received
widely attention. However, there are only a few studies concerning how association
rule can be beneficial in more specific targets. A major obstacle in data mining application is the gap between the statistic-based pattern extraction and the value-based
decision making [3]. Recent investigations in the retailing market have shown an
increasing interest on how to make decisions by unitizing association rules, which is
needed better knowledge about items. Consequently, Ke Wang *et al.* [3] first presented a profit mining approach to reduce this gap in 2002.

There are two main fields in profit mining, one is the problem of optimal
product selection and the other is viral marketing [4]. Here we focus on the first
problem. The problem is to find a subset of the products to be discontinued in a
typical retail store to maximize the profit. The types of products should be re-
freshed regular so that losing products are discarded and new products are
introduced.

---

[*] This work was supported by the Natural Science Foundation of China (Grant No. 60175024)
and the Key Science-Technology Project of the National Education Ministry of China (Grant
No. 02090). To whom correspondence should be addressed.

S. Grumbach, L. Siu, and V. Vianu (Eds.): ASIAN 2005, LNCS 3818, pp. 182 – 192, 2005.

From the market angle, two important criteria [5] should be met to being taken into account during the process of mining profit from retailing markets. In other words, the items in retails shops should meet the basic sale request, and should bring higher profits. Thereby, how to meet these two principles is the core problem of profit mining. The cross-selling effect of items [2] has also been noticed by current retailers, because the profit of an item is not only involved in the item itself, but is also influenced by its relative items. Given that some items fail to produce high profit by themselves, but they might stimulate customers to buy other profitable items. Consequently, the cross-selling factor which could be achieved by the analysis of historical transactions should be involved in the problem of item selection. Searching for such a relation of items has becoming an important issue. However, the current method of mining associate rules is not enough to support profit mining.

Many novel and important methods were proposed to support profit mining. Brijs *et al.* first proposed the PROFSET Model [2], which adopted the size-constrained strategy of 0-1 programming, took advantage of the cross-selling effect of items to solve the problem of item selection. In 2002, Ke Wang *et al.* first presented the profit mining approach and the relative several problems [3] [6]. Ke Wang *et al.* proposed the HAP algorithm [7] which is extended from the webpage-layered algorithm HITS [8] to solve the problem of item ranking with the consideration of the influence of confidence and profit, but it still has several drawbacks [9]. Raymond Wong *et al.* proposed the maximal profit problem of item selection (MPIS) [9] which has the goal of mining out a subset of items with the maximal profit and then ameliorates those above drawbacks. However, MPIS problem is too difficult to implement, because it is a NP-hardness problem even in the simplest situation. In other words, although MPIS algorithm could find the best solution, the cost of time is too expressive to be tolerated. Recently, Raymond Wong *et al* proposed Hill Climbing Method [4] to solve the problem of Item Selection for Marketing (ISM) by considering the cross-selling effect. Raymond Wong *et al.* [10] also adopted the genetic algorithm to generate local optimal profit to fit the optimal profit of the item selection problem.

The rest of the paper is organized as below. In Section 2 we introduce the preliminary definitions of optimal profit mining problem. In Section 3, we first describe the DualRank algorithm by and large. In Section 3.1, mining general profit phase is demonstrated systematically and theoretically, followed by the description of two novel optimizing strategies which play a key role in the optimizing profit phase in Section 3.2. Detailed experimental results are presented in Section 4. In Section 5, we draw the conclusion of DualRank algorithm.

2 Problem Definition

This section introduces some preliminary but important definitions which is essential for the further understanding of problem of item selection.

2.1 Basic Definition

Given a set I of item and a set of transactions, each transaction is a subset of I. An association rule has the form $X \to I_j$, such that $X \subseteq I$ and $I_j \to I$; the support threshold of association rule is the fraction of transactions containing all items in X and item I_j;

the confidence of association rule is the fraction of the transactions containing all items in set X that also contain item I_j.

2.2 Problem Definition

Maximal-profit item selection (MPIS) [6] is actually the problem of selecting a subset from a given item set with the consideration of the cross-selling effect to maximize the estimated profit of the resulting selection.

Given the dataset which contains m transactions: t_1, t_2,..., t_m, and the item set, I, which includes n items: I_1, I_2, ..., I_n. The profit of item I_a in transaction t_i is denoted by $prof(I_a, t_i)$. A subset of I, denoted by S, means a set of selected items. We also define two item sets, $t_i' = t_i \cap S$ and $d_i = t_i - t_i'$. The item set t_i' represents the selected items in the transaction t_i, and the item set d_i represents the unselected items in the transaction t_i. If the item set, d_i, is empty, all items in t_i are selected and the profit of t_i is unchanged. If the item set, t_i', is empty, no item in t_i is selected, and thus t_i generates no profit. If both t_i' and d_i are not empty, we stipulate d_i, $\Diamond d_i$, and t_i' as follow: $d_i = \{Y_1, Y_2, ..., Y_q\}$, $\Diamond d_i = \{Y_1 \vee Y_2 \vee Y_3 \vee ... \vee Y_q\}$, and $t_i' = \{I_1, I_2, ..., I_k\}$, such that Y_i ($1 < i < q$) represents a single unselected item.

Definition 1. Total Profit of Item Selection [6]: The total profit of an item selection S is defined as below formula:

$$P = \sum\nolimits_{i=1}^{m} \sum\nolimits_{I_a \in t_i'} prof(I_a, t_i)(1 - csfactor(d_i, I_a)) \tag{1}$$

We specify the cross-selling effect (denoted by $csfactor$) of some items for other items by *loss rule* which has a form of "$I_a \rightarrow \Diamond d_i$". For any a item I_a contained by the item set t_i', the *loss rule* [6], $I_a \rightarrow \Diamond d_i$, indicates that a customer who buys the item I_a must also buy at least one of the items in d_i. According to the discussion so far, the higher the confidence of $I_a \rightarrow \Diamond d_i$, the more likely the profit I_a in t_i should not be counted. Consequently, the profit in selected set S can also be defined as follow:

$$P = \sum\nolimits_{t_i \in T} \sum\nolimits_{I_a \in t_i'} prof(I_a, t_i)(1 - conf(I_a \rightarrow \Diamond d_i)) \tag{2}$$

In this paper, the *loss rule*, $I_a \rightarrow \Diamond d_i$, is treated as a special kind of association rule. Therefore, the confidence of this rule is defined in a similar manner as that of association rule.

Definition 2. The confidence of loss rule [6]: The confidence of a loss rule, $I_a \rightarrow \Diamond d_i$, is defined as below formula

$$The\ confidence\ of\ loss\ rule = \frac{number\ of\ tansactions\ containing\ I_a\ and\ any\ element\ in\ d_i}{number\ of\ transactions\ containing\ I_a}$$

3 DualRank Algorithm

Since hap algorithm may happen the phenomena of *rank leak* [8], and MPIS algorithm is a difficult problem of NP-hard even if we consider the very simple version where csfactor(d_i, I_a)=1, we develop a dual-phase algorithm to compute the optimal profit of item in retailing market. First, we utilize ItemRank sub-algorithm to efficiently determine a max-profit item set S. Second, the item set, S, is iteratively optimized by one of two optimal strategies, random and replace sub-algorithms.

Algorithm DualRank:

(1) Find a selection item set S by the ItemRank sub-algorithm;
(2) Mining potential profit of S by the sub-algorithm, Random(S) or Replace(S), to optimizing the profit;
(3) Return the selection item set, S, with the optimal profit.

Before explain the main principles of two phases respectively, customer behavior model is proposed and constructed. Our customer behavior model is motivated by the intuitive justification of the famous PageRank [8] algorithm, which is that a page can have a high PageRank if there are many pages that point to it, or if there are some pages that point to it and have a high PageRank. The well known search engine Google (http://www.google.com) has exploited this relationship for ranking query results on the web.

On the analogy of PageRank algorithm, the core thinking of customer behavior model is described as follow: if an item is influenced by many high-profited ones, it must be a high-profited item. Customer behavior model is denoted by a directed graph G = (V, E), where the set V of vertices denotes the items and the set E of directed edges denotes confidence relation between items. N_i denotes the out-degree of item I_i. We stipulate that an edge from I_i to I_j means that I_i gets the authorization from I_j, and item I_j is relatively important if there are many such edges. If many items point to an item, its item rank (IR for short) will be high, or there are some high IR items pointing to it. When we enlarge other items based on items in the list, these items will have high IR. Consequently, the weights of items could be transferred among the items based on the association rules.

3.1 Mining General Profit Phase

Based on customer behavior model, sub-algorithm, ItemRank, which is embedded in the mining general profit phase, is proposed on the basis of PageRank [8] [11] [12] algorithm to solve item selection problem. The number of frequent items is far more than the selected items, so the potential cross link, $I_i \rightarrow I_j$, depends on not only the confidence of items, but also the profit of items itself. Consequently, if the link $I_i \rightarrow I_j$ exists, we use "$conf(I_i \rightarrow I_j) \times prof(i)$" to evaluate the IR of item I_j, and if item I_j is not selected, the lose profit of itself is also denoted by the value of $conf(I_i \rightarrow I_j) \times prof(i)$, which is viewed as the trust weighs of subsequent items of I_j. The initial item rank IR(I_i) is defined as the following equation (3)

$$IR(I_i) = \sum_{(i,j) \in E} \frac{IR(I_j) \times prof(I_j) \times conf(I_i \rightarrow I_j)}{N_j} \qquad (3)$$

The equation (3) is the accurate result only under the precondition that all items must become a strongly connected graph. However, the precondition is difficult to be satisfied because the relation between items is not always in such an ideal situation.

Moreover, the phenomena of *rank sink* and *rank leak* [8] might happen for the occurrence of loop in the custom behavior model. Consequently, we introduce a damping factor d, $d \in [0,1]$, to avoid the above two phenomena. So the equation (3) is modified to:

$$IR(I_i) = \frac{1-d}{m} + d \sum_{(i,j) \in E} \frac{IR(I_j) \times prof(I_j) \times conf(I_i \to I_j)}{N_j} \text{ , such that } m \text{ is the number}$$

(4)

of nodes in the directed graph.

The equation (4) guarantees that the rank of item is decided by the trust weights of its subsequent items and all items proportionally.

Note that both the sum of possible distribution of items and the sum of IR of items are equal to 1, so

$$\sum_{i=1}^{m} IR(I_i) = \begin{bmatrix} 1, & ..., & 1 \end{bmatrix} \times \begin{bmatrix} IR(I_1) \\ ... \\ IR(I_n) \end{bmatrix} = e \times \begin{bmatrix} IR(I_1) \\ ... \\ IR(I_n) \end{bmatrix} = 1, where\ e = \begin{bmatrix} 1, & ..., & 1 \end{bmatrix}.$$

For the comprehension of incoming reason of DualRank algorithm, we first introduce some preliminary knowledge as below.

$$Matrix\ A = \begin{bmatrix} a_{11}, & ..., & a_{1n} \\ ... & ... & ... \\ a_{n1}, & ..., & a_{nn} \end{bmatrix}, Unit\ Matrix\ I = \begin{bmatrix} 1, & ..., & 1 \\ ... & ... & ... \\ 1, & ..., & 1 \end{bmatrix}, such\ that\ the\ element\ of\ A,$$

$$a_{ij} = \frac{prof(i) \times conf(i \to j)}{N_j}, only\ if\ there\ is\ an\ edge\ from\ i\ to\ j.\ Otherwise,\ a_{ij} = 0.$$

$$x = \begin{bmatrix} IR(I_1) \\ ... \\ IR(I_n) \end{bmatrix} = \frac{1-d}{m} \times \begin{bmatrix} 1 \\ ... \\ 1 \end{bmatrix} + d \times A \times \begin{bmatrix} IR(I_1) \\ ... \\ IR(I_n) \end{bmatrix} = \frac{1-d}{m} \times \begin{bmatrix} 1 \\ ... \\ 1 \end{bmatrix} \times 1 + d \times A \times \begin{bmatrix} IR(I_1) \\ ... \\ IR(I_n) \end{bmatrix}$$

$$= \frac{1-d}{m} \times \begin{bmatrix} 1 \\ ... \\ 1 \end{bmatrix} \times (\begin{bmatrix} 1, & ..., & 1 \end{bmatrix} \times \begin{bmatrix} IR(I_1) \\ ... \\ IR(I_n) \end{bmatrix}) + d \times A \times \begin{bmatrix} IR(I_1) \\ ... \\ IR(I_n) \end{bmatrix}$$

(5)

$$= (\frac{1-d}{m} \times \begin{bmatrix} 1 \\ ... \\ 1 \end{bmatrix} \times \begin{bmatrix} 1, & ..., & 1 \end{bmatrix} + d \times A) \times \begin{bmatrix} IR(I_1) \\ ... \\ IR(I_n) \end{bmatrix}$$

$$= (\frac{1-d}{m} \times \begin{bmatrix} 1 \\ ... \\ 1 \end{bmatrix} \times \begin{bmatrix} 1, & ..., & 1 \end{bmatrix} + d \times A) \times x$$

$$= (\frac{1-d}{m} \times \begin{bmatrix} 1, & ..., & 1 \\ ... & ... & ... \\ 1, & ..., & 1 \end{bmatrix} + d \times A) \times x$$

$$= Bx$$

$$where\ B = \frac{1-d}{m} \times I + d \times A.$$

Consequently, the item order result could be achieved by computing principal eigenvector of the matrix B. When the iteration number or the IR value of is invariable, the ItemRank sub-algorithm is terminated.

ItemRank Sub-algorithm:
Input: (1) N items; (2) n transactions; (3) frequent items; (4) all association rules;
Output: (1) selecting items S; (2) the corresponding profit coming from S.

(1)   Compute the out-degree for each item I_i.
(2)   Compute the value of matrix B;
(3)   Get the principal eigenvector of the matrix B;
(4)   Order the principal eigenvector of the matrix B;
(5)   Return the order of the items and the corresponding profit.

3.2 Optimizing Profit Phase

Although most general profit has been discovered during the mining general profit phase, a huge amount of potential profit fails to be discovered. Therefore, two novel optimal strategies which are embedded in the optimizing profit phase, random method and replace method, are proposed for mining potential profit. A higher-quality selection item set could be mined by adopting random or replace method to optimize the temporal result generated from the mining general profit phase.

3.2.1 Random Method
When the first phase finishes, a maximal profit item set, S, which contains approximate optimal profit, is generated. However, the first phase could not mining the maximize profit. In order to overcome the limitation, random method seems to be promising. Martin Ester *et al.* [14] used random method to optimize the result of customer-oriented catalog segmentation problem. In the optimizing profit phase, the profit of S is iteratively enhanced by randomly replacing one selected item by an unselected item. The sub-algorithm could be terminated when either a user-specified number of iterations has been met or the profitability stops increasing.

Random Sub-algorithm:
Input: (1) selecting items S, (2) the corresponding profit from S, (3) number of iterations N, (4) all items $I=\{I_1, I_2, ..., I_n\}$.
Output: (1) S selecting items, (2) the corresponding profit coming from S.

(1) Calculate the profit coming from S;
(2) For $n=1$ to N do
    a)   Randomly select an item $p \in \{S\}$;
    b)   Randomly select an item $p' \in \{I - S\}$;
    c)   Calculate the gain δ by replacing p with p' in S.
    d)   If ($\delta \geq 0$) Then
       i.   Replace p by p' in S;
      ii.   profit = profit + δ ;
(3) Return the profit with S selecting item.

3.2.2 Replace Process

Now, we present another efficient optimizing strategy, i.e. replace method, to mine the potential profit hidden in the item set S generated in the mining general profit phase.

Given a matrix L [10], and each entry $L_{i,j}$ in the matrix estimates the profit of item I_i if the item I_j is associated with I_i. Consequently, this entry is denoted as follows:

$$L_{i,j} = profit(I_i) \times conf(I_i \rightarrow I_j) \tag{6}$$

The sum value L_i, $L_i = \sum_{i=1}^{n} L_{i,j}$, may show out some key characters about item I_i and then identify the importance of item I_i. Replace method first ranks all sum values by descending order, and then substitutes items which contain the minimal profit in the item set S with the unselected items containing the maximal profit of all sum values iteratively. The replace process could be terminated when this process finishes or it has passed enough iteration.

Replace Sub-algorithm:

Input: (1) selecting item S, (2) the corresponding profit from S, (3) all items $I=\{I_1, I_2, ..., I_n\}$, (4) Matrix L.

Output: (1) S selecting items, (2) the corresponding profit coming from S.

(1)   Ranking all items by the descending order of profit;
(2)   While ($L_u > L_s$)
    a)   Choose an item p with minimum L_s in the S;
    b)   Choose an unselected item p' with maximal L_u not in the S,
    c)   Calculate the gain δ by replacing p with p' in S;
    d)   If ($\delta \geq 0$) Then
        i.   Replace p by p' in S;
        ii.   Profit = profit + δ;
(3)   Return the profit with S selecting item.

4 Experimental Evaluation

In this section, we report the performance study concerning the proposed algorithm over two synthetic datasets. We compare the efficiency of DualRank algorithm with the previous best method HAP and the naïve approach, because HAP algorithm is the state of the art in the consideration of item selection with cross-selling effect in the data mining literature.

All experiments are conducted on a 2.8GHZ Intel PC with 512MB main memory, using the Microsoft Windows XP. Profit of Items should be normally distributed, but we generate profit random average distribution for simple [7]. Profit of Items are generated as follow: 80% of items have a medium profit ranging from $1 to $5, 10% of items have a high profit ranging from $5 to $10, 10% of items have a low profit ranging from $0.1 to $1.

4.1 Results for Normal Synthetic Dataset

To evaluate DualRank algorithm, we use the IBM synthetic data generator [13] to create a synthetic database, T10.I4.N1K.D10K, which respectively has 888 and 902 frequent items and 24124 and 30250 frequent pairs with minimal support thresholds, 0.09% and 0.08%. It is obvious that there is strong cross-selling effect among items. DualRank algorithm is comprehensively compared with HAP algorithm and naïve algorithm [7]. The total profit in this dataset is $320092.

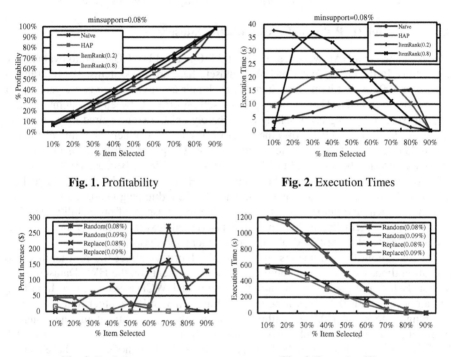

Fig. 1. Profitability   **Fig. 2.** Execution Times

Fig. 3. Profit Increase   **Fig. 4.** Execution Times

First, we experiment the ability of the ItemRank algorithm which is embedded in the mining general profit phase, and ItemRank algorithms with different dumping factors, d, are compared with other two algorithms. Fig.1 and Fig.2 indicate that ItemRank algorithms outperform other algorithms in both two aspects: profitability and execution time. Although ItemRank sub-algorithm with dumping factor d 0.2 spends the most time when selecting less than 40% items, ItemRank is turning to more efficient than both HAP and naïve algorithm with the increasing percent of selected items.

Although ItemRank sub-algorithm succeeds in mining more profit than Hap and naïve algorithms, it still fails to discover some potential profit in this dataset. Consequently, the core function of optimizing profit phase is to mine out the potential profit. We compare the profit mined by the Random process and Replace process embedded in the optimizing profit phase with the general profit generated by Item-

Rank sub-algorithm. Fig.3 shows that both of two methods in the second phase succeed in mining the potential profit with two different minimal support thresholds, and thus efficiently enhance the general profit of first phase.

Whatever the minimal support threshold is, the advantage of random method over the replace method is its prominent ability of mining potential profit, which is shown in the Fig.3. However, replace method also owns its advantage over random method, because it costs much less time than random method. Consequently, random or replace method could be chosen to be embedded in the optimizing profit phase, according to different requirements concerning profitability and execution time.

4.2 Results for HAP Worse-Case Synthetic Dataset

We also generate a HAP worse-case dataset 2 [10], called HWCDataset, to evaluate the algorithms. In the environment of HWCDataset, there are 1,000 items, 10,000 transactions, and 500 disjoint item pairs. Items of each pair are divided into two layers: upper layer and lower layer. There is strong cross-selling effect between two items of each disjoint pair, and strong cross-selling effect barely exists two un-paired items in upper and lower layer. Fig 5 [10] shows the idea of HWCDataset. When the minimal support threshold is less than 0.09%, all items are frequent. The profit distribution is the same as above dataset and the total profit of HWCDataset is $177883. Because HWCDataset is incompact and weakly associated between items, HAP algorithm barely gives excellent solutions. However, DualRank algorithm with different dumping factors surmounts this bad environment and outperform HAP algorithm in the aspect of profitability, which is shown in Fig.6. Actually, the bad environment generally exists in real retailing database, and thus DualRank algorithm deal with this problem appropriately.

To study how the parameters of DualRank algorithm affect the profitability and execution time, we conducted comprehensive experiments on the HWCDataset. 0.2 is obviously the best choice of the dumping factor of HWCDataset, because ItemRank sub-algorithm with 0.2 gives a better solution than ItemRank algorithm with other dumping factors and HAP algorithm. Consequently, the ability of mining potential profit of optimizing profit phase is evaluated when the dumping factor is set to 0.2. Fig.7 and Fig.8 indicate that both replace and random methods have the excellent abilities of mining potential profit, no matter what the minimal support threshold is.

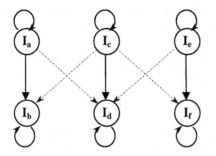

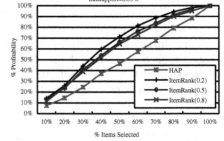

Fig. 5. Illustration of HAP Worst-Case dataset   **Fig. 6.** Profitability

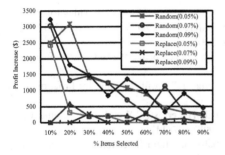 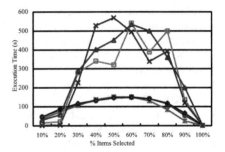

Fig. 7. Profitability Increase   **Fig. 8.** Execution Times

After comprehensively analyzing Fig.7 and Fig.8, DualRank algorithm which embeds the random method in the optimizing profit phase is clearly the best choice for mining profit from the HWCDataset, because it mines more profit with less execution time.

5 Conclusions and Further Work

This paper proposes a novel dual-phase algorithm to solve the problem of item selection in profit mining. The most special characteristic of DualRank algorithm is that it has two phases which mine general profit and optimize the profit by mining potential profit respectively. ItemRank, Random, and Replace sub-algorithms are proposed to accomplish those functions mentioned above. We conducted comprehensive and detailed experiment to evaluate DualRank algorithm. From the results, we could draw a conclusion that not only the mining general profit phase outperforms the well-known HAP and Naïve algorithms, but the optimizing profit phase indeed succeeds in mining potential profit efficiently.

We believe that there are many aspects to extend the current work. First, DualRank algorithm only thinks a Markov chain from the theory of Markov chain [15] and relies on the stochastic properties of random walk, but in fact maybe it need be proved further. Second, the algorithm should apply to real data and test the results. It will be more solid if we can give such an example. Finally, in real applications the number of transactions is increasing continuously, and then DualRank should be improved so that it should be able to rank items dynamically.

References

1. Han, J., Pei, J., Yin, Y.: Mining Frequent Patterns without Candidate Generation. In SIGMOD (2000) 1-12
2. Brijs, T.: Retail Market Basket Analysis: A Quantitative Modelling Approach. Ph.D. dissertation, Faculty of Applied Economics, Limburg University Center, Belgium (2002)
3. Wang, K., Zhou, S., Han, J.: Profit Mining: From Patterns to Actions. Proc. 2002 Int. Conf. on Extending Data Base Technology (EDBT'02), Prague, Czech (2002) 70-87
4. Wong, R., Fu, A.: ISM: Item Selection for Marketing with Cross-Selling Considerations. In Proc of PAKDD, Sydney, Australia (2004) 431-440

5. Brijs, T., Swinnen, G., Vanhoof, K., Wets, G.: The Use of Association Rules for Product Assortment Decisions: a Case Study. In: Proceedings of KDD 98, San Diego (USA), August 15-18, ISBN: 1-58113-143-7 (1999) 254-260

6. Zhou, S., Wang, K.: Profit Mining, to appear in Encyclopedia of Data Warehousing and Mining, (2004)

7. Wang, K., Su, M.: Item Selection By "Hub-Authority" Profit Ranking. In: Proc. of ACM SIGKDD, (2002) 652-657

8. Brin, S., Page, L.: The Anatomy of a Large-Scale Hypertextual Web Search Engine. Computer Networks and ISDN Systems, 30(1-7) (1998) 107~117

9. Wong, R., Fu, A., Wang, K.: MPIS: Maximal-Profit Item Selection with Cross-selling Considerations. In: Proc. of IEEE ICDM. (2003) 371-378

10. Wong, R., Fu, A., Wang, K.: Data Mining for Inventory Item Selection with Cross-selling Considerations. In the Journal of Data Mining and Knowledge Discovery, (2005)

11. Arasu, A., Novak, J., Tomkins, A, S., Tomlin, J, A.: Pagerank computation and the structure of the web: Experiments and algorithms. In Poster Proc.WWW2002, Honolulu, (2002)

12. Page, L., Brin, S., Motwani, R. and Windograd, T. The Pagerank Citation Ranking: Bring Order to the Web, Stanford Digital Library Technologies Project (1998)

13. Agrwwal, R.: IBM synthetic data generator, http://www.almaden.ibm.com/cs/quest/syndata.html (2004)

14. Ester M., Ge R., Jin W., Hu Z.: A Micro-economic Data Mining Problem: Customer-Oriented Catalog Segmentation, Proc. 10th ACM SIGKDD Int. Conf. on Knowledge Discovery and Data Mining (KDD 2004) 557-562

15. Lempel, R., Moran, S.: The Stochastic Approach for Link-Structure Analysis (SALSA) and the TKC Effect. Computer Networks: The International Journal of Computer and Telecommunications Networking, 33(1-6) (2000) 387-401

Efficient Evaluation of Sibling Relationship in XPath Queries

Changxuan Wan, Xiping Liu, and Dahai Lin

School of Information Technology,
Jiangxi University of Finance & Economics, Nanchang, China
wanchangxuan@263.net

Abstract. The structure queries of XQuery result in structural joins of various relationships. While several efficient algorithms have been proposed in evaluating ancestor–descendant and parent–child relationships, few efforts are put on the study on sibling relationship. In this paper, we study the structural joins of preceding-sibling–following-sibling relationship. To accelerate structural joins of parent–child and preceding-sibling–following-sibling relationships, optimizing techniques are employed to filter out and minimize unnecessary reads of elements using parent's structural information. Then, two efficient structural join algorithms in evaluating sibling relationship are proposed, in which nodes that do not participate in the join can be judged beforehand and then skipped using B+-tree index. Besides, each element list joined is scanned sequentially once at most. Furthermore, output of join results is sorted in document order. Our experimental results not only demonstrate the effectiveness of our optimizing techniques for sibling axes, but also validate the efficiency of our algorithms. To the best of our knowledge, this is the first effort that addresses this problem.

1 Introduction

As XML is adopted as a universal data exchange format, particularly in the World Wide Web, the study on efficiently managing and querying XML documents has attracted much research attention. Generally, an XML document can be viewed as an *ordered tree*, in which each node corresponds to a document element (or attribute) and an edge represents direct element–subelement (or parent–child) relationship. To retrieve such tree-shaped data, several XML query languages, such as XQuery [1] and XPath [2] have been proposed. XQuery is being standardized as a major XML query language in which the key building block is XPath, which addresses part of XML documents for retrieval, both by their structure and the values in their elements. Using path expressions in XPath, users are allowed to navigate through arbitrary *ordered tree*. Traditional indexing schemes, such as B+-trees, can be easily extended to support value-based queries on XML documents. Path expression queries pose a great challenge, requiring the computation of *structural joins* [3, 6]. A structural join focuses on the structural relationship of the XML elements and the join condition is specified not on the value of the XML elements, but on their relative positions in the XML document.

S. Grumbach, L. Siu, and V. Vianu (Eds.): ASIAN 2005, LNCS 3818, pp. 193–207, 2005.

Up to now, various coding schemes of *structural joins* for evaluating path expression queries have been proposed [3-13, 14, 16]. The coding schemes proposed in the literature can be characterized by the following features:

(a) The structure of the encoded data, such as trees and graphs;
(b) The supported structural queries, such as ancestor–descendant, parent–child, preceding– following and preceding-sibling–following-sibling relationships;
(c) The complexity of the coding algorithms;
(d) The maximum or average code size;
(e) The query evaluation time on the resulting codes;
(f) The recoding implications of incremental updates.

Complete comparison of these schemes is beyond the scope of this paper.

Normally, structural relationships in a path expression include parent–child, ancestor– descendant, preceding–following and preceding-sibling–following-sibling (sibling for short below) relationships, requiring respective structural join algorithms. There have been various implementation techniques of structural joins of ancestor–descendant relationship (or parent–child relationship) [3-9, 11-13]. Especially, algorithms proposed in [6-9] represent the state-of-the-art work in structural joins of ancestor–descendant relationship.

Various index techniques for efficient structural joins have been proposed [4, 7, 8, 9, 11-13]. Experiment has been conducted to analyze how well these techniques support XML structural joins [18]. We refer to [18] for detailed results and explanations.

We noted that all these algorithms are dedicated to the structural joins of ancestor–descendant (or parent–child) relationship, and little work has addressed the problem of structural join for preceding–following and sibling relationships. However, the preceding, following, preceding-sibling and following-sibling axes are indispensable parts of XPath axes, and preceding–following and sibling relationships are as important as ancestor-descendant (or parent-child) relationships in evaluating path expression.

There may be some naive illusions in evaluating the sibling relationship. Some may think that structural join of sibling relationship (sibling join for short below) can be simple modeled as two parent-child joins. However, this approach is heavyweight, because one join step is modeled as two join steps, which increases complexity of the problem. More important, it's impossible to maintain the results in document order unless additional sorting. Another naive approach is that, since a simple B+-tree index on (pOrder, order)[1] seems suffice to find siblings easily; it is possible to index two lists by (pOrder, order). Finding all pairs of following or preceding siblings in this case is an indexed nested-loop join procedure. This approach may be reasonable, but still suffers from the similar drawbacks. This can be illustrated from Figure 1. Suppose we are to evaluate the following-sibling axis and the index is built on (pOrder, order). Given preceding-sibling list (4, 5, 6, 7, 8, 9, 11, 14, 19) and following-sibling list (1, 2, 3, 7, 10, 12, 13, 15, 16, 17, 18, 20), the structural join result of these two lists via index lookup is a sequence of node pairs: (<6, 7>, <6, 16>, <7, 16>, <8, 10>, <8, 13>, <11, 12>, <14, 15>, <19, 20>). It turns out that the resulting sequence is not ordered in following-sibling's document order, which fails to meet the semantics of XPath

---

[1] We use **order** to denote the preorder rank of the node and **pOrder** to denote the parent's **order** of the node here.

queries. Moreover, the whole inner lists should be scanned, although some of them don't contribute to results at all. The situation for preceding-sibling axis is similar.

Essentially, the preceding–following and sibling relationships differ with ancestor-descendant and parent-child relationships in that the latter are essentially containment relationships while the former is not. In the meanwhile, the region coding schemes gracefully capture the containment relationship in position. In other words, the region coding schemes cater for ancestor-descendant and parent-child relationships. Accordingly, the techniques designed for ancestor-descendant and parent-child relationships cannot generally be employed to preceding-following and sibling relationships, and efficient evaluation scheme for these two relationships should be thoroughly studied.

Up to now, we have not found any paper devoted to the problem of structural joins of sibling relationship specially. The only paper that touches on this issue is [13], which proposed a database index structure called *XPath accelerator*, to support all XPath axes. The technique developed in [13] can process all of the axes. The idea of [17] is an extension and optimization of that of [13], which focuses on exploiting additional properties of the pre/post plane to speed up XPath query evaluation and the *staircase join* operator is proposed for this purpose. Our work differs with [13, 17] in followings. First, staircase join has a different flavor than structural join. Staircase join operates on a sequence of context nodes and generate new node sequence as output, and the resulting sequence becomes new context node sequence in turn, that is to say, it is a navigational access style. Second, we haven't found any discussion about improvement on the scan region of sibling axes in [13, 17], and the scan region specified by sibling axes is not so accurate. This can be seen from the experimental results. In our structural join algorithms for sibling relationships, we utilize parent's structural information to shrink scan region and enhance the ability of skipping.

The main contributions of this paper are summarized as follows:

- The optimizing techniques are employed in evaluating sibling axes. The key idea is to filter out and minimize unnecessary reads of elements using parent's structural information in order to accelerate structural joins of parent–child relationship [16] and sibling relationship.
- Two B+-tree based structural join algorithms for efficient evaluation of preceding-sibling and following-sibling axes of XPath queries are presented. These algorithms can avoid repeating scan of input list and generate node pairs sorted as the semantic of XPath demands.
- Large experiments have been carried to assess the effectiveness of optimizing techniques we propose for sibling axes and efficiency of structural join algorithms of sibling relationship.

In the following section, the optimizing techniques for sibling axes are introduced. Section 3 proposes two efficient B+-tree-based structural join algorithms to evaluate sibling axes of XPath queries. Experimental results are demonstrated in Section 4 and Section 5 concludes the paper.

2 Optimizing Techniques for Sibling Axes

For simplicity, we only consider a single, typically large XML document in this paper. Extension to multi-document databases is trivial using B+-tree index because only examination about docID is added and index location is made by docID.

As mentioned in [13], every axis in XPath specifies a scan region. Evaluating axis step thus amounts to select certain nodes from scan region. For a certain node, the scan regions specified by preceding, following, ancestor and descendant axes plus the node itself cover the whole document region exactly. In [13], the scan regions determined by following-sibling and preceding-sibling axes are the same as that of following and preceding axes, respectively. Suppose P is a sequence of context nodes (i.e., preceding-sibling element list), α is a following-sibling axis, f is an element tag, and F is following-sibling element list. Assume that both list P and F are sorted and indexed on their preorder of element nodes. For XPath path step P/α::f, the evaluating approach according to the idea in [13] is specified as: for each element node p in context list P, locating its scan scope in list F via index first, which is a following region of node p, then examining whether each node in the scope is a following-sibling of context node p or not.

Figure 1 depicts a sample XML document tree. Wherein, nodes in preceding-sibling list P and following-sibling list F are represented by squares and ellipses respectively. Hexagons represent the nodes that belong to both preceding-sibling and following-sibling list, and triangles represent other nodes. For the node 8, its *following region* and *descendant region* of its parent (i.e., node 7) are denoted in Figure 1.

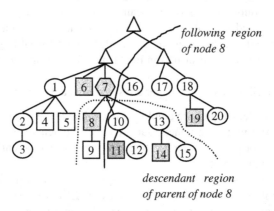

following region of node 8

descendant region of parent of node 8

Fig. 1. An XML document example

The scan cost on list F for processing following-sibling axis using XPath accelerator is sketched as Figure 2. For the sake of briefness, we denote node with preorder number n as node n in list F or node (n) in list P. Figure 2(a) shows the content of list P and F. Wherein, the node pairs 7(6), 10(8), etc in list F represent expected join results. Figure 2(b) illustrates scan cost sketch on list F for XPath accelerator. Wherein, the lines with arrow indicate scopes of nodes scanned in F for the associated nodes in P. For example, it is shown from Figure 2(b) that nodes 7, 10, ..., 20 in F are scanned for nodes (4), (5)

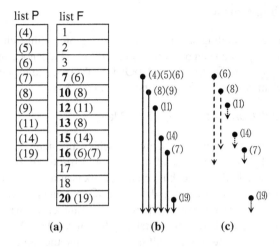

Fig. 2. Scan cost sketch for following-sibling axis

and (6) in P. It is clear that, when following-sibling axis is evaluated by XPath accelerator, there are many unnecessary visits and repeated scans for inner list (viz. list F), and the results joined are not ordered by preorder numbers of nodes, which don't coincide with semantics of XML queries.

Based on the analysis above, the evaluation of following-sibling axis can be improved in two ways:

First, the scan scope in list F can be shrunk in the presence of parent's structure information. Actually, the scan scope is the common area of the following region of p and the descendant region of p's parent. If parent's structural information can be easily accessed, it's possible to make the scan scope more accurate. Figure 2(c) depicts the scenario after improved. Compared with Figure 2(b), it is obvious that scanning on list F is avoided for nodes (4), (5) and (9) in list P, and what's more, the scan scopes in list F are shrunk dramatically for other nodes in list P. For instance, the scan scope of node (8) is confined to nodes 10, 12, 13 and 15 by cutting down nodes 16, 17, 18 and 20.

Second, a stack can be introduced to avoid repeated scan on list F. For any node p in list P, if there may be its following siblings after the current node f in list F, push it into stack. The stack maintains some preceding-siblings, ancestors and ancestor's preceding-siblings of current node that will be used later in the join.

These optimizing techniques will improve the evaluation of following-sibling axis. Performance study later also confirms the effectiveness of these techniques.

3   Efficient Evaluation of Sibling Relationship

In this section, we propose two structural join algorithms, based on region coding scheme, which embody optimizing techniques developed in the preceding section.

3.1 Region Coding Schemes

We first summarize our coding schemes here. The region coding scheme used in this paper is based on [16], which can be expressed as follows. Each node in an XML tree is assigned a quintuple <docID, order, max, pOrder, pMax>, and lists designed to store region codes of element nodes for XML data are shown as below:

Elem_*Tag* (*docID*, *order*, max, pOrder, pMax)

Here, the docID is the document identifier where the node lies. For each node, order is the extended preorder rank of the node and max is defined as the biggest order in the tree rooted in this node, but actually, max is assigned a value much bigger to reserve space for later insertion or update. The pOrder and pMax refer to the order and max of its parent respectively. There are a number of ways in which the Elem_*Tag* can be generated from the database that stores the XML data [4, 15]. To quicken evaluation of structural joins, all nodes that have the same tag name *Tag* are stored in the Elem_*Tag* list. Primary keys of the lists are in italic, and we suppose all lists are clustering-indexed with B+-tree index according to primary keys to quicken search. Although the algorithm is based on the region coding scheme in [16], it can be easily extended to other schemes.

3.2 Evaluating Following-Sibling Axis

Based on the region coding scheme above, we propose a structural join algorithm for finding all preceding-sibling–following-sibling node pairs, called *Pre-Fol-Sib-Join* shown in Figure 3. The *Pre-Fol-Sib-Join* algorithm is characteristic of three features: First, it can skip some nodes that are absent from the join results using B+-tree index; Second, preceding-sibling and following-sibling list are scanned once at most respectively; Furthermore, the output, a list of node pairs <p, f> where f from list F is following sibling of p from list P, is sorted by preorder number of node f, which meets the semantic demand of XPath queries.

Because steps 6, 10, 15, 22, 28 and 34 in *Pre-Fol-Sib-Join* algorithm can skip nodes that do not participate in the join using B+-tree index, preceding-sibling list and following-sibling list are scanned once at most respectively. If changing the indexing locations of p or f in steps 6, 10, 15, 22 and 28 into the next record of list P or F, and obliterating step 34, then the algorithm will become the one which only performs sequential scan on list P and F respectively. In practice, to avoid unnecessary B+-tree accesses, we first check whether the next record is in the same page b as the previous record (by checking the last record in b).

Figure 4 depicts the scenarios using parent's structure information to skip some unnecessary elements in steps 15 and 34. Wherein, the meanings of squares, ellipses and triangles are similar to ones in Figure 1. In particular, the squares with grid represent the nodes skipped which don't participate in join; the squares with shadow in Figure 4(b) indicate nodes popped from the stack. It is apparent that considerable nodes are jumped over in the join indeed.

The stack at all time has a sequence of nodes from list P, each node in the stack being a descendant or following-sibling or following-sibling's descendant of the node below it. If the current node in list F is after the parent of the current top of stack, we are guaranteed that no future node in list F is a following-sibling of the current top of stack, and so we may pop the top of stack and its preceding-siblings and repeat our test with the new top of stack.

For the example XML document depicted in Figure 1, the stack operations in the *Pre-Fol-Sib-Join* algorithm may be expressed sequentially as: node 4 is pushed, and then popped; nodes 6, 7, 8 and 11 are pushed successively, and node 11 is popped; node 14 is pushed, and nodes 14, 8, 7 and 6 are popped successively; finally, node 19 is pushed, and then popped.

Algorithm Pre-Fol-Sib-Join(P, F)

Input {P, F}: P and F are preceding-sibling list and following-sibling list, respectively.

Output {<p, f>}: A list of node pairs <p, f> where f from list F is following sibling of p from list P.

```
1.    Let p and f be the first record of list P and F, respectively;
2.    Let stack be empty;
3.    Sp=stack->push(p);      // Sp represents top record of the stack.
4.    Let p be the next record in P;
5.    while (f is not at the end of F and (p is not at the end of P or the stack is not empty)) {
6.        if (f.order<=Sp.order) { Let f be the record in F having the smallest order that is larger than Sp.order;
7.        } else if (f.order<=Sp.max) {
8.            if (p is not at the end of P and p.order<=Sp.max) {
9.                Sp=stack->push(p);   Let p be the next record in P;
10.               } else { Let f be the record in F having the smallest order that is larger than Sp.max; }
11.       } else if (f.pOrder==Sp.pOrder) {
12.           if (p is not at the end of P and f.order>p.order) {
13.               if (p.pOrder==Sp.pOrder) {
14.                   Sp=stack->push(p);   Let p be the next record in P;
15.                   } else { Let p be the record in P having the smallest order that is larger than MAX(Sp.max, p.pMax); }
16.               } else { Output f as a following-sibling of any record e in the stack if f is a following-sibling of e;
17.                   Let f be the next record in F; }
18.       } else if (f.order<=Sp.pMax) {
19.           if (p is not at the end of P and f.order>=p.order) {
20.               Sp=stack->push(p);
21.               if (f.order>p.max) {
22.                   Let p be the record in P having the smallest order that is larger than MAX(Sp.max, p.max);
23.                   } else { Let p be the next record in P; }
24.               } else {
25.                   if (p is not at the end of P and p.order<=f.max) {
26.                       Let begin_ord be p.order-1;
27.                       } else { Let begin_ord be f.max; }
28.                   Let f be the record in F having the smallest order that is larger than begin_ord; }
29.       } else {
30.           Pop top record and all its sibling records in the stack;
31.           Let temp be the first record popped;
32.           if (the stack is empty and p is not at the end of P) {
33.               if (p.order<=temp.pMax) {
34.                   Let p be the record in P having the smallest order that is larger than temp.pMax;
35.                   }Sp=stack->push(p);   Let p be the next record in P;
36.               } else { Sp=stack->top; }
          }
      }
```

Fig. 3. Pre-Fol-Sib-Join algorithm with output in sorted following-sibling order

For *Pre-Fol-Sib-Join* algorithm, depth of the stack is less than or equal to

$$MAX_{n \in P}(\sum_{m \in Ans\text{-}or\text{-}self(n)} Left\text{-}sibling(m))$$

Here, *Ans-or-self*(n) represents a node set that consists of node n and its ancestors in the XML tree, and *Left-sibling*(m) represents the total number of node m and its preceding-siblings that belong to list P.

It can be estimated that the depth of the stack will be acceptable. The reason lies in the fact that, general XML trees are not too deep, that's to say, the node set *Ans-or-self*() will not be large.

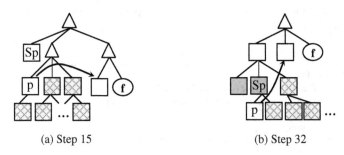

(a) Step 15   (b) Step 32

Fig. 4. Scenarios of using parent's structure information

3.3 Evaluating Preceding-Sibling Axis

It is not straightforward to modify the *Pre-Fol-Sib-Join* algorithm to produce results sorted by preceding-sibling because: if node p from list P on the stack is found to be a preceding-sibling of some node f in the list F, every node p_1 from list P that is a preceding-sibling of p (and hence below p on the stack) is also a preceding-sibling of f. Since the order of p_1 precedes the order of p, we must delay output of the join pair <f, p> until after <f, p_1> has been output. Nevertheless, there remains the possibility of a new element f' after f in the list F joining with p_2, which is ancestor or preceding-sibling of p, and hence below p on the stack, so we cannot output the pair <f, p> until the ancestor or preceding-sibling node p_2 is popped from stack. Meanwhile, we can build up large join results that cannot yet be output. Our solution to this problem is similar to that in [6].

We propose a structural join algorithm for finding all following-sibling–preceding-sibling node pairs, called *Fol-Pre-Sib-Join* shown in Figure 5, for efficient evaluation of preceding-sibling axis of XPath. The *Fol-Pre-Sib-Join* algorithm is similar to *Pre-Fol-Sib-Join* algorithm in three aspects: it can also skip some nodes using B+-tree index; the following-sibling list and preceding-sibling list are scanned once at most respectively; the output of the *Fol-Pre-Sib-Join* algorithm, which is a list of node pairs <f, p> where p from list P is preceding-sibling of f from list F, is sorted by preorder number of node p, which meet the semantic demand of XPath queries.

Because steps 13, 15, 20 and 21 (wherein, steps 15 and 21 take advantage of parent's structure information to accelerate structural join) in *Fol-Pre-Sib-Join* algorithm can skip some nodes that do not participate in the join using B+-tree index, following-sibling list and preceding-sibling list are scanned once at most respectively. If changing the indexing

---

Algorithm Fol-Pre-Sib-Join(F, P)

Input {F, P}: F and P are following-sibling list and preceding-sibling list, respectively.

Output {<f, p>}: A list of node pairs <f, p> where p from list P is preceding sibling of f from list F.

1.	Let p and f be the first record of list P and F, respectively;
2.	Let stack be empty and Sp be top record of the stack;
3.	Fflag=NULL;
4.	while (f is not at the end of F and (p is not at the end of P or stack is not empty)) {
5.	if (p is not at the end of P and p.order<f.order) {
6.	if (f.order<=p.pMax) {
7.	Sp=stack->push(p);
8.	if (Sp.pOrder==f.pOrder) {
9.	for (p1=stack->top; p1!=NULL and p1.pOrder==Sp.pOrder; p1=p1->down) {
10.	if (p1==stack->bottom) { Output node pair <f, p1>; }
11.	else { Append node pair <f, p1> to p1.selt-list; }
12.	if (Fflag==f) break;
	}
13.	Let p be the record in P having the smallest order that is larger than Sp.max;
14.	} else { Let p be the next record in P; }
15.	} else { Let p be the record in P having the smallest order that is larger than p.pMax; }
16.	} else {
17.	if (p.order<=f.max) {
18.	Let f be the next record in F;
19.	} else if (stack->size!=0 and Sp.order>f.pOrder or p.order<=f.pMax) {
20.	Let f be the record in F having the smallest order that is larger than f.max;
21.	} else { Let f be the record in F having the smallest order that is larger than f.pMax; }
22.	Fflag=f;
23.	while (stack->size!=0 and (f is at the end of F or f.order>Sp.pMax)) {
24.	temp=stack->pop(); Sp=stack->top;
25.	if (stack->size==0) { Output temp.inherit-list;
26.	} else { Append temp.inherit-list to temp.self-list; Append the resulting temp.selt-list to Sp.inherit-list; }
	}
27.	if (stack->size!=0 and Sp.pOrder==f.pOrder) {
28.	for (p1=stack->top; p1!=NULL and p1.pOrder==Sp.pOrder; p1=p1->down) {
29.	if (p1==stack->bottom) Output node pair <f, p1>;
30.	else Append node pair <f, p1> to p1.selt-list;
	}
	}
	}
	}

Fig. 5. Fol-Pre-Sib-Join algorithm with output in sorted preceding-sibling order

locations of p or f in steps 13, 15, 20 and 21 into the next record of list P or F, then the algorithm will only performs sequential scan on list P and F respectively.

As with the *Pre-Fol-Sib-Join* algorithm, the stack at all time has a sequence of nodes from list P, each node in the stack being a descendant or following-sibling or descendant's following-sibling of the node below it. Now, we associate two lists with each node in the stack: the first, called *self-list* is a list of node pairs <f, p> that are from the join results of this node p with appropriate nodes f from list F; the second, called *inherit-list* is a list of join results involving nodes in the stack from list P that were descendants or following-siblings of the current node. When the current node in list F is found to be a following-sibling of the current top of stack, it is just added to the self-lists of the top node and preceding-siblings of the top node in the stack.

As before, if the current node in list **F** is after the parent of the current top of stack, we are guaranteed that no future node in list **F** is a following-sibling of the current top of stack, so we can pop the top of stack and its preceding-siblings, and repeat our test with the new top of stack. When the bottom node in stack is popped, we output its self-list first and then its inherit-list. When any other node in stack is popped, no output is generated; instead, we append its inherit-list to its self-list, and append the result to the inherit-list of the new top of stack.

Similar to the processing in [6], a small, but key, optimization to the *Fol-Pre-Sib-Join* algorithm is as follows: no self-list is maintained for the bottom node in the stack. Instead, joined results with the bottom of the stack are output immediately. This results in a small space savings, but more importantly, it ensures that the algorithm would not be blocked.

4   Experimental Results

In this section, we present the comprehensive experiments conducted to evaluate the effectiveness of various algorithms and heuristics proposed in the paper.

4.1   Experimental Setup

We used synthetic data for experiments in order to control the structure and join characteristics of XML documents. The main part of the DTD used to generate testing data set was shown in Figure 6.

```
<!ELEMENT pub (book+)>
<!ELEMENT book (title, price, author+, chapter*, press, description?)>
<!ATTLIST book year CDATA #REQUIRED>
<!ELEMENT author (name, contact?)>
<!ATTLIST author id ID #REQUIRED>
<!ELEMENT contact (address, email?, phone?)>
<!ELEMENT chapter (title, section*, description?)>
<!ATTLIST chapter number CDATA #REQUIRED>
<!ELEMENT section (title, section*, description?)>
<!ATTLIST section number CDATA #REQUIRED>
<!ELEMENT press (name, address?, email?)>
<!ELEMENT description (text*)>
<!ELEMENT text ((#PCDATA | bold | keyword | emph)*)>
<!ELEMENT bold ((#PCDATA | bold | keyword | emph)*)>
<!ELEMENT keyword ((#PCDATA | bold | keyword | emph)*)>
<!ELEMENT emph ((#PCDATA | bold | keyword | emph)*)>
```

Fig. 6. DTD for testing data

To test performance of all algorithms for processing structural joins of preceding-sibling –following-sibling relationship, we chose *title* vs. *author, title* vs. *section, section* vs. *description,* and *section* vs. *section* element sets as the base element sets, and generated other element sets with different joining characteristics from the base element sets. The *title* vs. *author* represents ordinary sibling relationship; the *title* vs. *section* corresponds to nested following-sibling and the *section* vs. *description* depicts the scenario with nested preceding-sibling; the *section* vs. *section* illustrates the case where preceding-sibling and following-sibling share the same name and both are nested. These test examples have covered general sibling relationship.

About 72.8MB raw XML data was generated for the DTD by XML data generator designed by us. Statistics about related element nodes in the XML document are shown in Table 1.

Experiments are performed to study the comparative performance of structural joins of sibling relationship on *Pre-Fol-Sib-Join* algorithm, *Fol-Pre-Sib-Join* algorithm, and indexed nested-loop join algorithms using B+-tree based *XPath accelerator* proposed in [13]. Table 2 summarizes the join algorithms for which the results are presented. We did not test R-tree based *XPath accelerator* because it has similar performance as that of B+-tree based *XPath accelerator* when following-sibling axis is evaluated.

Table 1. Number of element nodes in the XML document

Tag name	Number of nodes
title	482 775
author	22 440
section	472 279
description	189 264

Table 2. Notations for algorithms

Notation	Represented Algorithm
XPA	Indexed nested-loop join algorithms using B+-tree based *XPath accelerator* proposed
XPA-P	The improved XPA algorithm using parent's structure
PFSJ	*Pre-Fol-Sib-Join* algorithm proposed in the
FPSJ	*Fol-Pre-Sib-Join* algorithm proposed in the

We evaluated the performance of different join algorithms using two performance indicators, *number of elements scanned* and *elapsed time.*

- *Number of elements scanned:* This metrics, the total number of elements scanned during a join, evaluates the capability to skip elements that do not produce join results for a structural join algorithm.
- *Elapsed time:* It is used to investigate the overall performance of different algorithms.

The testing system was built on top of our experimental XML database system, which includes storage manger, B+-tree index modules, XML document parser and loader. All the experiments were performed on a Pentium IV 1.5GHz PC with 256M RAM and 20G storage size running Windows XP. All the algorithms were implemented in MS VC++6.0. The page size used is 4K and we used the file system as the storage.

4.2 Varying Size of Preceding-Sibling Lists

The objective of this set of experiments is to study the performance of various algorithms when varying size of preceding-sibling list. During the experiments, we kept the whole element nodes (100%) in following-sibling lists and varied size of preceding-sibling lists via removing certain element nodes from the preceding-sibling lists.

Table 3 shows the total number of elements scanned (in thousand) for various algorithms. Note that some number of XPA is too large to be measured. *Sib-J* is short for both *Pre-Fol-Sib-Join* and *Fol-Pre-Sib-Join* algorithms.

Table 3. Number of elements scanned (in thousand) when varying size of preceding-sibling lists

(a) *title* vs. *author*			(b) *title* vs. *section*		
Size	XPA	XPA-P	Sib-J	XPA	XPA-P	Sib-J
100%	——	988	29	——	3061	955
75%	——	741	44	——	2299	834
50%	——	495	82	——	1535	712
30%	——	296	98	——	919	604
10%	539235	99	99	——	306	403
1%	53856	10	20	1144737	324	388
(c) *section* vs. *description*			(d) *section* vs. *section*		
Size	XPA	XPA-P	Sib-J	XPA	XPA-P	Sib-J
100%	——	2023	660	——	3114	945
75%	——	1515	542	——	2338	826
50%	——	1013	424	——	1548	705
30%	——	606	329	——	934	601
10%	——	200	223	——	314	414
1%	455490	208	46	1106539	31	46

It can be seen from Table 3 that the improved *XPath accelerator* scans much less elements than the original *XPath accelerator* does, validating the optimizing techniques for sibling axes. It is also noticeable that the proposed algorithms are able to complete the join by scanning fewer elements than the improved *XPath accelerator* in general. The benefit gets more obvious when the size of preceding-sibling lists increases.

The proposed algorithms in the case of *title* vs. *author* depicted in Table 3(a) are more capable of skipping unnecessary elements than in other cases; the reason is that it can skip more elements in this case. Whereas, the *Sib-J* algorithms seem to scan more elements as the size of preceding-sibling list decreases before to a certain extent, this is because the ability to jump unnecessary elements in preceding-sibling list becomes weaker as the size of preceding-sibling list decreases.

We also measured the CPU time, the number of I/O's and the elapsed time for each run. The results show that the elapsed time is dominated by the I/O's performance, specifically, the number of page misses. Figure 7 displays the elapsed time for each algorithm. As can be observed, the proposed algorithms outperform the improved *XPath accelerator*, which presents a striking contrast to the original one.

It is worth noting that the number of elements scanned is unnecessarily proportional to the elapsed time. The rationale is that while each element scan causes a pin to a buffer page, the elapsed time is dominated by page misses. Consecutive element scans on the same buffer page cause almost no additional running time.

4.3 Varying Size of Following-Sibling Lists

Next, we keep the whole element nodes in preceding-sibling lists and vary the size of following-sibling lists. Table 4 shows the total number of elements scanned (in

Table 4. Number of elements scanned (in thousand) when varying size of following-sibling lists

	(a) *title* vs. *author*			(b) *title* vs. *section*		
Size	XPA	XPA-P	Sib-J	XPA	XPA-P	Sib-J
75%	——	982	24	——	2538	837
50%	——	977	18	——	2013	718
30%	——	972	14	——	1594	622
10%	536218	968	9	——	1176	516
1%	58443	962	7	1122804	986	308

	(c) *section* vs. *description*			(d) *section* vs. *section*		
Size	XPA	XPA-P	Sib-J	XPA	XPA-P	Sib-J
75%	——	1752	609	——	2573	827
50%	——	1481	555	——	2028	707
30%	——	1267	501	——	1595	608
10%	——	1048	363	——	1162	475
1%	450446	951	92	1098036	966	160

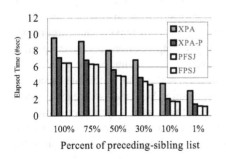

(a) *title* vs. *author*

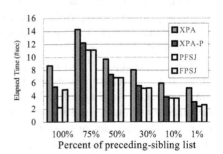

(b) *title* vs. *section*

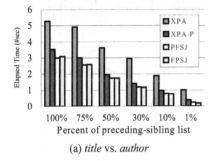

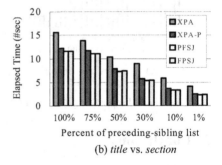

Fig. 7. Elapsed time (in second) when varying size of preceding-sibling lists

thousand) for various algorithms. Figure 8 shows the overall performance of the algorithms tested. It is obvious that the optimizing techniques presented improve greatly on *XPath accelerator* and proposed algorithms are superior to the improved *XPath accelerator* in general. The efficiency of proposed algorithms under various circumstances also demonstrates the scalability of these algorithms.

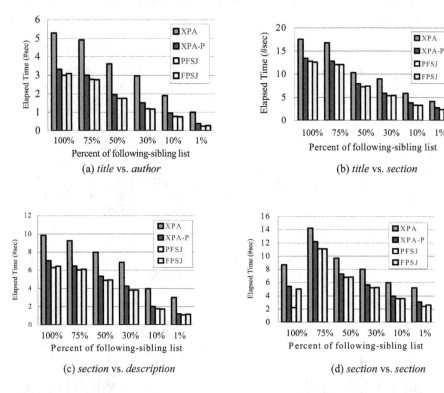

Fig. 8. Elapsed time (in second) when varying size of following-sibling lists

5 Conclusions

The sibling relationships are as important as ancestor-descendant (or parent-child) relationships in evaluating path expression. To the best of our knowledge, this is the first effort that addresses this issue. In this paper, we present two efficient algorithms for structural join of preceding-sibling–following-sibling relationship by integrating optimizing techniques in evaluating sibling axes. By utilizing parent's structural information, the algorithms jump over unnecessary nodes and accelerate structural joins of preceding-sibling–following-sibling relationship. Also, they scan each element list joined sequentially once at most, and produce output sorted by preorder number of following-sibling nodes or by that of preceding-sibling nodes. Performance study has shown that the optimizing techniques lead to significant improvement and the algorithms have high efficiency and scalability.

Acknowledgement

This work is partially funded by Natural Science Foundation of Jiangxi Province (No: 0411009). We would also like to give special thanks to Prof. Shiqian Wu from Institute for Infocomm Research of Singapore for his careful review and helpful suggestions.

References

[1] W3C. XQuery 1.0: A XML Query Language. W3C Working Draft.
[2] http://www.w3.org/TR/xquery/.
[3] W3C. XML Path Language (XPath) Version 2.0. W3C Working Draft. http://www.w3.org/TR/xpath20/.
[4] C. Zhang, J. Naughton, D. DeWitt, et al. On Supporting Containment Queries in Relational Database Management Systems. In: Proc of the SIGMOD Conf, 2001. 426-437.
[5] Q. Li, and B. Moon. Indexing and Querying XML Data for Regular Path Expressions. In: Proc of the VLDB Conf, 2001. 361-370.
[6] Liu Yun-sheng, Wan Chang-xuan, and Xu Sheng-hua. Efficiently Implementing RPE Query in a RDBMS. Mini-Micro Systems, 2003, 24(10): 1764-1771. (In Chinese)
[7] S. Al-Khalifa, H. V. Jagadish, N. Koudas, et al. Structural Joins: A Primitive for Efficient XML Query Pattern Matching. In: Proc of the ICDE Conf, 2002. 141-152.
[8] Chien Shu-yao, Z. Vagena, Zhang Donghui, et al. Efficient Structural Joins on Indexed XML Documents. In: Proc of the VLDB Conf, 2002. 263-274.
[9] N. Bruno, N. Koudas, and D. Srivastava. Holistic Twig Joins: Optimal XML Pattern Matching. In: Proc of the SIGMOD Conf, 2002. 310-321.
[10] H. Jiang, W. Wang, H. Lu, and et al. Holistic Twig Joins on Indexed XML Documents. In: Proc of the VLDB Conf, 2003. 273-284.
[11] Y. Wu, J. M. Patel, and H. V. Jagadish. Structural Join Order Selection for XML Query Optimization. In: Proc of the ICDE Conf, 2003. 443-454.
[12] H. Jiang, H. Lu, W. Wang, et al. XR-Tree: Indexing XML Data for Efficient Structural Joins. In: Proc of the ICDE Conf, 2003. 253-264.
[13] W. Wang, H. Jiang, H. Lu, et al. PBiTree Coding and Efficient Processing of Containment Joins. In: Proc of the ICDE Conf, 2003. 391-402.
[14] T. Grust. Accelerating XPath Location Steps. In: Proc of the SIGMOD Conf, 2002. 109-120.
[15] P. F. Dietz. Maintaining order in a linked list. In: Proc of the Annual ACM Symposium on Theory of Computing, 1982. 122-127.
[16] Wan Changxuan and Liu Yunsheng. Efficient Supporting XML Query and Keyword Search in Relational Database Systems. In: Proc of the WAIM Conf on Web-Age Information Management (Lecture Notes in Computer Science, Vol. 2419, Springer-Verlag), 2002. 1-12.
[17] Wan Chang-xuan, Liu Yun-sheng, Xu Sheng-hua, and Lin Da-hai . Indexing XML Data based on Region Coding for Efficient Processing of Structural Joins. Chinese Journal of Computers, 2005, 28(1): 113-127. (In Chinese)
[18] T. Grust, Maurice van Keulen, Jens Teubner: Staircase Join: Teach a Relational DBMS to Watch its (Axis) Steps. In: Proc of the VLDB Conf, 2003. 524-525.
[19] Hanyu Li, Mong-Li Lee, Wynne Hsu, Chao Chen: An Evaluation of XML Indexes for Structural Join. SIGMOD Record, 2004, 33(3): 28-33.

Practical Indexing XML Document for Twig Query*

Hongzhi Wang[1], Wei Wang[2,3], Jianzhong Li[1],
Xuemin Lin[2,3], and Reymond Wong[2]

[1] Harbin Institute of Technology, Harbin, China
{wangzh, lijzh}@hit.edu.cn
[2] University of New South Wales, Australia
{weiw, lxue, wong}@cse.unsw.edu.au
[3] National ICT of Australia, Australia

Abstract. Answering structural queries of XML with index is an important approach of efficient XML query processing. Among existing structural indexes for XML data, F&B index is the smallest index that can answer all branching queries. However, an F&B index for less regular XML data often contains a large number of index nodes, and hence a large amount of main memory. If the F&B index cannot be accommodated in the available memory, its performance will degrade significantly. This issue has practically limited wider application of the F&B index.

In this paper, we propose a disk organization method for the F&B index which shift part of the leave nodes in the F&B index to the disk and organize them judiciously on the disk. Our method is based on the observation that the majority of the nodes in a F&B index is often the leaf nodes, yet their access frequencies are not high.

We select some leaves to output to disk. With the support of reasonable storage structure in main memory and in disk, we design efficient query processing method). We further optimize the design of the F&B index based on the query workload . Experimental results verified the effectiveness of our proposed approach.

1 Introduction

XML has been widely used as a format of information exchange and representation over the Internet. Due to its hierarchical structures, XML data can be naturally modeled as a labeled rooted tree. As a result, most XML query languages, such as XPath and XQuery, allow user to retrieve part of nodes of the tree that satisfy certain structural constraints. For example, query $a/b[d]/c$ on XML tree in Figure 1 only retrieve nodes with tag c whose parent has tag b and contains at least one child with tag d.

Efficient query processing technologies of XML data are in great demand. One major challenge of XML query processing is the queries involving path

---

* This work was partially supported by ARC Discovery Grant – DP0346004 and the Defence Pre-Research Project of the 'Tenth Five-Year-Plan'of China no.41315.2.3.

S. Grumbach, L. Siu, and V. Vianu (Eds.): ASIAN 2005, LNCS 3818, pp. 208–222, 2005.

constraints. Using index to directly retrieve qualified nodes is a nature way to accelerate such path queries. Consequently, a number of such indexes have been proposed, including DataGuides [2], 1-index [8], F&B index [5]. Among them, F&B index is the smallest index that can answers all branching queries. However, the F&B index tends to have a large number of nodes, and hence occupying a large amount of memory. For example, the complete F&B index for 100M XMark benchmark datas [11] has 1.35 million nodes. It is obvious that if the available memory size is limited such that the F&B index cannot be accommodated in the memory, its performance will degrade significantly.

Such shortcoming limits the application of F&B index. One possible method to solve this problem is to use virtual memory managed by operation system. It is obviously not a good way. Because the main memory exchange strategy is not designed for query processing. Another solution is build approximate index. Current approximate F&B indexes mainly focus on approximate of 1-index that only supports single path query. Therefore this problem is still not resolved.

An observation of F&B index for tree-structured XML document is that about half of its nodes are leaf node(And during query processing with F&B index, leaf nodes are often accessed at last step. Based on this observation, we design our method of storing parts of leaves to disk. The storage structure of leaf nodes in disk should support the cooperation with index in main memory. And the choice of which nodes to output to disk is another problem to solve in this paper.

Our contributions in this paper includes:

- A strategy of cooperation of main memory and disk F&B index is presented. So that main memory size problem of F&B index is solved.
- We design a leave storage strategy and compacted structure of index in main memory. Such structure saves main memory further more without affecting the efficiency of query.
- Optimized strategies of choosing nodes to output to disk is designed. The strategies consider two instances, with workload and without workload.
  - In the instance without workload, based on cost model formulation and experiment, it can be seen that the optimization interval is limited so that random selection method is practical.
  - In the instance with workload, we design a heuristic method to select optimized node set to output to disk.

This paper is organized as follows. Section 2 presents some preliminaries. The storage structure and query processing strategy are discussed in section 3, The node selection strategies of instances without and with workload are presented in section 4. Section 5 gives results of experiments and the discussion. In section 6, related work is presented and conclusions are drawn in section 7.

2   Preliminary

XML data are usually modeled as labeled rooted trees: elements and attributes are mapped to nodes in the trees and direct nesting relationships between two

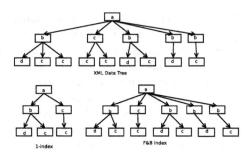

Fig. 1. The Example of Index

elements are mapped to edges between the corresponding nodes in the tree. In this paper, we only focus on element nodes; it is easy to generalize our methods to other types of nodes defined in [12].

All structural indexes for XML data take a path query as input and report *exactly* all those matching nodes as output, via searching within the indexes. Equivalently, those indexes are said to *cover* those queries. Existing XML indexes differ in terms of the classes of queries they can cover. DataGuide [2] and 1-index [8] can cover all *simple path queries*, that is, path queries without branches. [5] showed that F&BIndex is the minimum index that covers all branching path queries. We note that if the XML data is modeled as a tree, its 1-index and F&BIndex will also be a tree. Each index node n in an F&B index is associated with its *extent*, which is the set of data nodes in the data tree that the index node n represents for.

We show an running example in Figure 1; specifically, we show an example XML data tree, its 1-index, and its F&B Index. To distinguish nodes with the same tag, we append an sequence number after its label. For instance, both $b1$ and $b2$ in the 1-index have the label b. In the 1-index, all the second level b element in the data tree are classified as the same index node with tag b; this is because all those node cannot be distinguished by their incoming path, which is a/b. However, those b are classified into three groups in the F&BIndex; this is because branching path expressions, e.g., $a[c]/b$ and $a[d]/b$, can distinguish them. Compared to the 1-index which has only 6 nodes, the F&BIndex has much more nodes (10 in our example). It can be shown that in the worst case, an F&BIndex has the same number of nodes as the document does.

3   Disk Storage of F&B Index

In this section, we propose and discuss both in-memory and disk organizations when we shift parts of leaf nodes of an F&B index to disk in order to fit the rest of the index to the limited amount of main memory. Query processing methods based on this new organization are also discussed.

3.1   Store Leaves of F&B Index to Disk

One of the problems that limits the wide application of the F&B index is its large size for many irregular real datasets. When available main memory is not enough to accommodate an F&B index, one naive solution is to reply on the virtual memory managed by the operating system. It is obviously not a good solution, as the virtual memory replacement policy is not designed for database query processing, let alone specific access pattern for the XML index.

In order to solve this problem, a natural approach is to judiciously select part of the F&B index to the disk under the available memory constraint. We propose to shift the leaf nodes of the F&B index to the disk before considering the internal nodes. This strategy is based on the following two observations on the statistical nature and access patterns on the F&B index:

- We observe that leaf index nodes constitute the major part for many tree-modeled XML datasets. For example, we show the ratio of number of leaf index node versus the number of total index nodes for three typical XML datasets (DBLP, XMark, and Treebank) in Table 1. We can observe that the ratio is above 50% for all the three datasets. Therefore, shifting the leaf nodes of an F&B index to disk can effectively reduce the memory requirement.
- Traversal-based query processing techniques are commonly used on the F&B index. Our second observation is that, during tree traversal, query processing can stop in the internal nodes; even if the query results reside on extents of the leaf nodes, they are the last part to be accessed. Furthermore, for many complex branching queries, when the branching predicates do not contain value comparison, they can be evaluated without accessing the extents of the leaf nodes, because the semantics of the branching predicates are to test the existence of a particular type of node satisfying the branching path constraint.

Even though shifting some internal nodes to disk can further save main memory, processing queries on the structure obtained by such shifting will brings more disk I/O than on the structure obtained only by shifting leaves to disk in average. It is because when processing query by traversal index, interval nodes have more chances to be accessed than leave nodes.

The second design choice is the data organization of the in-memory F&B index as well the disk portion of the F&B index. A naive solution would be to replace all the in-memory pointers with the disk-based pointers. However, such simple solution is not likely to work well in practice, because following random disk-based pointers usually incur random I/Os, which is extremely costly. Therefore,

Table 1. Leaf Nodes Ratio for Three Typical XML Datasets

Dataset	#nodes	#index_nodes	#leaf_nodes	Ratio
DBLP	4620206	3477	4122	84.4%
XMark	2048193	294928	516935	57.1%
Treebank	2437667	1253163	2280279	55.0%

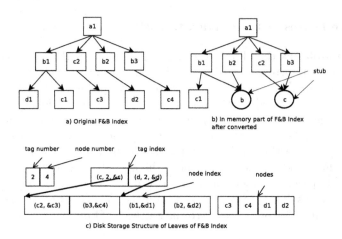

a) Original F&B Index

b) In memory part of F&B Index after converted

c) Disk Storage Structure of Leaves of F&B Index

Fig. 2. In-memory and Disk Organizations of the F&B Index

by taking into consideration of the query processing efficiency, we summarize the desiderata of a good organization as:

1. The in-memory part of the F&B index should cooperate seamlessly with the portion of index on the disk;
2. The I/O cost spent to answer queries on the disk portion of the F&B index should be minimized.

Our proposed solution consists of two parts accordingly:

1. In order to satisfy the first requirement, we introduce special **stubs** which serves as the connections between main memory part of the index and the disk part. A stub is extremely memeory-efficient in that it consists of a label name only; it is yet powerful enough for all the query processing.
2. We employ clustering and indexing techniques for the disk portion of the F&B index. Index nodes stored on the disk are clustered according to their tag names as well as incoming paths. Indexes are also built on it to support fast retrieval during query processing.

As an example, the F&B index with partial nodes shifted to the disk is depicted in Figure 2, where $a1$ is an index node with tag a, $b1$, $b2$ and $b3$ are index nodes with tag b, $c1$, $c2$, $c3$ and $c4$ are index nodes with tag c. In c) of Figure 2, $\&c$ and $\&d$ points to the address of the first node with tag c and tag d, respectively. We will discuss the details of the above design on this example in the following.

Stub. A special type of nodes, *stubs*, is introduced, which serves as the connection between main memory index and the disk part. For each stub, we only keep the tag of this node. We use an optimization that merges stubs with the same name into one to further save the memory. We will show shortly that this does not affect our query processing ability or efficiency. Furthermore, many branching predicates only needs to check the existence of index node with a particular tag rather than retrieving a specific index node or its extents, this optimization will not slow down the query processing of such branching queries. In our example index shown in Figure 2, suppose we choose nodes d1, d2, c3, c4 to be shifted to the disk. As shown in Figure 2(b), in the in-memory part of the index, d1 and d2 are replaced with a stub with tag name "d"; c3 and c4 are replaced by a stub with the tag name "c" (both in circle). To see why such organization does not hinder branching predicate checking, let's assume the query is $a/b[c]/d$. When node b3 is accessed, we need to check whether it satisfies the branching predicate, $[c]$; we only need to access the stub labeled "c" and can return true without the need to access the actual index node c4 which are now stored on the disk.

Clustering and Indexing. Index nodes on the disk are clustered based on their tag names and incoming paths. This is based on the observation that the leaf index nodes relevant to an XML query often have the same tag name and incoming path; as a result, such cluster strategy has the advantage of reducing physical I/O during the query processing. As shown in Figure 2(c), the four nodes that have been shifted to the disk, i.e., c3, c4, d1, and d2, are laid out contiguously according to the clustering criteria above.

Based on the clustering criteria, additional indexes are built to accelerate the access of F&B index nodes on the disk. Specifically, we build a *tag index* and a *node index*. The tag index is based on the property that all index nodes on the disk with the same tag are clustered together. Each entry in tag index points to the first *node index entry* of the same tag in the *node index*. For example, there are two entries in the tag index (shown in Figure 2(c)) for the running example. For the entry (c, 2), 'c' is the tag name; 2 is the number of F&B index nodes with the corresponding tag (i.e., 'c') on the disk; the associated pointer links to the first entry in the node index with the corresponding tag. The node index records the incoming path information for each corresponding F&B index nodes.

Information for query includes its the incoming path number and the pointer to the node with extent. For example, in c) of Fig 2, the entry (c2,&c3) of node index represents node c3 in F&B index in a). In this entry, c2 is the id of its father in F&B index and &c3 is the address of its real node. In c), part "nodes" is the storage of nodes with their extent. The pointer &c3 in entry(c2, &c3) points to c3 in this part. In order to accelerate the searching of index, in tag index, all entities are sorted by tag. In each cluster of node index, the nodes have the same tag name and sorted by their parent id.

In addition to the above three components, we also record the total number of tags and total number of nodes, for all the F&B index nodes shifted to the disk. The complete disk organization is thus shown in Figure 2.

The main motivation and the advantage of employing such clustering and indexing is to reduce the number of disk I/Os during the query processing. For example, in order to process query $a//d$ by traversing the F&B index shown in Figure 2(c), d1 and d2 will be accessed. Without clustering, d1 and d2 are likely to reside on different places on the disk. Without tag and node indexes, sequence scan of all the disk-resident F&B nodes will be required. As a contrast, with our clustering and indexing schemes, in order to retrieve d1, we first look up the tag index to find the starting position of node index entries with tag 'd'; we then search in the node index the address of the F&B node with tag 'b' and its parent node id equal to 'b1'; finally we fetch the node d1 from the disk by following the disk pointer. While searching node index for these two 'd' nodes, with the clustering, the disk blocks containing 'd' entries in node index need only be read into the main memory for one time because of the existence of buffers. Similarly the actual F&B index node d2 is likely to be in the buffer after d1 is accessed. Therefore, we can greatly reduce the physical I/O cost for many queries from two I/Os per F&B index node (one I/O to obtain the address the node in the node index and another to access the node) to a much smaller number. In fact, our experiments verified that with a reasonable amount of buffer pages, such saving is significant.

Building the F&B Index. We give the procedure to convert a totally in-memory F&B index to our F&B index structure once a subset of the leaf nodes, S, is given. We will discuss the criteria and algorithms to choose S in Section 4.

1. Sort the nodes in S by their tags and their parent IDs.
2. Gather the total number of tags and nodes in S.
3. Generate the node index from S and tag index from node index.
4. Compute the address of each node on the disk and fill it to corresponding entry in the node index. Compute the address of the first entry of each tag in the node index and fill it to corresponding entry in the tag index.
5. Store all these parts of storage in the structure discussed above.

We give an estimation of the memory that our method can save in Equation 1. The first item of Equation 1 is necessary memory size of when all nodes are in the main memory. The second item is the size of the stubs.

$$Size_{save} = \sum_{node \in S} size(node) - |T| \cdot size(tag) \tag{1}$$

where S is the set of nodes to output to disk and T is the set of tags of the nodes output to disk. $Size(tag)$ is a constant. The total storage size is estimated in Equation 2.

$$Size_{storage} = log|T| + log|S| + |T| \cdot size_{entry\_of\_tag\_index} +$$
$$+|S| \cdot size_{entry\_of\_node\_index} + \sum_{node \in S} size(node) \tag{2}$$

where $|S|$ and $|T|$ represent the size of S and T respectively. The first two items of Equation 2 are the storage cost of number of tags and number of nodes respectively. The second item is the size of tag index and the third item is the size of node index. The last item is the storage cost of nodes.

3.2   Query Processing Based on the Index

Our query processing algorithms for the F&B index with partial nodes on the disk is an extension of the common algorithms for in-memory F&B index. In the following, we briefly discuss the algorithms for the two types of queries: /-queries and //-queries.

Algorithm 1. QueryPath(n, q, $type$, fid)

```
 1: for all twig in q.twigs do
 2:     for all child in n.children do
 3:         if twig.tag == child.tag then
 4:             if QueryPath(child,twig, EXISTING, n.id) == ∅ then
 5:                 return ∅
 6: if q.nextLocStep != NULL then
 7:     for each child in n.children do
 8:         if child.tag == q.nextLocStep.tag then
 9:             result = result ∪ QueryPath(child,q.next,type,n.id)
10:             if type == EXISTING ∧ result != ∅ then
11:                 return result
12:     return result
13: else
14:     if n is a stub then
15:         return LoadExtent(n.tag,fid)
16:     else
17:         return n.extent
```

A /-query is a XPath query with only parent-child axis. Traversal-based method is commonly used for in-memory F&B index for such kind of queries. We present the sketch of the enhanced traversal-based method is in Algorithm 1, which is capable of working with F&B index with partial nodes on the disk. For each step of XPath query, at first, twig conditions are checked via recursive calls (Lines 1–5). The algorithm proceeds to process the next step in the query only after all the branching conditions have been satisfied. When encountering a leaf F&B index node, we shall take different steps depending on whether it is a in-memory index node or an in-memory stub. In the former case, the extent of the node will be appended to the result set; in the latter case, the extent should be loaded from disk However, we do no need to access the extent on the disk when checking twig conditions, because the tags of nodes on the disk are maintained in the corresponding stubs.

For //-queries, we need to traverse the whole subtrees of the current index node in order to evaluate the ancestor-descendant-or-self axis. We note that when the twig condition contains //, we can immediately return once a qualified node is met. In the interest of space, we skip the algorithm here.

A common procedure in the algorithms for both types of queries is the Load-Extent algorithm (shown in Algorithm 2), which loads the extents of index node on the disk. It has three steps and assumes that the tag index has been loaded into the main memory. Before query processing, tag index is loaded in main memory. At first, the entry of tag in node index is found. Then binary search is

---

Algorithm 2. LoadExtent(tag, fid)

1: $(begin\_index, end\_index) = searchIndex(tag)$;
2: $(begin\_pos, end\_pos) = searchPosition(fid, begin\_index, end\_index)$;
3: return LoadData($begin\_pos$, end_pos);

---

used to find the position of extent of requested node in node index. This binary search has two levels. The first level is to apply binary search on block level, that is to say, to find the block containing requested node by comparing with the first record and last record in disk. The second level is find the exact position in selected block. The usage of binary search is for the reason that it can locate to the disk containing required entry as soon as possible.

Cost Estimation

We now provide estimation of the disk I/O cost for processing a query on our data structure. With the assumption that buffer is "large enough" (its definition will be provided shortly), Equation 3 gives the upper bound of the physical I/O (PIO) and Equation 4 gives the upper bound of logical I/O (LIO) of processing a query Q.

$$PIO(Q) = \lceil \frac{\sum_{p \in Disk(tag(Q))} size(p)}{BLK} \rceil + \lceil \frac{num(tag_Q) * size_{node\_entry}}{BLK} \rceil \quad (3)$$

$$LIO(Q) = \sum_{p \in disk(Q)} size(p) + \lceil \log \lceil \frac{num(tag_Q) * size_{node\_entry}}{BLK} \rceil \rceil \quad (4)$$

where $Disk(tag(Q))$ is the set of F&B index nodes on the disk with the request of Q; $disk(Q)$ is the set of F&B index nodes required by Q on the disk; $size(p)$ is the size of F&B index node p; BLK is block size; $num(tag_Q)$ is the number of index nodes on the disk with the same tag as the goal of query Q; $size_{node_entry}$ is the size of each entry in node index.

In Equation 3, accessing each nodes on the disk satisfying Q requires us to locate the position of the node on the disk ($\lceil \log \lceil \frac{num(tag_Q)}{BLK} \rceil \rceil$ times of disk read) and to access the node ($\lceil \frac{size(p)}{BLK} \rceil$ times of disk read). When estimating the number of physical disk I/Os, because of the existence of buffer, many of disk pages can be located in the buffer during the query processing. So with enough buffer pages, the number of disk I/Os is *smaller* than the total number of disk pages containing the entries in the node index with tag specified by Q, $\lceil \frac{num(tag_Q)}{BLK} \rceil$. Since the nodes satisfying query Q may not be continuous on the disk, accessing all the nodes as Q's query result needs at most the number of all disk pages containing any node as the result of Q.

The condition that the buffer is "large enough" is the number of buffer pages should be no less than the number in Equation 5. The intuition is that the buffer should be able to accommodate the largest of the node index for a specific tag plus the number of blocks used during access the extent (this number is 1 since extent of each node is accessed only once).

$$\max_{T \in S}\{\lceil \log(\lceil \frac{num(tag_Q) * size_{node\_entry}}{BLK} \rceil) \rceil) + 1\} \qquad (5)$$

where S is the family of sets. Each is a set of nodes in disk with the same tag.

4   Node Selection Strategies

In this section, we focus on the choice of the subset of leaf F&B index nodes to be shifted to the disk. We consider two scenarios: without workload information and with workload information.

4.1   The General Problem

It is unnecessary to shift all the leaf nodes to the disk if there are enough memory. Therefore, we consider optimal choices of selecting the subset of leaf index nodes to be shifted to the disk. We will start with the scenario where we have no workload information. In this scenario, the choice of index nodes depends on the size of the nodes and their potential cost of disk I/O if they are shifted to the disk. We discuss in the following the formulation of this optimization problem.

The cost model of physical I/O can be represented as

$$Cost_{physicalIO} = \sum_{T \in S} (f_{node} \cdot \lceil \frac{\sum_{a_i \in T} size(a_i)}{B} \rceil + \lceil \frac{num\_tag(T) \cdot size\_head}{B} \rceil) \quad (6)$$

where S it the set family, each element in which is a set of node with the same tag; a_i is node in T; f_{node} is the frequency of accessing to $node$, $size(node)$ is the size of $node$ stored in disk and $num\_tag(node)$ is the number of nodes in disk with the same tag with $node$.

It is noted that Equation 6 represents the upper bound of physical I/O. The first item is the total storage size of nodes in the same tag. The second one is the max number of disk I/O necessary to find all the entries of extents of nodes in disk in the same query. Because binary search is used to find related node. The number of real accessed blocks during query is often smaller than $\lceil \frac{num\_tag(T) \cdot size\_head}{B} \rceil$.

The logical I/O cost is as following.

$$Cost_{logicalIO} = \sum_{node \in S} (f_{node} \cdot \lceil \frac{size(node)}{B} \rceil + \log \lceil \frac{num\_tag(node) \cdot size\_head}{B} \rceil + H)$$

where B is block size, S is the set of leaves selected to output to disk. Other symbols have the same meaning as Equation 6.

The first item of the formula is the number of I/O to read the extent of the index and the second item is the number of I/O to find the position of the position of a node with binary searching.

The problem can be represented as

$$\text{minimize} \qquad T = \begin{pmatrix} Cost_{physicalIO} \\ Cost_{logicalIO} \end{pmatrix}$$

$$\text{Subject to} \sum_{i \notin S} cost_{memory}(node_i) + size_{node} \cdot |T| \leq M \qquad (7)$$

This is a general definition of this problem. Without workload information, f_{node}'s are determined with the assumption that the frequency of all queries are same. So all f_{node}'s are set to equal value.

Obviously, this problem is hard to solve. But it is found in practise, the value of physical I/O, which determines the efficiency, in the cost model only changes in a small range. Therefore, without workload information, random selection is practical for the selection of nodes to output to disk. This point will be shown in the experiment.

4.2   The Solution Based on Workload

In this subsection, we consider the scenario where we have the query workload information. Intuitively, we can find better node selection strategies in this case.

Since the problem with workload information is still a hard one, we aim at finding good heuristic solutions. Our proposed heuristic has three levels.

The first level is based on weight in workload. This method is to add a weight property to each leaf node in the index. The queries are executed in the full F&B index. When a leaf node n is met, the weight of this query in workload is added to weight property of n. Then, all leaves are sorted based on weight. The nodes with the least weight number is outputted out disk. This method is reasonable. It is because the nodes accessed most should be contained in main memory.

If many nodes have same weight, in our heuristic method, the nodes with the largest extent should be outputted to disk. Intuitively such method can remain more nodes in main memory.

The third level is to output the nodes that have more nodes with same tag as them. From the Equation 6, because of the existence of ceiling function, adding a new tag to outside set brings more cost.

5   Experiments

In this section, we present part of the our extensive experiment results on the proposed improved F&B index.

5.1   Experimental Setup

All of our experiments were performed on a PC with Pentium 1GMHz, 256M memory and 30G IDE hard disk. The OS is Windows 2000 Professional. We implemented our system using Microsoft Visual C++ 6.0. We also implemented the F&B index building algorithm using random node selection or the heuristic

Table 2. Basic Information of XML Document for Experiment

Document Nodes	#Tags	#F&B Index Nodes	#Leaves in F&B Index	#leave ratio
413111	77	141084	83064	58.88 %

node selection algorithm based on workload, as well as the query processing algorithms. All the algorithms return the extents of the index nodes as the result. We used CLOCK algorithm as the buffer replacement policy.

The dataset we tested is the standard XMark benchmark dataset. We used a scale factor of 0.2 and generated XML document of size 20M. We used the following metrics in our experiments: query processing time, number of physical I/Os (PIO) and number of logical I/Os (LIO). Some statistics of the dataset and its F&B index is shown in Table 2.

In order to test the performance of the experiment, we generated various query sets as workloads. First, we generate all the single query with only parent-child edge (the set is called *single query set* for brief) and random select some ratio of them as the workload. Second, we extracted path queries from the standard test query set of XMark to test the general efficiency of our method.

5.2   Performance Results

Performance Without Workload. We test the performance without workload with random selection of nodes to output to disk. The parameters we used is available memory 0.5M, page size 1024 bytes, buffer size 128 pages. We select 10% queries from uniform query workload randomly. We did five times of experiments with same setting and selected nodes randomly. The result is in Table 3. From the result, the standard deviation of runtime, PIO and LIO are 28.028, 0.10 and 5.58 respectively. It can be seen from these data that without workload information, there is only little difference in efficiency with various random nodes selections.

Performance of the Method with Workload. We fixed the buffer size 64 blocks, page size 1024 bytes and memory size of leaves 1M bytes. We used random selection from all single paths with only single slash and the path queries extracted from standard of XMark query. All the experiment runs in cold buffer. The efficiency is compared with the instance of random selection nodes to output to disk. The results of random selection and optimized by workload are shown

Table 3. Experiment Results of Random Node Selection

nodes in disk	#average run time	#average PIO	#average LIO
70492	356.14	21.03	962.34
69916	307.31	20.94	949.86
70045	323.06	21.03	960.97
70233	309.34	20.86	966.74
70336	378.74	20.77	961.03

Table 4. Comparison of Different Node Selection Strategies

method	#nodes in disk	#avg. run time	#avg. PIO	#avg. LIO
Heuristic Algorithm	65565	289.06	0	0
Random selection	69937	521.97	20.57	935.54

in Table 4, where avg. PIO and avg. LIO represent average PIO and LIO of running all queries in workload on the index stored in these two node selection strategies, respectively.

5.3   Changing System Parameters

In this subsection, we test our system by varying various system parameters.

Varying the Size of Workload. We test the performance by varying the size of workload. We select the workload randomly from uniform query workload and various the number of queries in workload if from the 10% to 100% of uniform query workload. We fixed main memory for leaves 0.5M, page size 1024 bytes and buffer size 128 pages. The performance results are shown in Figure 3(a) and Figure 3(b).

It can be observed that when the ratio of workload increases, PIO and LIO increases. This is because when the number of nodes related to queries in workload increase to more than the memory's capacity, the average efficiency of processing the queries in workload will decrease. While the average efficiencies of processing the queries in the whole singe query set is stable.

Varying Available Memory Size. We test the performance with various available memory size. We fix the number of queries in workload 10% of the uniform workload, page size 1024 bytes and buffer size 128 pages. The results are shown in Figure 3(c) and Figure 3(d).

From Figure 3(c), we can observe that when memory size becomes large enough, the number of disk I/O changes to 0. It represents the instance that main memory is large enough to hold all the results nodes in the queries set. Since our storage is optimized for workload, so size of memory that makes the disk I/O of processing queries in workload 0 is smaller than that of processing queries in the whole singe-path query path.

Varying Cache Size. We test the performance with various buffer sizes. We fix the number of queries in workload 30% of the uniform query workload, page size 1024 bytes and available memory size 0.5M. The fixed parameters assure the number of I/O of querying workload queries non-zero. Since the number of logical does not chance with the varying of buffer size. We only test the change of PIO. The result is in Figure 3(e).

It can be observed from Figure 3(e), when the size of buffer reaches to a number, the number of PIO does not change. It is because all the entities of node index are cached, as we discussed in Section 3.1.

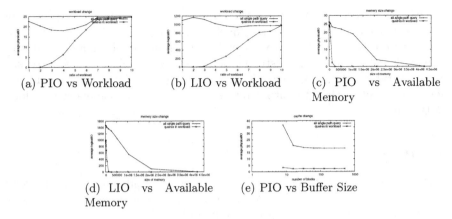

(a) PIO vs Workload   (b) LIO vs Workload   (c) PIO   vs   Available
Memory

(d) LIO   vs   Available   (e) PIO vs Buffer Size
Memory

Fig. 3. Experiment Results

6   Related Work

There have been many previous work on indexing the values [7], structure and
codes of XML data [4]. We focus on structural indexes in this paper. Most of
the structural indexes are based on the idea of considering XML document as a
graph and partitioning the nodes into equivalent classes based on certain equivalence relationship. The resultant index can support (or cover) certain class of
queries. A rigid discussion of the partitioning method and its supported query
classes is presented in [10]. DataGuide [2] are based on *equivalent* relationship
and 1-index [8] are based on the *backward bi-similarity* relationship. Both of
them can answer all simple path queries. F&BIndex [5] uses both backward and
forward bisimulation and has been proved as the minimum index that supports
all branching queries (i.e., twig queries). These "exact" indexes usually have
large amount of nodes and hence size, therefore, a number of work has been
devoted to find their *approximate* but smaller counterparts. A(k)-index [6] is
an approximation of 1-index by using only k-bisimilarity instead of bisimilar-
ity. D(k)-index [9] generalizes A(k)-index by using different k according to the
workload. M(k)-index and M*(k)-index [3] further optimize the D(k)-index by
taking care not to over-refining index nodes under the given workload. Updating
structural indexes has just receive attentions from researchers. Another different
approach to index the XML data is to build indexes only for frequently used
paths in the workload. APEX [1] is such an example and can be dynamically
maintained.

7   Conclusion and Further Work

F&B index is the smallest structure index to answer all the branch queries of
XML. But its size prevents its widely use. In this paper, a novel method of
making F&B index practical is presented. The basic idea is to put some leaves

of F&B index to disk. We design the storage structure and query processing strategy. For reduce disk I/O during query processing, we also present nodes to disk selection strategy. Without workload, we use random selection method. And with workload, we design heuristic method to select optimized nodes. Extensive experimental results proves the efficiency of our system. Our future include design an efficient method to output internal nodes to disk to support very large F&B index.

References

1. C.-W. Chung, J.-K. Min, and K. Shim. Apex: an adaptive path index for XML data. In *Proceedings of the 2002 ACM SIGMOD International Conference on Management of Data (SIGMOD 2002)*, pages 121–132, 2002.
2. R. Goldman and J. Widom. Dataguides: Enabling query formulation and optimization in semistructured databases. In *Proceedings of 23rd International Conference on Very Large Data Bases (VLDB 1997)*, pages 436–445, 1997.
3. H. He and J. Yang. Multiresolution indexing of XML for frequent queries. In *Proceedings of the 20th International Conference on Data Engineering (ICDE 2004)*, pages 683–694, Boston, MA, USA, March 2004.
4. H. Jiang, H. Lu, W. Wang, and B. C. Ooi. XR-Tree: Indexing XML data for efficient structural join. In *Proceedings of the 19th International Conference on Data Engineering (ICDE 2003)*, pages 253–263, 2003.
5. R. Kaushik, P. Bohannon, J. F. Naughton, and H. F. Korth. Covering indexes for branching path queries. In *Proceedings of the 2002 ACM SIGMOD International Conference on Management of Data (SIGMOD 2002)*, pages 133–144, 2002.
6. R. Kaushik, P. Shenoy, P. Bohannon, and E. Gudes. Exploiting local similarity for efficient indexing of paths in graph structured data. In *Proceedings of the 18th International Conference on Data Engineering (ICDE 2002)*, pages 129–140, San Jose, CA, USA, March 2002.
7. J. McHugh and J. Widom. Query optimization for xml. In *Proceedings of 25th International Conference on Very Large Data Bases (VLDB 1999)*, pages 315–326, 1999.
8. T. Milo and D. Suciu. Index structures for path expressions. In *Proceedings of the 7th International Conference on Database Theory (ICDE 1999)*, pages 277–295, 1999.
9. C. Qun, A. Lim, and K. W. Ong. D(k)-Index: An adaptive structural summary for graph-structured data. In *The 2003 ACM SIGMOD International Conference on Management of Data (SIGMOD 2003)*, pages 134–144, San Diego, California, USA, June 2003.
10. P. Ramanan. Covering indexes for XML queries: Bisimulation - Simulation = Negation. In *Proceedings of 29th International Conference on Very Large Data Bases (VLDB 2003)*, pages 165–176, 2003.
11. A. Schmidt, F. Waas, M. L. Kersten, M. J. Carey, I. Manolescu, and R. Busse. XMark: A benchmark for XML data management. In *Proceedings of 28th International Conference on Very Large Data Bases (VLDB 2002)*, pages 974–985, 2002.
12. W3C. XML Query 1.0 and XPath 2.0 data model, 2003. Available from http://www.w3.org/TR/xpath-datamodel/.

Efficient Stream Organization for Wireless Broadcasting of XML Data[*]

Chang-Sup Park[1], Chung Soo Kim[2], and Yon Dohn Chung[2,**]

[1] Department of Internet Information Engineering,
The University of Suwon, Korea
park@suwon.ac.kr
[2] Department of Computer Engineering,
Dongguk University, Korea
{ronalst, ydchung}@dgu.edu

Abstract. This paper presents a wireless streaming method for XML data which supports energy-efficient processing of queries over the stream in mobile clients. We propose new stream organizations for XML data which have different kinds of addresses to related data in the stream. We describe event-driven stream generation algorithms for the proposed stream structures and provide search algorithms for simple XML path queries which leverage the access mechanisms incorporated in the stream. Experimental results show that our approach can effectively improve the tuning time performance of user queries in a wireless broadcasting environment.

1 Introduction

Wireless information systems are currently realized in many areas as wireless technologies are rapidly gaining popularity [1, 4, 7, 8]. In the systems, mobile clients carry small, battery powered hand-held devices such as PDA's and mobile phones with limited data processing capabilities. In wireless systems, data broadcasting is widely used due to the bandwidth restriction of wireless communication [1, 8]. The server disseminates data through a broadcast channel, and mobile clients listen on the channel and selectively retrieve information of their interests without sending requests to the server.

In this paper, we consider a wireless information system where XML data are broadcasted in streams. With the recent proliferation of various XML technologies, XML data are often used in most information systems including wireless broadcast applications. For example, Electronic Program Guide (EPG) data and Traffic and Travel Information (TTI) data are represented and broadcasted in XML forms in digital broadcast systems such as Digital Audio/Video Broadcasting (DAB/DVB) systems [18, 20].

---

[*] This work was done as a part of Information & Communication Fundamental Technology Research Program, supported by Ministry of Information & Communication in Republic of Korea.
[**] Corresponding author.

S. Grumbach, L. Siu, and V. Vianu (Eds.): ASIAN 2005, LNCS 3818, pp. 223–235, 2005.

In our wireless broadcasting systems, XML data retrieved from XML storages or generated from external sources are transformed into a sequence of data units for streaming, called *S-Nodes*. The generated S-Nodes stream is pipelined to the data broadcaster and continuously transmitted to a lot of mobile clients over the air. In the client devices, user queries are issued and processed over the S-Nodes in the broadcast stream, which are received selectively based on the given queries.

The main contribution of this research is to propose a wireless streaming method for XML data which supports energy-efficient access to the streamed data in mobile clients. We first define an S-Node structure as a streaming unit for XML data. We suggest a few options of using different kinds of skip addresses to some related data in the stream, which can be utilized in processing user queries in client devices. We provide event-driven stream generation methods for the proposed stream structures. We also describe algorithms for processing simple XML path queries over the S-Nodes stream, which exploit the efficient access paths contained in the stream.

The rest of the paper is organized as follows. We first discuss background information and related work in Section 2. In Section 3, we propose new stream organizations and describe stream generation algorithms. In Section 4, we present query processing algorithms for the proposed stream formats. We evaluate the effectiveness of our methods by experiments in Section 5 and draw conclusions in Section 6.

2 Background and Related Work

Data broadcasting has many applications in wireless information systems due to its beneficial characteristics such as *bandwidth-efficiency* (i.e., the broadcast channel is shared by many clients), *energy-efficiency* (i.e., listening on the broadcast channel requires no energy for sending request messages to the server, where the energy for sending data is tens of hundreds of that for receiving data), and *scalability* (i.e., the number of clients listening on a broadcast channel is not limited) [1, 7, 8].

In wireless data broadcasting, we use two performance measures for streamed data access: *access time* and *tuning time* [7, 8]. The former is the duration from the time of query submission (i.e., start to listen on the broadcast channel) to the time of complete download of target information. The latter is the duration when a mobile device remains in the *active mode* during the access time, which directly relates to the amount of energy consumption of the mobile device. There have been studies for improving access time performance via effective scheduling of broadcast data [1, 5] and reducing tuning time via indexing methods which place index information intermixed with data on the broadcast stream [3, 4, 8]. However, those approaches are not directly applicable to the semi-structured XML data and typically require replication of indexing information in the stream which incurs bandwidth waste and the increase of access time.

Recently, extensive research on processing queries over streaming XML data has been conducted in the literature [12, 13, 15]. Those approaches exploit a network of finite automata or push-down transducers to represent and process a subset of XPath or XQuery queries over XML streams. V. Josifovski, *et al.* [9] proposed an efficient iterator-based XQuery processor for XML streams which can be integrated in a relational database engine. All the work, however, focused on processing complex XML queries over textual stream of XML data efficiently and did not consider requirements for energy-efficient access of streaming data in mobile computing environments. Our work is different from those query evaluation strategies in that it provides efficient stream organizations for XML data which support selective access of stream for primitive path queries.

There are also several proposals for binary encoding and compression of XML data for efficient representation and transmissions of pre-parsed XML documents [10, 11, 17, 21]. The Xstream middleware system in [19] provides fragmentation and packetizing strategies based on the semantic and structural characteristics of a given XML document in wireless environments.

3   Stream Generation

3.1   Basic Stream Organization

A well-formed XML document [22] can be represented by a tree of nodes as proposed in the XML data model [6]. Each element in the document is represented by an element node which may have nested element or text nodes as its child nodes representing content of the element. The child nodes are ordered by the occurrence of the corresponding elements in the document, i.e., in *document order* [22]. Element nodes may also be connected to attribute nodes which denote the name and value pairs of the associated attributes. For the sake of simplicity of presentation, we assume that element nodes have at most one text node.

For broadcast of a given XML document, we consider the binary tree representation of the above tree-structured data model where an internal node has at most two child links: one is to the first child node and the other is to the next sibling node. We can serialize XML data in document order by traversing the binary tree in pre-order

Table 1. Structure of the S-Node

Element	Size (B)	Description	Usage
flags	1	bit-flags	all
tagName	variable	name of the element with its length	all
siblingAddr	1	distance to the next sibling node	OSA
sameTagAddr	1	distance to the nearest sibling node having the same tag name	TSA
samePathAddr	1	distance to the nearest sibling/cousin node having the same tag/path name	SPA
diffTagAddr	1	distance to the nearest sibling node having a different and newly appeared tag name	TSA SPA
attributeList	variable	a list of name-value pairs of attributes with their length	all
charData	variable	character data contained in the element with its length	all
depth	1	nesting depth of the element in the document	all

Table 2. Meaning of the flag bits in the S-Node

Flag bit	Description	Usage
HAS_CHILD_NODE	The next node is the first child of it	all
HAS_SIBLING_NODE	The next node is its sibling	all
HAS_ATTRIBUTES	The node has attributes	all
HAS_CHAR_DATA	The node has character data	all
HAS_SIBLING_ADDR	The node has an address to the next sibling node	OSA
HAS_SAME_TAG_ADDR	The node has a same-tag address	TSA SPA
HAS_DIFF_TAG_ADDR	The node has a different-tag address	TSA SPA
HAS_SAME_PATH_ADDR	The node has a same-path address	SPA

depth-first manner. Since the first child node directly follows its parent node, the parent-child link information need not to be encoded in the stream and only the address to the next sibling node, if any, is calculated and placed in the stream.

An S-Node, which is the unit of streaming data proposed in this work, encapsulates useful information about an element and related items from the input XML data. As shown in Table 1, it has the tag name and nesting depth of the element and includes a list of associated attributes and/or character data, if the element has any. An important class of information contained in the S-Node is the addresses to other S-Nodes in the stream, which mean the time interval between two S-Nodes delivered on the air. The first byte of the S-Node is a set of bit flags representing various characteristics of the node, such as the relationship with the next S-Node and information about whether it has attributes, character data, and different kinds of addresses. Table 2 specifies the meaning and usage of the flags in the proposed methods. The flags, name, and addresses in the S-Node compose the S-Node header.

In a basic streaming strategy, called the *One-Sibling-Address* (*OSA*) method, we use the address to the next sibling node for each S-Node in the stream. It can be used to jump forward to the next sibling node from a current S-Node in processing path queries over the stream in mobile clients. Fig. 1 shows a part of example XML data from [22] and Fig. 2 depicts the binary tree structure of S-Nodes generated by the OSA method for the example data, where only the tag names and links are presented.

In our work, we use an event-driven XML processor which supports the SAX interfaces [16] to generate an S-Nodes stream in a single-pass scan of the given XML data without constructing any physical tree structure. We provide a content handler registered for the XML processor which defines a set of global variables as well as event handlers that are invoked when the start tag, end tag, and character data of elements are recognized during the parsing process. The pseudo-code algorithm of the content hander is presented in Fig. 3.

A difficulty in generating an S-Node having an address to the next sibling node is that we cannot know the actual value of the address until all the descendants of the element for the S-Node are read from the input data and their S-Nodes are produced. That means we cannot complete the generation of S-Nodes in document order of elements. In the proposed algorithm, however, we put out S-Nodes into the stream in document order by using a queue to store incomplete S-Nodes until their next sibling elements are detected from the input data. We also make use of a stack to store information about the S-Nodes in the queue, including the absolute position in the stream and the memory reference to the S-Node objects (in line 34). When the next sibling node of an S-Node occurs in the input data, the entry for the S-Node is popped from the stack and used to calculate the sibling address for the S-Node in the queue (in line 17~23).

```
<mondial>
    <continent id="f0_123">Asia</continent>
    <country id="f0_553" name="South Korea" capital="f0_1726">
        <name>Korea</name>
        <name>South Korea</name>
        <city id="f0_1726" country="f0_553" longitude="126.9" latitude="37.5">
            <name>Seoul</name>
            <population year="95">10229262</population>
        </city>
        <city id="f0_10230" country="f0_553">
            <name>Pusan</name>
            <population year="95">3813814</population>
        </city>
        <border length="238" country="f0_545"></border>
        <city id="f0_10235" country="f0_553">
            <name>Taegu</name>
        </city>
        <languages percentage="100">Korean</languages>
        <religions percentage="47.4">Buddhism</religions>
        <religions percentage="48.6">Christianity</religions>
    </country>
...
</mondial>
```

Fig. 1. Example XML data

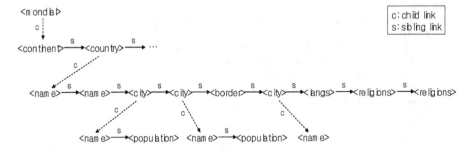

Fig. 2. The tree structure of S-Nodes in the OSA method

```
 1  ContentHandler StreamGenerator_OSA
 2  Input: A well-formed XML data
 3  Output: a stream of S-Nodes
 4  // Global Variables Definitions
 5  Stack S                              // stores an entry (pos, pSN)
 6  Queue Q                              // stores S-Nodes
 7  int curPos = 0                       // current position in the stream
 8  int depth = -1                       // depth of the current element
 9  boolean lastTag = START_TAG          // kind of the previous tag

10  EventHandler startElement (tagName, attributeList)  // invoked for a start tag
11  begin
12      depth++
13      if S is not empty then
14          if lastTag == START_TAG then  // the first child element
15              Get the top entry SE = (pos, pSN) in S.
16              Set the bit flag HAS_CHILD_NODE in pSN.
17          else                          // a next sibling element
18              Pop an entry SE = (pos, pSN) from S.
19              if the bit flag HAS_CHILD_NODE in pSN is clear then
20                  Set the bit flag HAS_SIBLING_NODE in pSN.
21              end if
22              Set the bit flag HAS_SIBLING_ADDR in pSN.
23              siblingAddr of pSN = curPos – pos – (the length of the header)
24          end if
25          if depth == 1 then    // flush a root node or a sub-tree of its child
26              Flush all the S-Nodes in Q into the output stream.
27          end if
28      end if
29      Initialize an S-Node structure SN with tagName, attributeList, and depth.
30      if attributeList is not empty then
31          Set the bit flag HAS_ATTRIBUTES in SN.
32      end if
33      Enqueue SN into Q and let pSN_c be the returned address of the entry in Q.
34      Push (curPos, pSN_c) into S.
35      Increase curPos by the total length of the S-Node header and attributeList.
36      lastTag = START_TAG
37  end.
38  EventHandler endElement (tagName)     // invoked for an end tag
39  begin
40      if lastTag == END_TAG then  Pop an entry from S.  end if
41      Increase curPos by the length of the depth field.
42      depth--; lastTag = END_TAG
43  end.
44  EventHandler characters (charString)    // invoked for a character data
45  begin
46      Get the top entry SE = (pos, pSN) in S.
47      charData of pSN = charString; set the bit flag HAS_CHAR_DATA in pSN.
48      Increase curPos by the length of charString.
49  end.
```

Fig. 3. The stream generation algorithm for the OSA method

3.2 Differentiating Sibling Nodes

The basic stream format has only an address to the next sibling node in S-Nodes. As an improvement on the previous method, we utilize two kinds of addresses to the sibling nodes following an S-Node in the *Two-Sibling-Addresses* (*TSA*) method. In the new streaming format, an S-Node may have two addresses, i.e., the *same-tag address* to the nearest sibling node having the same tag name as the S-Node and the *different-tag address* to the nearest sibling node having a tag name different from those of the S-Node and the previously generated sibling nodes.

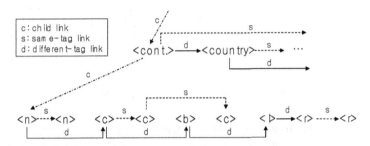

Fig. 4. An example tree of S-Nodes in the TSA method

Fig. 4 illustrates an example tree structure of S-Nodes created by the TSA method. Note that a set of sibling nodes is re-organized into a binary tree in which an internal node may have a node with a different tag name as its left child node and a node with the same tag name as its right child node. A sequence of same-tag links forms a chain of the sibling S-Nodes having the same tag name. The content handler for generating a TSA stream, which is extended from the OSA stream generator, is given in [14] for space limitation. The S-Nodes in the TSA method are also produced in document order of the input data using the same queue and stack as in the basic streaming method. We additionally use an associative array for a current set of sibling S-Nodes in order to store the position and reference information of the S-Node which is at the tail of a same-tag chain of sibling S-Nodes for each tag name. When the next sibling S-Node having the same tag name is generated, the same-tag address to the S-Node is calculated for a previous S-Node found from the associative array. We also keep the information of the last S-Node which has a tag name distinct from those of the previously generated sibling nodes. The different-tag address of the S-Node can be generated when a sibling element with a new tag name appears in the input data.

The pair of addresses proposed in the TSA method can be used as a useful mean to search all the S-Nodes matching with query nodes efficiently in processing path queries over the stream, which will be described in Section 4.2.

3.3 Chaining Nodes Having the Same Path Name

For more efficient processing of path queries, we extend the TSA method by connecting the S-Nodes from different sub-trees which have the same path specification.

Another streaming format, the *Same-Path-Address* (*SPA*) method, provides the last
S-Node among a subset of siblings having the same tag name with an address to the
nearest cousin node having the same path name, called the *same-path address*.

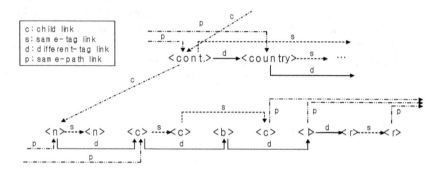

Fig. 5. An example tree of S-Nodes in the SPA method

An example organization of S-Nodes generated by the SPA method is shown in
Fig. 5. Note that the result structure is not a tree but a directed acyclic graph since an
S-Node may have an incoming link from a previous sibling node having a different
tag name and another one from a previous cousin node with the same path name.

In the content handler for the SPA method detailed in [14], we make use of another
associative array for storing the position and reference information of the S-Nodes
which were generated last among those having the same path name for all path names
previously occurred. The same-path address for an S-Node having no following sibling with the same tag name can be calculated using the information kept in the array
when an element having the same path specification appears in a different sub-tree
from the input data. The same-path address is also used to address the sibling node
having the same tag name, i.e., the same-tag address in the SPA method.

4   Query Processing over Streams

Users of mobile devices access wireless broadcast streams by issuing queries to
search data they have interest in. A form of path expression queries such as XPath [2]
queries is typically used for XML data. In this section, we describe stream access
methods for answering a simple path query, which consists of child axes and node
tests, over a wireless stream of S-Nodes generated by our streaming methods. The
complete pseudo-codes of the TSA and SPA search algorithms can be found in [14].

4.1   Stream in the One-Sibling-Address Format

The search algorithm for a stream of S-Nodes with one sibling address is provided in
Fig. 6. For a given query, we should search the stream to find S-Nodes having the
same tag name as a query node in each query step along the query path. If a node test
with a current S-Node in the stream succeeds, we proceed to the next query node, if
any, to examine child S-Nodes (in line 27~30). If either the S-Node has no child while

the next query node exists (in line 31) or the node test with the S-Node itself fails (in line 35), the S-Node and all its descendent nodes are irrelevant to the query and can be skipped using the sibling address in the S-Node (in line 32 and 36). Note that while the streaming data are skipped, client devices can be in doze mode with little energy consumption until the target node is available in the broadcast stream.

```
1  Procedure Search_OSA
2  Input: a stream of S-Nodes and a simple XML path query Q
3  Output: query results R satisfying Q
4      Let S be a stack for storing S-Node headers.
5      Let pQN be a pointer to a query node, initialized with the first one in Q.
6      Let SH be an S-Node header either from the input stream or the stack S.
7      Procedure Skip_by_sibling_address (sizeOfData)
8      begin
9          sizeOfPrevData = sizeOfData
10         while SH does not have siblingAddr do
11             Pop all the entries of the previous siblings of the S-Node from S.
12             Increase sizeOfPrevData by the total amount of data of the
               sibling nodes.
13             Pop an entry SH from S.      // the parent node
14             Move pQN one step backward along the path of Q.
15         end while
16         Push SH into S.
17         Skip the input stream by (siblingAddr in SH – sizeOfPrevData).
18     end.
19 begin
20     while the end of stream is not detected do
21         Read the header SH of an S-Node SN from the input stream.
22         if tagName in SH equals the query node pointed by pQN then
23             if pQN points to the last query node in Q then    // an answer is found
24                 Read SN and all its descendents from stream and insert into R.
25                 Skip_by_sibling_address (size of the sub-tree of SN)
26             else   // query nodes remain
27                 if SN has a child S-Node as the next node then
28                     Push SH into S.
29                     Skip the data of SN.
30                     Move pQN one step forward along the path of Q.
31                 else   // SN has a sibling as the next node or is a leaf node
32                     Skip_by_sibling_address (0)
33                 end if
34             end if
35         else   // node test has failed.
36             Skip_by_sibling_address (0)
37         end if
38     end while
39 end.
```

Fig. 6. The search algorithm for a stream in the OSA format

During search of the stream, we use a stack to store header information of all the ancestor and preceding sibling nodes of the current S-Node. As shown in the *Skip_by_sibling_address* sub-procedure in the algorithm, if the current S-Node is the last sibling node, we find from the stack its closest ancestor having a next sibling node and skip to that sibling node in the stream. Stack entries for the preceding sibling nodes and the parent node are used to calculate the actual number of bytes to be skipped before the next sibling of the parent, if any, can be found.

When an answer node is found during the search, we can transform the S-Node and all its descendents into XML data straightforwardly since the S-Nodes in a stream are in document order of the original XML data. A stack and the depth values of S-Nodes are used to generate closing tags for the result elements.

4.2 Stream in the Two-Sibling-Addresses Format

With the two different sibling addresses in the S-Nodes suggested in the TSA stream structure, we can process path queries more efficiently by skipping the larger number of irrelevant S-Nodes. For a set of sibling S-Nodes, only those connected by the chain of different-tag addresses should be accessed and examined for a node test since they provide the complete set of distinct tag names of the S-Nodes. Furthermore, once we find an S-Node matched with a query node, we can selectively access all matching S-Nodes among its subsequent siblings by following the sequence of same-tag addresses. In the new search algorithm, we use same-tag addresses instead of general sibling addresses in the sub-procedure for skipping streamed data while we exploit a different-tag address when a current S-Node fails a node test.

4.3 Stream in the Same-Path-Address Format

The Same-Path-Address streaming format proposed in Section 3.3 constructs chains of S-Nodes having the same path specification throughout the entire stream by using the same-path address in the S-Node structure. The address to the nearest full cousin node can facilitate more efficient search over the stream for a simple path query.

In the search of a TSA stream, if a current S-Node, which is not an answer node, is the last node in a chain of different-tag addresses or if a matching node does not have a subsequent sibling node with the same tag name, we should move up along its path until any ancestor having the same-tag address is found and repeat previous node tests with the following S-Nodes to find matching ones. Using the same-path addresses in the SPA stream, however, we do not have to do such work since all S-Nodes already know the address of the next subsequent node having the same path specification, if any. Thus, if an S-Node matched with a query node does not have a same-path address, no more answer node is expected in the future stream and the query processing can be immediately stopped.

In the SPA search algorithm, no actual stack structure is required and only a parent node and unmatched sibling nodes need to be temporarily stored for the calculation of the amount of data to be skipped to the next same-tag sibling/cousin node of the parent node when the current unmatched S-Node has no subsequent different-tag sibling node. We can also traverse S-Nodes in the normal way as in a TSA stream, if necessary for processing a complex query, since the same-path addresses to a sibling node can be distinguished from those to a cousin node by a flag bit stored in the S-Nodes.

5   Performance Evaluation

In this section, we present the results of experiments that we have conducted to evaluate effectiveness of our streaming methods. We constructed a simulation environment for a wireless XML streaming system on a Windows XP server and implemented the stream generation and search algorithms proposed in the previous sections in C#. We generated S-Nodes streams in different formats from the several XML datasets in [22]. We assume that data are transmitted and accessed in the unit of buckets whose size is 64KB. We performed the evaluation of various simple path queries over the streams, in which the access and tuning times were measured by the number of buckets.

Table 3. XML data and path queries used in the experiments

XML Data	Description	Size (MB)	Queries
Mondial	World Geo-graphic Data	3.6	Q1: /mondial/country/province
			Q2: /mondial/country/province/city/name
			Q3: /mondial/country/province/religions
SwissProt	Protein Se-quence Data	112.7	Q4: /root/entry/org
			Q5: /root/entry/features/chain

Fig. 7 shows some results for the queries in Table 3 over the streams of the Mondial and SwissProt datasets. The values are normalized by the access (i.e., tuning) times for the XML data streamed in textual form. In the results, the lengths of the S-Nodes streams in the proposed formats are reduced to about 75% of the textual streams, mainly due to the removal of the closing tags of elements in the stream. Tuning times in the OSA method are decreased more than 40% and further reduced in TSA and SPA methods to below 21% of those for the textual streams. We observe that the tuning times of Q3 and Q5 over the streams in the SPA format are less than 3% and 1% of those for the textual streams. Note that access time performance is also improved in the TSA and SPA streams of Mondial data. It is because the query evaluation can be finished earlier in the middle of searching the stream by exploiting the same-tag/different-tag address or same-path address. We expect that when the depth of a given path query is large and there are many repetitions of the same tag names in a set of sibling elements, the same-tag and different-tag addresses can enhance the performance of query processing over streaming data significantly. The SPA strategy is considered most effective for the queries that are much selective as well as have a deep path, since a large amount of irrelevant data can be skipped and the answer nodes can be successively found by following the same-path addresses in S-Nodes.

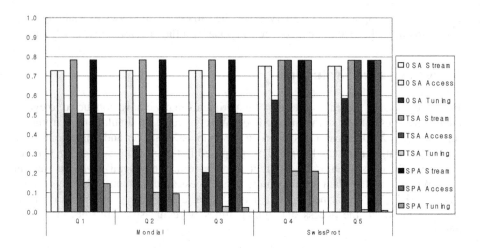

Fig. 7. Stream lengths, access times and tuning times

6 Conclusion

In this paper, we have proposed a wireless streaming method for XML data which supports energy-efficient processing of queries over a stream in mobile clients. We have defined stream structures for XML data and proposed different kinds of addressing strategies for the related data in the streams which can be utilized in processing path expression queries to skip irrelevant parts of data. We have provided event-driven stream generation algorithms for the proposed stream formats and also described search algorithms for simple XML path queries which leverage the access mechanisms incorporated in the stream. Our experimental results show that the proposed approaches can effectively improve tuning time performance for wireless streaming data. We plan to extend the proposed methods for processing more complex XML queries over the streams, which use various axes in the query steps and/or have filtering predicates on XML elements and attributes.

References

1. Acharya, S., et al.: Broadcast Disks: Data Management for Asymmetric Communication Environments. Proc. of ACM SIGMOD Conf. (1995) 199–210
2. Berglund, A., et al. (ed.): XML Path Language (XPath) 2.0, W3C Working Draft (2005)
3. Chen, M.S., et al.: Optimizing Index Allocation for Sequential Data Broadcasting in Wireless Mobile Computing. IEEE Trans. on Knowledge and Data Eng., 15(1) (2003) 161–173
4. Chung, Y.D., Kim, M.H.: An Index Replication Scheme for Wireless Data Broadcasting. Journal of Systems and Software, 51(3) (2000) 191–199
5. Chung, Y.D., Kim, M.H.: Effective Data Placement for Wireless Broadcast. Distributed and Parallel Databases, 9 (2001) 133–150
6. Cowan, J., et al. (ed.): XML Information Set. W3C Recommendation (2004)

7. Imielinski, T., Badrinath, B.R.: Data Management for Mobile Computing. SIGMOD RECORD, 22(1) (1993)
8. Imielinski, T., et al.: Data on Air: Organization and Access. IEEE Trans. on Knowledge and Data Eng., 9(3) (1997)
9. Josifovski, V., et al.: Querying XML Streams. VLDB Journal (2004)
10. Lam, W.Y., et al.: XCQ: XML Compression and Querying System. Proc. of Int. WWW Conf. (2003)
11. Liefke, H., Suciu, D.: XMill: An Efficient Compressor for XML Data. Proc. of ACM SIGMOD Conf. (2000)
12. Ludascher, B., Mukhopadhyay, P., Papakonstantinou, Y.: A Transducer-based XML Query Processor. Proc. of Int. Conf. on VLDB (2002)
13. Olteanu, D., Kiesling, T., Bry, F.: An Evaluation of Regular Path Expressions with Qualifiers against XML Streams. Proc. of Int. Conf. on Data Eng. (2003)
14. Park, C.S., Kim, C.S., Chung, Y.D.: Efficient Streaming of XML Data in Wireless Broadcasting Environments. Technical Report, Dongguk University (2005)
15. Peng, F., Chawathe, S.S.: XPath Queries on Streaming Data. Proc. of ACM SIGMOD Conf. (2003)
16. Simple API for XML, http://www.saxproject.org/
17. Sundaresan, N., Moussa, R.: Algorithm and Programming Models for Efficient Representation of XML for Internet Applications. Proc. of Int. WWW Conf. (2001) 366–375
18. Transport Protocol Experts Group, http://www.tpeg.org/
19. Wong, E., Chan, A., Leong, H.: Xstream: A Middleware for Streaming XML Contents over Wireless Environments. IEEE Trans. on Software Eng., 30(12) (2004) 918–935
20. DVB Document A081, Digital Video Broadcasting (DVB) Transmission System for Handheld Terminals DVB-H (2004)
21. The XML Binary Characterization Working Group. http://www.w3.org/XML/Binary/
22. XML data repository, http://www.cs.washington.edu/research/xmldatasets
23. Yergeau, F., et al. (ed.): Extensible Markup Language (XML) 1.0 (3rd Ed.). W3C Recommendation (2004)

Using Control Theory to Guide Load Shedding in Medical Data Stream Management System[*]

Zijing Hu, Hongyan Li[**], Baojun Qiu, Lv-an Tang, Yu Fan,
Haibin Liu, Jianlong Gao, and Xinbiao Zhou

National Laboratory on Machine Perception,
School of Electronics Engineering and Computer Science,
Peking University, Beijing, 100871, P. R. China
{huzijing, lihy, qbj, tangla,
efan, liuhaibin, jlgao, zhouxb}@cis.pku.edu.cn

Abstract. The load shedding problem is vital to a Data Stream Management System (DSMS). This paper presents the design, implementation, and evaluation of a load shedding method under the guide of the feedback control theory, in order to solve practical problems in medical environment. Thus, the using of operator selectivity, which has been proven not stable enough, is avoided. This paper focuses on the restriction of memory resource, this prevents the overflow of both CUP and memory resource. Our method can well support ad-hoc queries, while it is not so in a DSMS using current load shedding method because of the instability of operator selectivity. Our method also ensures a higher query precision when the system is over loaded and is easy to be implemented. The analytical and experimental results show that our method can be applied to medical data stream systems efficiently.

1 Introduction

Data stream applications such as network monitoring, online transaction, and sensor processing pose tremendous challenges for traditional database systems. The research of this new data model has become a hot field of database community recently. A number of Data Stream Management Systems (DSMS) have been proposed as proto-type systems [1, 2, 3, 4]. The data in typical data streams are usually unbounded, continuous, huge in amount, fast arriving and time various. Under this circumstance, the huge amount of data arrived in DSMS may exceed the total processing ability of DSMS. To insure that DSMS could run steadily in this situation, DSMS has to find a way to depress the system load when huge amount of data arrives, so come forth the load shedding problem.

Currently, there are many research works on the load shedding problem [5, 6, 7, 8, 9]. These methods have a vital shortcoming that they all rely on the selectivity of continuous query operators to guide load shedding. The selectivity of operator is just

---

[*] This work was supported by Natural Science Foundation of China(NSFC) under grant number 60473072
[**] Corresponding author.

S. Grumbach, L. Siu, and V. Vianu (Eds.): ASIAN 2005, LNCS 3818, pp. 236–248, 2005.

a concept, which is defined as the ratio between the number of output tuples produced by the operator and the number of input tuples consumed by the operator. Following are some reasons why selectivity is not fit for solving load shedding problem:

- The selectivity of operator depends on the data consumed by the operator and is just a description of the system status of last period, which could be short or long. As stream data is usually time various, the stream data of different time periods could differ a lot from each other, which makes the selectivity of operator continually change;
- The computation of operator selectivity needs to collect statistical information of system before it formally run. However, ad-hoc queries would be promoted by system users when DSMS is already running. Thus, there is no time for ad-hoc queries to collect statistical information so we could not get the operator selectivity.

Various system resources including CPU, memory, and network bandwidth[7] may become the bottleneck in DSMS query processing. Most of current research works mainly concentrate on the management of CPU cycles and assume there are sufficient memory and network throughput. However, the memory resource is another important factor as well as CPU:

- Memory resource is not always sufficient. And load shedding itself needs to cost some time, thus the data volume arrived in this period could be huge enough to overrun memory resource. Under the condition of high data arrival rates, DSMS may also run out of memory even at the period when load shedding are carrying out according to the CPU oriented method.
- As we mentioned, doing load shedding itself needs to cost some time and DSMS may run out of the memory at this time, Moreover, the control of memory resource could indirectly achieve the effect to control CPU resource utilization.
- In many data stream applications, except for the manufacture field, slight process delay of data is acceptable. For example, even the time restriction of process data in the Intensive Care Unit (ICU) system of hospital is very pressing, the ICU system only need to generate its judgment in a few of seconds, which is because the deterioration of patient's state couldn't cause the death of patient in a few seconds. So DSMS just need to guarantee the memory resource not be over pumped and the buffer effect of data will be gained to handle the sharp turbulence effectively.

Reference [7] first gave the idea of using feedback control theory to guide load shedding. But it still uses the operator selectivity as its major judgment parameter to solve this problem. In addition, it also focuses on the CPU resource utilization. Our method is different from it as we focus on the memory resource utilization in order to give the data some buffer and avoid using the operator selectivity to guide load shedding.

The rest of the paper is organized in the following manner: Section 2 presents some related works; Section 3 gives the system design under the guide of control theory, along with the problem specification; Section 4 explains our system design methods in theory; Section 5 gives some experiments; at last, Section 6 summarizes the paper and discusses future work.

2 Related Work

Algorithms in data streams have received many attentions recently. The survey [1, 2] contains a vide overview of work in the field and it proposes the load shedding problem in DSMS. Since then many researchers engaged in this problem. Although goals are different, most of them focused on methods for dropping tuples from the data stream.

The approaches in reference [5, 6] deal with load shedding in slow CPU case in order to achieve minimum utility loss. The corresponding output in Aurora is associated with a QoS specification function, chosen among three available types: a latency graph, a value-based graph and a loss-tolerance graph. Three major issues are raised to solve load shedding problem – when (what time to start load shedding), where (where to place the drop operators) and how much (load should be shed)[5]. It tries to make sure the CPU cycles are always adequate. Another method tries to minimize the total minimum utility loss generated by load shedding, assuming that QoS specifications are not given for the outputs[6]. Assuming the general case of a system evaluating concurrently a set of individual continuous queries, the aim of the shedder is to drop excess load, while minimizing the maximum error over the queries. The problem is firstly formed as an optimization problem, subject to certain constraints. Reference [7] first uses the feedback control theory to solve load shedding problem. It concentrates on the deadline miss problem of stream data. All the works above have a common problem that they use operator selectivity to judge the system status and to take action. This associated the effectiveness of their method with the stability of operator selectivity.

Some other approaches temporarily exceed system capacity and focus on limiting the memory utilization of DSMS. Improving the efficiency of the allocation of memory among query operators, as proposed in reference [17] or among inter-operator queues are alternatives to load shedding that can improve system performance when limited main memory is the primary resource bottleneck.

Much research work has applied control theory to computing systems in order to achieve acceptable performance in unpredictable environment. For example, a control-theoretical approach has also been applied to provide Qos guarantees in web servers[12]. Feedback control theory is adopted to implement adaptive real-time system[13]. However, feedback control theory has been mostly applied in mechanical and electrical systems. In trying to apply feedback control theory to DSMS, the modeling and implementation face significant research challenges. Some of these challenges will be solved in this paper.

3 System Design with the Guide of Control Theory

First, let us see how a DSMS runs. Figure 1 illustrates a basic DSMS architecture: Inputs from data sources are fed to data queues, and then pushed into operators to be processed. Conceptually, the scheduler picks a box for execution, ascertains what processing is required. The box processor executes the appropriate operation and then forwards the output tuples to its following operators in the query network. The

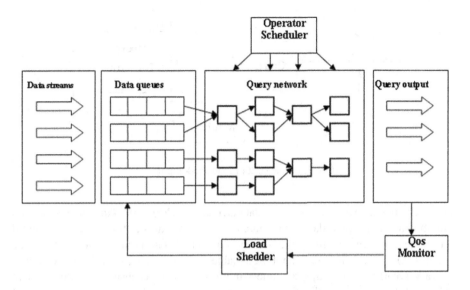

Fig. 1. The architecture of a typical DSMS

scheduler then ascertains the next processing step and the cycle repeats. The QoS monitor continually monitors system performance and activates the load shedder when it detects an overload situation and poor system performance. The load shedder then sheds load till the performance of the system reaches an acceptable level. Our approach is focus on the design and implementation of the Load Shedder. In our feedback based load shedding method, we need to define some system variables as follows:

The first step in designing the load shedding part of DSMS is to decide the following variables in terms of control theory. Readers can refer to [14, 15, 16] for the basic knowledge of control theory.

Controlled variable is the performance metric controlled by the real-time search engine system. In our model, the variable memory utilization $M(k)$ is used as controlled variable, which is defined over a time window $\{(k-1)W, kW\}$, where W is the sampling period and k is called the sampling instant. For the simplicity, time window $\{(k-1)W, kW\}$ is also called time window k. The memory utilization $M(k)$ at the kth sampling instant is defined as the total size of data items in the DSMS in the time window k.

Performance reference represents the desired system performance in terms of the controlled variable. For example, to assure the reliability of a particular system, it may require a most memory utilization $Mref = 80\%C$, where C is the total system capacity of memory resource. The difference between a performance reference and the current value of the controlled variable is called an error. The total error $E(k)=Mref-M(k)$.

Manipulated variable is system attribute that can be dynamically changed by the system to affect the value of the controlled variable. In our system, the manipulated

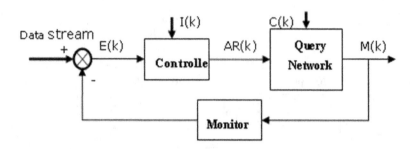

Fig. 2. Framework of load shedding model

variable is data arrival rate $R(k)$. The data arrival rate $R(k)$ at the kth sampling instant is defined as the average data arrival rate of all data streams at time window k, and it can be measured by recording the average number of data items arrived at this time period. $R(k)$ is time-varying and not predictable, however, it is assumed that $R(k)$ does not vary greatly in two adjacent time windows. This is because the stream data of real-world data stream applications are context-sensitive, which means the change of the state of data stream source is not in a random pattern but a gradual pattern. We get this conclusion because this is the general rule of the state change of things in real world.

Figure 2 illustrates the framework of the feedback based load shedding model of DSMS. The monitor measures the controlled variable $M(k)$ and feeds the samples back to the controller. The controller compares the performance references $Mref$ with $M(k)$ to get the current error $E(k)$, and computes a change $D(k)$, called control input, to the data arrival rate $I(k)$, then we get respected data arrival rate $R(k)$. The controller uses a simple P (proportional) control function to compute the respected data arrival rate to keep the total memory utilization decrease to the reference $Mref$. Then our system dynamically changes the data arrive rate at each sampling instant k according to the control input $D(k)$ by adjusting the filter proportion of filters. For example, if the arrive rate is supposed to be lower, we simply give the filter a higher probability, compared with the original one, and then the filter drop the items pass through it with this probability. The goal of the filter manager is to enforce the new data arrive rate $R(k+1) = R(k) - D(k)$.

Next, we should decide how to assign drop works between queries. In our method, we assign drop works according to operators' processing times. This is because the operators with less execution time could process data faster than the one with more execution times.

In our system, filter manager can calculate the new filter proportion by formula:

$$F(k+1) = F(k) - R(k+1) + R(k) = F(k) - D(k) \tag{1}$$

Formula (1) is feasible because of the previous assumption that the data arrival rate of data stream does not vary greatly in two adjacent time windows.

4 Performance Specs

4.1 Open Loop Transfer Function

The second step in designing load shedding part of DSMS is to establish an analytical model to approximate the load shedding system. Although it is difficult to precisely model a nonlinear and time-varying system, we can approximate such a system with a linear model for the purpose of control design because of the robustness of feedback control with regard to system variations. Starting from the control input, the filter manager changes the data arrival speed at every sampling instant k.

$$R(k+1) = R(k) - D(k) \tag{2}$$

Since stream data arrival rate are time-varying and unpredictable, the precise value of actual data arrival rate at time window $k+1$. $AR(k+1)$ may differ from the predicted value $R(k+1)$.

$$AR(k+1) = R_{AS}(k+1) \cdot R(k+1) \tag{3}$$

We can also rewrite it as following:

$$AR(k) = R_{AS}(k) \cdot R(k) \tag{4}$$

Here $RAS(k)$ is a time-variant variable that represents the extent of data arrival rate variation in terms of the predicted value. Let $RAS = MAX\{RAS(k)\}$, which is called the worst-case extent of data arrival rate. Hence Equation (3) can be simplified to the following formula for the purpose of control design:

$$AR(k) = R_{AS} \cdot R(k) \tag{5}$$

$M(k)$ usually increases nonlinearly with the data arrival rate $AR(k)$. When load shedding begins, data buffers are full and the operator scheduling is fixed at this time, so the average data cost by load shedding has a limitation, in fact it is always the same between two adjacent time windows. So the relationship between $M(k)$ and $AR(k)$ is linear when load shedding begins. According to this, we define RM as (when load shedding begins):

$$R_M = \frac{dM(k)}{dAR(k)} \tag{6}$$

In practice, RM can be estimated experimentally by plotting a $M(k)$ curve as a function of $AR(k)$ based on experimental data. Now, we have the following linear formula:

$$M(k) = M(k-1) + R_M \cdot (AR(k) - AR(k-1)) \tag{7}$$

Based on Equations (2) and (4), the analytical model for the data arrival rate output is as follows:

$$M(k) = M(k-1) + R_M \cdot R_{AS} \cdot D(k-1) \tag{8}$$

We now convert the model to z-domain transfer function that is suitable to control theory methods. Let $Y(z)$ be the z-transform of the output variable $M(k)$, and $X(z)$ be the z-transform of the input variable $D(k)$. A linear system can be represented by a transfer function $H(z)=Y(z)/X(z)$. For our system, formula (8) can be converted into z-domain as $Y(z)=z\text{-}1\ Y(z)+\ RM\ RASX(z)z\text{-}1$. So the transfer function in open loop is:

$$H(z) = \frac{R_M R_{AS}}{z-1} \tag{9}$$

4.2 Closed-Loop Transfer Function

The third step is to establish the closed-loop transfer function. At each sampling instant k, the controller computes a control input $D(k)$ based on the memory utilization error $E(k)$. We choose a simple P (proportional) control function to compute the control input.

$$D(k) = K \cdot E(k) \tag{10}$$

It is obvious that the parameter K has great impact on the system performance. According to the control theory, we have the system transfer function $H(z)$ as follows:

$$H(z) = \frac{Y(z)}{X(z)} = \frac{A(z)}{1 + F(z) \cdot A(z)} \tag{11}$$

Here $A(z)$ is the open loop system transfer function, and $F(z)$ is the feedback transfer function. The closed-loop system transfer function should be recalculated based on the open loop one. We have the $A(z) = RMRAS/(z\text{-}1)$ and $F(z)=1$. The system input $I(z)$ is the performance reference, which is modeled as a step signal, $Mref\ z\ /(z-1)$in the z-domain. From control theory, we can establish a closed-loop transfer function of deadline satisfied ratio in response to the reference input:

$$H_1 = \frac{K \cdot R_{AS} \cdot R_M}{z-1 + K \cdot R_{AS} \cdot R_M} \tag{12}$$

The output can be computed by:

$$Y(z) = H_1(z)I(z) = \frac{K \cdot R_{AS} \cdot R_M}{z-1 + K \cdot R_{AS} \cdot R_M} \times \frac{M_{ref}z}{z-1} \tag{13}$$

The second input to the closed-loop system is the disturbance $N(z)$ that adds to the total memory utilization.. The execution of DSMS queries itself consumes some data in query plan's data buffer queue, and this makes the total amount of data decrease, so we call this the disturbance $N(z)$. As we explained before, when load shedding begins this cost has its upper limit N, because the total amount of data processed in this time period is deemed as N or $N(z)=Nz/(z-1)$ in the z-domain. Here the value N means the extent of the disturbance. Considering the disturbance input, the closed-loop system transfer function for the memory utilization rate in response to the disturbance is as following:

$$H_2 = \frac{R_M(z-1)}{z-1+K \cdot R_{AS} \cdot R_M} \tag{14}$$

The system output while considering both reference input and disturbance input can be computed by:

$$Y(z) = H_1(z)I(z) + H_2(z)N(z) \tag{15}$$

4.3 System Stability

According to control theory, a system is stable if and only if all the poles of its transfer function are in the unit circle of z-plane. The only one pole in formula (12) and (14) is $1-KRASRM$. So, if $0 < K < 2/RASRM$, the stability can be guaranteed. In our system, $M(k)$ is the output, and its corresponding format in z-domain is $Y(z)$.

The final value theorem of digital control theory states that the system output converges to a final value: $limM(k) = M(\infty) = lim(z-1)Y(z)$. From the formula (15):

$$\lim_{z\to1}(z-1)Y(z)$$
$$= \lim_{z\to1}[(z-1)(\frac{K \cdot R_{AS} \cdot R_M}{z-1+K \cdot R_{AS} \cdot R_M} \times \frac{M_{ref}z}{z-1} + \frac{R_M(z-1)}{z-1+K \cdot R_{AS} \cdot R_M} \times \frac{Nz}{z-1})]$$
$$= M_{ref}$$

This means that the steady state error is zero. According to control theory, for the system transfer function (formula 12), the overshoot remains zero in response to reference input if the closed loop pole equals to or larger than zero. So, if the parameter K satisfies the condition $0 < K \leq 1/RASRM$, the deadline satisfied ratio $M(k)$ reaches zero overshoot. The settling time of this feedback system can be adjusted by parameter K, because the parameter K has direct relation to the pole of the transfer function. It is a basic technique to determine the settling time according to poles in a first order system in control theory.

While the load shedding system is steady, the output $M(k)$ will be stabilized at the value M ref . When disturbance occurs, the system will converge to the desired value $Mref$. The speed of this converging can be adjusted by parameter K. If $M(k)$ is stabilized at the value $Mref$, the memory utilization guarantee is satisfied according to the concept of stochastic scheduling.

5 Performance Evaluations

Our aim is to provide a memory resource oriented load shedding method, but the current research works are all CPU resource oriented. If we consider the resource utilization as the comparison parameter, there isn't any method to be compared with.

No matter which load shedding method we use, the aim of load shedding is to ensure the system work stably in the cost of lowest generated error when load shedding occurs. As a result, we can compare our method with some load shedding methods such as Aurora's. Although the idea of introduce feedback control theory into load shedding method is from reference [7], its aim is to solve the deadline miss problem, which is not comparable with our resource utilization oriented method.

5.1 Experimental Setup

All experiments were conducted on a PC with a 2.0GHz Intel Pentium 4 processor and 1GB RAM. The data we use is the real medical stream data from ICU of Peking University Affiliated NO.3 Hospital. They are collected from patients in ICU during two months, with an accumulative total time of 7200 minutes. The data arrival rate ranges from 40ms to 240ms, which forms the wave pattern as Figure 3 shows.

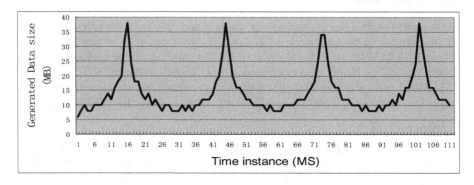

Fig. 3. Data generation

We constructed a 7-queries network consisting of typical monitoring queries including selection operators, filter operators and simple join operators. These queries are real queries from ICU information systems. In a typical query, which concerns the rhythm of the heart, several selection operators are used to judge whether the heart rhythm overflows certain limitations.

To keep the fairness of comparison, we simply use a FIFO scheduling method to choose the operator to run. We compared the performance of Aurora's load shedding method and ours. Before it is put to work, Aurora's method need to run the queries system to collect statistic information, such as operator selectivity and operator execution times. Aurora also needs QoS graphs to guide its calculation and judgment, so we just pick up some simple QoS graphs for Aurora with the purpose of conciseness. The stream rates were monitored by the system during query execution instance to collect information used for comparison.

5.2 The Linearity of the Input and Output Signals

First, we should test the linear relationship between the memory utilization ratio $M(k)$ and actual data arrival rate $AR(k)$. Figure 4 shows the result of our experiment. The

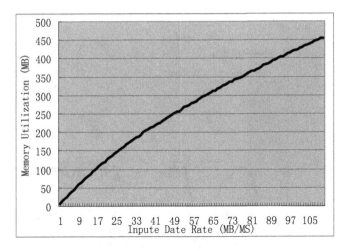

Fig. 4. Relationship between input and output Signals

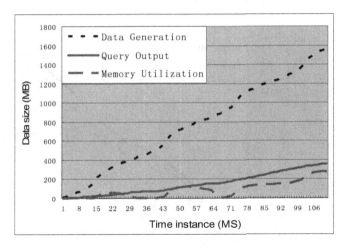

Fig. 5. System status

relation is nearly linear in this figure. We choose the point region when memory utilization is around 80% as the working region, because our load shedding method will be invoked at this region. Therefore, we have the RM equals 0.3 when memory utilization is around 80% of total restriction. We use $RAS=1.5$, $Mref=80\%C$, where C is the memory upper-limitation of 70MB.

5.3 Experimental Result

To show the effectiveness of our method, in the first step, we run the query system without any memory utilization restriction and without any load shedding method. Figure 5 shows the data generation, query out and the memory utilization under this circumstance.

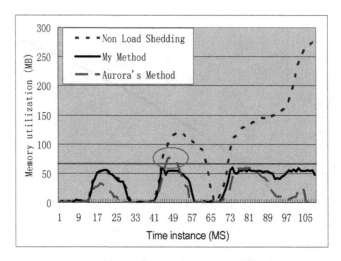

Fig. 6. Memory utilization comparison

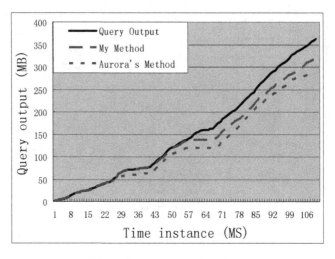

Fig. 7. Query output comparison

In the second step, we compared the memory utilization condition with an upper-limitation utilization of memory resource about 70MB. We could see that when load shedding occurs, our method well satisfied the limitation. Near the time 50 ms, Aurora's method did not restrict the memory utilization to below this limitation. This means the systems using Aurora's method could not satisfy memory limitation anyway and would certainly crash.

Figure 7 shows the query output result of our method and Aurora's method. We could see clearly that, out method can guarantee more correct query output than Aurora's method does.

6 Conclusions and Future Work

This paper proposes a method for guiding load shedding in DSMS. Experiment results proved the effectiveness and feasibility of our method. In addition, out method doesn't need to rely on the operator selectivity to guide load shedding so it doesn't need to run system to collect statistical information before system is put to work. Thus our method is more veracious to judge the system condition. As we do not need to collect statistical information, our method could cope with ad-hoc queries very well.

Future work will further investigate the meanings of stream data, because this could make the shed of data more effective and could result in more correct query outputs. The exploration of operator scheduling method also will be consider[11], as it has great impact on the choice of data to drop in load shedding.

References

1. B. Babcock, S. Babu, M. Datar, R. Motwani, and J. Widom. Models and issues in data stream systems. In Proc. 2002 ACM Symp. on Principles of Database Systems, June 2002.
2. R. Motwani, J. Widom, A. Arasu, B. Babcock, S. Babu, M. Datar, G. Manku, C. Olston, J. Rosenstein, and R. Varma. Query processing, approximation, and resource management in a data stream management system. In Proc. First Biennial Conf. on Innovative Data Systems Research (CIDR), Jan. 2003.
3. D Carney, U Cetintemel, M Cherniack, C Convey, S Lee, G Seidman, M tonebraker, N Tatbul, and S Zdonik. Monitoring streams–a new class of data management applications. In: Proc. 28th Intl. Conf. on Very Large Data Bases. Hong Kong, China, August 2002.
4. Daniel J Abadi, Don Carney, Ugur Çetintemel, Mitch Cherniack, Christian Convey, Sangdon Lee, Michael Stonebraker, Nesime Tatbul, Stan Zdonik. Aurora: a new model and architecture for data stream management. In VLDB August 2003. 120-139.
5. Nesime Tatbul, Uˇgur C, etintemel, Mitch Cherniack, Michael Stonebraker. Load Shedding in a Data Stream Manager. Proceeding of the 29th VLDB Conference, 2003.
6. Brian Babcock, Mayur Datar, Rajeev Motwani. Load Shedding for Aggregation Queries over Data Streams. Proceedings of the 20th International Conference on Data Engineering, 2004.
7. Yi-Cheng Tu, Yuni Xia, and Sunil Prabhakar. Quality of Service Adaptation in Data Stream Management Systems: A Control-Based Approach, Department of Computer Science, Purdue Univ. 2004. Available at
8. http://www.cs.purdue.edu/homes/tuyc/pub/draft/QoS.ps.
9. Frederick Reiss, Joseph M. Hellerstein. Data Triage: An Adaptive Architecture for Load Shedding in TelegraphCQ. Proceedings. 21st International Conference on 05-08 April 2005 Page(s):155 – 156.
10. Jain, E. Y. Chang, and Y.-F. Wang. Adaptive Stream Resource Management Using Kalman Filters, ACM International Conference on Management of Data (SIGMOD), pp.11-22, Paris, June 2004.
11. Q Jiang, S Chakravarthy. Data Stream Management System for MavHome. Proceedings. Annual ACM Symposium on Applied Computing, Mar, 2004
12. Babcock, B., Babu, S., Datar, M., Motwani, R. Chain: Operator Scheduling for Memory Minimization in Data Stream Systems. SIGMOD, 2003.

13. C. Lu, T.F. Abdelzaher, J.A. Stankovic, and S.H. Son. A feedback control approach for guaranteeing relative delays in web servers. In IEEE Real-Time Technology and Application Symposium, 2001.
14. S. Parekh, N. Gandhi, J.L. Hellerstein, D. Tilbury, T.S. Jayram, and J. Bigus. Using control theory to achieve service level objectives in performance management. In IFIP/IEEE International Symposium on Integrated Network Management, 2001.
15. Cheng Shengtan, Guo Baolong, Li Xuewu and Feng Zhongzhe. Signal and System. Press of Xian Electronic Technology Univ., Xian, P.R.China, 2001.
16. Shun Zhengqi. System analysis and control. Tsinghua univ. Press, Beijing, P.R.China, 1994.
17. G.F. Franklin, J.D. Powell and M.L. Workman. Digital Control of Dynamic Systems (3rd Edition). Addison-Wesley, 1998.
18. J. Kang, J. F. Naughton, and S. Viglas. Evaluating window joins over unbounded streams. In Proc. 2003 Intl. Conf. on Data Engineering, Mar. 2003.

A New Active DDoS Defense System Based on Automatic Learning

Junfeng Tian, Min Peng, and Yuling Liu

Faculty of Mathematics and Computer Science,
Hebei University, Baoding 071002, China
wsrainstone@126.com

Abstract. Active DDoS Defense System (ADDS) compensates the deficiencies of isolated defenses made by routers, firewalls or kernel defense programs, and ADDS implements technique of net traffics analysis to control routers for optimizing net traffics distribution. The use of neural network made ADDS the capacity of automatic learning, and ADDS filters DDoS attack traffics automatically according the intensity of attacks in each router; the use of accelerated arithmetic of iteration made ADDS the capacity of quick response.

Keywords: DDoS, active defense, neural network, statistical analysis, traffic monitoring.

1 Introduction

At present, the other kinds of mechanism of defense and response on DDoS attacks, e.g. ingress filtering, packet mark, packet trace and technology of firewall, have many deficiencies and can not solve DDoS attacks problems efficiently. And each other kind of various methods against DDoS attacks do only effect to some curtain attacks and is short of integrity. As to solve this problem, the paper proposed an ADDS (Active DDoS Defense System) melted system defense, traffics analysis and technology of authorization.

2 Analysis of ADDS Defense Mechanism

The numbers of traffics can be classified into normal traffics and abnormal traffics, which includes attack packets. The research to the variations of the SYN arrival rates of all traffics had showed that the arrival rates of the abnormal traffic rose sharply when were attacked. According to a lot of experimental results, in various segments of time, SYN packet arrival rates with the cumulative normal distributions have the same averages and variances. So most parts of the SYN rate distributions of the normal flows can be modeled by the normal distribution.

The ADDS employs Widrow-Hoff arithmetic, which is classical neural network arithmetic and is provided with characteristics of excellent capacity of automatic learning, prominent stabilization and quick discriminability.

S. Grumbach, L. Siu, and V. Vianu (Eds.): ASIAN 2005, LNCS 3818, pp. 249–250, 2005.

The ADDS exploits the merits of neural network to regulate the distribution of the whole network automatically and to optimize the capacity of the network. The main idea of the arithmetic is that every router limits the traffics passing it according to its intensity attacked.

The ADDS is characteristic of accuracy of measuring the response rate. And then it can accelerate arithmetic of iteration by employing this character. The neural network is not only provided with the high efficiency of distribution of traffics, but also provided with high speed of distribution.

3   Emulation Experiment and Analysis of Result

The experiment has proved excellent defensive capacity of ADDS against DDoS attacks. And it not only has the merit of very quick speed of response and very high response rate but also has fairly overall defensive capacity and excellent defensive capacity against DDoS attack of category of Uselessly Normal Connection (UNC).

References

1. Savage, S., Wetherall.: Network Support for IP Traceback. In: IEEE/ACM Transactions on Networking. (2001), 9
2. Xiaoling Zhao, Zuling Peng, Yabin Wang.: The Technical Tutorial of Network Security. Bei Jing: National Defence Industry Press. (2002) 70-72,147-159
3. S., Zhang, P., Dasgupta.: Hardened Networks. PHD Proposal, Arizona State University, Tempe, (2002)
4. Steven, M., Bellovin.: ICMP Traceback Messages. In:Work in progress, Internet draft bellovin-itrace-00, (2000)
5. Thomas, W., Doeppner, Philip, N., Klein, Andrew, Koyfman.: Using Router Stamping to Identify the Source of IP Packets. In: Proceedings of the 7th ACM Conference on Computer and Communications Security. (2000), 184-189
6. Stefan, Savage, David, Wetherall, Anna, Karlin, Tom, Anderson.: Practical Network Support for IP Traceback. In: Proceedings of ACM SIGCOMM (2000)
7. William, Stallings.: Network Security Essentials-Applications and Standards (Second Edition). Bei Jing: Tsing Hua Univercity Press. (2002)
8. L., Peluso, D., Cotroneo, S., P., Romano, G., Ventre.: An Active Security System against DoS Attacks (2001)
9. J., F., Kurose, K., W., Ross.: Computer Networking: A Top-Down Approach. In: Featuring the Internet, 2nd edition. (2002)
10. Martin, T., Hagan, Howard, B., Demuth, Mark, H., Beale.: Neural Network Design. Bei Jing: China Machine Press. (2002) 168-196
11. Katerina, Argyraki, David, R., Cheriton.: Active Internet Traffic Filtering: Real-Time Response to Denial-of-Service Attacks. In:USENIX 2005 Annual Technical Conference. (2005), 135-148
12. David, K., Y., Yau, John, C., S., Lui, Feng Liang, Yeung Yam. Defending Against Distributed Denial-of-Service Attacks With Max-Min Fair Server-Centric Router Throttles. In : IEEE/ACM Transaction on Networking. (2005)

An Equity-Based and Cell-Based Spatial Object Fusion Method[*]

Haibo Li and Lizhen Wang

Department of Computer Science and Engineering,
School of Information Science and Engineering, Yunnan University,
650091 Kunming, China
{Haierbopuhuixing, Lzhwang}@ynu.edu.cn

Abstract. The spatial object fusion problem occurred in geographic information system is also met in spatial data warehouses, and it plays an important role in the spatial data preprocessing. A novel, equity-based and cell-based spatial object fusion method in spatial data warehouses, which only uses locations of objects and few computes distance among objects, is proposed and its efficiency and effectiveness are measured in terms of *Recall* and *Precision* in this paper. Especially, this method is very suitable for the cases, whose targets can be abstracted into point objects, such as the study about representative plants, animals and landscapes living in special environment. Our work extends the research about this field.

Huge amounts of spatial data have been accumulated in the last two decades by government agencies and other organizations for various purposes such as tour resources management and environment management. It is an imminent task to integrate information from heterogeneous spatial databases. For example, in ecology, for same representative plant in same area, different investigator will work out different plants distribution maps. When integrating these data into one whole map, a challenge is how to fuse distinct objects that represent the same real-world plant. It is known as the *spatial object-fusion* problem.

In the research on object fusions, the opinion that objects have identifiers (e.g., keys) are held by some research results [1], [10], and it is studied without global identifiers in [2, 6]. For the lack of global identifiers, the object-fusion problem is much harder. Using only location of objects, dozens of efficient algorithms are published, such as the one-sided nearest-neighbor join [6], the mutually nearest method [2], the probabilistic method and the normalized-weights method [2]. All of the above methods are based on the distance measure. However, an unassailable fact is that two nearest-neighbor objects on the distance will not always represent the same entity. This motivates us to present a *cell-based* algorithm to finding corresponding objects that should be fused. Subsequently, similarly to [2], a random-datasets generator is implemented and the *recall* and *precision* are appointed to measure the quality of algorithm. After testing this method by various datasets, unexpectedly, the experimental results seem to be unsatisfactory.

---

[*] Supported by the National Natural Science Foundation of China (No. 60463004).

S. Grumbach, L. Siu, and V. Vianu (Eds.): ASIAN 2005, LNCS 3818, pp. 251–252, 2005.

We analyzed results and found that our method is sensitive to three factors, the *minimum distance* M, the *error interval* D and the *length of cell* L. Therefore, motivated by the purpose to reduce the side effect from M and D, the *equity-cells* concept is introduced. Preliminary experimental results show that the *equity-based* and *cell-based* methods have higher *recall* and *precision* than those of the cell-based method. At the same time, we also find that the *equity-cells* concept will be easy to be extended to the case of multi-datasets.

An effective approach for the spatial data preprocessing is presented in this paper. Combining our approach with clustering method about spatial data mining [7],[9], considering how to fuse spatial objects that only use locations are our future work. In addition, we are now focusing on the development of fusion algorithms for more than two datasets [2].

References

1. Samal A., Seth S., and Cueto K.: A feature based approach to conflation of geospatial sources. International Journal of Geographical Information Science, 18(00): 1-31, 2004
2. Catriel Beeri Yaron Kanza Eliyahu Safra Yehoshua Sagiv.: Object Fusion in Geographic Information Systems. In proceedings of the 30th VLDB Conference, pages 816-827, Toronto, Canada, 2004
3. Fonseca T. F., Egenhofer J. M., and Agouris P.: Using ontologies for integrated geographic information systems. Transactions in GIS, 6(3), 2002
4. Fonseca T. F., Egenhofer J. M.: Ontologydriven geographic information systems. In Proceedings of the 7th ACM International Symposium on Advances in Geographic Information Systems, pages 14-19, Kansas City (Missouri, US), 1999
5. Uitermark H., Oosterom V. P., Mars N., Molenaar M.: Ontology-based geographic data set integration. In Proceedings of Workshop on Spatio-Temporal Database Management, pages 60-79, Edinburgh (Scotland), 1999
6. Minami M.: Using ArcMap. Environmental Systems Research Institute, Inc., 2000
7. Agrawal R., Gehrke J., Gunopulos D., and Raghavan P.: Automatic subspace clustering of high dimensional data for data mining applications. In Proceedings of the ACM SIGMOD Conference on Management of Data, pages 94–105, Seattle, WA, 1998
8. Bruns T., Egenhofer M.: Similarity of spatial scenes. In Proceedings of the 7th International Symposium on Spatial Data Handling, pages 31-42, Delft (Netherlands), 1996
9. Wang W., Yang J., Muntz R.: STING: A Statistical Information Grid Approach to Spatial Data Mining. In proceedings of the 23rd VLDB Conference, pages 186-195, Athens, Greece, 1997
10. Papakonstantinou Y., Abiteboul S., Garcia-Molina H.: Object Fusion in Mediator Systems. In proceedings of the 22nd VLDB Conference, pages 413-424 Mumbai (Bombay), India, 1996

Research on the Similarity of Constraint Driven Semantic Web Services

Junfeng Man, Aimin Yang, Jianshe Li, and Qianqian Li

Computer Science Department, Zhuzhou Institute of Technology,
412008 Zhuzhou, China
mjfok@tom.com

Abstract. Currently, it is difficult to ensure the found services are optimal in web services discovery. Thus, we suggest that the applicant's requirements be represented with Service Template (ST) in forms of constraint by adding ample semantic description to web services, and then ST is matched with Service Advertisements (SA) which have been published and saved in enhanced UDDI library, so we can get a set of candidate services, at last, we can find a optimal service from this set. This method can greatly improve the precision and efficiency of web services process, and focus more on how to select optimal service rather than to find a suitable one merely.

1 Introduction

In order to achieve the target of dynamic and composing business process, we should search more quick and efficient method to describe service, and identify them with proper means automatically[1]. So, we should emphasize on solving the following problems: (i) need a system which allows business process to select partners dynamically, (ii) be able to seamlessly incorporate any new partners in future, (iii) be able to select partners based on applicants' constraints (e.g., supply-time, location, cost, reliability of provider), and (iv) ability to select the optimal set of partners.

In order to solve above problems, we have done many research work on semantic web services, for reason of limit space, we will mainly discuss (i) how to present a suit of criterion to evaluate services, and (ii) how to select candidate services from SA in enhanced UDDI library according to applicant's requirements, and then evaluate these services with linear estimation method, finally select the optimal one.

2 Three Types of Semantics

We incorporate data semantics, functional semantics and QoS semantics to support activities in the complete web process lifecycle in our representational framework. (i) input/output data is annotated using domain ontology, it can be used to match the semantics of the input/output data of the Web service with the semantics of the input/output data of the requirements, (ii) functional semantic can describe services with less granularity, it tells service process what to do, (iii) QoS semantic is used to

S. Grumbach, L. Siu, and V. Vianu (Eds.): ASIAN 2005, LNCS 3818, pp. 253–254, 2005.
© Springer-Verlag Berlin Heidelberg 2005

evaluate the quality of services, it tells service processing programs how to complete the service process very well.

We use above three types of semantics to annotated WSDL by adding semantic mark into original WSDL according to the semantic metrics of domain ontology, thus, annotated WSDL may describe web services more detailedly in the level of semantic. Undoubtedly, it will provide more convenience for service discovery and optimization.

3 Process of Semantic Web Services

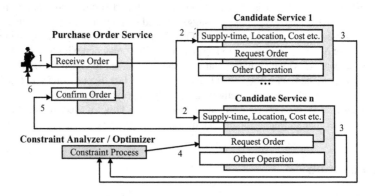

Fig. 1. Here, we illustrate the process of semantic Web services with a sample

4 Constraint Analyzer/Optimizer

Constraint Analyzer/Optimizer includes three sub-modules: (i) Constraint Representation Module uses OWL and SWRL[2] to provide more descriptive rules for specifying business constraints, (ii) Cost Estimation Module queries the information stored in the cost representation module for estimating costs for various factors which affect the selection of the services for the processes, and (iii) in Constraint Optimizer Module, the Integer Linear Programming Solver will produce a number of feasible sets which would be ranked from optimal to near optimal solutions. Finally, the feasible set which is best suitable for applicant's requirement is sent to Run-Time Module.

References

1. Aggarwal R., Verma K.: Constraint Driven Web Service Composition in METEOR-S. Proceedings of IEEE International Conference on Services Computing, (2004)1-4
2. Horrocks.: SWRL, A Semantic Web Rule Language Combining OWL and RuleML, http://www.daml.org/2003/11/swrl/, (2003)

Schema Homomorphism – An Algebraic Framework for Schema Matching

Zhi Zhang[1], Haoyang Che[2], Pengfei Shi[1], Yong Sun[3], and Jun Gu[3]

[1] Institute of Image Processing and Pattern Recognition, Shanghai Jiaotong University,
Shanghai 200030, China
{zzh, pfshi}@sjtu.edu.cn
[2] Institute of Software, The Chinese Academy of Sciences,
Beijing 100080, China
[3] Department of Computer Science, Science & Technology University of Hong Kong,
Hong Kong, China

Abstract. A formal framework for SMP is important because it facilitates the building of algorithm model and the evaluation of algorithms. First, we propose a formal definition of schema matching that is named multivalent matching, i.e., an individual of source schema can be associated with a set of individuals of target schema. Second, we develop the algebraic framework of multivalent matching that is called schema homomorphism and propose the algorithm model of SMP. Then, we discuss the relations between match cardinality and variants of schema homomorphism.

1 Multivalent Matching

Based on universal algebra, a schema can be denoted by a 4-tuples $S = (I^S, Lab^S, F^S, R^S)$ over the signature σ [4]. We rename this model of schema as *multi-labeled schema*. By using multi-labeled schema, we propose a definition of schema matching: multivalent matching, i.e., an individual of source schema may be associated with a set of individuals of target schema. The matching results are called *multivalent correspondences*, which are binary relationships that establish many-to-many correspondences between the individuals of two schemas.

Definition 1. *If S is the source schema, T is the target schema, the matching result of two schemas is a set $m \subseteq I^S \times I^T$ that contains every matched couple $<s, t> \in I^S \times I^T$.*

2 Algorithm Model of SMP

Zhang *et al.* [4] prove that: *two schemas S and T are matched iff there exists a semantic homomorphism from S to T.*

Definition 2. *A schema homomorphism (SHOM) $\varphi : S \to T$ from the source schema S to the target schema T is a mapping $\varphi : I^S \to I^T$, which is a set of multivalent correspondences such that:*

S. Grumbach, L. Siu, and V. Vianu (Eds.): ASIAN 2005, LNCS 3818, pp. 255–256, 2005.
© Springer-Verlag Berlin Heidelberg 2005

Condition 1. *There exists a labeling function symbol f of arity n*

$$f^S(s_1, \cdots, s_n) = l_n^S \Rightarrow f^T(\varphi(s_1), \cdots, \varphi(s_n)) = \varphi(l_n^T) , \text{ for } s_1, \cdots, s_n \in I^S, l_n^S \in Lab^S$$

Condition 2. *There exists a semantic relation symbol R of arity m*

$$R^S(s_1, \cdots, s_m) \text{ holds} \Rightarrow R^T(\varphi(s_1), \cdots, \varphi(s_m)) \text{ holds}, \text{ for } s_1, \cdots, s_m \in I^S$$

Based on SHOM, and Theorem 1 in [4], we give the algorithm model of SMP:

Algorithm Model of SMP: *Given two schemas S and T, the goal of matching algorithms is to find the semantic homomorphism between S and T.*

Then, we develop the algebraic framework and built the algorithm model for SMP. The homomorphism model [1] can guide practitioner to design the effective algorithms for SMP and evaluate the algorithms. We investigate the $n:m$ matching algorithms based on multi-labeled graph matching [3].

3   Match Cardinality and Variants of Homomorphism

In [2], Rahm and Bernstein illustrated match cardinality by examples. Each element of the resulting mapping may match one or more elements of one schema to one or more elements of the other, yielding four cases: 1:1, 1:n, n:1, n:m. For SMP, we discuss some variants of SHOM, such as *schema isomorphism*, *schema epimorphism*, and *schema monomorphism*. Here, we show the definition of schema epimorphism.

Schema Epimorphism: *A schema epimorphism from S to T is a surjective mapping $\varphi: I^S \rightarrow I^T$, which satisfies two conditions of Definition 2.*

Schema epimorphism is a many-to-one (n:1) semantic mapping from S to T. Some schema matching approaches have n:1 matching cardinality, such as SKAT and CUPID [2].

References

1. Hell, P.: Algorithmic aspects of graph homomorphisms, Combinatorics 2003, London Math. Society Lecture Note Series 307, Cambridge University Press, 239-276.
2. Rahm, E., Bernstein, P. A.: A survey of approaches to automatic schema matching, The VLDB Journal, 2001(10): 334-350.
3. Z. Zhang, H. Y. Che, P. F. Shi, Y. Sun, J. Gu. Multi-labeled graph matching - An algorithm model for schema matching. ASIAN'05.
4. Z. Zhang, H. Y. Che, P. F. Shi, Y. Sun, J. Gu. An Algebraic Framework for Schema Matching. WAIM 2005.

Dynamic Geospatial Web Services Composition in Peer-to-Peer Networks

Xiujun Ma, Kunqing Xie, Chen Liu, and Chenyu Li

Department of Intelligence Science,
National Laboratory on Machine Perception,
Peking University, Beijing 100871, China
{maxj, kunqing, liuchen, licy}@cis.pku.edu.cn

Abstract. This paper presents a peer-to-peer based execution model to improve the availability and reliability of Geospatial Web Services (GWS) composition. A service community concept and a QoS model of GWS are proposed to discover the best quality GWS engines in the peer-to-peer network. The engines coordinate other participants in charge of initiating, controlling, monitoring the associated GWS execution, and adopt an alternative approach for failure recovery. The paper also presents the implementation of a peer-to-peer GWS composition system prototype based on JXTA platform.

Geospatial Web Services (GWS); composition is often referred to service chaining, the process of combining or pipelining results from several complementary services to create customized applications[1]. Unfortunately, concepts for GWS composition lack some important features. They do not allow the integration of web services into higher abstraction levels, no descriptive language is standardized to define complex chains and executable rules, and semantic aspects are not addressed at all. Typically, existing implementations of GWS chaining are centralized paradigm, in which a central scheduler controls the execution of the components of the chaining service. However, the centralized paradigm will incur severe problems including scalability, availability, and security problems[2,4,7,9,11]. The purpose of this paper is to propose a P2P based execution model for dynamic GWS composition.

A GWS composition is the orchestration of a number of existing GWSs to provide a solution for a geo-processing task. There are many GWSs with overlapping or identical functionality. The availability and reliability of a GWS composition can be improved if the execution can invoke alternative ones when a service invocation fails. We propose a GWS community model to support dynamic GWS composition that the execution can find alternative services in runtime. A service community is an aggregator of different GWSs with similar functionality without referring to any actual provider. It intends to support dynamic GWS composition that the execution can find alternative services in runtime. Furtheron, we present a QoS model with quality criteria of performance, reliability and availability to support selecting the best quality service dynamically[5,6,8,10].

In our peer-to-peer system architecture, each engine delegates one or more GWSs as its resources, and all the delegated GWSs have already mapped into a certain GWS community. Engines publish their delegated services by means of advertisement, thus these services can be discovered dynamically in runtime by other engines. During the

S. Grumbach, L. Siu, and V. Vianu (Eds.): ASIAN 2005, LNCS 3818, pp. 257–258, 2005.
© Springer-Verlag Berlin Heidelberg 2005

execution a GWS composition, all participated engines are orchestrated through peer-to-peer message exchange. A Composition Execution Context message is used to keep track of the execution state of the GWS composition [3].

Given a GWS composition, a number of engines are allocated in charge of initiating, controlling, monitor-ing the associated GWS execution. The engines coordinate their participants by the services community rule and have the knowledge of a number of GWSs that provide similar functionality. During the composition execution, one engine invokes the appropriate participant engines based on their QoS rank and keeps others in a candidate list. If a participant fails due to whatever reason, the engine can invoke another candidate engine from the list. Then the whole composition goes on. In many situations, this saves the expensive rollback or abort of GWS invocation. In the worst scenario, where all the alternative services for a critical participant fail, it does allow the whole execution to abort.

The Geospatial Web Services are developed in Java programming language and are deployed with Apache Axis. The P2P services execution engine is implemented based on JXTA. Engines advertise their message as JXTA pipes and connect between pipes using the virtual communication paradigm in JXTA networks.

References

1. Alameh, N.: Chaining geographic information Web services. IEEE Internet Computing (2003) 7(5):22-29
2. Benatallah, B., Dumas, M., Sheng, Q.Z.: The SELFSERV Environment for Web Services Composition. IEEE Internet Computing (2003) 17(1):40-48
3. Benlakhal, N., Kobayashi, T. and Yokota, H.: Ws-sagas: transaction model for reliable web-services-composition specification and execution. DBSJ Letters (2001) 2(2): 17-20
4. Chen, Q. and Hsu, M.: Inter-Enterprise Collaborative Business Process Management. In: Proc. of 17th Int. Conference on Data Engineering (ICDE), pages 253–260, April 2001, Heidelberg, Germany. IEEE Computer Society.
5. Liangzhao, Z., Benatallah, B., Anne, N., Marlon, D., Jayant, K., and Henry, C.: QoS-aware Middleware for Web Services Composition. IEEE Transactions on Software Engineering (2004) 30(5):311-327,
6. Menascé, D.A. QoS Issues in Web Services. IEEE Internet Computing (2004) 8(1):72-75
7. Papazoglou, M.P., Kramer, B. J., and Yang J.: Leveraging Web-Services and Peer-to-Peer Networks. In: J. Eder and M. Missikoff (eds.): CAiSE 2003. Lecture Notes in Computer Science, Vol. 2681. Springer-Verlag Berlin Heidelberg (2003) 485–501
8. Peng, Z.R. and M.H. Tsou.: Internet GIS - Distributed Geographic Information Services for the Internet and Wireless Networks. John Wiley & Sons, Hoboken (New Jersey) (2003)
9. Pitoura, E., Abiteboul, S., Pfoser, D., Samaras, G., Vazirgiannis, M.: DBGlobe: a service-oriented P2P system for global computing. SIGMOD Record 32 (2003) 77-82
10. Richard O.: Modelling for Quality of Services in Distributed Geoprocessing. In: XXth ISPRS Congress, July, 2004, Istanbul, Turkey
11. Wang Q., Yuan Y., Zhou, J., Zhou, A.: Peer-Serv: A Framework of Web Services in Peer-to-Peer Environment. In: Dong, G., Tang,C., Wang, W. (eds.): Advances in Web-Age Information Management. Lecture Notes in Computer Science, Vol. 2762. Springer-Verlag GmbH (2003) 298-305

An Approach for Service Discovery Based on Semantic Peer-to-Peer*

Hao Wu, Hai Jin, Yunfa Li, and Hanhan Chen

Cluster and Grid Computing Lab,
Huazhong University of Science and Technology, Wuhan, 430074, China
hjin@hust.edu.cn

Abstract. Service discovery is a key step during *Peer-to-Peer* (P2P) converging with Web Service. In this paper, a semantic-P2P based approach is presented for web service discovery. To enable the semantic web service, service profile is used to describe web service and as the service data source. The service-expertise based model is proposed for service node selection.

1 Semantic Peer-to-Peer Based Service Discovery Framework

There are totally three kinds of patterns for web service discovery, *Matchmaking*, *Broker* and *Peer-to-Peer (P2P) model*. We introduce an expertise-based model for service discovery under P2P. In our model, every peer performs service provider and service consumer simultaneously. Each peer is also *Local Service Registry* (LSR) and knowledge repository, shown as Fig.1. The peers share an ontology O, which provides a common conceptualization of web service domain. The ontology is used to describe the expertise of peers and the subject of requests. An expertise description e is an abstract, semantic description of the knowledge base of a peer based on the common ontology O. *Service Expertise* (SE) is a subclass of the expertise. The peer selection [1] is based on semantic matching the subject of a service request and the SE, this facilities query with designedly forwarding.

The semantic topology relies on the knowledge of the peers about the service expertise of other peers. It is independent of the underlying network topology. Due to this, the TTL of service request need not be conceived, as it can be processed by underlying P2P protocol. The semantic topology can be described by the relation: $Knows \subseteq P \times P$, where $Knows(p1, p2)$ means that p1 knows about the expertise of p2.

We abstract service as a quaternion (*Category, F_i, Q_i, C_i*), where *Category* is taken to compute similarity with expertise to select peers and forward query. F_i is the functional description of a service; Qi is the QoS attributes description, while C_i indicates the cost.

The service discovery flow is described as followings. (1) Semantic topology is set up in P2P network. Each joined peer will advertise its service expertise, then peers

---

* This work is supported by National 973 Basic Research Program of China under grant No.2003CB317003.

S. Grumbach, L. Siu, and V. Vianu (Eds.): ASIAN 2005, LNCS 3818, pp. 259–260, 2005.

create semantic overly topology according to the known relationship of the expertise between them. (2) A peer initializes a request described with service profile, and sets the key information. (3) The original peer computes the similarities between request *r* and all other expertise (set of *se*) cached in local storage, and selects next forwarding peer whose corresponding similarity value is larger than a certain threshold. (4) The forwarding peer performs the same procedure as above and forwards the request; meanwhile, it searches the service in local registry. The search focuses on semantic similarity computing for (F_i, Q_i, Ci). When the suitable services are found, it returns the result to the original peer. (5) The original peer receives the query results, analyzes them and communicates with the service provider by SOAP message.

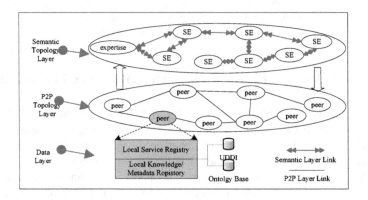

Fig. 1. Layered Architecture of the Framework

2 Conclusion

An approach for service discovery based on semantic P2P architecture is proposed. Different from both service-oriented system such as [2][3], our works conceive of the service request routing in P2P and the service matching in local peer. It is totally designed for the web service, while their works are partial to provide the web service invocation for the corresponding function.

References

[1] P. Haase, R. Siebes, and F. van Harmelen, "Peer selection in peer-to-peer networks with semantic topologies", *Proceedings of International Conference on Semantics of a Networked World: Semantics for Grid Databases*, 2004, Paris.
[2] P. Haase, S. Agarwal, and Y. Sure, "Service-Oriented Semantic Peer-to-Peer Systems", *Proceedings of Workshop on Intelligent Networked and Mobile Systems*.
[3] C. Qu and W. Nejdl, "Interacting the Edutella/JXTA Peer-to-Peer Network with Web Services", *Proceedings of 2004 International Symposium on Applications and the Internet*, 2004. pp 67–73.

Security Concerns for Web Services and Applications

Sylvia Encheva[1] and Sharil Tumin[2]

[1] Stord/Haugesund University College,
Bjørnsonsg. 45, 5528 Haugesund, Norway
sbe@hsh.no
[2] University of Bergen, IT-Dept.,
P.O. Box 7800, 5020 Bergen, Norway
edpst@it.uib.no

Abstract. In a secure system and for Web services specifically, security measure must be provided by implementers and system's owner to support maximum level of trust relations by incorporating security product and technologies at all levels. In this paper we discuss some security issues concerning designing, implementing and deploying Web Services.

1   Introduction

Security is perceived differently from different prospective. A user is usually interested in protection of privacy and identity theft and against framing. A system views security as protection for data and process integrity, information flow and resources, and secure communication link protocols.

The use of a single credential for a global Web services authentication provides users with the convenience of remembering one user-identification and password only [1], [6]. However, a single credential policy increases the risk of the system wide security breach, should that credential got stolen [5]. Using a single credential for Web sign-on from a Web browser situated in non-trusted environments like Web Cafe, public libraries and the like will increase the risk. We propose a method of using password card for Web sign-on that does not disclose users' system credentials.

Three core tools form the foundation on which our Web applications/services are built upon - Apache HTTP server, Python programming language and PostgreSQL relational database management system.

2   Security Implementation

The XML-RPC based request/response messages using signed digital envelopes involve the use of symmetric cryptography and public-key cryptography [4]. An XML message is encrypted by a symmetric cryptographic function using a secret-key. Public-key cryptography is used to encrypt the secret key using the public-key of the receiving party [3]. Together, they make a message in a digital envelope.

S. Grumbach, L. Siu, and V. Vianu (Eds.): ASIAN 2005, LNCS 3818, pp. 261–262, 2005.

Hash value of the digital envelope is produced by running it through a hash function. The hash value is then encrypted using the sender's private key to create a digital signature. The symmetric cryptographic function, the secret-key, the hash function, the digital signature, and the XML message are then used as parameters to an XML-RPC request and return values to the call. The actual procedure name and its parameters or the actual return values are embedded in the XML message. For an XML-RPC request, the receiver unpacks the XML message to get the procedure name and its parameters. On XML-RPC response, the receiver unpacks the XML message to get return values.

The sign-on application presents the user with a dynamically created image. The user needs to write the correct key, alias and pin-code for authentication. If the user succeeds, the system then proves its validity by presenting the user with the card serial number. The sign-on is successful if the user can then provide a valid pin-code. Single-sign-on function is provided by using single-sign-on mechanism based on page redirect and authenticated session cookies [2]. The cookies are signed by the sign-on server and contain an opaque user's authentication data. All authenticated users will have a valid session tokens saved in the session database. There is one-to-one correspondence between a token and a cookie.

3   Conclusion

Security concerns must be addressed from the very beginning of a Web-based application project and not as an afterthought once the system is put in production. To achieve this we propose the use of simple and open-ended software tools, and that any part of the system being developed is under a full control of the developers.

References

1. Fürst, K., Schmidt, T., and Wippel, G: Managing access in extended enterprise networks, Proceedings of IEEE Internet Computing, (2002)
2. Pashalidis, A., Mitchell, C.J.: Imposter: A Singel Sign-On System for Use from Untrusted Devices. Proceedings of the EIRE Globecome 2004, USA, EIRE Press, (2004)
3. Spillman, R.J.: Classical and Contemporary Cryptology, Pearson Prentice Hall, (2005)
4. Stallings, W.: Cryptography and Network Security: Principles and Practice, Prentice Hall, (2005)
5. Schwoon, S., Jha, S., Reps, T., Stubblebine S.: On generalized authorization problems. Proceedings 16th IEEE Computer Security Foundations Workshop, (June 30 - July 2, 2003, Asilomar, Pacific Grove, CA), (2003) 202–218
6. Topchy, A., W. Punch, W.: Dimensionality Reduction via Genetic Value Clustering. GECCO- 2003, 1431-1443 Lecture Notes in Computer Science, Vol. 2724. Springer-Verlag, Berlin Heidelberg New Jork (2004) 1431–1443

Modeling Web Services Based on the Bayesian Network[*]

Kun Yue[1], Weiyi Liu[1], Xiaoling Wang[2], and Aoying Zhou[2]

[1] Department of Computer Science and Engineering,
School of Information Science and Engineering,
Yunnan University, 650091, Kunming, P.R. China
kyue@ynu.edu.cn
[2] Department of Computer Science and Engineering,
Fudan University, 200433, Shanghai, P.R. China

Abstract. In this paper, aiming at the semantics description of Web services, a novel approach to the probabilistic graphical modeling of Web services is proposed, and the services Bayesian network is constructed based on the application of the least fixpoint and conditional mutual information. From the deduction and statistics of historical invocations, the inherent dependencies among elementary services are described, and measured qualitatively and quantitatively. Preliminary experiments and analysis show that our approach is effective and feasible.

In order to perform the automated services composition and intelligent services management, the following two questions should be conquered in the services modeling and management: How to describe the inherent dependencies of services qualitatively? How to give the measure of dependent or independent services quantitatively?

The Bayesian network is a useful tool of nondeterministic knowledge representation and inference under conditions of uncertainty. In this paper, a novel approach to the probabilistic graphical modeling of Web services is proposed, and the corresponding method for constructing the services Bayesian network is presented. Generally, the concrete contributions of this paper can be summarized as follows:

• From the composition procedures, the invocations of elementary Web services are described formally in temporal semantics based on time intervals. The sequential, conditional and parallel invocations are described qualitatively and quantitatively in a universal measure.

• The semantically inherent dependencies and associations among elementary services are evaluated based on the deduction and statistics of historical invocations. As the basis of our method, the least fix point semantics is computed based on the direct service associations, denoted as $P=(id, p_s, c_s, \tau_b, \tau_e)$. And the fixpoint function is defined as $\mathcal{L}=f(\mathcal{L}, P)=\pi_{1,2,8,4,10}(P \bowtie_{1=1 \wedge 3=2 \wedge 5=4} \mathcal{L}) \cup P$, in

---

[*] This work is supported by Natural Science Foundation of Yunnan Province(No. 2005F0009Q), the reserach foundation of Yunnan University (No.2004Q024C) and the National Natural Science Foundation of China (No. 60263006).

which $\mathcal{L}=(id,p_s,c_s,\tau_b,\tau_e)$ represents an arbitrary service association. Thus, the subjectively and optionally pre-defined knowledge is avoided to a great extent.

• The method for constructing the Web services Bayesian network is proposed. As the important intermediate steps for the construction of services Bayesian network, the ordering among the given elementary services is obtained by a partially ordered set based on the fixpoint semantics, and the conditional independences are obtained based on the conditional mutual information.

• With preliminary experiments and performance analysis on the real *City-Travel* services given by ecommerce Inc., the effectiveness and feasibility of the proposed method are verified.

References

1. Tsur, S., Abiteboul, S., Agraval, R., Dayal, U., Klein, J., Weikum, G.: Are Web Services the Next Revolution in E-Commerce? VLDB (2001) 614–617
2. Narayanan, S., Mcilraith, S. A.: Simulation, Verification and Automated Composition of Web Services. WWW (2002) 77–78
3. Yue, K., Wang, X., Zhou, A: The Underlying Techniques for Web Services: A Survey. J. Software. Vol. 15. 3 (2004) 428–442
4. Hull, R., Su, J.: Tools for Design of Composite Web Services. SIGMOD (2004) 958–961
5. Amer-Yahia, S., Kotidis, Y.: A Web-Services Architecture for Efficient XML Data Exchange. ICDE (2004) 523–534
6. Abiteboul, S., Benjelloun, O., Cautis, B., Manolescu, I., Milo, T., Preda, N.: Lazy Query Evaluation for Active XML. SIGMOD (2004) 227–238
7. Benetallah, B., Dumas, M., Sheng, Q., Ngu, A.: Declarative Composition and Peer-to-Peer Provisioning of Dynamic Services. ICDE (2002) 297–308
8. Tosic, V., Pagurek, B., Esfandiari, B., Patel, K.: On the Management of Compositions of Web Services. OOPSLA (2001)
9. Wang, X., Yue, K., Huang, J. Z., Zhou, A.: Service Selection for Dynamic Demand-Driven Web Services. ICWS (2004) 376–383
10. Bultan, T., Fu, X., Hull, R., Su, J.: Conversation Specification: A New Approach to Design and Analysis of E-Service Composition. WWW (2003)
11. Pearl, J.: Probabilistic Reasoning In Intelligent Systems: Networks of Plausible Inference. San Mateo. CA: Morgan Kaufmann Publishers, INC. (1988)
12. Heckerman, D., Wellman, M. P.: Bayesian Networks. Communications of ACM. Vol. 38. 3 (1995) 27–30
13. Cheng, J. Bell, D., Liu, W.: Learning Bayesian Networks from Data: An efficient Approach Based on Information Theory. 6th ACM Conf. on Information and Knowledge Management. (1997)
14. Helsper, E. M., Van der Gaag, L. C.: Building Bayesian Network Through Ontologies. 15th European Conf. on Artificial Intelligence (2003)
15. Van Emden, M., Kowalski, R.: The Semantics of predicate logic as a programming language. JACM. Vol. 23. 4 (1976) 733–742
16. Balbin, I., Ramamohanarao, K.: A Generalization of the Different Approach to Recursive Query Evaluation. Logic Programming. Vol. 4. 3 (1987) 259–262
17. Liu, W., Song, N.: Fuzzy Functional Dependencies and Bayesian Networks. J. Computer Science and Technology. Vol. 18. 1 (2003) 56–66
18. Web Services: Design, Travel, Shopping. http://www.ec-t.com

QoS-Driven Composite Web Services Selection

Lei Yang, Yu Dai, Bin Zhang, and Yan Gao

School of Information and Engineering, Northeastern University, China, 110004
qwe_yanglei@163.com, zhangbin@mail.neu.edu.cn

Abstract. A new QoS evaluation model for composite Web Services selection is proposed in this paper, which not only takes account of basic QoS properties but also considers relationships between services. This paper proposes a novel mechanism to map a service selection problem into a multistage decision-making problem to utilize global optimization algorithm to solve it.

Composite Web services have gained a lot of attention recently and moreover, since the number of available Web Services with same function may be large, service selection which picks out suitable service for composite one is needed. In this paper, a new QoS evaluation model is proposed, which revolutionizes the QoS model as most paper [1-3] addressed. And we also describe how to put such model into selection.

A composite service can be described by a statechart (Fig.1), in which tasks and dependencies between services are identified. Service selection is based on such statechart which according to QoS of each service pick out suitable service for each task in order to make the whole composite service achieve best qualification.

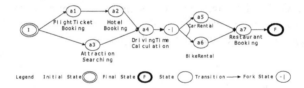

Fig. 1. A composite process of "Traveler Planner"

Here we initially assume that only services linked with each other can exchange message. And the new QoS model which takes enough consideration of matching degree between services can be expressed as follows:

$$QoS(S)=<Q_{pr}(S),\ Q_{du}(S),\ Q_{av}(S),\ Q_{rat}(S),\ Q_{rep}(S),\ Q_{md}(S)>$$

where Q_{pr}, Q_{du}, Q_{av}, Q_{rat} and Q_{rep} are defined as [1]. Q_{md} (S) is matching degree and can be calculated as follows ($\rightarrow$ presents that s_{i-1} is invoked before s_i and p signifies number of output parameters of s_{i-1}, q signifies number of input parameters of s_i):

$$Q_{md}(s_{i-1}\rightarrow s_i)=\begin{cases}\sigma & \text{if } (p<q)\\ 0 & \text{if } (q<p)\end{cases}\ ;\ \begin{cases}\sigma=\left(\sum_{k=1}^{q}\sum_{l=1}^{p}\dfrac{MD(s_i\uparrow k,s_{i-1}\uparrow l)}{q}\right)\times\left(\sum_{l=1}^{p}\sum_{k=1}^{q}\dfrac{MD(s_{i-1}\uparrow l,s_i\uparrow k)}{q}\right)\\ MD(s_{i\uparrow k},s_{i-1\uparrow l})=\dfrac{1}{1+\alpha}\end{cases} \quad (1)$$

S. Grumbach, L. Siu, and V. Vianu (Eds.): ASIAN 2005, LNCS 3818, pp. 265–267, 2005.

where, $s_{i-1} \uparrow 1$ signifies output parameter numbered 1 of s_{i-1} and $s_i \uparrow k$ signifies the input parameter numbered k of s_i. MD($s_{i-1} \uparrow 1$, $s_i \uparrow k$) is the function to calculate the concept matching degree of such two parameters. If parameter $s_{i-1} \uparrow 1$ and $s_i \uparrow k$ is the same concept, then α=0; Else, α can be a number above 0.

Then the overall qualification of S can be calculated as (2) from which, we know purpose of selection is to find a set of services for S that makes (2) gets the max value.

$$QoS(S) = \sum_i Q(s_{i-1} \to s_i) = \sum_i \frac{\left(Q_{pr}(s_i)*W_{pr} + Q_{du}(s_i)*W_{du} + Q_{av}(s_i)*W_{av} + Q_{rat}(s_i)*W_{rat} + Q_{rep}(s_i)*W_{rep} + \frac{Q_{md}(s_{i-1} \to s_i)*W_{md}}{n}\right)}{\left(W_{pr} + W_{du} + W_{av} + W_{rat} + W_{rep} + W_{md}\right)} \quad (2)$$

Considering complex composite service is hard for selection and here we adopt techniques described in [4] to simplify the composite one. Thus here we initially turn our attention to a fraction of simplified composite service.

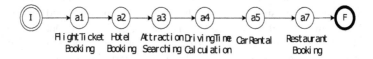

Fig. 2. A Fraction of Simplified Statechart of Fig.1

Thus after substitute corresponding services for each task, graph can be viewed as a weighted graph G= (V, E) (Fig.3) where V signifies a set of candidate services and E as a set of arcs presenting execution order between services. And based on (2), weight of arc ($s_{i-1,m} \to s_{i,n}$) can be calculated as Q($s_{i-1,m} \to s_{i,n}$).

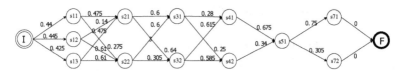

Fig. 3. Graph composed by concrete services

Then selection problem become a multistage decision-making problem and the mathematics model of such problem can be expressed as (3) based on which can calculate $F_1(s_{1,1})$, which is the max QoS from initial stage I to final stage F.

$$\begin{cases} F_{i-1}(s_{i-1,m}) = \min\{\text{weight}(s_{i-1,m} \to s_{i,n}) + F_i(s_{i,n})\} \\ F_{max}(s_{max,1}) = 0 \end{cases} \quad (3)$$

This paper presents a new QoS evaluation model for service selection. Such model, compared with current popular QoS model, takes account of the matching degree in order to find services that have the best operability. Moreover, this paper also shows how to use this model to do the selection job.

References

1. Liangzhao Z. and Boualem B.: QoS-Aware Middleware for Web Services Composition. IEEE Transactions on Software Engineering. Vol.30 (2004) 311-327.
2. Cardoso J. and Bussler C.: Semantic Web Services and Processes: Semantic Composition and Quality of Service. On the Move to Meaningful Internet Computing and Ubiquitous Computer (2002).
3. Sumra R. and Arulazi D.: Quality of Service for Web Services-Demystification, Limitation, and Best Practices. http://www.developer.com/services (2003)
4. Tao Y. and Kwei-Jay L.: Service selection algorithms for web services with end-to-end QoS constraints. In proceedings of IEEE international conference on E-commerce technology (2004) 129-136.

Cubing Web Data Based on Multidimensional Arrays

Yan Zhu[1] and Alejandro P. Buchmann[2]

[1] School of Information Science and Technology, Southwest Jiaotong University,
610031 Chengdu, China
yzhu@home.swjtu.edu.cn
[2] Department of Computer Science, Darmstadt University of Technology,
64287 Darmstadt, Germany
buchmann@dvs1.informatik.tu-darmstadt.de

Abstract. Data Warehousing and OLAP technologies enable enterprises to achieve Business Intelligence (BI). Since the Web is the largest independent information repository, systematically integrating suitable Web data into a data warehouse will benefit the enterprise. This paper introduces a Web data warehousing system in the MOLAP environment. A transformation approach is proposed to construct a base cube and then aggregates are precomputed over the base cube. To specify the aggregation rules we have developed a SQL style language that uses external functions for retrieving array data, computing aggregates, populating aggregated cubes.

1 The Web Data Cube Construction and Multi-dimensional Aggregates Computation

To construct a Web data base cube, Web data is first represented as MIX objects [1]. A set of generic transformation principles is then developed for covering several transformation aspects in the MOLAP environment. Following the generic principles, the specific mapping rules (SMDs) are defined. A web data base cube is then constructed.

After the construction of the base cube, a rule-driven aggregation approach is used for precalculating multi-dimensional aggregates. Because there is no standard language in the MOLAP environment for specifying aggregation rules, and the existing languages for querying arrays are also not suitable for our task, a language, Array Aggregation Language (AAL), is developed. AAL treats a multi-dimensional array as a function from the index set to the value as in [2], based on which the aggregation over arrays can be implemented as the function transformation. The main advantage of such an approach is that the functions can be recursively evaluated and we will have clean syntax and semantics in the language. In addition, this language supports external functions for reading arrays, calculating aggregates, and writing aggregates in new arrays. The following is an example of AAL rules (SADs).

- *Total import value of product "Fruit/Nuts" of Europe in 1999*

select {Agg : fun(getSum(Imports[ProdGrp/Country/Year])),
  SumA : fun(writeArrayofAgg(ProdGrp/Region/Year/Agg))}
where {ProdGrp : "Fruit/Nuts", Region : {Europe : {Country : ""}}, Year : "1999"}*
in Bcube

S. Grumbach, L. Siu, and V. Vianu (Eds.): ASIAN 2005, LNCS 3818, pp. 268–269, 2005.

The processors for warehousing Web data are shown in Figure 1.

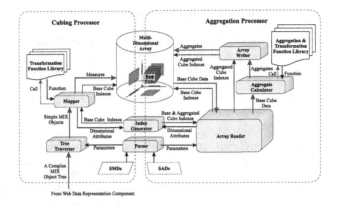

Fig. 1. The structure of the Cubing Processor and Aggregation Processor

2   Related Work and Conclusion

There is little research on investigating Web data warehousing systems in the MOLAP environment. However, several related languages can be compared with AAL.

AQL [2] provides four low-level array constructs but does not include any particular set of high-level operations. The array data operation in AQL has to include procedural expressions, which hinder the separation of the aggregation description and its operational implementation. RasQL [3] can define, retrieve and update multidimensional arrays. However, the domain of the array dimensions must be defined in queries for manipulating array data. Another big difficulty is that RasQL does not provide a statement like the view definition in relational SQL. Due to the limitations of these languages, AAL is proposed for specifying aggregation rules in the MOLAP environment.

We are investigating new approaches to improve the base cube construction and the aggregation computation in the system. For example, compression approaches can be integrated for constructing a compact Web data cube.

References

1. C. Bornhövd. *Semantic Metadata for the Integration of Data Source from the Internet.* PhD thesis, Department of Computer Science, Darmstadt University of Technology, Germany, 2001.
2. L. Libkin, R.Machlin, and L.Wong. A Query Language forMultidimensional Arrays: Design, Implementation, and Optimization Techniques. In *Proc. of ACM SIGMOD'96, Canada,* pages 228–239, 1996.
3. R. Ritsch. *Optimization and Evaluation of Array Queries in Database Management Systems.* PhD thesis, Institut für Informatik, Technische Universität München, Germany, 1999.

Mining Correlations Between Multi-streams Based on Haar Wavelet[*]

Anlong Chen[1], Changjie Tang[1], Changan Yuan[1,2], Jing Peng[1], and Jianjun Hu[1]

[1] College of Computer Science and Engineering, Sichuan University,
Sichuan ChengDu 610065, China
[2] Department of Information Technology, Guangxi Teachers Education University,
NanNing 530001, China
{tangchangjie, chenanlong}@cs.scu.edu.cn

Abstract. Mining correlation between multi-streams is a significant task. The main contributions of this paper included: (1) Proposes the equivalence model and equivalence theorems to computing correlation coefficient. (2) Designs anti-noise algorithm with sliding windows to compute correlation measure. (3) Gives extensive experiments on real data and shows that new algorithm works very well on the streams with noise in the environment of short size windows.

1 Introduction

Data steams have been hotspots in the research area of data mining recently. There are many research issues such as summarization [1], reducation [2]. Researching correlation between streams is significant in such settings.

To mine correlation in multi-streams with noise, the main work of this paper included: (1) Introducing Haar wavelet to eliminate high frequency noise form streams. (2) Proving the equivalence between wavelet coefficients and original data about computing local correlation. (3) Designs anti-noise algorithm with sliding windows to compute correlation coeffrcients. An equivalence theorem is showed as follows.

Equivalence Theorem. Let $Y_1^T = [y_{1,1}, y_{1,2}, \ldots, y_{1,m}]^T$ and $Y_2^T = [y_{2,1}, y_{2,2}, \ldots, y_{2,m}]^T$ $(m=2^n)$ be respectively wavelet coefficients for streams $X_1 = [x_{1,1}, x_{1,2}, \ldots, x_{1,m}]$ and $X_2 = [x_{2,1}, x_{2,2}, \ldots, x_{2,m}]$. $g(X_1) = (x_{1,1} + x_{1,2} + \ldots + x_{1,m})/m$, $g(X_2) = (x_{2,1} + x_{2,2} + \ldots + x_{2,m})/m$. If the correlation coefficients between two streams is calculated by $Corr(X_1, X_2) =$

$$\sum_{i=1}^{m}(x_{1,i} - g(X_1)) \times (x_{2,i} - g(X_2)) \bigg/ (\sum_{i=1}^{m}(x_{1,i} - g(X_1))^2 \sum_{i=1}^{m}(x_{2,i} - g(X_2))^2)^{\frac{1}{2}}$$

then $Corr(X_1, X_2) = \sum_{i=1}^{m-1}(y_{1,i} \times y_{2,i}) \bigg/ (\sum_{i=1}^{m-1}y_{1,i}^2 \times \sum_{i=1}^{m-1}y_{2,i}^2)^{\frac{1}{2}}$

* This work was supported by Grant from National Science Foundation of China (T60473071), Specialized Research Fund for Doctoral Program by the Ministry of Education (SRFDP20020610007), CHEN Anlong, YUAN Changan, PENG Jing, HU Jianjun are Ph. D Candidates at DB&KE Lab, Sichuan University. And TANG Changjie is the associate author.

S. Grumbach, L. Siu, and V. Vianu (Eds.): ASIAN 2005, LNCS 3818, pp. 270–271, 2005.
© Springer-Verlag Berlin Heidelberg 2005

2 Algorithm on Double Sliding Windows

Different from previous methods, these Algorithm is featured with (a) eliminating high frequency noise from stream data by discrete wavelet transform, (b) computing the local correlation by wavelet coefficients without reconstruction series data. The correlation between two streams is computed over the sliding windows with 2^{2p} series data points and 2^p sliding steps which the first sub-window is called computing window to be used for wavelet transform and the second sub-window is called buffer window to be used for memory coming data. The correlation coefficients between two streams are computed on sliding windows as follows: The first step, the wavelets coefficients are computed by the method in the reference [2, 3]. In the last step, the correlation coefficients are computed by formula that is given by Equivalence Theorem.

3 Experimental Result

The experiments are designed on real data that come from daily stock trade price of ShenZhen and ShangHai stock exchange in china. The platform as following: (1) Hardware with Pentium IV 2.6GHz and 256 MB of main memory. (2) System software with Windows2000 and SQL Server2000. The correlation coefficients are investgated on 500 pair-wise data series with the different sliding sub-window size such as 32,64,128,256,512 and the dynamic filter threshold. The results show that new algorithm has well filter on the streams with noise in the environment of short size windows.

4 Conclusions

The filter technique of Haar wavelet is applied to multi-streams. Equivalence Theorem describes the rationality of computing correlation with wavelet coefficients without reconstruction streams. The novel algorithm was designed on sliding windows to computing correlation coefficient and the experiments on real data are performed.

References

1. Yunyue Zhu and Dennis Shasha StatStream: Statistical Monitoring of Thousands of Data Streams in Real Time *VLDB*, pages 358–369, Aug. 2002
2. Sudiopto Dula, Chulyun Kim and Kyuseok Shim. XWAVE: Optimal and Approximate Extended Wavelets for Streaming Data. *VLDB*. Toronto, Canada (2004)
3. Chen Anlong, Tang Changjie, Yuan Changan, Peng Jing, Hu Jianjun. The full version of this paper, "Mining Correlations between Multi-Streams Based on Haar Wavelet" Science-PaperOnline; http://www.paper.edu.cn No20050911

Parallel Learning of Bayesian Networks Based on Ordering of Sets

Tao Du, S.S. Zhang, and Zongjiang Wang

Shanghai Jiaotong University, Shanghai 200030, China
dutao@sjtu.edu.cn

Abstract. In this paper, we firstly formulate the concept of "ordering of sets" to represent the relationships between classes of variables. And then a parallel algorithm with little inter-processors communication is proposed based on "ordering of sets". In our algorithm, the search space is partitioned in an effective way and be distributed to multi-processors to be searched in parallel. The results of experiments show that, compared with traditional greedy DAG search algorithm, our algorithm is more effective, especially for large domains.

In this paper we propose a novel parallel algorithm which could greatly speed up the process of learning Bayesian networks from data. Compare to existing parallel algorithms [2, 3], our algorithm is not bound to special hardware and MDL score metric.

In many real circumstances, although the dependency relationships between specific variables can not be defined explicitly, experts of domains could identify the causal relationships between classes of variables.

Based on observation mentioned above, we firstly propose a concept of "ordering of sets" to represents the relationships among classes of variables. For an ordering of sets, variables in preceding sets could be candidates of parents for variables in the posterior sets; however variables in posterior sets can not be the parents of the variables in preceding sets. For variables in a same set, they could be candidates of parents for each other.

Our algorithm is based on the following two propositions which could be easily derived from the prior knowledge represented by "ordering of sets".

1. All variables which are parents of variable X_i must belong to the preceding sets of the set which X_i belongs to.
2. When searching for optimal structures, if there exists a cycle in the resulted network, the variables in the cycle must belong to a same set.

Suppose that network structure G is represented as an adjacent block matrix, with proposition 1, the truth of equation (1) could be proved easily. And with proposition 2, we could know that, for decomposable score metrics, given an "ordering of sets" $S = \{S_1, S_2, \cdots, S_k\}$, the searching of best network structure G_{best} could be partitioned into at most k sub-tasks, where k is number of sets in the ordering. For sub-task m, $\forall m \in \{1, \cdots k\}$, the best combinations of parents

S. Grumbach, L. Siu, and V. Vianu (Eds.): ASIAN 2005, LNCS 3818, pp. 272–273, 2005.

for variables in set S_m are determined. In other words, in sub-task m, the best block elements $[B_{1,m}, \cdots, B_{m,m}]'$ in equation (1) should be searched.

$$G = \begin{bmatrix} B_{11} & B_{12} & B_{13} & \cdots & B_{1k} \\ B_{21} & B_{22} & B_{23} & \cdots & B_{2k} \\ B_{31} & B_{32} & B_{33} & \cdots & B_{3k} \\ \cdots & \cdots & \cdots & \ddots & \cdots \\ B_{k1} & B_{k2} & B_{k3} & \cdots & B_{kk} \end{bmatrix} = \begin{bmatrix} B_{11} & B_{12} & B_{13} & \cdots & B_{1k} \\ 0 & B_{22} & B_{23} & \cdots & B_{2k} \\ 0 & 0 & B_{33} & \cdots & B_{3k} \\ \cdots & \cdots & \cdots & \ddots & \cdots \\ 0 & 0 & 0 & \cdots & B_{kk} \end{bmatrix} \quad (1)$$

Our algorithm is shown in Fig.1. For our parallel algorithm, there are two merits we could get. The first is that the searching could be accelerated greatly. The second merit could be get is that, by partitioning large space into several smaller search spaces, an optimal structure could be obtained more easily.

Algorithm : Parallel Greedy DAG Search
    Allocate k sub-tasks to l processors.
    Transmit training data D , ordering of sets S to processors
    for every processor
        for sub-task m allocated to the processor
            Search best block elements $[B_{1,m}, \cdots, B_{m,m}]'$ and return it
        end
    end
    Assemble the all block elements to form the finally G_{best}
    Return G_{best}
end

Fig. 1. Parallel Greedy DAG Search Algorithm

The effectiveness our algorithm is evaluated using two well-known benchmarks of Bayesian Networks including ALARM and INSURANCE. The results of experiments have shown that, compared to traditional greedy search algorithm, with the ordering of sets, the parallel algorithm proposed in this paper could reduce the time for learning Bayesian network greatly. And in addition, the score of the finally obtained network structure could be also improved.

References

1. Tao Du, S.S. Zhang and Zongjiang Wang, "Structure Learning Based on Ordering of Sets", accepted by IEEE CIT2005
2. Wai Lam; Segre, A.M., Knowledge and Data Engineering, IEEE Transactions on Volume 14, Issue 1, Jan.-Feb. 2002 Page(s): 93 - 105
3. Y. Xiang and T. Chu, Parallel Learning of Belief Networks in Large and Difficult Domains, Data Mining and Knowledge Discovery, 3: 315-339, 1999.

A Grid Clustering Algorithm Based on Reference and Density

Xue Yong-Sheng[1], Zhang Wei[1,2], Wen Juan[1], Huang Zong-Yi[1],
Kuang Tian-Qi[2], and Xu Xin-Zheng[2]

[1] Department of Computer Science, Xiamen University, 361005 Xiamen, Fujian, China
wenjuan@xmu.edu.cn
[2] School of Software, Xiamen University, 361005 Xiamen, Fujian, China

Abstract. In the paper, a new kind of clustering algorithm called GCARD is proposed. Besides the merits of Density-Based clustering analysis and its efficiency, GCARD can capture the shape and extent of clusters by core grid units, and then analyze data based on the references of core grid units. We present a method of RGUBR to improve the accuracy of grid clustering method, so it can be used to discover information in very large databases.

1 Introduction

Density-Based clustering[1][2] and grid clustering[3][4] can discover clusters with arbitrary shape and separate noise. DBSCAN[1] finds dense regions that are separated by low density regions and the region queries can be supported efficiently by spatial access method such as R*-tree. So, DBSCAN has an almost quadratic time complexity for high dimensional data. Grid clustering is effective and can handle high-dimensional data. Due to the distribution of data is few or never considered when partitioning the data space, it is difficult to ensure clustering quality.

In this paper, we present a grid clustering algorithm based on reference and density——GCARD by first partitioning the data space into a number of units, and then dealing with units instead of points. Only those units with the density no less than a given minimum density threshold are useful in extending clusters. Our algorithm improves the efficiency of DBSCAN by only searching the neighbors of dense units. Besides, high-dimensional data is handled in single dimension space by using distance[5][6]. In this regard, GRDCA can deal with high-dimensional data. The method of calculating distance in multidimensional space and planar space is similar. In order to be convenient for describing algorithm, we analyze GRDCA in planar space.

2 GCARD ——A Grid Clustering Algorithm Based on Reference and Density

In general, GCARD can be divided into four steps:

Step 1. Preprocess: Map each point into the corresponding unit and stores position, density, sum of the non-empty units as well as pointers to the points using a k-d tree.

S. Grumbach, L. Sui, and V. Vianu (Eds.): ASIAN 2005, LNCS 3818, pp. 274–275, 2005.
© Springer-Verlag Berlin Heidelberg 2005

Step 2. Clustering C_d: Find the cluster of units based on density-reachable and density-connected. Initially, all units are identified as "unclustered". To find a cluster, GCARD starts from start c using a breadth-first search. If a neighbor unit of start c is unclustered, it is identified as the current cluster. Moreover, if it belongs to C_d, it is added to the end of seeds. Then it is deleted from the seeds. Next, the first unit of seeds is extracted to perform the same procedure. When all density-reachable units in the cluster had been visited, a cluster is discovered. Consequently, the procedure repeats by starting with an unclustered dense unit until there is no unclustered dense unit.

Step 3. Find the cluster of the non-empty units which are identified as "unclustered" by RGUBR.

If c_1 and c_2 are two non-empty units and dist(c_1,c_2) $\leq \tau$, we consider that there is an edge connected c_1 with c_2.

Step 4. Use RGUBR method to deal with "unclustered" points.

In the current partition pattern of data space, let c_1, c_2 be two units, c_2 is neighborhood of c_1, $c_1 \in C_d, c_2 \in C_{ne}$ and $c_2 \notin C_d$. It is potential that there is a partition pattern of data space in which partial or whole points of c_2 belong to certain dense unit. In anther word, these points and points of c1 belong to the same cluster. So, we use RGUBR method to deal with "unclustered" points for improving the accuracy of clustering.

Both theory analysis and experimental results confirm that GCARD can discover clusters with arbitrary shape and is insensitive to noise data. In the meanwhile, its executing efficiency is much higher than traditional DBSCAN algorithm based on R*-tree. Future work is testing the efficiency of GCARD for high-dimensional data.

References

1. Ester M., Kriegel H.P., Sander J., Xu X.:A density based algorithm for discovering clusters in large spatial databases with noise. In: Simoudis E., Han J.W., Fayyad U.M. (eds.):Proceedings of the 2nd International Conference on Knowledge Discovery and Data Mining. Portland (1996) 226-231
2. Zhou B., Cheung D., Kao B.: A fast algorithm for density-based clustering. In: Zhong N., Zhou, L. (eds.): Proceedings of the Third Pacific-Asia Conference on Knowledge Discovery and Data Mining. heidelberg (1999) 338-349
3. Agrawal R., Gehrke J., Gunopolos D., Raghavan P.: Automatic subspace clustering of high dimensional data for data mining application. In: Haas L.M., Tiwary A.(eds.):Proceedings of the ACM SIGMOD International Conference on Management of Data. Seattle (1998) 94-105
4. Schikuta, E.: Grid clustering: an efficient hierarchical clustering method for very large data set. In: Proceedings of the 13th International Conference on Pattern Recongition. Vol. 2. (1996) 101-105
5. Miinshen Yang, Kuolung Wu.: A Similarity-Based Robust Clustering Method. IEEE Transactions on Pattern Analysis and Machine Intelligence, Vol. 26. (2004) 434-448
6. Berchtold S., Bohm C., Kriegel H.P.: The pyramid- technique: towards breaking the curse of dimensionality. In: Haas L.M., Tiwary A. (eds.): Proceedings of the ACM SIGMOD International Conference on Management of Data. Seattle (1998) 142-153

Systematic Study on Query Expansion

Yue Li, Xing Li, and Jingfang Xu

Department of Electronic Engineering, Tsinghua University,
100084 Beijing, P.R. China
{liyue, xjf}@compass.net.edu.cn
xing@cernet.edu.cn

Abstract. Although query expansion (QE) has been extensively studied to provide more specific and accurate information for user query, little has been explored to study the importance of combined solution which includes extract terms, select terms correlation, and weight terms correl- ation for QE. The experimental results, based on two real Chinese query logs with 8-14 millions queries, show that the precision varies from 10% to 90% of the top 5 expansion terms.

1 Introduction

In Information Retrieval (IR) systems, user queries are always short and contain only a few words, thus QE is used to describe the user request more detailed[1]. There are two major components in QE: to extract expansion terms, and to weight the correlati- on of the expansion terms[2, 3]. With the development of large scale IR systems, esp- eciallly search engines, user query log is also used as a source in QE[1, 2, 4]. A *term* in this paper is defined as an alphabet-based word, a Chinese character or a phrase. In this paper, we study how to combine the methods for term extraction, term correlation selection and weighting as the best QE solution.

2 QE Solution

The query expansion solution in this paper includes: 1)extract terms: "*Quotation-mar-k-phrase*"(QMP)[1] and "*N-gram-phrase*"(NGP)[2]; 2)identify source to select terms correlations: "*Term-query-only*"(TQO) and "*Term-query-session*" (TQS)[1,2,3,4]; 3)weight term correlations: "*Correlation-coefficient*"(CC)[1] and "*Normalized-tf*idf*" (NTI) [3]. QMP is using the *quotation mark*(") operator in queries to enclose phrases, and NGP is to extract all N continuous word sequences from queries as candidate phr- ases. A *query* is what user submits to search engines, consisting of words and operato- rs. TQO only considers the term co-occurrences in a query, TQS considers in a query session. A *query session* is a sequence of queries issued by a single user within a short time(10min) [1, 2]. CC calculates the deviation in terms of non-occurrence as well as co-occurrence, and NTI calculates the degree of co-occurrence of terms.

S. Grumbach, L. Siu, and V. Vianu (Eds.): ASIAN 2005, LNCS 3818, pp. 276 – 277, 2005.

3   Experimental Evaluations

We make use of nine-month (2004.09.09~2005.05.06) apache access logs to three sites of CERNET. Then we extract the query logs from Google or Baidu(based on the "Referer" field). The frequency of distinct queries in Google is 14,478,375, and in Baidu is 8,848,233. Top 20 popular queries from Google or Baidu are used in our experiments. Three people in our research group analyzed the top 20 queries and their top 5 related terms made by each combined solution, then decided whether the terms are suitable. Precision is used to evaluate the QE performance for each combined solution in two datasets:

In Google: QMP/TQO/CC-23(%); QMP/TQO/NTI-6(%); QMP/TQS/CC-94(%); QMP/TQS/NTI-14(%); NGP/TQO/CC-84(%); NGP/TQO/NTI-12(%); NGP/TQS/CC -86(%); NGP/TQS/NTI-12(%). In Baidu: QMP/TQO/CC-31(%); QMP/TQO/NTI-15 (%); QMP/TQS/CC-95(%); QMP/TQS/NTI-15(%); NGP/TQO/CC-86(%); NGP/TQ-O/NTI-16(%); NGP/TQS/CC-88(%); NGP/TQS/NTI-14(%).

From above precisions, the best combined solution is QMP/TQS/CC in both query datasets. NTI has a bad performance according to its definition[3], for the experimental queries are most popular queries and most of them are short queries. TQS is more effective to describe the user demand than TQO for query session's definition. And a phrase defined by QMP is less ambiguous than defined by NGP, the former is labeled by users.

4   Conclusion

In this paper, we evaluate 8 combined solutions, each of which includes term extraction, term correlation selection and term correlation weighting. The results show that the precision varies from 10% to 90% in both datasets, which indicates that proper combination is extremely important for the QE performance. Although Chinese query logs are used in this paper, the results can be used to other languages' QE.

References

1. C. Silverstein, M. Henzinger, H. Marais, and M. Moricz. Analysis of a very large altavista query log. *SIGIR Forum*, 33(1):6-12, 1999.
2. H. CUI, J.-R. WEN, J.-Y. NIE, and W.-Y. MA. Query Expansion by Mining User Logs. *IEEE transactions on knowledge and data engineering*, vol. 15, no. 4, july/august, 2003.
3. J. Komarjaya, D.-C.C. Poo and M.-Y. Kan. Corpus-Based Query Expansion in Online Public Access Catalogs. In *Proceedings of the European Conference on Digital Libraries*, pages 12-17, September, 2004.
4. B. M. Fonseca, P. B. Golgher, E. S. De Moura, and N. Ziviani. Using association rules to discover search engines related queries. In *1st Latin American Web Congress*, November, 2003.

Relational to XML Schema Conversion with Constraints

Teng Lv[1,2], Ping Yan[1], and Qiongxiang Huang[1]

[1] College of Mathematics and System Science, Xinjiang University, Urumqi 830046, China
[2] Teaching and Research Section of Computer, Artillery Academy, Hefei 230031, China
lt0410@163.com

Abstract. This paper studies the problem of schema conversion from relational schemas to XML DTDs. As functional dependencies play an important role in the schema conversion process, the concept of functional dependency for XML DTDs is proposed and used to preserve the semantics implied by functional dependencies and keys of relational schemas. A conversion method is proposed to convert relational schemas to XML DTDs in the presence of functional dependencies, keys and foreign keys. The methods presented here can preserve the semantics implied by functional dependencies, keys and foreign keys of relational schemas and can convert multiple relational tables to XML DTDs at the same time.

XML [1] has become one of the primary standards for data exchange and representation on the Web and is widely used in many fields. Historically, lots of data and information are stored in and managed by relational database management systems. So it is necessary and urgent to develop some efficient methods to convert relational data to XML data in order to take advantage of all the merits of XML. As DTDs [2] are the most frequently used schemas for XML documents in these days [3], we will use DTDs as schemas of XML documents. Schema semantics plays a very important role in the schema conversion, and functional dependencies, keys, and foreign keys of relational schemas are very important representations of semantic information. So it is significant that the conversion method from relational schemas to XML DTDs must consider the semantics implied by functional dependencies, keys, and foreign keys, and the obtained XML DTDs can represent such semantics in some way. In this paper, we give the definition of functional dependencies over XML DTDs to represent the semantics of DTDs. Then we propose a conversion method to convert relational schemas to XML DTDs in the presence of functional dependencies, keys, and foreign keys. The method presented in the paper has a significant improvement over NeT and CoT[6~8] in the aspect of preserving the semantics implied by functional dependencies of relational schemas.

Acknowledgements

This work is supported by Science Research Foundation for Young Teachers of Xinjiang University (No. QN040101).

S. Grumbach, L. Siu, and V. Vianu (Eds.): ASIAN 2005, LNCS 3818, pp. 278–279, 2005.

References

1. Tim Bray, Jean Paoli, et al. Extensible Markup Language (XML) third edition. http://www.w3.org/TR/REC-xml.
2. ArborText Inc. W3C XML specification DTD. http://www.w3.org/XML/1998/06/xmlspec-report-19980910.htm.
3. Byron Choi. What are real DTDs like. In: Proc. of the 5th Workshop on the Web and Databases (WebDB'02). ACM Press, 2002: p43~48.
4. M. Arenas and L. Libkin, A normal form for XML documents, Proceedings of Symposium on Principles of Database Systems (PODS'02), ACM press, 2002, pp.85-96.
5. M. L. Lee, T. W. Ling, and W. L. Low, Designing functional dependencies for XML, Proceedings of VIII Conference on Extending Database Technology (EDBT'02), LNCS 2287, Springer, 2002, pp.124-141.
6. Lee D., Chu Mani M., et al. Nesting-based relational-to-XML schema translation. In: Proc. of the 4th International Workshop on the Web and Database Systems (WebDB2001), Santa Barbara, California, USA, 2001:p61~66.
7. Dongwon Lee, Murali Mani, and Wesley W. Chu. Schema conversion methods between XML and relational models. Knowledge Transformation for the Semantic Web. Frontiers in Artificial Intelligence and Applications, Vol. 95, Amsterdam, IOS Press, 2003: p1~17.
8. Dongwon Lee, Murali Mani, et al. NeT and CoT: Translating relational schemas to XML schemas using semantic constraint. In: Proc. of the 2002 ACM CIKM International Conference on Information and Knowledge Management. ACM Press, 2002: p282~291.
9. C. Kleiner and U. Lipeck, Automatic generation of XML DTDs from conceptual database schemas, GI Jahrestagung (1) 2001, pp.396-405
10. J. Fonga , H.K. Wonga, Z. Cheng, Converting relational database into XML documents with DOM, Information and Software Technology, 2003, 45(6), pp.335-355.
11. J. Fong and S. K. Cheung, Translating relational schema into XML schema definition with data semantic preservation and XSD graph, Information and Software Technology, 2005, 47(7), pp.437-462.
12. Teng Lv, Ping Yan, and Zhenxing Wang. Mapping DTD to relational schema with constraints. Journal of Computer Science, 2004, 31(10Supp): p443~444,457.
13. Teng Lv, Qiongxiang Huang, and Ping Yan. Mapping XML DTDs to relational schemas in the presence of functional dependencies over DTDs. In: Proc. of the 10th Joint International Computer Conference (JICC2004), International Academic Publishers, 2004: p242~246.
14. Jayavel Shanmugasundaram, Kritin Tufte, et al. Relational databases for querying XML documents: limitations and opportunities. In: Proc. of the 25th VLDB Conference, Edinburgh, Scotland: Morgan Kaufmann Publisher, 1999: p302~314
15. Shiyong Lu, Yezhou Sun, et al. A new inlining algorithm for mapping XML DTDs to relational schemas. ER workshops 2003, Spinger, Lecture Notes in Computer Science, Vol. 2814, 2003: p366~377.
16. Yi Chen, Susan B. Davidson, and Yifeng Zheng. Constraints preserving XML storage in relations. Technical Report, MS-CIS-02-04, University of Pennsylvania, 2002.
17. Teng Lv and Ping Yan. Mapping DTDs to relational schemas with semantic constraints, Information and Software Technology, 2005, 47 (To be appear).
18. W. Fan and L. Libkin. On XML integrity constraints in the presence of DTDs. In: PODS'01, ACM Press, 2001: p114-125.
19. Teng Lv and Ping Yan. Functional dependencies of XML and their inference rules. Journal of Computer Research and Development, 2005, 42(5): p792-796.
20. Teng Lv, Ning Gu, and Baile Shi. A normal form for XML DTD. Journal of Computer Research and Development, 2004, 41(4): p615~620.

An Extended Mandatory Access Control Model for XML[*]

Dong-Zhan Zhang and Yong-Sheng Xue

Department of Computer Science, Xiamen University, Xiamen 361005
zdzwxl@126.com

Abstract. More and more information is distributed in XML format. Information stored in XML documents should be protected by access control policy. An extended MAC model for XML is presented. The subject and object are discussed at first. The labeled XML document model, which includes three rules and one algorithm, is presented allowing for definition and enforcement of access restrictions directly on the structure and content of XML documents. The extended MAC model for XML documents is described in detail by discussing four operations on XML documents. The architecture and some mechanisms used to implement the model are discussed at last.

1 Introduction

More and more information is distributed in XML format. Information stored in XML documents should be protected by access control policy. High security system uses MAC (mandatory access control) to secure information in system. Our work will focus on XML Access Control and is aimed at providing a sophisticated dynamic mandatory access control model for XML documents.

Access Control for XML has been the topic of many recent research publications. An XML-based language Author-X has been discussed in [1]. A related effort has been reported in [2]. All these efforts have been based on XML DTD, and not on XML schemas, and hence lack the set of enhanced capabilities that XML schema provides over DTD[3]. With the advent of XML schema, access controls based on XML schema are presented. An XML access control language, XACL, has been discussed in [4]. An XML-based approach to specify enterprise RBAC policies has been reported in [5]. XACML is presented in the OASIS. It is based on an extension of XML to define an access control specification that supports user credentials and context-based privilege assignments. XACML 2.0 and all the associated profiles were approved as OASIS Standards on 1 February 2005[6].

All above efforts lay stress on DAC (Discretionary Access Control) and RBAC (Role Based Access Control). No one discusses MAC directly. A closely related approach is presented in [7]. It presented Fine-grained MAC model for XML documents. The fine-grained MAC model is only based on XML schema, without referring to XML instances and the relationship between schema and instance. The

[*] Supported by the National Natural Science Foundation of China under Grant No.50474033.

S. Grumbach, L. Siu, and V. Vianu (Eds.): ASIAN 2005, LNCS 3818, pp. 280–281, 2005.

label in the model is static and single. It can't afford the explicated query as the following example. The access control for XML should take into account schema-based vs. instance-based authorizations, global vs. local authorizations, document vs. element/attribute authorizations and Hard vs. soft statements. To the best of our knowledge, no earlier effort within XML and MAC model has been reported to target the aforementioned specific security requirements of XML.

2   Extended MAC Model for XML

In our model, the subject is a user of Internet who has a sensitivity label. It is a pair (u, l) where u refers to a user or an autonomic system such as agent, which can access information from XML documents and l refers to the sensitivity of u.

In MAC, both the subject and the object have labels. The label of subject is simple, but the label of object is very complicated, so we give a labeled XML document model.

Definition 1. *Labeled XML Document: a labled XML document is a ten-tuple, Xdoc=(Ve , v r, Va, Ns, Ls, Lt, subelem, attrs, name, XSD, label).*

Ls refers to the set of labels.
Lt refers to the set of label types.

Through the above model, both the subject and the object have label. When a user submits an access request. The system can get the labels of the subject and object. It can actualize access control by those labels. The core of MAC is the secure labels, hence the labels must be saved safely. These secure labels in security information files repository. It includes two parts, one is XLS(XML Label Sheets) which stores labels of XML document, the other is ULS(User Label Sheets) which stores labels of the users.

References

1. E. Bertino, S. Castano, E. Ferrari, "On Specifying Security Policies for Web Documents with an XML-based Language", Proceedings of Sixth ACM Symposium on Access Control Models and Technologies, 2001.
2. E. Damiani, S. D. C. di Vimercati, S. Paraboschi, P. Samarati, "A Fine Grained Access Control System for XML Documents", ACM Transactions on Information and System Security, Volume 5, Issue 2, May 2002.
3. "Why XML Schema beats DTDs hands-down for data" http://www.106.ibm.com /developerworks /xml/library/x-sbsch.html, 2005
4. S. Hada, M. Kudo, "XML Access Control Language:Provisional Authorization for XML Documents", April 17, 2002, Tokyo Research Laboratory, IBM Research.
5. N. N. Vuong, G. S. Smith, Y. Deng, "Managing Security Policies in a Distributed Environment Using eXtensible Markup Language (XML) ", Symposium on Applied Computing, March 2001
6. XACML 2.0 specification, http://docs.oasis-open.org/xacml/2.0/XACML-2.0-OS-ALL.zip, 2005
7. LI Lan, HE Yong-Zhong, FENG Deng-Guo, "A Fine-Grained Mandatory Access Control Model for XML Documents", Journal of Software, 2004, 15(10): 1528~1537

A Query Processing Approach Based on Window Semantics in Data Stream System[*]

Baoyan Song[1], Shanshan Wu[2], Feng Yuan[2], and Ge Yu[2]

[1] School of Computer Science and Technology, LiaoNing University, China 110036
[2] School of Computer Science and Engineering, Northeastern University, China 110004
bysong@lnu.edu.cn

Abstract. Since data streams are continuous, unbounded and real-time, continuous queries over data streams are generally based on windows. Windows placed on data streams are maintained by operators themselves for a query in most DSMSs. However, some operators can't maintain the windows properly, and a lot of redundancy and inconsistency may be incurred because the tuples are heavily copied and operators interfere with each other. In this paper, we thoroughly discuss the query processing mechanism based on windows and analyze the window semantics in a query sentence, then propose a query processing approach *MullayerQuery* that abstract windows into two types, stream window and operator windows. A strategy and some algorithms are given to keep the consistency among windows in a query. The experiments show *MullayerQuery* can't only maintain the query semantics, but also implement to share data in multiple queries as well as decrease the usage of memory. *MullayerQuery* has been carried out in a prototype system-*RealStream* that is a DSMS for real-time embedded applications.

1 Issues in Window Queries

A query plan is a sequence of operators, each of which can achieve appropriate function. The operator may be relation operators or set operators [1-2]. Here, we class the operators into two types: Non-Stored operators and Stored operators. Non-Stored operators process the input tuples without the other tuples, such as Selection, projection, and so on. Stored operators process the input tuples without the other tuples, such as Join, aggregation, and so on. Every Stored operator has its own window. Stored operators maintain their windows according to the window information given by the query generally. The issues are as follows[1, 3-6].

(1) If an operator O (such as selection) is followed by a Stored operator, and the window of the Stored is based on the number of tuples, the operator O disturbs the Stored operator window. We cannot know exactly the size of the Stored operator window according to the window information given by the query statement. (2) If an operator O would filter some tuples from the stream, the Stored operator following

---

[*] This work is supported by the National 863 High-tech Program (2002AA1Z2308, 2002AA118030), and Doctor's Startup Foundation of Liaoning Province, China (20041029).

S. Grumbach, L. Siu, and V. Vianu (Eds.): ASIAN 2005, LNCS 3818, pp. 282–283, 2005.

could not update its window in time. (3) As a rule, query window (called stream window) is placed directly on the data stream in a query statement. Although the size of operator window keeps consistency with that of the window, their semantics are completely different.

2 *MullayerQuery* : Approach of Maintaining Multi-layer Windows

A approach that is driven by tuple and structure pointer is proposed in this paper, that is called *MullayerQuery*. We bind the information of window maintenance to new structure pointer. The change of operator window is driven by the new structure pointer, and the change of stream window is driven by the new tuple.

For the stream window, if original window is $[t_k, t_{i-1}]$, after t_i arrived, we will delete the expired tuples whose ID are smaller than j according to the window's definition in the query. t_i is inserted into the stream window, and a structure pointer p_i is created. The structure pointer contains deletion messages j and a pointer that points to tuple t_i. We denote p_i as $p_{i(j)}$. Then put it into the query plan on the stream.

For the operator window, when a structure pointer $p_{i(j)}$ enters Stored operator windows, according to the deletion message of tuples, these operators will delete all the structure pointers which point tuples with IDs smaller than j, in order to make its own window consistent with stream window.

For some tuples, if operators such as selections absorb them, they cannot enter the following operator windows. Because the windows may be changed by the tuples, the deletion information cannot be ignored. So $p_{i(j)}$ is still required by following operators. Here, the pointer that point to tuple t_i is null, and the deleting information j is set in structure $p_{i(j)}$. The operators do nothing when the structure pointers that take only the deleting messages go through the Non-Stored operators. When they pass through the Stored operators, the Stored operators maintain their windows with the structure pointer. The experiments show the approach can decrease the cost of duplicating tuples and improve data sharing among multi-layer windows.

References

1. B Babcock, S Babu, M Datar, R Motwani, and J Widom. Models and issues in data stream systems. In Proc. of the 2002 ACM Symp. on Principles of Database Systems, June 2002.
2. S. Chandrasekaran and M. Franklin. Streaming queries over streaming data. In Proc. 28th Intl. Conf. on Very Large Data Bases, August 2002.
3. S Chandrasekaran, O Cooper, A Deshpande, et al. TelegraphCQ: Continuous dataflow processing for an uncertain world. In Proc. of Conf. on Innovative Data Systems Research (2003).
4. D J Abadi, D Carney, U Çetintemel et al., Aurora: a new model and architecture for data stream management, The VLDB Journal,2003, 12(2):120-139.
5. S Madden, M Shah, J M Hellerstein, V Raman. Continuously adaptive continuous queries over streams, In Proc. of ACM SIGMOD '2002, Madison, Wisconsin, USA.
6. D Carney, U Cetintemel, M Cherniack et al. Monitoring streams–a new class of data management applications, In Proc. 28th Intl. Conf. on Very Large Data Bases, August 2002.

A Hybrid Method for Detecting Data Stream Changes with Complex Semantics in Intensive Care Unit[*]

Ting Yin, Hongyan Li[**], Zijing Hu, Yu Fan, Jianlong Gao, and Shiwei Tang

School of Electronics Engineering and Computer Science,
Peking University, Beijing, 100871, P.R. China
sophie_yin@163.com, {lihy, huzijing,
efan, jlgao}@cis.pku.edu.cn, Tsw@pku.edu.cn

Abstract. Detecting changes in data streams is very important for many applications. This paper presents a hybrid method for detecting data stream changes in intensive care unit. In the method, we first use query processing to detect all the potential changes supporting semantics in big granularity, and then perform similarity matching, which has some features such as normalized subsequences and weighted distance. Our approach makes change detection with a better trade-off between sensitivity and specificity. Experiments on ICU data streams demonstrate its effectiveness.

1 Introduction

The equipments in intensive care unit (ICU) dynamically measure patient's physiological functions continuously, and generate a large amount of data streams. The clinicians care changes of the patient's disease, but they have difficulty in getting information timely from streams due to various distractions in the clinical environment, thus detecting changes in ICU data streams is urgently needed.

The change semantics of ICU data streams has the following properties: polymorphism, time-varying and priority. And change may involve several data streams. All those add to the challenges of change detection.

2 Related Work

There are two major techniques for change detection. One is data stream query processing, on which much research have done. But noises in data streams have not been considered. The other is similarity matching, we can extract features from and design the similarity model. Research on financial data streams [1] only covers single stream. Our method is application driven, and focuses on supporting the semantics of changes.

---

[*] Supported by Natural Science Foundation of China (NSFC) under grant number 60473072.
[**] Corresponding author.

S. Grumbach, L. Siu, and V. Vianu (Eds.): ASIAN 2005, LNCS 3818, pp. 284–285, 2005.

3 Change Detection Method

It's not practical that change detection method can guarantee both the sensitivity and specificity in real applications, thus we introduce the minimum cost rule to the evaluation of detection method. Our method combines the two existing techniques. As showed in Fig.1, we first use query processing to assure the sensitivity to changes and if the cost tends to be lower, triggers the similarity matching to increase the specificity.

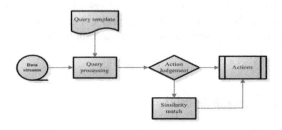

Fig. 1. The framework of the change detection

We use predefined query template and ad hoc query in support of the polymorphism of change semantics. Query processing is data triggered, and we support the time varying of the data streams by updating the queries.

We introduce approximation matching [3]. And Noise removal is processed before feature extraction. The method we use is similar to the similarity matching in [2], but we consider the semantics of the stream changes and prove the properties of the similarity measure. We also introduce weighted distance over multiple streams.

4 Experiments and Conclusion

Upon studying the special requirements of ICU, we present a hybrid method for detecting changes in ICU data streams. And our method is compared with three common methods. All data come from the surgery of ICU of Peking university affiliated NO.3 hospital. And our method performs much better on reducing false alarm, and keeping high sensitivity on both significant and insignificant changes.

References

1. Y. Zhu and D. Shasha. StatStream: Statistical Monitoring of Thousands of Data Streams in Real Time. VLDB, pages 358–369, 2002
2. Dina Q. Goldin, Todd D. Millstein, Ayferi Kutlu: Bounded similarity query for time series data. Information and Computation 194(2004) 203-241
3. Huanmei Wu, Betty Salzberg, Donghui Zhang. Online Event-driven Subsequence Matching over Financial Data Streams SIGMOD 2004 Paris, France.

Three-Level Schema Model in a Web Data Engine

Zhiqiang Zhang, Qi Guo, Hang Guo, and Lizhu Zhou

Department of Computer Science and Technology,
Tsinghua University, 100084 Beijing, China
zqzhang@mail.tsinghua.edu.cn

Abstract. In this paper, we introduce a three-level schema model for querying the web data which have been used in a specific-domain web data engine—SESQ, which can be customized on different domain by defining the different domain ontology.

1 Three-Level Schema Model

For running the SESQ system to realize the web data searching, we firstly need resolve the problem "how to model the web and the data on the web?" But this is a difficult task because of the web data dynamic nature and the complex relationships among the data. In SESQ, we adopt a model framework to model the different aspects, for example, the search agent adopts the graph model to model the web in which the nodes represent the web pages and the arcs represent the links between the pages; the extractor adopts the tree model to model the content of one page; and the three-level schema model is responsible for giving a global view for user and the upper applications, and also in charge of managing and storing the extracted data.

♦ **Concept Schema**

For easily modeling the Web data, we adopt a simple and flexible modeling method, which uses domain ontology to model a domain at high level of abstraction and uses concept schema at a logical level to describe the actual data extracted from the Web.

Modeling the domains of interest facilitates a better understanding of the domains and related concepts. In SESQ, there are four main parts in domain ontology for establishing the concept schema, namely, Semantic Inheritance Rules (SIR), Object Property Descriptions (OPD), Semantic Information Pairs (SIP) and Domain Lexicon (DL).

SESQ can establish edges between two concepts C_1 and C_2 based on some rules, such as, a_1 and a_2 should be the same data type (In SESQ, there is only one "String" data type now), where a_1 and a_2 are attributes of concept C_1 and C_2 respectively, and a_1 and a_2 must have the same semantics. According to this rule, it makes no sense to establish a relationship edge [PaperTitle, ResearcherName] between PAPER and RESEARCHER, if PaperTitle and ResearcherName have different semantics.

SESQ could automatically construct the concept schema from given domain ontology. More details may be found in [2]. For instance, we know that the attribute AuthorName includes information about person's name from SIP. And we also know researcher is a subclass of person from SIR, so we could establish the relationship

S. Grumbach, L. Siu, and V. Vianu (Eds.): ASIAN 2005, LNCS 3818, pp. 286–287, 2005.

edge [AuthorName, ResearcherName] between PAPER and RESEARCHER, which expresses *"paper's author is the researcher"*.

◆ **Underlying Schema**

Query Processor will receive the user query and establish a query plan based on the optimization scheme [1]. It used the index and data dictionary to obtain the instances which would make contribution to the final query result. The interface of index manager is very simple. Taking the query constraint 4-tuple *{simple concept name, attribute name, operator, constraint's value}* as its input, the index manager would return the instance IDs that satisfy the query constraints.

Except establishing and maintaining the concept schema, the Basic Storage Manager is also in charge of maintaining an underlying schema of all concepts, namely, the data schema that the underlying storage system adopted for storing the instances. For example, if we use RDB as the underlying storage system, the underlying schema will be presented as a group table schema definition. Herein, we could add new adapter to support the new underlying storage system. The task of adapter is to translate the query to a group local query and return the query result. The key problem of adapter is to choose one efficient storage method and to realize the relevance evaluating algorithms, for example, suppose taking the RDB as the underlying storage system and adopt the *Edge* and *Binary* storage methods, adapter need to realize the translation algorithms between the CSQL [1] query to SQL query.

◆ **View Schema**

For easily expressing query requests and capturing the user query intent, SESQ adopts an interactive method which allows users to express their query requests with the query language CSQL (*Conceptual Structure Query Language*) [1] over the tree view schema simplified from the concept schema. User can design the tree view schema according to their query requests and formulate their queries taking care only of the semantics of the data in which such users are interested. The method is implemented by a visual query interface through which a user can submit her/his query and view the results.

Comparing with the SQL, the expressiveness of CSQL is a more lightweight query language now. For example, it can not express the query "Please find the papers that cite two different papers of Mendelzon". In future, CSQL will be enhanced more powerfully with some aggregation functions and some new operations.

References

1. Z. Zhang, C. Xing, L. Zhou and J. Feng, A New Query Processing Scheme in a Web Data Engine, DNIS 2002, LNCS 2544, pp. 74-87, Japan December 16-18, 2002.
2. Z. Zhang, C. Xing, L Zhou and J. Feng, An Ontology-based Method for Querying the Web Data. Proceedings of IEEE 17th International Conference on Advanced Information Networking and Applications (AINA), pp 628-631, Xi'an, China, March 27-29, 2003.

Resource Integration Framework of Logistics Resource Grid[*]

Biqing Huang[**], Yang Wang, Zhiyuan Chen, and Hongbo Sun

Department of Automation, Tsinghua University, Beijing 100084, PR China
Tel: 00 86 10 62789636
hbq@tsinghua.edu.cn

Abstract. In this paper, the Logistics Resource Grid (LRG) for complex logistics applications is constructed. Furthermore, a Resource Integration Framework (RIF) of LRG is developed with Globus Toolkit and OGSA-DAI. LRG and RIF provides a logistics resource integration and optimization environment for Third party logistics companies.

A bottleneck problem for Third-party Logistics companies (3PL) is the lack of social-wide logistics resource integration. To solve this problem we propose the architecture of *Logistics Resource Grid (LRG)* from the view of 4th party logistics. And based on grid developing tools - Globus Toolkit [2], we constructed the *Resource Integration Framework (RIF)* which is a part of the architecture. The RIF is a distributed logistics information platform, by which it is possible to manage the logistics resources from different owners in a uniform way of grid service and to realize large scale, multi-institutional information sharing and resource cooperation.

In order to integrate all kinds of social logistics resources, we presented the service-oriented architecture of LRG. In this architecture, all the functional modules are deployed in Internet as grid services [1]. Clients are able to access these grid services seamlessly through identical service interfaces and communication protocols (such as HTTP, SOAP) which are independent from programming languages and run-time platform. The services are divided into six levels from the bottom to the top according to their different granularities - *Grid Infrastructure (GI), Resource Integration Framework (RIF), Operation Process Constructer (OPC), Operation Service (OS), Meta-Information Representation (MIR)* and *Grid Portal (GP)*. The fine-granular services in lower levels form the coarse-granular services in higher levels.

Here we focus on the implementation of *Resource Integration Framework*. RIF is divided into two sub-levels, Resource Domain and Resource Dispatch Enabler. The former consists of distributed resource domains, each of which containing the local logistics resource information (under the administration of each 3PL) and the corresponding grid services used to handle the information. By these resource domains, Resource Dispatch Enabler provides some fine-granular grid services such as logistics resources matching and scheduling in the global or local scale. We implement RIF with GT3 and OGSA-DAI [3]. OGSA-DAI is adopted to make the

---

[*] This work was funded by Chinese Hi-Tech R&D Program under the Grant 2003AA414330.
[**] Corresponding author.

S. Grumbach, L. Siu, and V. Vianu (Eds.): ASIAN 2005, LNCS 3818, pp. 288–289, 2005.

data access in LRG transparent. Through OGSA-DAI, various relational databases (as MySQL, Oracle) and XML databases (as Xindice) are encapsulated into *Grid Data Services (GDS)*. Data stored in heterogeneous databases of different resource domains can thus be manipulated conformably through the invocation of GDS.

Each resource domain consists of atomic grid service modules including domain control agent service, resource management service, user management service and invoice management service which are deployed in a grid node. They are respectively responsible for managing the logistics resource information, user information and invoice information of different 3PLs. The kernel of resource domains is *Domain Control Agent Service (DCAS)* whose data elements maintain all the information of grid services deployed in its resource domain. At the same time, DCAS also takes charge of scheduling the grid services to satisfy the requests from clients according to the policies of the relevant 3PL. Additionally, through the service data of DCAS, clients are enabled to inquire the metadata of each resource domain (including the information of the 3PL which is in charge of it and the status of the domain).

The services in resource dispatch enabling sublevel are all called *Resource Dispatch Enabling Services (RDES)*. RDES implements the optimized matching, associated allocation and real time monitoring of logistics resource information both globally (within the entire logistics alliance) and locally (within a 3PL) through such grid services as follows: 1) *Domain Registration Service (DRS)* is in charge of the registration of each resource domain. Its service data maintain the information about the *Domain Control Agent Service (DCAS)* of all resource domains. When a DCAS instance is created, it invoke the ServiceGroupRegistration::add method to register itself to DRS; when such an instance is being terminated, it logout from DRS by ServiceGroupRegistration::remove method. 2) *Resource Matching Service (RMS)* implements the resource matching method and optimizes the resource matching process according to the inquiries by each client. 3) *Resource Allocation Service (RAS)* dispatch the logistics resources to logically specific resource consumers by changing the current status of them to "available", "reserved", or "in use" and designating the "available time" and "actual occupation time" values of them. 4) *Resource Monitoring Service (RMS)* is responsible for real time monitoring of the status of the resources in RIF and reactivate the resources which are "reserved" for too long.

Now we have developed a prototype of RIF with all these services implemented and deployed in a general service container - Apache Tomcat 4.1.

References

1. FOSTER, I., KESSELMAN, C., NICK, J. M., Tuecke, S.: Grid Services for Distributed System Integration. IEEE Computer, Vol. 35, No. 6. (2002) 37-46.
2. Sandholm, T., Gawor, J.: Globus Toolkit 3 Core - A Grid Service Container Framework. http://www-unix.globus.org/toolkit/3.0/ogsa/docs/gt3_core.pdf. (2003)
3. The University of Edinburgh, IBM Corporation: OGSA-DAI (Open Grid Services Architecture - Data Access and Integration). http://www.ogsadai.org.uk/docs/OtherDocs/WhatIsOGSADAI3.pdf. (2003)

General Consistency Management Within the Development of Ontology-Driven Web Information System[*]

Baojun Qiu[1,2], Hongyan Li[1,2,**], Zijing Hu[1,2], Dongqing Yang[2],
Lv-an Tang[1,2], Jianjun Wang[1,2], Meimei Li[1,2], and Shiwei Tang[1,2]

[1] National Laboratory on Machine Perception,
[2] School of Electronics Engineering and Computer Science,
Peking University, Beijing 100871, P.R. China
{Qbj, Lihy, Huzijing, Tangla, Wangjj, Limm}@cis.pku.edu.cn
{ydq, tsw}@db.pku.edu.cn

Abstract. This paper proposes a general consistency management methodology within ontology-driven WIS development. The contributions of this paper are follows: 1) introduces the concept structures for representing model ontologies, mappings ontology and their instances. These ontologies and their instances greatly enhance the representation and reasoning capabilities of mapping and also simplify the manipulation 2) Defines and implements a series of general operators to manipulate mapping and model ontologies. 3) Formalizes the consistency management problem and gives an algorithm basing on general operators. 4) Implements a prototype and integrates it with WISE.

1 Introduction and Related Work

Ontology Driven Architecture (ODA)[1] follows a very similar approach of Model-Driven Architecture (MDA), but employs ontologies to construct models and can define models more effectively and accurately. Our research group have proposed ontology-driven Web Information System development Environment (WISE) and have done some work on the definition of model ontologies and model ontology transformation [2] [3]. This article aims to solve the problem of consistency management of model ontology instances within WISE. Since WISE can produce many kinds of ontology instances, the consistency management methodology should be general and can take different kinds of instances similarly.

2 General Consistency Management

In WISE, although model ontologies are arranged as graphs, their instances can be organized and manipulated as trees [2] [3]. Mapping ontology, used to preserve the

---

[*] Supported by Natural Science Foundation of China (NSFC) under grant number 60473072.
[**] Corresponding author.

S. Grumbach, L. Siu, and V. Vianu (Eds.): ASIAN 2005, LNCS 3818, pp. 290–291, 2005.

mapping information of transformation between model ontology instances, comprises a set of OWL Classes and properties and the relationship between them. An instance of Class *Mapping* can also be managed as a tree. The merits of employing ontology to represent the mapping, includes: 1) powerful representation capability.2) supporting reasoning and logic deduce.3) both models and mappings are ontology instances and can be manipulated similarly.

A series of general operation on model and mapping ontology instances have been defined, such as *composition* returning a mapping instance by combining two other mappings instances; *IntraCons* checking if an ontology instance satisfies the integrity constraints of ontology; *Merge* taking two model ontology instances and mapping between them as input and returning a new model ontology instance and mappings between the new and two old instances, and *ModelGen* generates from a model ontology instance basing on a set of generating rules a new instance as well as mapping between the tow instances. Two important points should be kept in mind when define the general operators: 1) the operator creating or modifying new model ontology instance from old one(s) must also return the mapping(s) between new and old instances. It is very important for keeping the transformation track; 2) model or mapping ontology instances returned by operators must be well-formed.

Consistency management in ontology-driven WIS development can be formalized as: A_1 and B_1 are two model ontology instances, R_{ab} is the transformation rule set for transforming from instances of Class A to instances of Class B. $<B_1, M_{a1b1}> = ModelGen(A_1,R_{ab})$, A_2 is a modified version of A_1, how to produce revised version of B_1 marked as B_2 that is consistent with A_2? Basing on general operators, a consistency management algorithm is given and main steps are follows: 1) *IntraCons* (A_2); 2) *Match* (A_1, A_2) returns two mapping instances between A_1 and A_2 to identified which elements are same or intra-modified respectively; 3) deletes from B_1 elements generated by those elements in A_1 but not in A_2, thus B_{11} has been created, also the mappings between B_{11} and B_1, B_{11} and A_1. 4) Produces minimum sub model marked as A_3 containing all intra-modified elements from A_2; 5) $<B_3, Ma3b3>=ModelGen(A_3, R_{ab})$ and *Merge* B_{11} and B_3 to generate B$_4$;6) Produces minimum sub model marked as A_4 containing all new elements from A_2; 5) $<B_5,M_{a4a5}>=ModelGen(A_4, R_{ab})$ and gains B_6 from operation $Merge(B_4 ,B_5 ,M_{b4b5})$. 6) Restructure B_6 according to the structure of A_2 then invokes *IntraCons* (B_6); and gains B_2; 7) Generates M_{a2b2}.

References

1. http://www.w3.org/2001/sw/BestPractices/SE/ODA/
2. Lv-an Tang, Hongyan Li, Zhiyong Pan, Shaohua Tan, Baojun Qiu, Shiwei Tang, Jianjun Wang: PODWIS: A Personalized Tool for Ontology Development in Domain Specific Web Information System. In Proceeding of 7th Asia-Pacific Web Conference, LNCS3399: 680-694.
3. Lv-an Tang, Hongyan Li, Zhiyong Pan, Dongqing Yang, Meimei Li, etc.: A Domain Ontology based Approach to Construct Behaviors in Web Information Systems. In Proceeding of 6th Conference on Web-Aged Information Management, LNCS 3739:194-208.

Author Index

Lecture Notes in Computer Science

For information about Vols. 1–3711

please contact your bookseller or Springer